The Greene Family and Its Branches

LORA S. LA MANCE

THE GREENE FAMILY
AND ITS BRANCHES

FROM A. D. 861 TO A. D. 1904

By

Lora S. La Mance

TOGETHER WITH POEMS DESCRIPTIVE OF THE TEXT

BY MRS. ATTIE A. STOWE

MAYFLOWER PUBLISHING COMPANY

FLORAL PARK, NEW YORK

𝔊𝔯𝔢𝔢𝔫𝔢

THE GREENE COAT-OF-ARMS.

ALL BRANCHES OF THE FAMILY ARE ENTITLED TO USE THE THREE BUCKS
TRIPPANT, *OR*, ON AN AZURE FIELD, AS IT WAS BORNE BY THE FOUNDERS OF
THE LINE. THE CRESCENT, A MARK OF CADENCY DENOTING THE LINE OF A
SECOND SON, IS USED BY ALL THE WARWICK AND QUIDNESSELT GREENES.

This book is dedicated to the memory of

- Nancy King-Nichols,

An Early Family-Historian, 1767-1820

The prejudices of her times against literary women prevented her from writing down her carefully searched out history But the fragments of her verbal narrative that came down to me, were the inspiration and foundation of this book, by her grand-daughter.

Lora S La Mance

Pineville, Mo ,
Feb 1, 1904.

Table of Contents

Authorities Consulted

Account of Green's Norton, Eng..Rev. S. Beal, D. C. L.
A Catalogue of the First Puritan Settlers..
Age of Charlemagne..Wells
Age of the Crusades...Ludlow
A History of New England. ....Palfrey
American Heraldrica...E. Dev Vermont
American Historical Register, 11 vols..
Americans of Royal Descent..Browning
Andrews Genealogy.. ....Miss Hattie F. James
Annals of the American Pulpit.   Many vols..Sprague
Annals of the Four Masters..
Annals of Narragansett Church...
Annals of the Town of Providence, 1636—1862..
Appleton's Cyclopedia of American Biography..
Beginning of the Middle Ages..Church
Biography of Henry Dunster.................... ....Parton
Bradford's History..
Bradford's Letters...
Braintree, Mass. Records............................
Bristol Church Records..
Chalmers' Biographical Dictionary...
Chambers' Cyclopedia.   15 vols...
Charleston, Mass. Church Records...
Chronicles of Massachusetts...Young
Crowell's Spirit of the Times..Revolutionary Lists
Curious Myths...S. Baring Gould
Daughters of America...Phebe A. Hanaford
Discoverie of Witchcraft...Scott
Display of Heraldry..Wewton
Dictionary of British and American Authors...Allibone
Dorchester, Mass. Records...
Early Emigrants...Hotten
Early History of Britain...Milton
Early Settlers of Reading, Mass...
Early Ship Building in Mass...
Ecclesiastical History of Ireland...Lanigan
Economic and Social History of New England..
Encyclopedia Brittanica.   20 vols..
Epochs of Church History.   10 vols...
Fairy Legends of Ireland...Crofton Croker
First Settlers of Rhode Island...John Farmer
Founders of New England ....
Fox's Book of Martyrs...
French Celebrities..Claretie
Friends in America.   7 vols..
Friends' Library.   Several vols..
Friends' Record of Portsmouth, R. I...
Genesis of the U. S..Alexander Brown
Genealogy of the Havens Family...Lewis & Farmer
Genealogical Dictionary of the First Settlers of N. England.................................Savage
Genealogical Record of Family of Parsons......................................Sam. L. Parsons
Genealogy of Nichols Family. A..Aaron Sargent
Genealogy of the Lewis Family...
Green Family of Genealogy.   ....S. S. Green
Genealogical Dictionary of R. I...Austin
Greenes of Warwick in Colonial History..Turner
Holstead's Succinct Genealogies.   24 copies privately printed in 1585......................
History of Bridgewater, Mass...Hon. Nahum Mitchell
History of the Crusades..Coxe
History of the Early Colonists...Judd
Historical Discourse of the First Baptist Church................................Rev. H. M. King

Authorities Consulted

History of England .... .Macauley
"   "   "   ....Hume
"   "   "   ....Wilson
   Other standard English Histories...
History of New England....... ....Winthrop, Puritan Governor
History of Lynn, Mass...Lewis
History of Northampton, England..Baker
History of Northampton..Trumbull
History of Narragansett..Potter
History of Quidnessett..Daniel Gould Allen
History of the Queens of England..Agnes Strictland
History of Rhode Island..G. W. Greene
History of Woodbury, Conn..
Huguenot Emigration...
Huguenots of France and America. 2 vols..Baird
Irish Notes..Moore
Irish Saints...O'Hanlon
Irving's Life of Washington...
Interleaved Almanac..Rev. William Cooper, 1716-1743
Journal of the Plague..De Foe in 1721
Lamb's Biographical Dictionary..
Life of Roger Williams..Knowles
Life of Roger Williams..Straus
Life of Wesley(English)...
Malden, Mass. Records...
Marshfield, Mass. Records...
Mary Dyer, the Quaker Martyr..H. Rogers
Mary, Queen of Scots..Abbott
McClintock & Strong's Theological Dictionary. 12 vols,..................................
Magazine American History, bound vols...
Mass. Historical Society's Collection. 5 vols...
Middleburg, Mass. Records...
Middle Ages..Hallam
Milton, Mass. Church Records..
Myths of the Druids...Davies
New England Judged...Bishop
New England Historical and Genealogical Record, 56 vols.................................
New England Memorial, Morton, (Puritan,) before 1685....................................
Narragansett Friends' Records...
Narragansett Historical Register. Bound copies..
Narrative and Critical History of America; Several vols...............................Wilson
National Cyclopedia of American Biography..
Parish Register of the Barbadoes ....
Parish Register of St. Michael ....
Philip of Pokanoket..Washington Irving
Pierce Genealogy ....Gen. Ebenezer Pierce
Pilgrim Fathers of New England..Brown
Pioneers of Massachusetts...Pope
Pirates and Amazons...Stevens
Portsmouth (N. H.) Records..
Puritan Settlers. 3 vols..Hinman
Queen Elizabeth ....Abbott
Records of Boston...
Records of Dr. McSparran...1720-1757
Records of Essex and Old Norfolk, Mass..
Records of Hull, Mass...
Records of Maple Root Six-Principle Baptist Church of R. I..............................
Records of Newport Episcopal Church, R. I...
Records of St. Paul Church, Narragansett..
Records of Weymouth, Mass...
Richard the Second...**Abbott**
R. I. Land Evidences..
R. I. Genealogies...
Scituate and Barnstable, Mass. Records..

Authorities Consulted

Shipping Lists..1619-1640
Sudbury, Mass. Records...
The Bennett Family..S. B. Bennett
The Green Family..Frank L. Green, A. M
The Reformation... Walker
The Waite Family...D. Byron Waite
Topsfield, Mass. Records...
Transactions of the Lancashire Historical Society.   (England.)...................................
Vital Records of Rehoboth, Mass..James N. Arnold
Vital Records of R. I.   12 Vols..James N. Arnold
William the Conqueror...Abbott

The Old Greene Tree

Long years ago, " The old Greene Tree "
  Sank deep its roots in Albia's Soil ;
Its branches spread and, banyan like,
  They bore to earth ; thus no turmoil
Could shake this old and mighty tree.
  Was warfare on ?   Its branches then
Made stoutest staffs to slay the foe,
  And Lords de Greenes de Boketon's men,
Led by their fearless chiefs, became
  A scourging rod for those who dared
Oppose the will of England's king.
  But warrior Greenes their honors shared
With those of legal lore ; and Lord
  Chief-Justice Henry Greene we find
Was long supreme in Judges' Hall.
  His truly just and legal mind
Was tower of strength to Henry Third ;
  And second son of this de Greene
Lives for all time, in Shakespeare's plays ;
  And on the throne as England's queen,
A daughter of this line is seen.

The Greene Tree grew and " waxed strong,"
  Nor would its sturdy branches bear
Unjust control ; and thus it fell
  That men of Greene were those to dare
Oppose unjust, infamous Laud,
  Who sought with all his churchly power
To crush religious freedom out ;
  But persecution proved a dower
Of Good unto those dauntless souls,
  Who, for religious liberty,
Forsook their dear ancestral homes
  And crossed the wide and stormy sea,
That they might live and worship God,
  In freedom, as their conscience taught.
But persecution was not o'er ;
  The wilderness again was sought ;
Again was fireside altar raised
  Where men were free.   Thenceforth, they throve.

Their men have filled high place of trust
    In peace and war.   Who does not love
This name of Greene?   Who does not know
    And honor him, that stalwart son,
Branch of this tree, who, from the first
    Until the righteous war was done,
Undaunted led his brave men on
    To victory on many a field ?
'Tis only to Great Washington's
    That fame of Greene doth yield.

Read you this book, and reading love
    Those honored ones of long ago.
Read and reflect.   'Twill make you strong
    For God and Right, then men shall know
You are a true and worthy branch
    Of that old, staunch, well-rooted tree.
That for the Right has ever stood,
    That for the Wrong shall never be.

                              Attie A. Stowe.

CHAPTER I

INTRODUCTORY

"Other things being equal, in most relations of life I prefer a man of family......
Four or five generations of gentlemen and gentlewomen—among them a member of His
Majesty's Council for the Province, a Governor or so, one or two Doctors of Divinity, a
member of Congress, not later than the time of top-boots with tassels.

"Family portraits !......Some family silver ; a string of wedding and funeral rings,
the arms of the family curiously blazoned...... I go, other things being equal, for the
man who inherits family traditions and the cumulative humanities of at least four or five
generations."—*Oliver Wendall Holmes in Autocrat of the Breakfast Table.*

At the very outset, the question of dates is to be considered. There is
a difference of 12 days between Old Style chronology and New Style, which
change was made in 1752. The beginning of the year changed at the same
time from the 25th of March to our present 1st of January. I have followed
the usual custom of historians, i. e. given the month and the day of the
month O. S. (Old Style,) but made the year correspond with the N. S. reckoning. So if any wish to turn dates of before 1752 into present style of
reckoning, they have only to add 12 days.

I also explain that the small numerals at the upper right hand of family
names, denotes the number of generations from the stem father. In the
English history this is reckoned from Sir Alexander, the first Lord de Greene.
For convenience, in the American history, the numerals begin anew with
the first emigrant ancestors.

This book is what it is, a history of "The Green Tree and Its
Branches," because it could be nothing else. All the other lines, Nichols,
King, Pierce, Howard, LaValley and Matteson ran straight back to the main
line of all, the Greenes of Surgeon John of Warwick and John of Quidnessett descent. They in turn belonged to the old and honored house, the head
and founder of which, Lord Alexander de Greene de Boketon, received his
titles and estates A. D. 1202.

Some will ask, " Have you not ostentatiously paraded the barons and lords, earls, high admirals, kings and queens connected with the lines from which this family and its branches have sprung ? " I think not. If it is a misfortune to have forefathers with the bluest of blue blood, and bearing titles of high honor, then our's is an afflicted line. If it is an honor, we have been signally blessed in this form of ancestral riches. We could have gotten along with a few less lords, or half-civilized kings ; but they have certainly added life and picturesqueness to the dull, early-day history, that otherwise we would have known little about.

The Greenes in all their branches have always been fond of history. I hope this book may add to their children's zest for it. I trust it may make clearer to them the misty days of fourteen centuries ago, when King Fergus McEarc sailed from Ireland and became the lineal head of kings that for centuries sat upon Scotland's throne ; that it may bring nearer the troublous days of wicked King John ; make real the checkered career of Richard II ; bring before them the court of bestial Henry III, whose last queen was of the house of Greene, and set vividly before them the horrors of St. Bartholomew's Massacre, when perished noble Admiral de Coligny, by marriage of our line. With all these epochs, those of our blood have been closely concerned.

Our children ought to love our own land the better, because their foreparents followed Roger Williams into the wilderness ; because at the head of men protecting their homes, others of our ancestors fought the Indians in King Philip's war, and because the greatest of Revolutionary generals, after Washington, was Nathaniel Greene of collateral blood. Surely the story of such deeds is worth recording.

There is probably not another English-speaking family upon the globe with such a remarkable religious record. Of our blood have been Catholics, direct disciples of St. Patrick himself, and builders of churches and chantrys. One branch of the family goes back to Henry Barrows, one of the first to profess Congregational or Separatist doctrines, and who sealed his profession by his own blood, being executed at Tyburn in 1593. Goaded by Archbishop Land's tyrannies, not less than a dozen men and women, direct heads of families with which the line of John Greene of Quidnessett has since incorporated itself, fled to the American Colonies for safety.

These same families became Baptists, and were exiled into the unknown region of rocky, sea-girt Rhode Island. Lastly, the Kings and LaValleys, Huguenot Episcopalians, under Louis XV's persecutions, fled to America for religious asylum.

So thrice this family has been exiled for conscience sake, and has furnished French and English martyrs, who have sealed their faith by their own blood. They have ever excelled in patriotism, and their sons have ever been ready to fight for their country. In the Revolutionary War, Samuel Greene of R. I., sent eight sons into the war, a record no one else ever equalled, and Joseph Greene of N. Y., 12-year old volunteer, was the youngest soldier of the same war.

This book covers nearly 300 years of American history. There are thousands of names recorded here. I have not found one among them all that has ever been convicted of a crime, one that was a deserter, one that was an out-and-out infidel, or one that was a drunkard. It was two and a quarter centuries after the coming to America of John Greene of Quidnessett, ere a single divorce occurs in the whole allied lines of his blood.

Mrs. Attie A. Stowe, a poet and song writer of the Pacific Coast, contributes several original poems written expressly for this book. I am deeply grateful to her for this favor. It is pleasant to feel that we have a poet in the family's ranks; that she sings in an easy, natural key; that her themes are the stirring scenes through which our fathers passed, and the noble deeds that they did; and that the old martial fire that the Greenes' sons have ever felt, glows in genial warmth through these stanzas of this daughter of the house. I feel that the rich treat Mrs. Stowe has given us is worth the price of the book to its readers. My slower, duller, more lagging prose is thrown in as ballast.

The Song of the Bard

At Norton's Hall, de Boketon's home,
   High wassail reigned at Christmas-tide :—
The aged harper thumbed his strings,
   Then drained the flagon by his side
And, when its contents warmed his blood
   And roused his pride till wits were keen,
He voiced this lay, wherein he sang
   Of Alexander, Lord de Greene.

King John was in sore need ;
   Rebellion stalked the land ;
Forsooth it fell because
   Unto his crown and hand.
He'd taked for his own
   Another's plighted wife—
Despoiled de la Marche
   Was leader in the strife.

Then called the harried king
   To his barons brave and bold :
"I'm your annointed king,
   My will you *must* uphold !
stamp this rebellion out,
   And, when it fully ends,
You shall have large estates,
   For John rewards his friends."

Then to his king's support
   Sir Alexander came.
And struck such sturdy blows
   He won the chieftain's fame.

In truth, foremost was he
   In service of his king ;
Foremost, on warring lords,
   Swift punishment to bring.

Because those sturdy blows,
   That timely given aid,
Enabled John to keep
   The lovely Norman maid,
His gratitude was shown
   In grants of large estates ;
From that old Lord de Greene,
   Our lordship clearly dates.

His fingers cease their touch
   Upon the clanging strings ;
The singer's head sinks down
   As though recital brings
A weight of memory
   Too great to bear with ease.—
A memory that earned
   From earthly cares, surcease.

The servitors, amazed,
   Lift up the drooping head,—
Alas ! the bard has gone !
   With song his life has fled !

Yours truly, Attie A. Stowe

MRS. ATTIE A. STOWE.
(Poet and writer. See Biography, Chapter XL.)

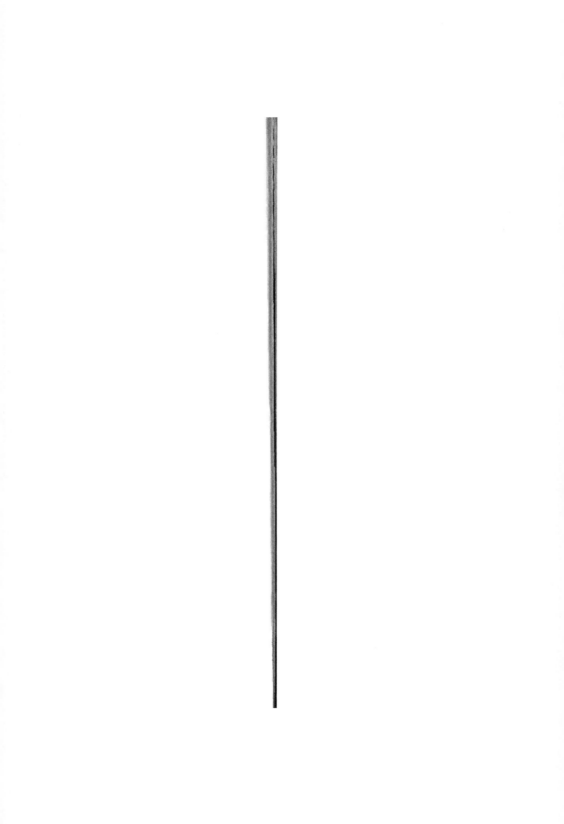

CHAPTER II

THE DIM PERIOD OF GREENE HISTORY

FROM LORD ALEXANDER TO LORD THOMAS, 1202–1296

Inquire I pray thee of the former age, and prepare
thyself to the search of their fathers.
Job VIII. Verse 8.

The meager data of the first one-hundred years of the family's history. How the estate came to be bestowed by King John. The family name. The title. State kept by the early Lords of the line. Their recreations. Alexander's trials as a stem father. The Crusading sons' coats-of-arms. The early escutcheons of the Greenes.

He who steps out into the night finds at first that all is gross darkness, but as he gropes his way, dim landmarks begin to shape themselves out of the darkness. The faint rays of light grow plainer, and the traveler at last walks in a path that has familiar objects to the right and the left, to show him how far he has come, and in what direction he is going. So in this history the beginning of the Greene family is shrouded in the midnight of the unchronicled story of centuries ago. A date or two comes down to us. The hazy figure of Lord Alexander rises like a ghost from his seven centuries of dust. There is a certain branching and widening out of the family. Not until the fourth lord of the line comes a record and history.

The cool, exacting critic, who will accept nothing but what has a date and an official certificate attached to it—exactly as a mineral specimen is tagged in a museum—will be disappointed in this chapter. All that we really know of the first Lord de Greene may be summed up in this brief paragraph. Alexander, a Knight at the king's court, was the great-grandson of one of the Norman nobles who invaded England with William the Conqueror, 1066. King John bestowed the estate of Boughton in Northampton upon him in 1202.*

---

* The authority for this date is Surgeon Colonel John Joseph Greene, of Dublin, Ireland, author of "Pedigree of the Family of Greene," of which one-hundred and fifty copies were printed in Dublin in 1899. Surgeon Colonel Greene spent many years of research, and his statements are authoritive. The Irish Greenes are descendants from a younger son of the ninth Lord de Greene.

But when we remember that mean, parsimonious King John had a way of rewarding a dirty act done in his service by an extravagant gift filched from some noble who may have offended him; when we recall the date of Lord Alexander's patent that followed on the heels of a peculiar crisis in King John's history, we have a right to connect these events. It is not to the credit of the founder of the house of Greene, but it proves him to have been human. Very much such a man, we fear, as some of his sons that have lived centuries after him.

No other English king was ever as hated as was King John. When he had been dead one-hundred and sixty-five years, the rebels in the Wat Tyler Rebellion took solemn oath never to permit a king who bore the name of John to sit on the throne of England. When a Prince John came to the neighboring Scottish throne, he changed his name to Robert, because John as a ruler's name was so odious he would not bear it. John broke his father's heart, and the elder king died, to the horror of the priests, with curses of his unnatural offspring upon his lips. This same treacherous prince usurped his brother's throne while Richard was in the Crusade. Later, he murdered his own nephew, Prince Arthur, with his own hands. His people sullenly bowed to the rule of this false and cruel king that they were not strong enough to depose.

At twenty-three, King John married his cousin Avisa, (or Hadwisa,) daughter of the Earl of Gloucester. She was a dull, plain featured woman, who bore patiently with his misdeeds. John was King both of England and of Normandy, France. At the close of the year 1200 he visited France and became enamored of Isabelle, wife of Count de la March. For state reasons she had been married when a child to the Count, who was to take her to wife when she was seventeen. John carried Isabelle off, ordered his prelates to pronounce a divorce between Avisa and him, and then married Isabelle.

Count de la March set up a rebellion. King John ordered his nobles (in 1201) to cross over to Normandy and put down the rising. They flatly refused, rebellion thus threatening him at home also. The king was furious. He swore " by God's teeth,"—his favorite oath—he would make the barons sick of their daring. From attendant knights and other subservient material, he found leaders for his troops. He broke up the confederacy of angry lords in England and defeated Count de la March. He rewarded those who aided him, and confiscated the estates of some of the lords who disobeyed him.

The date of Alexander's patent shows that he must have been one of these knights that steeled their hearts to Queen Avisa's woes, and fought for the king who could make their fortunes. No doubt his very estate had belonged to some of the lords whom King John had attainted.

We do not know the extent of his estate. The least a great baron could

KING JOHN.

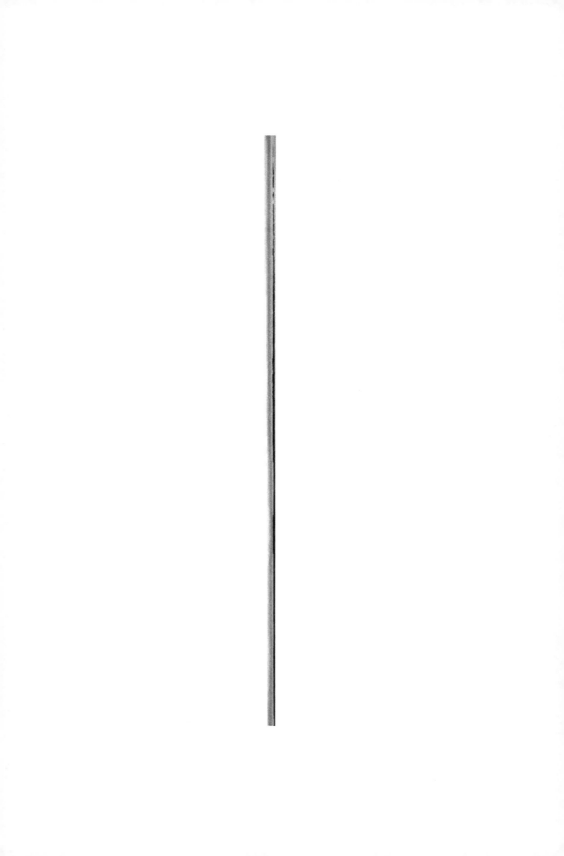

own and hold his rank was fifty hides of land, i. e., six thousand acres. He might own very much more. Halstead says that at one time the Greenes were the largest land-owners in the kingdom. It was somewhat difficult to keep the exact boundaries of the great lords' possessions. They got around this problem after a unique fashion of the Middle Ages. On Holy Thursday or Ascension Day, they each year "beat the bounds." All the men on the Lord's estate turned out. His Lordship with his suite, rode about his estate, following the received boundary lines all the way, a crowd of boys at his heels beating brush, trees and stones as they passed along. Moreover, at convenient points, by landmark trees or other objects, a boy was "sharply whipped with peeled willow wands," so that he would always remember being flogged at this part of his lord's boundary mark. As the urchins received a liberal reward for their stripes, they never lacked for volunteers. The Lords de Greene must have punished a small army of boys in this way, for the fifth lord, Sir Henry, Chief Justice of England, settled upon his second son, after providing for the regular heir, over thirty manors, each of which would to-day support a baronetcy.

Lord Alexander assumed a surname after his chief estate, de Greene de Boketon, i. e., the Lord of the Park of the Deer Enclosure. A green in the early day was a park. Boketon is an old, old word meaning the *bucks'* (bokes) *ton* or paled-in enclosure. Centuries ago the terminal syllable *ton* had lost its original sense, and meant a town. So that Boketon, still used in the original sense, shows Lord Alexander came to an estate named long before, and noted for its extensive parks and deer preserves. Boketon became Bucks and Buckston, and later Boughton, its present name. It lies in Northampton.

For a long time the full name de Greene de Boketon was used in legal documents. Naturally in everyday speech it was shortened to de Greene. During the reign of Henry VI, 1422–1471, with its attendant French wars, the patriotic de Greenes dropped the patrician de as too Frenchy in sound for Englishmen, as they now considered themselves.

The title of the early de Greenes was strictly Sir (Militis), and their wives were Dame. Familiarly they were called Lord, or the Right Honorable Lord, and their wives Lady. At that date there were but two titles of nobility, earls and knights. The knights were subdivided into greater and lesser barons. The great barons held their estates from the crown. The lesser barons were like the present baronet, and held their manors from an over-lord or great baron. Lord Alexander was a great baron. He had a power in his estates almost as a petty king. He had to furnish so many men for the king's wars, pay a portion toward the dowry of the princesses, and entertain the king when in his territory. He had to pay homage also, to show that he held his estate from the crown. We are expressly told of how each of the Lords de Greene did this, 1202–1506, "by lifting up his right hand toward the King yearly on Christmas day, in what place soever the King is." [Halstead's Genealogy, A. D. 1585.]

The Lords de Greene lived in state. They wore rich apparel, belted with a gold or silver girdle to which was attached a purse, a rosary, a pen and inkhorn, a set of keys and an elaborately chased and sheathed dagger. These showed their rank. When they rode they wore gold spurs. Their armor was magnificent. They wore robes in Parliament, hats and plumes at court, and at the king's coronation they wore a crimson velvet cap, lined with ermine, and having a plain gold band. Their servants wore the Greene livery, which was blue laced with gold. There has been unearthed a steward's household account, of that same early period, in a nobleman's family that kept perhaps less state than the early de Greenes. The steward says his master's family consists of one-hundred and sixty-six persons, including such servants as the forbisher who kept the armor bright, the fencing master, harper, priest, bedesman or praying-man, the almoner who looked after the poor for his lord, and the barnes or berner, who kept the twenty-four fires in the castle in order. The Lord kept an open table, and fed on an average fifty-seven visitors a day. The knights sat with the Lord at one end of the long table, and were served with the choicest food. "Below the salt" the retainers and commoners sat, and ate coarser victuals, or as we yet express it, "humble pie."

I will add that for five generations the de Greenes spoke Norman French. They were a family that delighted in athletic sports. They hunted and hawked, and attended tournaments, and played games of tennis, cricket, bowls, etc. All of them in their generations were noted for their fine bowling alleys, two or three of which were the finest in England. Charles I. used to go to Lord Vaux's at Harrowden, or to Lord Spencer's at Althorpe to play bowls at their famous alleys, which were once the Greenes'. Here Cornet Joyce arrested him and carried him off to Whitehall and a violent death. Each winter they had miracle shows and religious plays, held in their barns and roofed alleys. The actors were always men, as "became decent behavior." These early Greenes were also much given to hours of riddle making and conundrum guessing.

The Germans call the head of a line the *Stemmvader* [Stem-father.] In a peculiar sense Alexander was indeed a *stemmvader*. He had a passionate love of horticulture, that has throughout these seven centuries dominated his entire line of descendants.* There is probably no other English

---

* A marked personal trait or character is sometimes carried down in a family for centuries. The Jews claim that the royal line of David from which Our Lord Himself sprang, was for two thousand

speaking family to-day that has so many members that delight in beautiful home grounds, and in flowers and fruit, and finely kept farms. It seems to have been Alexander's set rule to avoid court entanglements and political manoeuvers, and to spend his energies in beautifying his estates. With two notable exceptions the lords who followed him pursued the same policy. Thereby, even the turbulent times of the War of the Roses failed to embroil them to a ruinous extent in their ruler's quarrels.

Thirteen years after Lord Alexander settled at Boughton, the lords rose against King John. They met at Runnymede, only a few miles away from the family seat of the de Greenes. Only seven barons adhered to John, and he was not one of them. Therefore he must have been enrolled among the two thousand nobles who put their united protests in the hand of twenty-five lords who presented the Magna Charta to the king, and forced him to sign that document that guaranteed both the lives and the property of his subjects from arbitrary spoilation. It will interest a branch of R. I. Greenes who have the blood of the LaValleys as well, to know that two of the Magna Charta signers were Gilbert DeLaval and William de Lanvalley. Another signer was Roger, Earl of Winchester, whose great-great-granddaughter, Lucie de la Zouche, married Sir Alexander de Greene's great-great-grandson, Lord Thomas[5]. John revenged himself " like a devil," as one old historian puts it, burning castles and doing other foul deeds. He died the next year, 1216, and his old favorite fortunately escaped his fury.

Lord Alexander's son, the second Lord, was probably a crusading knight in the seventh Crusade, which ended in 1240. His grandson was almost undoubtedly one of the knights that accompanied Edward I on the last great Crusade, and died in the Holy War. Nothing more is known of this period of family history, except that Lord Alexander had other sons and grandsons

years distinguished for remarkable personal beauty. The Bible bears this out. Rebecca, the damsel that was " very fair to look upon," was born seven hundred and fifty years before her lineal descendant, King David, " ruddy and of a fair countenance." Of that King's sons was Prince Absolom, of whom the Scriptures said, "In all Israel there were none to be so much praised as Absolom for his beauty; from the sole of his foot even to the crown of his head, there was no blemish in him." Nearly five hundred years later, Daniel of "the king's seed," was chosen because of his physical beauty to stand before Nebuchadnezzar.

The Thatchers, known in Colonial history, boasted of ancestors, who from father to son for nine generations, were ministers. The late Rev. Dr. Goodell could say the same of his line. The Emerson family from which Ralph Waldo Emerson sprang, in one branch counted eight clergymen in lineal descent. Rev. John Witherspoon, one of the signers of the Declaration of Independence, was maternally descended from an unbroken line of ministers to the great Scotch divine, John Knox, borne two hundred and seventeen years before. The Welsh family of Chenoweth, old enough to have intermarried with the Cromwells before the great Protector's day, cannot point to a time when the family was not a medical one. In 1884, there were living in the United States no less than twenty-six Doctors Chenoweth.

The thick, pouting " Hapsburg lip," of the Austrian royal family, was first seen five hundred years ago in their foremother, Princess Cymburga of Warsaw. Col. Higginson when in Europe, was annoyed by a lord's peculiar brusque manner. His hostess apologised, saying it was only the —— manners, for which the family had been noted for generations. Examples might be multiplied. These are enough to convince any doubting Thomas.

who became heads of lines of their own. We know this by the evidence of their coats-of-arms.

The Crusades brought about the use of coats-of-arms. The Crusade leaders rode at the head of their followers, clothed from head to foot in armor, —gorget, cuirass, gauntlets, brassets, cuishes and greaves encased the man in an envelope of steel, while the closed helmet masked all of the face but the eyes. There was nothing to distinguish one knight from any other of the same build and wearing the same accouterments. The Norman-French knights in 1147 hit upon the ingenious plan of engraving upon the knight's shield a device that would tell who the bearer was. Richard Coeur de Lion was one of the first of the Norman-English to take up the new fashion, nearly fifty years after the French crusaders had begun it. His knights followed the kingly example, improving on the original idea by not only emblazoning the device upon the real shield, but by embroidering a shield or escutcheon upon the surtout or coat worn over the armor, and on this placing the same designs. Hence arose the expression, a coat-of-arms.

A coat-of-arms has been from the first a badge of good birth. Severe fines and confiscation of property were imposed on any of common blood who assumed a family escutcheon. Coats-of-arms were occasionally allowed to those of merely "good blood," i. e. to those who could name their grandparents. Usually, however, it was restricted to those with blue-blood, or full pedigree, i. e. those who could name their father and mother, their four grandparents, eight great-grandfathers and eight great-grandmothers. After a line has taken a coat-of-arms, all of the legitimate descendants are entitled to use it, provided they can prove their pedigree. Less than fifty years ago a titled English family died out, and it was supposed the estate would revert to the crown. A family who bore the same arms, proved their pedigree back four hundred and three years to a brother of an ancestor of this titled line, and the courts awarded them both the estate and the title of their centuries-removed kinsmen. To have a coat-of-arms was and is *prima facie* evidence of good blood, and in some European countries those who use them must pay a tax on them as a valuable personal possession.

All of the oldest coats-of-arms were very simple. The shield was without ornamentation, and there was no crest, scroll, motto, or mantling adorning it, up to the year 1300. The device was usually three charges (devices) upon the field, (the face of the shield,) two above and one below. About 1360 elaborate quarterings, palings, emblazonments, etc., began to appear. So a simple, three charge escutcheon indicates an antiquity of six or seven hundred years. After elaborate coats-of-arms became admired, noble houses of which the heirs married heiresses who brought rich estates to them, quartered the wife's arms with their own. The old house of de Greene in time

showed many quarterings and emblazonments.   See Greene coats-of-arms
both on opposite page and in chapter III.

About 1300 a torce or wreath, representing the twisted garland of silk
that was the knight's favor received from his lady's hand, was placed above
the shield.   It forms the support for the present crest.   Borders (bordures,)
to the shield began to be used, each variation representing a different branch
of the family.   The signs of cadency, as they are called, a crescent on the shield
to denote a second son, a mullet for the third, etc., did not come into use
until the time of Henry VII, 1485-1508.   This was about the time the head
of the Dorsetshire and Gillingham Greenes, (from whom the American lines
of Warwick and Quidnesset Greenes descend,) would have assumed his coat
of arms.   When Deputy Governor John Greene went from R. I. to England
a few years prior to 1700, he had a new seal made from the family arms.
This seal is now in the possession of Henry Lehré Greene, and shows the
crescent, which tells us that this ancestor of four hundred years ago was the
second son of a recognized branch of the noble house of Greene.

Nearly a hundred years after the wreath began to be used, the mantling
appeared.   This is the wavy folds hanging down from the crest at each side
of the shield, and represents the bauldrick or silken military sash the knights
wore on parade.   Crests were the last things introduced upon coats-of-arms,
though royalty and crusade commanders used them before.   There is usually a helmet as part of the crest.   If in profile, showing the bars, it denotes
nobility of high rank.   Those who will study the coats-of-arms given in
this chapter and the next will find these various changes illustrated one by
one.   These seals and escutcheons are photographed by permission from a
set of Halstead's (Earl of Peterborough's) Genealogies, three hundred and
nineteen years old.

About 1272 Henry III had a roll made of all the coats-of-arms in the
kingdom up to that year.   Edward I and Edward III also had them carefully listed and described.   Heraldry reached its height under Richard II,
who reigned from 1377 to 1398.   He established the College of Heralds,
who registered each coat-of-arms, and the pedigree on which it is founded,
and gave permission for new coats-of-arms, or to make changes.   In Richard
II's time there were but seven hundred escutcheons in all England, and an
overwhelming majority of these became extinct in the War of the Roses.
So that a coat-of-arms that antedates 1400 is ancient indeed.

To return to the early escutcheons of the first de Greenes.   This was
at the beginning of Heraldry.   The first idea was solely to show by a device
who each knight was.   All these first coats-of-arms suggested the knight's
surname, by the name of the object emblazoned on the shield.   Inherited
coats-of-arms were at first only considered as belonging to those who inher-

ited a title. Until nearly 1300, younger brothers chose whatever coats-of-arms pleased them. Thus the Lords de Greene de Boketon chose a device that suggested the de Boketon part of their name. It was three bucks (bokes) trippant, *or*, upon an azure field. That is, the bucks were traced in gold, as walking upon a blue field. The terminal syllable ton, tine, prong, fork, twig, etc., all came from the same root-word, that at that time meant nearly the same thing. So that the deer's broad antlers suggested to them buck's tons or antlers. At least three younger scions of the house chose other devices, each a play, however, either upon the de Greene or the de Boketon part of the name. One represented an English bird commonly called the green Woodpecker. It was pecking on a tree trunk in the park or green. A second represents a dove with a sprig of a green olive leaf in her bill. The third represents a stag's head with wide antlers, which again suggests buck's ton or buck's prong. As coats-of-arms soon became hereditary to all of one line, these three altogether different coats-of-arms prove that Lord Alexander de Greene de Boketon had other sons and grandsons beside the direct heirs, who assumed these arms before 1275.

The Crusader's Tale

"Ho! far-off ancestors!
   Ho! men of other days!
Help me recount your deeds
   In lays of fitting praise."

For answer, misty shapes
   Take form before my eyes;
And "Tell them of *my* deeds,"
   An eager ghost-shape cries.

"No! No! Of mine!"   "Of mine!"
   Resounds on either hand:
Just then commanding shape,
   With mien both fierce and grand,
Uprose amidst that throng
   And did those ghosts berate.

"Give way, ye upstart shades,
   Give way, while Hugh the Great
Relates *his* daring deeds;"
   Then unto me he turned,
His face aglow with zeal
   That once within him burned.

"In that great First Crusade,
   When Christians sought to wrest
The Holy Sepulchre,
   Christ's sacred place of rest,
From out of Moslem hands,—
   In that Crusade, dear scribe,
Hugh Magnus Vermandois,
   King Henry's second son,   .
Bore stress of leadership.
   A score of times we won
Our lives 'gainst fearful odds;
   A score of times we bore
With famine's fearful woes;
   Or bore with thirst so sore
That naught but honor's might
   Enabled valiant men
To keep the conflict up.
   Most fearful time was when
Besieged at Antioch,
   By hunger's pangs oppressed,
We ate our leathern shoes,
   We were so sore distressed;
Then sallying forth we smote
   Th' encircling Turkish foe;

13

We smote with lance and sword,
　Nor did we Christians know
One moment's rest, until
　Upon that bloody field,
Two thousand Infidels
　Were forced their lives to yield.
The Moslems rallied well ;
　We drove them back again,
And fought them till we slew
　One hundred thousand men.

"The wily Moslem foe
　Surrounded us again ;
Alas ! from out that fight,
　With scarce a thousand men,
I cut and forced my way.
　Dear scribe, I'd tell you more,
For Hugh de Vermandois
　Adventures had by score ;
But I have said enough
　To prove my rightful claim
To rank the peer of all
　Who earned Crusader's fame."

He faded slow away,
　And, as he went from sight,
I caught my pen, that I
　Might chronicle aright
The fame of Vermandois.
　His star of life has set,
But through all coming time
　Our songs shall praise him yet.

　　　　　　　Mrs. A. A. Stowe.

Addenda

The second baron of the line, as listed in old rolls of 20th year of Henry III, (1236) and 45th year of same king, (1261) was Sir Walter de Boketon. The same properties or affairs listed again in a roll of the 7th year of Edward II, (1314) repeat the name of Sir Walter, and also give name of John de Boketon, whom we may consider the next heir. As the fourth lord was certainly Sir Thomas, who received the title in his infancy, at the beginning of the reign of Edward I, (1272) this (Sir) John de Boket on was doubtless the young crusading Knight who perished in Palestine in 1271. This completes the names of the Lords of the line, and is given here, although received too late to be entered at the proper place in the regular chapters.

NOTE TO CHAPTER III. ANCESTRY OF DUKE ROBERT THE STRONG.

Wittekind, the famous hero of old German lore, was converted to Christianity A. D. 785. After this there are but the scantiest authentic records of him. However, very old traditions uniformly assert, and historians usually accept as a fact, that three families descended directly from him. These were (1) the Dukes of Lower Saxony, whose head, Duke Ludolf, 850, was the great-grandson of Wittekind; (2) the Counts of Wettin, who were descended from either a younger son or a daughter of the hero, and (3) the line of Robert the Strong, created Duke de France A. D. 861. The latter is by some historians called the son of Wittekind. It is much more probable that he was the grandson of that chieftain.

The Saxons were Pagans of Northern Germany. They worshipped Odin and all the host of Norse deities. Pepin, one of the strongest kings of the Franks, subdued the Saxons, broke down their strongholds, forced them to pay a tribute of 300 horses annually, and made them allow Christian missionaries to settle among them. When his son Charlemagne came to the throne he felt it to be the mission of his life to crush the power of the Saxons, and to convert the nation to Christianity. He conducted 18 wars against this brave but unfortunate people,—wars bitter and blood-thirsty on either side.

A. D. 772, he ground Saxony beneath his iron heel. In particular he destroyed the Sanctuary of Odin, and threw down the venerated idol of Irminsul, a mysterious, column-like image, the loss of which roused the Saxons to a religious frenzy. Wittekind, "Noblest of heathen heroes," as one styles him, the "Last Saxon King" as another calls him, undertook the leadership of the forlorn Saxon host.

In 774 this Westphalian chieftan led his army against Charlemagne. By 777 that powerful king forced most of the great Saxon nobles to surrender and receive baptism. Wittekind fled to Siegfried, the King of Jutland, a part of Denmark. This is the same Siegfried whose exploits are told in the *Nibelungenlied* and other folk-lore songs, which sing of his magic-mantle of invisibility and his beautiful wife, Kriemhilt, and of the treasure of the *Nibelungen* that he brought from the far North. However mythical these things may be, Siegfried was a loyal friend to Wittekind, and gave him his own sister, the Princess Geva, for a wife.

It was the next year, 778, when Charlemagne's army was hemmed in in the Pass of Roncesvalles, and the Knight Roland and others, the very flower of chivalry, perished there. This reverse of Charlemagne's fortune inspired Wittekind to a new rebellion. He came back and again headed his people in a revolt, laying west the country of the Rhine. Again he fled to Jutland. Again he returned. This last time, in 782, he fell upon the Frankish army upon the Sintle River, and all but wiped it out. Charlemagne took revenge in the Massacre of Verden, where he slew 4,500 with the sword in one day. Terrible battles followed, but the Franks were ever victorious.

In 785 Wittekind and his followers came to the great king at Attigny surrendered and were baptized, Charlemagne himself attending Wittekind to the font, and making him magnificent presents. He created him Duke also. Wittekind built himself the Castle of Babilonie near Lubeck, and ruled his subjects with kindness until 807, when helping Charlemagne, he expired in a campaign. He was buried in the church at Engers, where a beautiful monument was later erected over his remains.

ARMS OF THE 2ND LORD MORDAUNT, (AT LEFT,) QUARTERED WITH ARMS OF LEWIS (AT LEFT.)
About 1550. In the generations close following the Greene-Mordaunt Arms were
born by Earl Peterborough, author of Halstead's Genealogy, so often quoted
in these pages and by the great English General, Charles Mordaunt, also
Earl of Peterborough. The arms were surmounted by an Earl's coronet.

CHAPTER III

FROM 1296 TO DEATH OF LORD CHIEF-JUSTICE GREENE, 1370

These mentioned by their names were princes in their family ; and the house of their
fathers increased greatly.

—I Chronicles, IV. Verse 38.

*Halstead's Genealogies. Lord Thomas⁴. Lord Thomas⁵ and his marriage into the royal
line of French Kings. The de la Zouche genealogy. The Lord Chief-Justice, Sir
Henry⁶. Services to state. Establishment of the great Boughton Fair. His estates.
His marriage and family. The peculiar entailment of his estate. His burial.*

Ambitious family antiquarians are always proud if they can claim a
royal descent. The Greenes find no trouble in presenting their royal tree,
as their lineal line to the Capet Kings of France is complete without a break
or an uncertain ancestor. We have followed Halstead's Genealogy, Brown-
ing's Americans of Royal Descent, and Rev. S. Beal's, D. C. L. Account of
Green's Norton, together with the known genealogy of the Capetian Kings
of France, all of which agree with each other.

Halstead's Genealogy stands at the head of English works of this kind.
It was written in 1585 by the second Earl of Peterborough, himself of the
blood of Greene. He assumed the pen name of Robert Halstead, and hence
his work is always spoken of as Halstead's Genealogy, although his true
name is well known. But twenty-four copies were printed. The work is
valued so highly that a few years ago when a set was offered for sale in
England, the price was fixed at one hundred and twenty-five guineas, or
$625.00! One feature of Halstead is eighty pages of proofs, verbatim copies
of official state records, some of them in English, but more of them in either
Latin or Norman-French. All of the scholars of that day used Latin, and
Norman-French was the language of Court and Parliament until near the
close of Edward III's reign. We were allowed to have this invaluable work
copied, and by special permission to have photographs taken of its centuries-
old illustrations of coats-of-arms, tombs, etc.

15

King John was succeeded by weak, irresolute Henry III, who reigned fifty-six long, dreary years. Sir Thomas, the fourth Lord de Greene de Boketon, was born in the closing years of this reign. In 1270, Prince Edward, afterward known as The Hammer of Scotland, set forth on the last of the great Crusades. The flower of the nobility attended the Prince as knights. The second Lord de Greene was yet alive. His heir was a young man whose rank entitled him to accompany the Prince. Edward reached the Holy Land and won some victories, but at a frightful cost of life. Young de Greene is supposed to have perished in Palestine, leaving in far-off England a little son so young that his own heir was not born until twenty years after Prince Edward became king, which was in 1272. The old Lord, the child Sir Thomas' grandfather, died a few years after his crusading son. "Sir Thomas flourished," says Halstead, "about the beginning of King Edward I," i. e. he came to his title about this time.

King Edward conquered Wales, and then attempted the conquest of Scotland, earning the sobriquet of "The Hammer of Scotland" from his four wars against it. He captured and executed Sir William Wallace, the hero of "Scottish Chiefs." He also carried off the Stone of Destiny that the superstitious Scotch believed was the stone upon which Jacob pillowed his head when he saw the vision of angels ascending and descending from a ladder that reached unto heaven. Scotch kings were always crowned sitting upon that stone. Edward I took it to Westminster, and had an elaborate coronation chair built, with the stone within it. Every English monarch since then has been crowned while sitting on that sacred stone.

Halstead continues: "Sir Thomas we find recited in an ancient catalogue of the knights who accompanied Edward I against the Scots in 1296." Sir Thomas' wife was Alice, daughter and co-heir of Sir Thomas Bottisham, of Braunston. Sir Thomas de Greene⁴ was mentioned in the records of 1319 as then alive.

Sir Thomas, the fifth lord, was born in 1292. He contracted a high marriage with one of royal descent, and when about 40 was made High Sheriff of Northampton, (1330–1332), in the early part of the reign of Edward III. "The office was not as in these days, but esteemed equal to the care of princes, an office of great trust and reputation, and justly esteemed *honos sine onere.*" (*Halstead.*)

Our chronicler continues: "He married Lucie the daughter of Eudo de la Zouche and Millicent, one of the sisters and heirs of George de Cantelupe. Lord of Abergavenny, [on the River Usk in Wales,] with whom he had in free marriage nine Messuages, [houses with adjoining lands,] one Toft, [a grove,] and four Virgates of Land, [yard lands of from 15 to 40 acres each,] with their appurtenances in Harringworth. The house of de la Zouche was lineally descended from Alan the famous Earl and Sovereign of Little Britain." Sir Thomas' by Lady Lucie had one son, Sir Henry de Greene⁶, afterward Lord Chief Justice of England.

Lady Lucie had royal blood. From her only son have descended the Earls of Wiltshire, Montague, Peterborough and Sandwich, as well as a host of good Americans, including the Warwick and Quidnessett Greenes. For their benefit Lady Lucie de la Zouche's pedigree is given.

Charles the Bald, the grandson of Charlemagne, was King of France from 823–877. When at war with his brothers and in sore straits, he called to his aid Robert the Strong, a Saxon leader in England, and rewarded him with rich territorial grants and the titles of Count of Anjou and Duke of Ile de France. This was in 861. Duke Robert was every inch a military man, and won renown for his victories over the Norsemen, after they were successful almost everywhere else. It is from him that the martial spirit came that has blazed out anew now and then down the centuries, among his descendants, as in Lord Montague and the Earl of Sandwich in England, and our own General Nathaniel Greene of Revolutionary War fame.

Robert the Strong fell in battle with the Norsemen. A son Hugh was later killed in a Norse battle also. Robert's two sons, Duke Eudes and Duke Robert, are by some reckoned among the kings of France, as they exercised the power of a ruler. Eudes long fought the Norsemen with dogged courage. Robert², who succeeded this brother, had civil wars to contend with. When Robert's son, Count Hugo the White, or Hugo the Great, became Duke of France, there was nominally a descendant of Charlemagne on the French throne. In reality Hugo was king in all but name. His son, Hugh Capet, in 987, wrested the throne from the weak puppet upon it, and was crowned king at Rheims. Hugo Capet married a sister of Guilhem Fier-a-Bras, (William of the Iron Arm,) the Duke of Aquitaine.

Their son, Robert the Pious, came to the throne in 996 and reigned until his death in 1031. He was a good man, but weak king. He obediently put away his first wife at the Pope's command, and married Constans of Provens, by whom he had Henry, who became King in 1031. For nearly 900 years this line of kings sat upon the throne of France. Henry, this third Capetian king, found it an uneasy seat. The whole of his 29 years reign was a constant struggle with his great nobles. Guerrilla warefare was carried so far that the Church proclaimed a "Truce of God," by which no hostilities could take place from Thursday evening until Monday morning, or on feast days, or during Lent and Advent. King Henry's children were by his second wife, Anne of Russia. She was the daughter of Grand Duke Jaroslay, and was lineally descended from Jaroslav the Great, a famous Russian of 1000 years ago.

King Henry's second son was Hugh Magnus, Count of Vermandois, who is better known as the Great Crusader.*

The Count's daughter, Lady Isabel, married Robert de Bellemont, Earl of Mellent and first Earl of Leicester. They had Earl Robert the Second, who married Aurelia de la Waer, the daughter of Ralph, Earl of Norfolk. This second Earl of Leicester was Lord Chief Justice of England also. Robert, the next and third Earl of Leicester, married Petronella, the daughter of Hugh de Grantes-Mismil.

The daughter of Earl Robert and Countess Petronella was Lady Margaret de Bellemont, who married Sieur de Quincy. This nobleman was the first beside kings and princes to assume a crest to his coat-of-arms. Newton in his *Display of Heraldry* says the honor was conferred upon him because he was an eminent commander in the Holy Wars. This crest of his was noted for its extraordinary size. Sieur de Quincy was in the Crusade of 1188–1192, under Richard Coeur de Lion, King of England. One of his fellow crusaders was Robert, third Earl of Leicester, afterwards his own father-in-law. In 1207 King John created this nobleman Earl of Winchester. Nevertheless, when the barons rose against King John, eight years later, he was one of the 25 great barons who signed Magna Charta, and compelled the king to do likewise. His son, Roger, second Earl of Winchester, married Helen, a daughter of Alen, Lord of Galloway.

Earl Roger's daughter, Lady Elene de Quincy, married Alen, Lord de la Zouche, Governor of the Castle of Northampton, who died in 1269. Eudo

---

*His history reads like a romance. He was called Hugh the Great, both because he was a powerful leader, and because of his tall stature. As the brother of the King of France, he was given command of the French armies of Langue d' Oil. He was the first of the great leaders to reach the Orient. He took ship on the coasts of Italy early in 1096. Anna Comnena says his fleet was badly crippled by a great tempest. He passed on, however, and as he must pass through the Byzantine Emperor Alexius' territories, he sent 24 of knights in golden armor to Alexius to announce his coming. He styled himself, "The brother of the King of Kings, and Lord of all the Frankish hosts." Smooth spoken Alexius let him come within the walls of Constantinople, then made him prisoner. And not until all of the Crusader readers with their hosts besieged the city, did he set him free.

It was a campaign of horrors. In one day 500 men perished from excessive heat. At one time over 500 died of thirst, and the plague numbered its thousands. At Antioch the Sultan Kerboghu besieged the Christians until the soldiers from hunger devoured the leather of their shoes and shields, and even ate the bodies of the dead. The last pitiful remnant of bread and wine was used to celebrate the mass. Then, at the head of a mob of ragged, starving men, Count Hugh made a sudden and desperate sally where the Turks were strongest. 3000 of the Turks were killed on this spot They fled, and before the affray ended, 100,000 Moslems were slain.

Some time later, the Turks took a terrible revenge. They hemmed in 150,000 Christians and began to slaughter them. 149,000 Christians were killed. Count Hugh, who seemed to live a charmed life, cut his way through with barely 1000 men.

The Crusade closed in 1100. Count Hugh remained to make the little Kingdom of Jerusalem secure, the more so that thousands of enthusiasts, both men and women, flocked to Palestine, determined to end their days in the Holy City. Alexius again showed treachery, and the Christians marched against him, hundreds of ladies accompanying them to witness the combat. They were out witted and out numbered. The women were captured, sold as slaves in Bagdad, and ended their days harems. Count Hugh escaped to Tarsus, the city where the Apostle Paul was born. Worn out by his hardships, there he died, ...

de la Zouche was the next in the line. He married Lady Millicent de Cantelupe. It was their daughter, Lady Lucie, that married the fifth Lord de Greene. She was the fifteenth in lineal descent from Robert the Strong, eleventh from Hugh Capet, eighth from Count Hugh the Crusader, and fourth from Earl Winchester, who signed Magna Charta. She had the blood of lords, earls, counts, dukes, grand dukes and princes, and of three kings in her veins. Those who descended from her need not feel unduly elated. There have been nineteen generations since her day, and whatever royal blood she transmitted to her line must be pretty effectually diluted by now.

To return to the de Greenes. Both Sir Thomas[5] who married Lady Lucie, and their son, Sir Henry[6], the Lord Chief Justice, received high honors from the hand of King Edward III, one of the best and strongest kings England ever had, and whose long reign of 50 years allowed him to bring about many reforms. He was a warrior and statesman, with a lawyer-like bent of mind. More important laws were passed in his reign than in 300 years before. He created Justices of the Peace; made the rank of a duke; established the Order of the Garter; divided Parliament into the House of Commons and the House of Lords, and had its powers first clearly defined. He ordered the use of the English language in Court and Parliament instead of French. An energetic, change-working king such as he, had particular need of a counselor of trained judicial qualities.

He found such a trusted adviser in Sir Henry de Greene, the foremost lawyer of his day. Sir Henry's rank would not allow him to plead before the bar, but he put all his mental acumen and legal knowledge at his royal master's command. The King was deeply attached to him. Little did either of them think that in a day to come the King's grandson would cut off the head of his counselor's favorite son.

Halstead tells of the Lord Chief Justice's rise in these words: "He was a Commissioner to examine certain abuses of which there was great complaint. He was much employed, and in special trust and authority under those ministers the King left to govern the land in all the long wars he made in France. . . . . . His integrity, wisdom and great abilities did occasion his advancement [1353] to the office of Lord Chief Justice of England. He was Speaker of the House of Lords in two Parliaments [1363-4,] and became at last of the Kings nearest Counsel. [State Cabinet.] And such was his good fortune, ... he left to his posterity one of the most considerable estates of that age."

" He died possessed of his ancient manor of Buckton, of Greene's Norton, East Neaston, Heydmon Court, Heybourn, Ashby Mares, and Dodington, with lands in Whittlebury, Paulsbury, and Northampton; the lordships of Drayton, Luffwich, Pesford, Islip, Shipton, Wolston, Wamingdon, Chalton,

Haughton, Boteshaseall, with lands in Harringworth, Cottingham, Middleton, Carleton, Isham, Aldwinckle, Pishteley, Harrowden, Hardwick, Raunds, Ringstead, Coates, Titchmarsh, Warrington and sundry other places."

One of the Lord Chief Justice's enterprises was the establishment of a Fair, held each year upon the spacious green or park at Boughton. A charter* was granted to him to hold a three day's fair on the "vigil, day and morrow" of the Day of Saint John the Baptist, i. e. the 24th, 25th and 26th of June, each year.

The Boughton Fair became second only to the London Fair itself. Noblemen brought their horses and stock for exhibition, racing and sale. Silk merchants, sword cutlers, armor-makers, jewelers, saddlers, wig-makers, carvers and marble-workers sold their wares. There were feats of tumbling, wrestling, stilt-walking and sword-fencing. There were merry-Andrews, buffoons and clowns, "wranglers in verse," (poets, who fitted a rhyme while their patrons waited,) and musicians who played harp, fife and flute. There were eating booths and ginger-bread stalls, and shows of giants, dwarfs, double-headed calves, and wild beasts. This great Fair was a boon to all Northampton. Incidentally it helped to fill the coffers of the Lords of the Green. The Boughton Fair still exists, five and a half centuries after its rise.

The Lord Chief Justice died in 1370, a little under 60, and was buried at Boughton. He was the last Lord of the line to be buried there. He was early married to Katherine, the daughter of Sir John, and only sister of Sir Simon Drayton of Drayton. They had four sons and two daughters, Sir Thomas[7], the heir ; Henry, afterwards knighted by King Richard II, and

---

*The original text of King Edward's Charter is in Medieval Latin and is as follows.
Sir Henry Greene, Lord of Buckton and other Lands and Lordships.

Carta pro Feria in Buckton.

Anno 35° Regis Edwardi Tertii.

Rex, Archiepiscopis, Episcopis, etc. Salutem. Sciatis Nos de gratia nostra speciali concessisse & hac Carta nostra confirmasse dilecto nobis Henrico Green, quod ipse haeredes sui imperpetu um habeant singularis annis unam Feriam apud Manerium suum de Buckton in Comitatu Northamptoniae per tres dies duraturam, videlicet in Vizilia & in Die & in Crastuio Nativibatis Sancti Johannis Baptistae, nisi Feria illa sit ad nocumentum vicinarum Feriarum. Quare volumus & firmiter praecipimus pro nobis & haeredibus nostris, quod praedictam Henricus & haeredes, sui praedicti imperpetuum habeant Feriam praedictam apud Manerium suum praedictum cum omnibus libertatibus libertis consuetudinibus in, hu, uemodi Feriam pertinentibus, nisi Feria illa sit ad nocumentum vicinarum Feriarum, sicut praedictum.

His Testibus,

Venerabili, bus Patribus S. Cantuar, Archiepiscopis, totius Angliae Primate [Venerable Father, Arch bishop of Canterbury, Primate of all England.] R. London.

J. Wigorn, Chancellorio nostro, Episcopis, [Chancellor and Bishop.]
Will de Bohun, North.
Will de Clynton Huntingdon, Comitibus,
Radulph. Baron Stafford.
Joh. de Gray de Rotherfield, Senescallo Hospitii nostri & aliis. [

Dat. per manum nostram apud Westmonasterium vicesimo octavo die Februarii. [Dated at Westminster Feb. 8, (1361.)]

Per breve de privats Sigillo.

made heir to his uncle, Sir Simon Drayton ; Nicholas and Richard, who never married, and supposedly died young ; Margaret, who married Lord de la Zouche, and Amabila, who married Lord Ralph Raynes of Clifton.

According to the English law, the title and estate should have been the oldest son's, but as Jacob of old loved Joseph above his other sons, so the Lord Chief Justice favored his second son above all the rest. There must have been something particularly engaging about Henry de Greene. The King afterwards advanced him to high honor ; his uncle left him his title and estate, and the heir himself, Thomas⁷, consented to the extraordinary and almost unheard of thing, to alienating an entailed estate, and passing the major part of it on to the second son. A special license was given by the King, Boughton remained to the heir's portion, and Green's Norton was purchased and added to it. With that and large moneys, the older son was content.

CHAPTER IV

THE LORD GREENES OF GREEN'S NORTON, 1359 TO 1570.

History of Green's Norton. Line to close of the Lord Greenes. Lady Vaux's Line. Countess of Pembroke's line. Line of Lady Parr, Queen Catherine Parr and Henry VIII.

Those interested only in their immediate family history may as well skip this chapter. None of the American Greenes are of this branch. The blood of the Lord Greenes flows in the Pembroke family and other noble families, through the daughters. But the males of the titled line died out in 1506. The interest of this branch centers in Queen Catherine Parr, the last consort of that burly old monarch, Henry VIII.

Norton was a beautiful manor as far back as Richard Coeur de Lion's day. He bestowed it on a favorite soon after his return from the Crusades. From Earl this and Earl that it passed for 165 years. Several who held it died young. Three died childless, and three left only daughters, so that each time the property passed to collateral lines. Baron Morley, to whom it came, was afraid of it. Lord Chief Justice de Greene broke the entail for him, and acquired it himself, changing the name to Green's Norton. It was ever after the seat of the Lords de Greene, instead of Boughton.

The Lord Chief Justice's son, Sir Thomas[7], married Sir John Mablethorpe's daughter. Only one son survived. There is an old and handsome church at Green's Norton. Here the Greenes, from Sir Thomas[7], are buried. The family took a pride in the magnificence of their tombs. Some of their tombs had rare brasses, which were inlaid panels of fine brass with raised letterings. Others had altar tombs of finest marble, supporting effigies or recumbent statues representing those buried beneath. Canopies, recessed arches, and carved coats-of-arms were used wherever they could heighten the effect.*

---

* In this connection we give the contract for the making of the tomb of Lord Ralph and Lady Greene. Lord Ralph was the oldest son of Sir Henry Greene who was beheaded in 1399. Anyone with a little

In the church at Green's Norton, at the east end of the north aisle, is a depressed arch, under which was once a handsome tomb, now sadly mutilated. This is shown to sight-seers as the Lord Chief Justice's tomb. It is really that of Sir Thomas[7] and his wife.

Sir Thomas[8] was born in 1369 and died in 1417. His only son, Sir Thomas[9], had a large family by Phillipa, daughter of Baron Ferrars. His wife was descended from William the Conqueror, through the Earl Spencers.*

Sir Thomas[10] lies with his wife in the center of the nave of the church. The brass of their tomb-slab bears this inscription, that I commend to those who would like to try a specimen of middle-age Latin.

" Hic jacet Thomas Greene miles. D'n's de Norton et Matilda ux ejus, qui vero. Thomas fuit filius et heres Thome Greene Militis. D'ni de ead'm et Philpoe ux's ejus filie Roberti D'ni Ferras de Charteley et Elizabeth uxoris ejus filie Thomas Le Spencer, qui quidem Thomas Greene pater prefati Thomas Greene, fuit filius et Heres Thomas Greene Militis. D'm de Norton predicati, et Marie ux's ejus (filie) Ric'i D'm Strange de Blacmere, qui quidem prefatus Thomas filius predicati. Thome et Philippoe, obiit ix

knowledge of both French and Latin can read it.

Indentura inter Katherinam uxorem Radulphi Greene & Thomam Prentys & Robertum Sutton de Chelaston. Kervers.

CEste Endenture faite perpentres Katherine que fuist la feme Rauf Greene Esquier, William Aldwynele & William Marchall Clerk d'un parte, & Thomas Prentys Robert Sutton de Chelaston en Count de Derbie Kervers, d'autre parte testemoigne, que le ditz Kervers ount covenantez & empris pur fair & entailler bien, honestement & profitablement, une tombe de piere appele alabast re bon, fyn & pure, content en longure ix pees d'assise, en largure iiij pees deux d'assise, sur quele tombe serent taitz deux images d'alabastre, l'un counterfait à un Esquire en armes et toutz pointz, contenent en longure vii pees d'assise avec un helm de soubz son chies,& un curs à ses pees,& l'autre image serra counterfait à une dame gisant en sa suroote overte, avec deux Anges tenants un pilow de soulz sa teste, & deux petitz chiens à ses pees, l'un des ditz images tenant l'un des ditz images tenant l'autre per la main, avec deux tabernacles appelés gabettes à lour testes, quele tombe counteindra per less costés avec le leggement trois pees d'assise, sur queux costés seront images d'Anges ove tabernacles portants escutz, selont la devise des ditz Katherine, William & William. Et auxi ferront les ditz Kervers un arche d'alabastre amounte tout la dite tombe, en longure & largure, avec pendantz & knottes, & un crest de soytes & autres ouvrages appertinent un tiel tombe, les queux image tombe & arche ferront proportionez endorres peintes & arraies ove couleurs bien & sufficientment en le pure honeste & profitable manere come appertient à tiel overage. Et ferront toutz les ditz overages prestment flatz, & performez, en toutz pointz, en manere suisdite, & sarrois & enhaute, per les ditz Thomas & Robert en l'eaglise parochiel de Luffwick, en Counte de Northampton, as costages & perill des ditz Thomas & Robert, en toutz maneres choses, perentre ey & le feste de Pasque serra l'en de grace Mcccxx. Pur quelles overages eu manere avantdit affaire & performers les ditz Katherine, William, & William, paieront ou feront paire as ditz Thomas & Robert ou l'autre deulx, quarant liures desterlinges, dont seront paier al sesance di cestes dys marcs & al fest de Pasque ore prochein aveuir dix marcs, & al fest del Nativité le Seint John Baptistre adonque prochein ensuant dys marcs, & at fest de Saint Michell adonque prochein ensuant dys marcs, & les dix marcs remanantz seront paiez qunnt tout les ditz overages seront faitz & sirnys, en manere avantdit; pur toutz quelles covenantz avantdit; pur toutz quelles covenantz avantditz & chescun deulx, de part les ditz Thomas & Robert faites, à performer mesmes Thomas & Robert eus obligent, & chescum deulx per foy, en lentier, lour heirs & executors as ditz Katherine, William, and William, en cessant livres per y cestes Eu tesmoignance de quele chose les parties avantditz a y cestes Endentres enterchangeablement ount mys lours Sealx. Donne le xiij jour le Feverer l'an du Regne du Roy Henry Quint puis la Conquest sisme.

*The Irish Greenes, who are exceedingly proud of their blood, claim descent from one of the younger sons of this ninth Lord Greene.

die Sep. An. dom. mili'mo cccclxii, et prefata Matilda una filiarum Joh'ni's Throcmorton, armigeri, quondam Subthesarauraii Angl. obiit . . . . die . . . . an. dom. millessimo cccc . . . . . Quorum anemabus propitictur Deus. Amen."

Sir Thomas[10] died before his wife, Lady Matilda—called Maud, after the old English custom of nicknaming Matilda—and she married again. She built and endowed a chantry in 1496, wherein it was directed by her will that priests " Should sing and pray perpetually for a perpetual obit for Richard Myddleton, [the second husband,] for Dame Maud, Thomas Greene, (sometime her husband,) his father, mother, and all his ancestors and friends." The building has always been known as Lady Maud's Chantry, though when the Reformation came in less than half a century after, all monasteries and chantries were abolished.

Sir Thomas[11] left an only son, Sir Thomas[12], the sixth lord in succession to be named Thomas, and the last Lord Greene. He had two daughters, to whom Green's Norton passed. Boughton went to the Lord Montagues, through former marriages of daughters of the Greene line.

The last five Lord Greenes lived in the Bloody Century. There was bad blood between the Lancasters whose emblem was the red rose, and their royal cousins, the Yorks, who displayed the white rose. First one side and then the other gained the throne. There was a see-saw of fighting, banishing and beheading. Hume says the nobility was almost annihilated, and 80 princes of the blood were killed. The House of Greene survived. Lord Alexander's policy, lived up to by his successors, not to intermeddle with the politics of kings, kept the Lord Greenes' heads upon their shoulders. There was never any doubt of where their sympathies were. When Henry the IV of Lancaster, at the beginning of the trouble, basely cut off Sir Henry Greene's head for no other crime than having been a good servant to his lawful king, he made every Greene a Yorkist to the marrow of his bones.

If they saved their lives, they suffered other ways. Their estates were raided, and the Lords sometimes mulcted for large sums of money. King Henry the VII, who never forgot he was of Lancaster, even though the War of the Roses was a thing of the past, had the meanness to throw the last Lord Greene into prison in 1506 on a charge of plotting treason. The infirm old man was then so near death that he died before the year was out. He was released, but not until the grasping king was richer. By a curious turn of fortune's wheel, the feeble old lord's granddaughter Catharine came to sit upon the throne of England, as the wife of the harsh king's son.

Lady Anne Greene, daughter of the last Lord Greene, married Baron Vaux of Harrowden. We are not able to trace her line. Thomas, Lord Vaux, a cousin of Queen Catharine Parr, had command over the Isle of Jer-

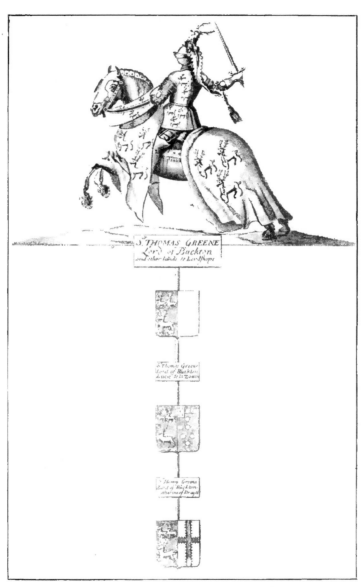

ARMORIAL BEARINGS OF SIR THOMAS GREENE.[7]

(Photographed expressly for this work from Halstead's Genealogy, published in 1685.)

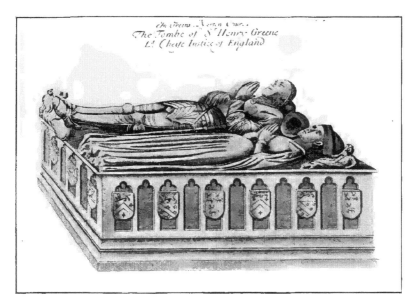

In Greene Norton Church
The Tombe of Sr Henry Greene
Ld Cheife Iustice of England

THIS IS THE TOMB POINTED OUT AS THAT OF LORD CHIEF JUSTICE SIR
HENRY GREENE, AND LADY KATHERINE, AT GREENE'S NORTON.
IT IS REALLY THAT OF HIS SON, THE SEVENTH LORD.

(Photographed expressly for this work from Halstead's Genealogy, published in 1785.)

sey. He published a volume of poems, some of which are yet found in collections of poetry. We give one stanza of his to show his philosophical temperament and poetic style :

> "Our wealth leaves us at death ;
>   Our kinsmen at the grave ;
> But virtues of the mind unto
>   The heavens with us we have.
> Wherefore, for virtue's sake,
>   I can be well content,
> The sweetest time of all my life
>   To dream in thinking spent."

The other daughter of the last Lord Greene was Matilda, who married Lord Thomas Parr, and had one son and two daughters. The son, Lord William, was a man of high integrity. King Henry the VIII made him one of his executors, and he was also one of Queen Elizabeth's nineteen Counselors. He was made Marquis of Northampton, but as he died childless in 1570 the honor died with him.

A daughter of Lady Matilda Parr's is mentioned in history as "sister of Queen Catherine Parr." She married William Herbert, Earl of Pembroke. He was a brilliant man, a man of note in his day. Burke says that this Earl on one occasion rode in parade with 300 in his retinue, "100 of them being gentlemen in plain blue cloth, with chains of gold, and badges of a dragon on their sleeves." The mourning given away to be worn at his burial cost more than $10,000! Earl William's son, Earl Henry, married Lady Sidney. One of her brothers was Sir Philip Sidney, and at her home he wrote his celebrated *Arcadia*. Not a few scholars and authors have been in this family, and from it have sprung the later lines of the Earls of Powis and Carnarvon.

The remaining daughter of Lady Parr was the celebrated Catherine Parr, born in 1513. She had fine mental powers, a stately presence, and an even, well-controlled disposition. She was undoubtedly ambitious. When a child her mother chided her for not being attentive to her embroidery. Catherine answered her—"My hands were not made to use the distaff or needle. My head was made to wear a crown, and my hands to hold a scepter."

She was the young and childless widow of Lord Latimer, when Henry VIII fell in love with her. She has been blamed for marrying this crowned Bluebeard, but in truth she dared not refuse him. The King used to boast that "no man could stand before his anger, and no woman before his lust." He was a great lump of fat, a coarse, conceited bully, and cruel as the grave. There was an average of 2,000 persons executed each year of his reign. He divorced his first wife to marry Anne Boleyn ; he cut off Anne Boleyn's head to marry Jane Seymour. When Jane was dead, he married Anne of Cleves whom he politely called " a great Dutch mare,"—and quickly divorced her because he found her fat and stupid. Then he married the all-too-gay Catherine Howard, and soon beheaded her for infidelity. Then he offered his bloody hand to Catherine Parr.

He would have had her head cut off if she had refused him. Naturally, she decided to keep her head on her shoulders, and so married him, July 12, 1543, when she was about 30 years old. He was a fretful invalid, a mass of bloated flesh. Catherine nursed him with tenderest care, and yet she came near following his other wives to the block.

The royal weather-cock had had several changes of heart (?) during his reign. Each change of creed he had marked by cutting off the heads of some of his chief advisers, and burning a number of his subjects. As a wit of that day put it, " Those that were for the Pope he burned, and those that were against him, he hanged !" The King after 1539 drew nearer and nearer the Roman Catholic faith, though the head of a Protestant nation. Queen Catherine came of a family who were strong for the Reformation. The King's advisers, Chancellor Wriothesely and Bishop Gardiner, feared her influence, and sought to make the king so angry at her that he would put her to death. The wary Queen guarded her speech so carefully, however, that even their spies could report nothing against her.

Mistress Anne Askew, a young, beautiful and intelligent woman, was a guest of the Queen at the palace. The King's pet tenet at the time was the Catholic one of the Real Presence, that is that at the consecration of the sacramental bread and wine, it becomes the actual body and blood of our Savior. This young lady was rash enough to argue against this to the King who, like most men of his stripe, had a poor opinion of women's brains, and was furious that she, a woman, would dare to answer back to a king. He accused her of heresy. She was put to the torture. Chancellor Wriothesely told her she should go free if she would but tell " who of the King's household " held the same views as she. She refused to name the Queen, though racked until almost pulled in two, and the Lieutenant of the Tower refused to torture her longer. She was tied in a chair, as she could no longer stand, and carried to Smithfield to be burned. After she was tied to the stake she was offered her liberty if she would accuse the Queen. But she would not. She was burned July 16, 1546, three years after the Queen's marriage.

It was a narrow escape for Queen Catherine, but a closer danger awaited her. The King was eternally arguing on religion. The Queen was unguarded enough to differ somewhat from him, and when he challenged her for proof her keen wits were more than a match for his bombast. He was soon in one of his black moods, and sent for Bishop Gardiner, who urged

QUEEN CATHERINE PARR

(From an old English print)

Photographed Especially for this Work

THE CHURCH AT GREEN'S NORTON

As restored by the munificence of Queen Victoria and others. Here were
the tombs of the six Sir Thomases, last Lords of
the line, and their families.

Henry to " make an example of her," i. e. behead her. The King consented and told the Bishop to go home and draw up an accusation against her for heresy. Spies were placed in the royal closet to witness to all the Queen might say. Word was secretly sent the Queen by a friend. It was like the doom of death to her, but she resolved to make an effort to turn the King's fickle fancy. He could swallow unlimited flattery, as she knew. He was known to have been really pleased when a fulsome speaker to his face compared him " For justice and prudence to Solomon, for strength and fortitude to Samson, and for beauty and comeliness to Absolom!" If she could tickle his vanity she felt there might be a chance to save her life.

She paid her daily visit with all composure. The King said that he would like to discuss religion with her. The Queen sweetly declined, and remarked * " That such profound speculations were ill suited to the natural imbecility of her sex. Women, by their first creation, were made subject to men. The male was created after the image of God, the female after the image of the male. It belonged to the husband to choose principles for the wife. The wife's duty in all cases was to adopt implicitly the sentiments of her husband. As for herself it was doubly her duty, being blest with a husband who was qualified by his judgment and learning to not only choose principles for his own family, but for the most wise and knowing of every nation."

The King took this so well, she ventured further. "She well knew," she said, " that her conceptions could serve no other purpose than to give him a little momentary amusement, that she found the conversation apt to languish when not revived by some opposition, and she had ventured sometimes to feign a contrarity of sentiment in order to give him the pleasure of refuting her." She concluded by observing how much profit and instruction she had reaped from his discourses.

"And is it so, Sweetheart?" replied the king. "Then we are perfect friends again," and he affectionately embraced her. When the Chancellor and 40 pursuivants came to arrest the Queen, the King gave him a fearful tongue-lashing, calling him " Pig! Fool! Knave! Beast!" and ordering him out of his presence. And so the Queen was saved. But she never again expressed a hair's breadth's difference of opinion from the king.

In January 1547 King Henry died. According to English custom Catherine was ever after addressed as a queen and kept a queen's estate. She married again, this husband being Lord Admiral Seymour, uncle to the young King Edward VI that succeeded Henry the VIII. Her short married life is supposed to have been unhappy, as the Lord Admiral was a thorough rascal. She died in 1548, not without suspicion of being poisoned, and is buried under a beautiful tomb at Sudeley. Poor Queen Catherine Parr!

* See Hume.

CHAPTER V

LINE OF THE BEHEADED SIR HENRY GREENE

List of estates entailed upon Sir Henry Greene. Sir Henry's career. History of King Richard II. Edward IV's anger at Sir Henry. Sir Henry's attempt to protect the young queen. His violent death. His heirs. Passing of the estate to the de Veres. Line of Thomas. John the Fugitive, and the legends about him. The Gillingham Greenes from Robert, and those who came to the Colonies in 1635.

It is true that the second son of Sir Henry, the Lord Chief Justice, was a young man of exceptional promise, and that he was his father's favorite. Yet it is hard to understand how a practical, level-headed man like the Lord Justice could fly in the face of the law of primogeniture, then held as all but a sacred institution. Nor is it an easy matter to account for the real heir's consent to relinquish his birthright, and let the younger son take the major part of his father's estate. Hard to understand as may be, it was exactly what was done. It took a long time to get around the cumbersome red-tape of English administration of English laws. The Lord Chief Justice's many estates had to be broken up, one by one, and re-entailed. It was in 1352 that he purchased Greene's Norton,—a part of the consideration by which Lord Thomas surrendered his birthright—and 1359 when Halstead speaks of the re-entailment as fully completed.

No full list has been preserved of the many manors settled upon Henry, the younger son. The more important and richest estates old historians list thus:

Buckworth.	Emerton.	Grafton.
Harringworth.	Hardwick.	Middleton.
Luffwich.	Harrowden.	Carlton.
Islip.	Raunds.	Isham.
Shipton.	Chalton.	Sudborow.
Titmarsh.	Warrington.	Irtlingburg.
Alwincle.	Haughton.	Ringstead.

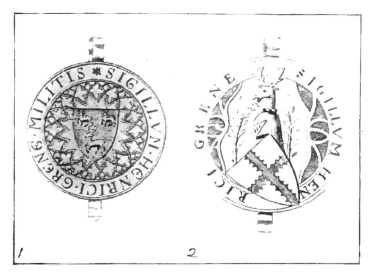

(1) The Greene Arms   (2) The Drayton Arms

SEALS OF THE BEHEADED SIR HENRY GREENE

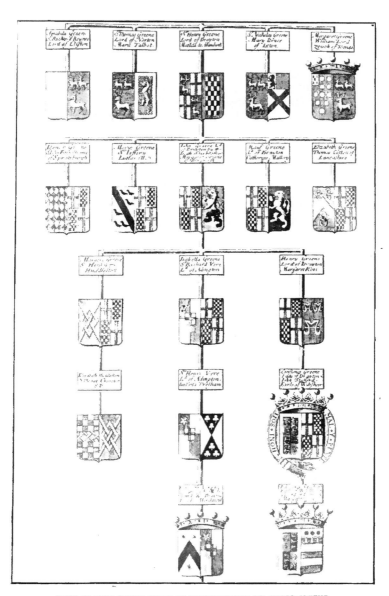

COATS OF ARMS OF THE HOUSE OF THE BEHEADED SIR HENRY GREENE.

Wolston.	Battershaseall.	Coats.
Pitchelery.	Cottington.	Warringdon.
Charlton.		

Halstead adds that through Henry's marriage with Matilda, sole heiress of her father, Lord Thomas Manduit, the lordships of Werminister, Westburg, Lye, Grateley, Dychurch, "and other fair possessions" were added to his estates.

More than this, Henry's childless uncle, Simon, Lord of Drayton, settled his large estate upon this nephew, stipulating that when he was dead Henry should assume the title and bear on his escutcheon the Drayton coat-of-arms. In time this all came about, as will be seen by consulting the coat-of-arms on the next page.

Many of these manors were then noted ones, or afterwards became historical because of famous men or events connected with them. Edward the Confessor, one of the last Saxon Kings, was born in Islip. The unfortunate Charles I, when "retired" to Northampton in practical imprisonment, used often to go over to Harrowden to play games on its famous bowling green. At Luffwich's handsome church, many of this line of Greenes were buried. The poet Dryden was born at Aldwincle, and at Drayton (Bury) both George Fox, the founder of the Friends or Quakers, and Sir Robert Peel, the great statesman, was born.

Like his father, Henry refused to follow the usual Greene policy of burying himself on his estates. He loved public life. His ability was so great that he became as prominent a statesman as his father before him. He was sent to the House of Commons, and was soon one of the leaders. The king knighted him. Sir Henry, as he henceforth became, was made one of the king's near Counsellors, and later was appointed one of the Parliamentary Commissioners who helped the king govern the country.

Halstead gives this interesting account of this bright period of his ancestor's fortune: "The ambitions of the young Henry Greene, fomented by these favors of fortune, drew him to the Court, where he resolutely joined his hopes and expectations to the fate of that unhappy prince, King Richard II, at whose hand he received the honor of knighthood. The merits of his person soon acquired him the nearest favor of this king, and those of his mind, the approbation and encouragement of all his Council, into the members whereof he was chosen for his great faithfulness and abilities."

"And when the Conspiracies of divers of the turbulent and seditious Lords had obliged the King to condemn some and banish others, he conferred (1395) several parcels of their confiscated lands upon Sir Henry Greene, as the Manors of Kibworth, Cotgrave, and Preston Capes, that appertained to Thomas, Earl of Warwick, those of Knighton, Covelle, and Bulkington* in the County of Wilts, by reason of the attainer of Richard, Earl of Arundell; and the Place of Lord Cobham in London with all its furniture. To the end that he might secure the fidelity of those about him by exemplary satisfaction for their services and hazards. And indeed, had not the perverseness of this King's Planet (which obstinately prospered the Rebellion of his Enemies,) overwhelmed all of his hopes, there was not any greatness unto which the deserts of this Sir Henry might not well have attained."

Yet this very favor of the King was Sir Henry's undoing. To understand how this came about, we must turn to the history of this king.

Edward III died in 1377, leaving a grandson, Richard II, on the throne. Great hopes were entertained of this king, far better morally than most of his predecessors, and showing at time, great courage, will and ability. Unfortunately, he was at other times eccentric and ill-balanced almost to insanity. Twice Parliament adopted the extraordinary measure of appointing a Board of Commissioners who had to formally sanction the King's acts before they could be lawful.

Time would fail to tell of Richard II's queer doings. He was but sixteen when, in 1382, he married Princess Anne of Bohemia. She was a warm-hearted, amiable, pious queen, yet she loved fashion, and is remembered as the one who introduced fans into England, and who taught the ladies of the kingdom to ride on side-saddles. It was at the gay and crowded Courts of Richard and Anne that gentlemen wore pointed shoes that turned up so high at the toes that they were sometimes tied to the shin to keep them from turning down. The ladies, not to be outdone, wore hennings or cornettes, horn-shaped head-dresses made over wire, and towering high above the head, and adorned with lace, fringes and spangles. (Imagine dapper Sir Henry at Court, wearing shoes with an six-inch peak to them, while Lady Matilda moved majestically about with a two-foot cornette upon her head!)

Queen Anne died in 1394 and Richard mourned her with almost a madman's outburst of grief. Nevertheless, he married again the next year. He was childless, and his cousins were plotting for his throne. Instead of trying to secure an early heir, however, the one thing that could keep down his rivals' intrigues, in one of his folly-fits he married Isabelle the daughter of the King of France, a pretty, dark-eyed child of eight, and put her in Windsor palace to be educated for her high duties.

Upon a certain occasion he banished for ten years the rival he

*This makes 40 known manors that Sir Henry possessed, besides his town houses in London.

most feared, Henry Bolingbroke, Duke of Hereford and Lancaster, his own cousin. Such a sentence carried with it a confiscation of the banished man's property to the crown. King Richard, however, to his Court, and to the young Duke himself, pledged his kingly word that Bolingbroke should not lose either his lands, or the estate that would come to him on the death of his father, the old Duke of Lancaster. When the old Duke died, however, Richard coveted his great wealth. He knew, beside, that it would be spent by the new Duke in fomenting uprisings and hiring troops against himself.

The Parliament of 1399 had just placed another Commission over the ill-balanced king. Richard appealed to them to allow him to confiscate the dukedom. By every consideration of honor, the King was bound to keep his royal oath. Nevertheless, being King, with the power that kings at that day possessed, he had the legal right to annul his former decision, and keep the estate and money. Sir Henry Greene, who had been trained under his father, and had all of the intricacies of the law at his tongue's end, seems to have pointed out to the Commission that Richard's demand was lawful. Whereupon the unanimous Board of Commissioners sanctioned the King's action.

All England was indignant over the disgraceful breaking of a King's oath. The banished Duke was furious, and laid all the blame on Sir Henry Greene, who was considered to be "the brains of the Commission." About this time there was something of a rebellion in Ireland. King Richard made another of his foolish moves by posting off in person to Ireland, and leaving England open to invasion. Bolingbroke promptly sailed to England, and most of the army went over to him. Sir Henry might have escaped, but he would not leave his royal master's child-queen to her fate. He made all speed with little Queen Isabelle into the strong castle of Bristol, where there was a strong garrison. The commander of the garrison treacherously surrendered the city to Bolingbroke without a blow, and at Bolingbroke's command, delivered Sir Henry Greene and two companions, Sir John Bushy or Bushey and the Earl of Wiltshire, disarmed and bound, to him. The next day they were beheaded.

Shakespeare, who devotes much of Acts I and II of his Richard II to Sir Henry Greene, puts into the mouth of Bolingbroke, as these members of the Commission were brought before him, these words:

> "Bring forth these men.—
> Bushy and Greene, I will not vex your souls
> (Since presently your souls must part your bodies)
> With too much urging your pernicious lives,

For 'twere no charity; yet ,to wash your blood
From off my hands, here in view of men,
I will unfold some causes of your deaths.

'You have misled a prince, a royal king,
A happy gentleman in blood and lineaments,
By you unhappied and disfigur'd clean.
......Myself a prince, by fortune of my birth;
Near to the king in blood: and near in love,
Till you did make him misinterpret me,—
Have stooped my neck under your injuries,
And sigh'd my English breath in foreign clouds,
Eating the bitter bread of banishment;
While you have fed upon my seigniories,
Disparked my parks, and felled my forest woods;
From mine own window torn my household coat,
Raz'd out my impress, leaving me no sign—
Save men's opinions, and my living blood—
To show the world I am a gentleman.
This, and much more, much more than twice all this,
Condemn you to the death.——See them delivered over
To execution and the hand of death."

As with much else in this play, this harangue is probably purely fiction. Bolingbroke seems to have hustled them out without ceremony or the shadow of a trial, for no other crime than being loyal to their anointed king, to the market-place at Bristol. In Market Square stood an imposing, high market-cross, of which the city was justly proud. At its foot he cut their heads off. So ignominiously perished September 2, 1399, Sir Henry Greene[7]. Only a few months more, with King Richard in captivity, Bolingbroke had himself crowned as Henry IV. He made a strong and diplomatic king, but to the day of his death, fourteen years after, he had fits of remorse and was constantly haunted by visions of those three treacherously slain at Bristol. He made all the amends in his power to the family of Sir Henry.

The beheaded Sir Henry Greene[7] and Lady Matilda left seven children, Ralph, John, Thomas, Henry, Eleanor, Elizabeth and Mary. Two of the daughters married noblemen; Ralph and John were successively Lord Greene. The great estate, in the end, passed through the last heiress of John's line to the Earls of Wiltshire and Peterborough, her descendants. Of Henry, the youngest son of Sir Henry, we know no more. He probably died in some of the wars of the "Bloody Century," leaving no children. Thomas, the third son, was the ancestor of the Gillingham Greenes.

Seal of John Greene
Drayton and Manduit Arms

Seal of Ralph Greene
Drayton and Manduit Arms

Seal of Ralph Greene
Greene and Manduit Arms

SEALS OF THE SONS OF THE BEHEADED SIR HENRY GREENE

(Photographed from Halstead's Genealogy printed in 1685)

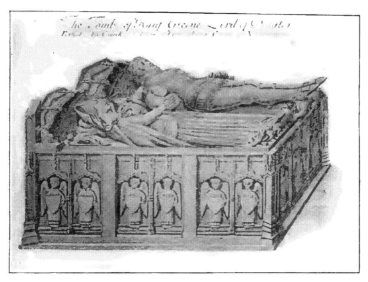

TOMB OF SIR RALPH GREENE[b], SON OF THE BEHEADED LORD GREENE

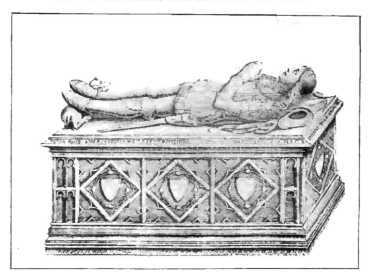

TOMB OF EDWARD[?], EARL OF WILTSHIRE

TOMBS WITH EFFIGIES.   LINE OF BEHEADED SIR HENRY GREENE
(Photo...   ...the K...   ... ...   by   ...   a H   ...   ...po, published in 1883)

In the very first year of King Henry IV, Ralph[5], Sir Henry's oldest son, was restored to his title and estates,[*] and received in after years particular honors from the king. The beautiful tomb of this Lord Greene of Drayton is shown on opposite page. As he left no children, the estate passed to his brother John,[5] who left three children.

Lord Henry[9] next succeeded. He left an only daughter, who married John, Earl of Wiltshire, the second son of the Duke of Buckingham. Their only heir was Edward,[10] Earl of Wiltshire, who died in 1501, while yet a young man, leaving no issue. The estate then reverted to the grandchildren of Lady Isabelle de Vere, a sister of Lord Henry.[9] None of the beheaded Sir Henry's line remained to bear the name of Greene, save the line of his son Thomas[4] alone. From him came the Gillingham Greenes, and from these again, came the Warwick and Quidnessett Greenes, two of the most important lines of that name in America. I have therefore taken pains to get all possible facts relating to the line of Thomas.[5] [†]

Between Thomas[8] and Robert[11] of Gillingham, two generations intervene. The name of the 9th of this line has not been preserved. This does not weaken the chain of descent. Henry K. Elliott, the English genealogist, whose ancestors for 300 years have lived at Greene's Norton, says the Gillingham Greenes have always been recognized as of the beheaded Sir Henry's line through his son Thomas.[8] This is confirmed through the absolute testimony of the Herald's Visitation, some of which are yet preserved. Henry VIII, in 1528, commissioned provincial Kings-of-arms to visit the different shires of England, and enroll all who could show their full pedigree and their right to wear coats-of-arms. Every 25 or 30 years this Visitation was repeated, and the enrollment registered, until 1686. The Gillinghams, being officially certified as entitled to bear the arms of Sir

---

* Halstead gives the long petition in mingled Latin and Norman French, in which Ralph Greene prays Parliament and the King to restore him his father's estates, which the King, in his first anger, seems to have confiscated. It begins:

"Petitionis Radulphi Greene in Parliamento. Henricus Dei gratia Rex Angliae & Franciae & Dominus Hiberniae, omnibus ad quos praesentes literae pervenerint, Salutem: Inspeximus tenorem cujusdam Petitionis Nobis in ultimo Parliamento nostro apud Westmonasterium tento per Radulphum Greene exhibitae in haec verba: Tres-excellent & tres-redoubté Siegneur, nostro Siegneur le Roy, supplie tres-humblement vostre humble liege Rauf Greene Esquire, que come en l'an primer de vostre gratieuse Regne le avantdit Rauf," etc., etc.

† I was fortunate enough to secure the aid of Henry K. Elliott, a scholarly English antiquarian. His family have for 300 years lived at Greene's Norton, the family seat of the Lords Greene. He himself resides in the Chantry House, which was built more than 400 years ago by Dame Maud Greene. He has recently completed a genealogy that necessitated a thorough and special search of all the records of the County of Northampton, England, and was therefore well calculated to undertake the English Greene researches. He examined and copied records, wills, subsidy rolls and Herald's Visitation lists for us. He looked up in particular all that could bear upon the pedigree of John Greene of Quidnessett, R. I., a weak link in whose chain of ancestry had hitherto baffled all searchers. The documentary evidence he found, confirmed and emphasized by the American records, make this pedigree clear. Mr. Elliott sent me no less than eight chart pedigrees, each 13 by 16 inches in size, that listed the Greenes of this line in their generations, at Boughton, Greene's Norton, Gillingham, Drayton and Orpidell, in Northamptonshire, Dorsetshire and Hampshire, England.

Henry Greene of Drayton, did at that time possess ample proofs of that fact, and so exhibited them to the King-at arms. This silences all cavil.

It is not strange that the name of the son of Thomas was lost. He was born about 1420, and came to manhood in the middle of the Bloody Century. Hume, speaking of the War of the Roses, says this: "No part of English history since the Conquest, [1066,] is so obscure, so uncertain, so little authentic or consistent, as that of the War between the two Roses. All we can discover with certainty through the dark cloud that covers this period is a scene of horror and blood-shed, savage wars, and treacherous, dishonorable conduct in all parties."

His son is supposed to have been born about 1450. This son was John.[11] The signs of cadency, i.e., descent of sons in order of birth, began to be added to coats-of-arms in the reign of Henry VII, 1485 to 1509. Even then cadency insignia were only used when the head of a line was a well-known man, prominent enough to found a new branch of the family. As John's sons added to the Greene coat-of-arms a crescent, the sign of a second son, we know two things; (1) John was the next-to-the-oldest son; and (2) he was a man of prominence in his day. The last is borne out by other facts, patent enough to those who take history as they find it. Those who are never willing to own their ancestors *could* do wrong, will of course try to think these incidents refer to some other John Greene.

The Greene *penchant* for athletics, fostered by the atmosphere of war in which he was born and brought up, made John[11] a most skillful sword-player, who could parry, feint and thrust, and perform the most astonishing feats with his trusty blade. Tradition says he had no superior in the use of the sword in the kingdom. He was a Yorkist, and for the Yorkist king, right or wrong, first, last and all the time.

In July, 1483, Richard III, one of the wickedest of England's several wicked kings, was crowned King, though his two nephews had the first right to the crown. He feared an uprising to place these princes on the throne, and therefore shut them up in the tower of London, and made Sir Robert Brackenbury their keeper. Toward the end of this same month, July, 1483, he and the queen came in state to the Earl of Warwick's and were his guests for a week at the Earl's magnificent castle at Warwick. It was but a few miles from the home of the Greenes, and John[11] made haste to tender his homage, for Richard, though mean, false, cruel and blood-thirsty, was yet of the House of York, and a crowned king.

The King had some dirty work to do. He sized up this cool, nervy, daring man, ready to give life or take it at his sovereign's command. The King himself sent him to Sir Robert Brackenbury, nearly a hundred miles away. "To him," says Dickens, "by the hands of a messenger named John

Greene, did King Richard send a letter, 'ordering him to put the two princes to death.' But Sir Robert sent John Greene back again, riding and spurring along the dusty roads, with the answer that he would not do so horrible a piece of work." The curtain falls on the too-faithful messenger there. The very next month King Richard found some one less scrupulous, who murdered the two lads for him. But the foul deed did not shake John's allegiance to this murderous king.

Two years later Richard III was slain in battle. Henry, the head of the House of Lancaster, married Elizabeth, the heiress of the House of York, and the War of Roses came forever to an end. Henry VII hated the Yorkists so heartily that he treated his own queen like a brute, because she was of York blood. He held a grudge against all who had rendered King Richard III, his former rival, a service. He had a spite against the family of Greene, a few years later arresting, as we know, Lord Thomas Greene at the very brink of the grave, on the charge of plotting treason. It would naturally be supposed that John Greene[11] would lose no time putting the seas between himself and the revengeful king. This is exactly what family tradition represents him as having done.

The Gillingham Greenes who came to America had this story, one from his father, and the other from his grandfather, who had been told it by *their* grandfather, Robert[11], own son of the man of whom the tradition is about. John Greene of Warwick, R. I., handed down no more than a reference to a change of name. His second cousin, John Greene of Quidnessett, handed down much more of the tradition. Being the namesake of his great-grandfather, John, who in turn was the namesake of *his* grandfather, the John of the story, his pride in the name gave him a special interest in the tradition. After his death his descendants adhered to the gist of the story, but transposed the names, and shifted the time and country to fit one of their first American ancestors, Lieutenant John of Quidnessett, whom they called John of London. This is a common thing in family traditions and what any genealogist would expect.

The Rhode Island version is that their ancestor was named John Clarke, and was one of the Regicide Judges who condemned King Charles I to death in 1649, and had to flee for his life when Charles II was restored to the throne in 1660. Then he came to Boston under the name of John Greene. One day he joined a game of sword-play, and performed some marvelous feats. Finally, he gave his sword a fling that sent it swirling in the air, from which it dropped, piercing and cleaving a loaf of bread to the center as it descended. Some one spoke up, "That is John Clarke, Judge Whaley, or the Devil, for no one else could do that!" Fearing he was discovered, Clarke *alias* Greene, fled into R. I. Here he married Abigail Wardwell, and here he died.

This is a very pretty story, but absolutely without a leg to stand on, if applied to either John Greene of Quidnessett, or his son, Lieut. John. The records show that the elder John resided continuously in R. I. for 59 years, from 1636 to 1695. He would have been a stripling of *78* when he married 19-year old Abigail Wardwell, and would have raised a family of 11 children after that, dying in 1729 at 123 years old! The story is as impossible if applied to his son, Lieutenant John[2], born in 1645, and therefore but *four years old* when King Charles was beheaded, and could scarcely have had a hand in sentencing him to death!

But taking the story as it should be, back to the days of John Greene,[10] the tradition throws a real light on affairs. John fled from King Henry to Europe. Homesick for England and family, he ventured back to an English city in which he was a stranger, and passed as John Clarke. Here he could see his family occasionally. Becoming less cautious, as he was not discovered, he was drawn into a bout with swords, and his identity guessed from his previous fame in that direction. Again he fled, and remained abroad until the death of the king.

A son of John the Fugitive was Robert Greene, Gentleman. He purchased an estate at Gillingham, in Dorsetshire, which was called Bow-ridge Hill. On the old records it is usually spoken of as Porridge Hill, the local pronunciation of Bowridge Hill. His wife's name is unknown. Whoever she was, it is believed that by her came that extraordinary mathematical ability that has made the majority of her descendants "quick in figures," as we usually express it, and has every now and then since her day cropped out in one of those phenomenal cases of instantaneous calculators.

Most of the subsidy rolls of that century have been destroyed. In the one of 1543.* Robert Greene[11] of Gillingham is listed. He was then an elderly man with grand-children. He had five children, Peter, Richard, John, Alice and Anne.† Peter died without heirs, and Richard inherited the estate. From Richard[12]'s line came Surgeon John Greene,[14] the head of the Warwick Greenes, and from the only other son, John, came John of Quidnessett,[15] the head of a numerous Rhode Island family of

---

* A quotation from this Subsidy Roll of 1543 is given to show the remarkable spelling of this period: "In thys Cedule indentyd is conteignyd as well as ye namys of all and ev'y p'son and p'sons havyng landis to ye yerly valeu of xlti or above, as also goods to ye valeu of xlti or above & also ye sumes p'ticularly set oute uppon ev'y off ther seyd namys dew to our Soverenge Lorde the King for ye fyrst of ye four yerys sbsyde [subsidy] grantyd unto hys hygnes in ye last P'lymet. [Parliament.]"

† An old English custom was to give a child one name, then call it another. Thus Mary became Polly, Matilda became Maud, and Anne became Nancy. The Gillingham Greenes had a diminutive of their own for the name of Anne. They called all their Annes—and they were partial to the name—by the soubriquet of Welthian, or Wealthy Ann. The two cousins who came to the Colonies named their daughters Welthian without circumlocution about it. Among the tens of thousands of names found in the records of New England for the 125 years after its first settlement, we have found not a Welthian outside of these two families. With them it is common.

Greenes. As these two were all of this family who came to the Colonies, we shall not attempt to give a full list of those who remained in England.

Richard[12] left a son Richard[13] and a daughter. Richard[13] and wife Mary had five sons and four daughters. Of these the fourth son was Surgeon John Greene[14]. In most American genealogies he is called the son of Peter Greene of Aukley Hall. This is a mistake. Peter was his oldest brother, the heir to Bowridge Hall.

John[12], of Robert[11], died in 1560. He had three sons, Robert[13] of Langham, Jeremy of Gillingham, and Henry[13], who seems to have lived at some distance from the old home. Henry "died suddenly," as the parish records puts it, Aug. 22nd, 1578. He had certainly a son, "Thomas of Wyke," and a son Robert. This Robert[14] had a son John[15] born in 1606, who came to the New World 1635, and is known to us as John Greene of Quidnessett.

CHAPTER VI

The Puritans to many seem mere savage iconoclasts, fierce destroyers of forms, but it were more just to call them haters of *untrue* forms   Poor Laud seems to me to have been weak and ill-starred, not dishonest, an unfortunate pedant rather than anything worse   Like a weak man, he drives with spasmodic fury toward his purpose, cramps himself to it heeding no voice, no cry of pity   Alas was not his doom stern enough? Whatever wrongs he did, were they not all frightfully avenged on him?"   —*Carlyle*

The three periods of emigration prior to 1650   Early Virginia and Barbadoes settlers New England a magnet   Laud and King Charles I and their tyrannies   The three classes of Greenes that came to Massachusetts   Line of Ruling Elder John Greene The Greenes of unknown descent   The two Gillingham Greenes who founded the two famous lines of Rhode Island Greenes   The great emigration of 1635   Archbishop Laud

The Forefathers are those emigrants who came to the American Colonies before 1650.   From the first Colonization to Cromwell's day, all emigration may be divided into three distinct periods   The early Virginia settlements on the James River, the first of all, the coming of the Pilgrim Fathers to Massachusetts 1620–31, and the emigration of anti-Laud men, the influx of which was at its greatest in the year 1635

The first of these periods was dominated by a spirit of adventure   The new world was pictured as Indian inhabited and wild beast infested, but in all other respects a paradise   The early Virginians were men who loved adventure, and were seeking quick wealth   The claims of religion rested very lightly upon them indeed

The illusion of tropical forests and rivers with sands of gold, was pretty well over with by the time of the Pilgrim Fathers' day   New England's bleak coasts were settled by a stern, stout-hearted class that had come for refuge, not for gain, that they might worship God after the dictates of their own consciences   We may shrug our shoulders at the sternness of their religion; we may deprecate their narrow bigotry; we may ridicule their prim, stiff ways, and their cheese-paring stinginess; we may make the most we can of their persecutions of the Baptists and Quakers, and of their hanging witches. The fact remains that we owe them a debt we can never repay. Their industry, honesty, and hard good sense, their positive religious convictions and unflinching adherence to what they thought right, has laid the foundations of our nation's greatness.

The colonists who crossed the ocean to escape Laud's tyrannies were almost to a man Independents or Puritans in religion. It was practically from their ranks that the Quakers and Anabaptists were afterwards drawn. They were men of a rugged, religious type, ready to lay down their lives for what they esteemed the truth.

The pioneer Greene in America appears to have been Solomon Greene, aged 27, who came to Virginia in 1618. By 1623 there were living in the James River settlements this same Solomon and five others, three of whom died within a year. From the survivors, Solomon, Robert and John, with Alexander and Roger who came in 1635, the Southern Greenes descend. Beside these who are named, ten others came from England in 1635, but settled in the Barbadoes, in the West Indies. Most of these Greenes became rich sugar planters and extensive slave owners. All of the other early Greenes I have been able to trace, belong in New England.

The New England Greenes may be divded into three groups, (1) those of the Ruling Elder John Greene line; (2) the Gillingham Greenes; and (3) those whose ancestry is unknown.

Ruling Elder John Greene came to Charlestown, Mass., in 1632. His wife was Perseverance, the daughter of a noted Puritan minister, the Rev. Francis Johnson. Elder Greene was 39 years of age at that time, and was accompanied by his wife, daughter, his two sons, John and Jacob, and Joseph Greene, a relative. A little later the Elder's kinsman, Bartholomew Greene, and family, came and settled in Boston. His two sons were Nathaniel and Samuel. This Samuel, in 1648, succeeded Samuel Day in business, thus becoming the second printer in all America. From his famous press were issued the Bible, Baxter's Call, the Colonial Laws, and Eliot's celebrated work on the Indian language. Hs became the head of a line that in all its generations has furnished an unusual nnmber of editors and printers. Two or three of his descendants did the first printing in their respective states. Thomas Greene, senior, and Thomas Greene, junior, of Malden, were of the Elder John Greene branch also.

This line of Greenes have for a crest, the green, or British woodpecker, pecking at a tree trunk. See the close of Chapter II. This coat-of-arms shows them to have descended from one of the younger sons or grandsons of

Lord Alexander de Greene de Boketon, who became the first Lord de Greene, in 1202.

There were two of the Gillingham Greenes, second cousins to each other, and each named John. Their history is sketched in the next chapters.

The forefather Greenes of unknown descent are these : James and William of Charlestown ; Robert of Hingham ; Rev. Henry of Reading ; Henry of Watertown, who was probably identical with Henry of Essex ; Percival of Cambridge ; Ralph of Boston ; and Thomas of Ipswich, who may be the same as Thomas, Junior, of Malden. Beside these were two John Greenes that died bachelors.

Of these forefathers, Elder John, Bartholomew and James Greene, with their families, came to Massachusetts by 1634. Rev. Henry Greene probably came about 1639 or 1640. All of the others came in 1635, the famous year of general Nonconformist emigration.* The conscientious husbands and fathers were more willing for their families to endure the hardships of a new country and rigorous climate, and face perils from Indians, than to remain in their own land, where religious persecution was already rife, and the muttering of approaching civil war was heard.

The Puritans, or Nonconformists, or Independents, as they are variously styled, had been frowned upon by every English monarch, Catholic or Protestant. They were radicals, keen of tongue, interpreting the Bible for themselves, and standing in little awe of either bishop or king. Elizabeth, the good Queen Bess of old song, burned a few of them for their obstinacy, punishing them quite as much for the fuss they made about ministers wearing a surplice or robe. or to making the sign of the cross, or to bowing at the name of Jesus, as for their alleged heresy.

James I thought himself quite a saint. This did not hinder him from making things so unpleasant for the Nonconformists that many of them went to Holland, and later, in the Mayflower and Ann, to New England. There was no improvement under Charles I, the next king.

Charles I hated the Puritans. He said it was because of their long faces and doleful Psalm singing. More probably it was because they were radicals and mal-contents in politics, and he was a king who rode straight over law. For seventeen years he refused to call a Parliament ; but at his own pleasure, and by his own might, imposed unlawful taxes, and levied ship money and subsidies that were no better than blackmail or robbery.

---

* The government became so alarmed by this wholesale emigration, that for several years they restrained their subjects from leaving. In 1637, eight ships were about to start, when they were forcibly detained. Oliver Cromwell was one of the passengers who would have gone to America, had the ship sailed. It would have been better for Charles, and the head on his kingly shoulders, had he permitted that ship to have gone upon its way.

His chief counselor was Archbishop Laud, who practically was Premier of England, and ruled the land. The old saying was, "It is Laud here, Laud there, and Laud everywhere." Charles' court-fool solemnly asked grace at the King's table one day, and brought over in his petition, "Great Laud and little Devil." *

The all-powerful Laud hated the Puritans even worse than did the king. Charles had to be a Protestant, because he was the head of a Protestant nation. Laud had to be a Protestant also, because he was the king's nearest adviser. What sort of a one he was is shown by the Pope offering to make him a cardinal. And really poor Laud meant to be extremely good. Being a narrow-minded man, or as Dickens says, "Of great learning and little sense," he could only be good in his own narrow way. He delighted in tinkling of bells and the burning of candles about the altar, in clouds of incense, and in much bowing and genuflection. He ordered those things to be done in every church.

One Puritan divine boldly said from his pulpit, that this was all trumpery and there was no authority in the Scriptures for bishops, anyway. For this speech, Laud had this minister's nose slit, his cheek branded, both ears cut off, fined 5000 pounds (nearly $25,000), and then imprisoned for life. Several others were handled almost as roughly. As for the lesser offenders, there were ears cut off, noses slit, and unmerciful whippings administered without number.

Small wonder our fathers thought Indians less savage than Laud !

___

*If pronounced slurringly, Lord has the sound of Laud. The Archbishop was short of stature, hence the force of the allusion. The poor fool was well whipped for his pains.

CHAPTER VII

FOLLOWING ROGER WILLIAMS INTO THE WILDERNESS

And my God put it into my heart to gather together the nobles, and the rulers, and the people, that they might be reckoned by genealogy. And I found a register of them which came up at the first, and found written therein.

Nehemiah VII. Verse 5.

Intolerance of the Pilgrim Fathers. Instance of Rev. Clarke's trial and of the hanging of the Quakers. Roger Williams. His banishment. The first Baptist church in America. Some of its first members. The present church building of the historic First Church of Providence. The three John Greenes who settled in R. I.

The Pilgrim Fathers came to Massachusetts that they might have religious freedom, but it was their own freedom they sought and not other men's. It was not a tolerant age. Catholic, Established Church, Presbyterian or Puritan, whoever had the upper hand tried to compel every other person to come to his way and his mode of thinking.

It was an age when religious topics were daily discussed ; when religion was more than art, education, or politics ; when received orthodox tenets were so rigidly insisted upon that not so much as a hair's breadth of disbelief in them would be put up with, and when such a thing as every man choosing a belief for himself was a thing unknown. There was the Catholic religion on the one hand, the Protestant on the other, and the Protestants were almost as undivided as the Catholics. There was no such thing known as Methodist, Universalist, Unitarian, Disciples, or Evangelical Churches. Those who liked a good deal of formality in church services belonged to the Established Church, or as we say now, to the Episcopalians. Those who believed in simplicity of service, but were strong as to their creed, were Independents or Puritans, corresponding to the Presbyterians and Congregationals of to-day.

Our forefathers were honest, upright men, but they could see no use of more modes of religious thinking than these. As they saw it there was absolutely no room for any other sect, and if any other tried to make a place for itself, it was of a surety of the Evil One. Just at this time the Baptists were struggling for a foothold, and the Friends or Quakers had also come into existence. *We* smile at these two tried and worthy Christian hosts being regarded as of Satan; but in that day their doctrines were considered rank heresy. Nay, they were thought absolutely blasphemous, so utterly vile and misleading that they needed putting down with a strong hand.

This is well illustrated by the trial of Rev. John Clarke in 1651. He was the Baptist minister at Newport, R. I. While on a visit at Lynn, Mass., he preached at a friend's house, at this friend's request. Before the sermon was ended two constables arrested him and two of his friends as " erroneous persons." They were taken to Boston for trial, and the charge entered against them of being Antipedobaptists. If anyone wants to know the meaning of that word, I refer him or her to Rev. Increase Mather's lucid definition of it more than two hundred years ago, thus :

" Antipedobaptism is a blasted error."

At the trial Governor John Endicott asked them if the charge was true. Whereupon the Rev. Mr. Clarke made use of this language: " I am neither an Anabaptist, nor a Pedobaptist, nor a Catabaptist; and though I have baptized many, I have never re-baptized any, for infant baptism is a nullity."

Rev. John Cotton preached a sermon on this answer. He declared the Rev. Clarke ought to be hung, because he preached doctrine that made him a soul murderer. Governor Endicott was more lenient.

" You deserve to die," said the Governor sternly. Then he imposed a mild (?) sentence upon them. All were to be whipped, and fined from five to thirty pounds each. The clergyman was finally let off without the whipping,* but elder Obadiah Holmes, one of his companions, received thirty lashes on the bare back from a 3-cord whip, and for several days had to lie on his face, as his back was one great sore.

A few years later three Quaker preachers were hung in Boston as " pestilent heretics." One of them was Mary Dyer, a woman of 36, and of a blameless life. But as the authorities thought no woman had a right to preach, they hung her higher than the men, that she might be a spectacle to Heaven, angels and men. Things like these teach us the temper of these good but mistaken men, who thought they were doing God-service by putting down all that they considered heresy.

No clergyman was allowed to have a copy of Shakespear in his library.

---

*Parton says that some unknown person paid Rev. Clarke's fine without the clergyman's knowledge. A personal friend became security for John Crandall, so that Holmes alone was whipped. Some additional particulars are given in Chapter XX.

No one was allowed to preach who did not heartily expound the gospel according to the received standard. No one was allowed to carry fire-arms, or to vote, or to hold the commonest office, unless he was a church member. One of the author's ancestors, William Wardwell, had his fire-arms taken from him, because he was believed to be tainted with the heresy of the Rev. Mr. Wheelwright, who had just been banished.

We must keep in mind their point of view, and how deep their feeling was in this matter, to understand the persecution of Roger Williams and his followers that arose 1631–1636.

Roger Williams was a remarkable man. He was magnetic, drawing converts to his views, wherever he went. He was a born leader, a quick thinker, a persuasive speaker, a man of enthusiasm, daring and originality, and a man who took up new thoughts, and new ways of doing things. He not only planned, but he carried out his plans. Some hold that he has been over-rated, that he was more brilliant than deep, and that in a religious sense he was everything by turns and nothing long. If all this be true, it must yet be conceded that he fills a greater space in history than any other man of the Colonies in a hundred years. He drew the best brain and blood of New England to Rhode Island, and when Massachusetts began to lord it over Rhode Island, Williams sailed to England and obtained a charter that put the younger colony in charge of its own affairs, and allowed a degree of religious liberty beyond anything ever known before.

Roger Williams was of Welsh descent, and was educated at Pembroke College. Afterwards he was the protege of Chief-Justice Sir Edward Coke, and from this great lawyer got his ideas of law and government. He was an exceptional linguist, a Greek, Hebrew and Latin scholar, and spoke and wrote English, Dutch, French and German. In America he soon added the Indian tongue to his other attainments.

Williams was ordained a clergyman of the Church of England. He soon developed Puritan views, and came to the Colonies, though he said it was "as bitter as death" to him to leave England. By the time his six-weeks sea voyage was over he was a Separatist or extreme Puritan. He arrived at Boston with his wife Mary, Feb. 5, 1631. He settled at Salem, only to be driven away. Then he was two years at Plymouth, returning to Salem again at the end of this time. Here, in 1634, there was erected for him a frame church, the oldest church edifice in America that is yet standing. The authorities thought he preached heresy. He certainly told his hearers in so many words that they had no right to take the Indians' land without paying for it, and that the magistrates had no right to dictate to men's consciences. This was more than the authorities would stand, and in October, 1635, they gave him a certain length of time to leave the colony.

Many of the Salem Church followed him into the unbroken wilderness of Rhode Island. In June, 1636, the colony was planted at Providence on the shore of Narragansett Bay. Everything was done systematically. The land was purchased from the Indians, and a compact was drawn up and signed, remarkable for its simplicity, and for the absolute liberty accorded to all. Here he preached for two years. Then another change of his religious views followed. He became a Baptist, and was persuaded that immersion was the only lawful baptism. In all New England there was not a clergyman that had been immersed. However, a little band of his closest followers met, twelve in all, including Roger Williams himself. Ezekiel Holyman or Holliman, (it is spelled both ways,) was chosen to baptize Williams. Then Williams baptized the other eleven. This strange proceeding was first reported by Governor Winthrop in his journal under date of March 16, 1639, and this was long thought to be the correct date. It is now known that it was really late in the autumn of 1638.

The old church records have been lost, and the names of only ten of the twelve constituent members of this first Baptist church in America have been preserved. The descendants of Surgeon John Greene are confident that he and his wife are the two missing members. So family tradition has it. Some of the other names have an interest to Greene descendants. Among them are Ezekiel Holyman and wife. Ezekiel Holyman's wife came to Providence in 1636 as Mrs. Sweet. Her husband died soon after, leaving two small sons, James and John. Then Mrs. Sweet married Mr. Holyman. Her son James, when grown, married Surgeon John Greene's youngest child, Mary. She inherited her father's skill and passed it on to her descendants, the celebrated " Bone-setting Sweets."

Two others of this original little band became ancestors of a large line of descendants who afterwards intermarried with the Greenes. These were a young couple, Stukeley Westcott and wife, who was Rosanna Hill before her marriage. This re-baptism of adults who had been previously baptized by sprinkling, gave great offense to the home church in Massachusetts, when they heard of it. The Salem church excommunicated the eight re-baptized members that had belonged to them. Mary Sweet-Holyman, and Stukeley Westcott and wife were among the number.

Dr. Henry M. King, the present pastor of this historic First Baptist Church at Providence, says of this church : " A church born in loneliness and exile, but born in the spirit of God, to human view self originated, and without lineal descent or pedigree, untouched by priestly hands, unanointed by apostolic grace, and yet a church of Jesus Christ came into being . . . . . . It was a very simple affair. There was no creed but the scriptures, and no ritual but the spontaneous offering of prayer, and the familiar unfolding of the word of truth. They were still possibly unsettled in their religious opinions, and far from unanimous . . . . . . Roger Williams became a high-church Baptist, and distrusted the validity of his own ordination and baptism. The little church survived the withdrawal of the minister, and gradually increased."

In after years the Warwick Greenes and the Westcotts became exceedingly proud of their foreparents having been of the "first" Baptist church in the Western Hemisphere, and bragged more about it than was really becoming, perhaps. Those who think the whole affair irregular, claim the real first Baptist church was at Newport, of which the Rev. John Clarke became the first pastor in 1644.* The Providence church is generally accorded that honor. In 1775, the year before the Revolutionary war commenced, the third church building of this church was erected, and is being used to-day. The first bell, made for it in London, weighed 2515 pounds, and had on it a quaint inscription :

> "For freedom of conscience the town was first planted.
> Persuasion, not force, was used by the people ;
> This Church is the eldest, and has not recanted,
> Enjoying and granting bell, temple and steeple."

It is a peculiar circumstance that Mr. J. F. Greene, one of the Church's present officers, is a lineal descendant of Surgeon John Greene and his wife who their descendants believe were two of the original twelve members.

Other towns and communities sprang up. The Quakers and the followers of Mrs. Anne Hutchinson were banished to Rhode Island, then known as Providence Plantations. By 1650 the Waites, Anthonys, Wardwells and Pierces, with whom the Greenes largely intermarried, were residents of the liberty-loving colony. Of the Greenes themselves there were three adult men. These all came about the same time, in the very earliest day of the colony. Each was named John, and two of these three had wives named Joan. These three men were John of Newport, Surgeon John of Warwick and John of Quidnessett.

John of Newport's line yet continues. His family was never as extensive as the others, and kept to their own part of the country pretty well. So far as I have been able to trace them, his posterity did not intermarry with the other Greenes of Rhode Island at all. The other John Greenes were of the English Gillingham branch and were second cousins-german to each other. †

*"Possibly in 1644. This is the traditional date of the origin of the church. There is no historic record prior to 1648."

Note by Henry M. King, D.D. pastor of the First Baptist Church at Providence, and an authority upon early Baptist history.

† The younger John's father was second cousin to Surgeon John, which would make the younger John third cousin to the Surgeon's children. He was of course more nearly related to the father than to the children, to whom he was mid-way between a second and third cousin, or as genealogists phrase it, a second cousin-german. German here denotes not nationality but degree of relationship.

FIRST BAPTIST CHURCH OF PROVIDENCE, R. I.

Oldest Baptist organization in the Western Hemisphere. Established 1638 by Roger Williams. Present edifice erected 1775.

The older cousin was variously called John Senior, John the Elder, John of Salisbury, Chirurgeon John and Surgeon John, John of Providence and John of Warwick. In these pages he is spoken of as Surgeon John of Warwick. Various dates have been given of his birth. His direct descendant, Henry Lehré Greene, who has studied the matter carefully, puts the date at 1585. He was born at Bowridge Hall, Gillingham, England, and was the younger son of Richard Greene, Gentleman, and Mary his wife. He was something of a bachelor when on November 4, 1619, he married Joan Tattersall, (or Joane Tatarsole, as the old records have it,) at St. Thomas' Church, Salisbury, England.* His home was at Aukley Hall, Salisbury. He was too strong an anti-Laud man to make it safe for him in England, so with his wife and five children, he set sail from Southampton in April, 1635, in the good ship James, and arrived at Boston, May 3, of the same year. He lived for a time at Salem and was among the first who followed Roger Williams to Providence. The latter showed his confidence in him by making him one of the trustees to whom Providence was deeded.

The younger cousin is spoken of as John Greene the Younger, John of London, John of Wickford and John of Quidnessett. In this history he is always John of Quidnessett. He was born in England in 1606, and resided at or near London; probably his home was at Enfield, one of the suburb towns of the great city. He was a man given to commemorating family events by the names of his children. Thus a son was John Clarke, the very name assumed by his ancestor, John the Fugitive, 166 years before. A daughter was Enfield, a most singular name for a girl, but understandable if given in honor of the dear old English home.

John of Quidnessett left England in the ship Matthew, early in 1635. He was at that time 29. He went first to St. Christopher, one of the British West Indies. This tropical island was a capital place at that time to make wealth. But its population was a Godless set, and John had too much of the Puritan about him to relish such companionship. He sailed therefore for Massachusetts, and from there passed to R. I. In 1637 we find him with Richard Smith, the Indian trader, at Aquidneck or Quidnessett, on Narragansett Bay. He lived for some years in Smith's family, in the Block House, or family fort. Here Roger Williams was a frequent visitor. Here Richard Smith gave free lodging and entertainment to all travelers, and here he opened up a trading post with the Indians, John Greene assisting him. When about 36 years of age John of Quidnessett married a young widow. Of his children and history the next chapter will tell.

---

*The St. Thomas Church records are interesting. They give the baptism of "ye sonnes and daughters of Mr. John Greene and Mris. Joane Greene." "Mris." is an old abbreviation of Mistress, our present Mrs. John Greene is variously described as " Gentleman " and " Chirurgeon."

CHAPTER VIII

The first Greenes of Rhode Island. Resemblance of character between Surgeon John of Warwick and John of Quidnessett. Honors that fell to the Warwick line. Early days of Providence. The wrangle with the Massachusetts authorities. Arrest of Surgeon John in Boston. The Massachusetts version of the affair. Settlement of Shawomet, afterwards Warwick. Death of Mrs. Joan Greene among the Indians. Wholesale arrests. Surgeon John in London. His last days.

Rhode Island might better have been named the State of Greene. It is said to not be safe to speak evil of any man in the State, for if not a Greene, he is liable to be of kin to them. Rhode Island is the one state where the Smiths, Browns and Johnsons are outnumbered. There are more Greenes in the State than of any other name whatever, and they have enjoyed more state and civic honors than any other family within her borders.

The Mississippi, as its headwaters flow from Lake Itaska, is but a small stream. It gathers momentum as it descends, and becomes a mighty torrent ere it empties into the ocean. So the stream of descent for this numerous family, great as it is, has its rise in the triple father fountains, the three John Greenes of Rhode Island.

The early records are by no means complete. Knowing this, many take it for granted that the first hundred years of R. I. history must be confused and tangled as to the Greenes, as each of the stem-fathers had the same name. Others suppose that other Greenes came to R. I. in an early day, and that their descendants are mixed up with the others. I have made a careful and special study on this very subject. I state emphatically, (1) that up to the year 1700 there is no record, tradition or trace of any stem-father by the name of Greene, other than these three Johns. (2) There is no confusion whatever, up to the same year, A. D. 1700. After that there is, in some cases. But to that time, every son or daughter of that house may be readily and correctly placed among the descendants of the particular John to whom he or she belonged.

48

John of Newport's children have been the least numerous. They kept to their own part of the state and did not intermarry with the others. Surgeon John moved to Warwick before any of his children married, and for a long time his descendants lived almost exclusively at Warwick and East Greenwich. John of Quidnessett's line lived at Kingstown, now Wickford, Westerly, Charleston, Coventry, and West Greenwich quite as commonly. I repeat that no one need fear that any of the early generations are assigned to the line of the wrong John. It has been easier to get the first century's links of descent accurate than those of a later date, when the families began to scatter.

John of Newport passes at once from this narrative, as no incidents are recorded of his history. The other Johns were both leaders, both prominent men, and there is a great deal in the records about them. They showed a resemblance in their traits. No doubt they were good and able men, and left a record their descendants are justly proud of. But they were not saints. They were both positive, aggressive, stand-on-the-defensive men. Their fighting armor was ever on. In fact, they were two typical Englishmen, that could neither be scared nor driven, and were on general principles not averse to a scrap now and then.

Both men were prominent. Of the two, Surgeon John of Warwick's fame is the greater. He was a generation older than the younger John, and the more naturally selected as a representative of the Providence Plantations* to cross the ocean and lay their side of the controversy with Massachusetts before the English authorities. In England he became the best known man of the Colony, with the exception of Roger Williams. Naturally official favor was shown to both him and his sons.

Of the Surgeon's three sons who lived to be middle-aged, all three were at various times Assistant President of the Colony. The oldest son, whose name was also John, held office from the Crown for forty-nine years, having been Recorder, Attorney General, President's Assistant, one of the Council of Sir Edmund Andros, Major of the Main, which is equivalent to our Major General, and for ten years, 1690–1700, was Deputy Governor, the highest office in the Colony, Sir Edmund Andros being Governor over all the New England Colonies as a whole.

---

* The colony was first called Providence Plantations. In 1638, Rev. John Clarke, whose trial for heresy is given in the previous chapter, and Mrs. Anne Hutchinson, a banished "heretic," purchased Aquidneck Island of the Narragansett Indians. The Hutchinsons started the town of Pocasset or Portsmouth. Clarke started the town of Newport in 1639. Rev. Clarke thought Aquidneck a good name for the entire region and found many who followed his example in calling it that. In 1644, the year Surgeon John went back to England, the Assembly met and debated which of the several names used should be adopted by the colony. They settled upon the name Island of Rhode, or Rhode Island. The name spread so slowly that Surgeon John, fifteen years later, used in his will the term Providence Plantations. In 1663, the name of Rhode Island was finally and officially confirmed.

This brave record has been well kept up. Of this family have been General Nathaniel Greene, greatest, save Washington, of all the Revolutionary War heroes; General George Sears Greene and General Francis Vinton Greene. It has supplied Rhode Island with representatives, senators, supreme judges and governors. As a result, when a Greene first begins to study his pedigree, his first question is,—"Am I of the Warwick Greenes?"

To take up Surgeon John of Warwick, R. I.'s history first of all.

Roger Williams purchased the land upon which the city of Providence stands, from the Indians. Then as grantor he deeded it to twelve trustees for the use of the colony. Stukeley Westcott is the first trustee mentioned, John Greene the fifth, and Ezekiel Holyman the last. Two years later, the time being ripe for division, the land was divided into fifty-four lots or shares, one lot being allowed to each single man or head of a family who had been an "associate," as the records phrase it, with Roger Williams at the time of the Providence settlement. Where a husband had died the widow was given his share, so that none were either overlooked or given a double portion.

John Greene Senior and John Greene Junior each received an allotment. The first of these was of course Surgeon John. It has been held that John Greene the Younger was the Surgeon's oldest son. But inasmuch as he was a lad of less than sixteen in June, 1636, when Providence was settled, this seems improbable. It seems more reasonable that the younger John was John Greene of Quidnessett, a man of thirty at the time of the exodus.

When Providence bid fair to become a prosperous settlement, Massachusetts began to make trouble by claiming it was within the limits granted to her, and belonged to her jurisdiction. She did not hesitate to step in and nullify Providence Plantation's laws, and she threatened to prosecute those of heterodox religious views. This was the beginning of a long struggle that lasted for years, and in which neither Rhode Island nor Massachusetts show up to advantage. They quarrelled, took unfair advantages of each other, appealed to the mother country, and were as stiff-headed and unreasonable a set of mortals as could well be imagined.

Roger Williams in 1641 sailed to England to get a charter for R. I. that would stop these clamors. The spite-work and quarrelling waxed worse after his departure. There were Samuel Gorton, Richard Carder, Randall Holden and Robert Potter, particularly violent in speech, and ring-leaders on the R. I. side. Surgeon John was a warm friend of these men, and in the thickest of the fray. The Surgeon wrote a bold pamphlet on what was called the Verin Controversy, a question of heresy and the State's right to put down such beliefs. He flatly charged the Legislature of the Bay (Mass.) with "Usurping the power of Christ over the Churches and men's consciences."

There was nothing of the craven about the doughty Surgeon. The year after his settlement at Providence, he paid a visit to Boston. Here he expressed himself freely as to the tyranny of town officers trying to control men's consciences. Palfrey tells us that the Boston authorities, Sept. 19, 1637, fined him twenty pounds (nearly $100.00) for "seditious discourse," and sent him away with an injunction to keep away for the future.

Captain Edward Johnson in his "Wonder-working Providence," tells us the Massachusetts' side. He says Surgeon John Greene "spoke contemptuously of Magistrates," and because of it was heavily fined and "forbidden this jurisdiction on pain of further fine and imprisonment." Meanwhile three of his especial friends, Potter, Carder and Holden were "disenfranchised of their privileges and prerogatives, and their names cancelled out of the record." Captain Johnson thought these men deserved this punishment, for he says they were "full gorged with dreadful and damnable errors." Another author tells us that these men disturbed the authorities by "their insolent and riotous carriages," and that they wrote "insulting and abusive letters" in defending their course to their superiors.

Gorton, the most turbulent of the lot, determined to start a new settlement. In 1642, he purchased Occupessuatuxet, or Pawtuxet, of Miantonomo, the head sachem of the Narragansett Indians. This was called Shawomet or Shawmut until 35 years later, when it was changed to Warwick. Following Roger Williams' example, this land was deeded to a dozen trustees or proprietors, the coterie of the five close friends already mentioned, and John Wicks, Francis Weston, Richard Waterman, John Warner, Samson Shatton, William Wardwell* and Nicholas Power. How close and strong was the friendship between these men who faced peril and hardship together, is shown by the fact that Surgeon John's near descendants married into the Wicks, Holden, Gorton, Potter and Carder families.

Massachusetts took this new settlement to be a challenge to her from her most seditious and rebellious subjects. The long threatened storm burst upon them in a fury. The Massachusetts authorites sent commissioners and forty soldiers, who broke up the settlement by force, and took nearly all the settlers of Shawomet prisoners. This was in 1643. Joan, wife of Surgeon John, was drawing near death. In her weak state, she was dreadfully alarmed, and her husband carried her off for refuge to the friendly Indians at Conanicut, R. I. Tradition says that here, with dusky faces watching about her death-bed, she passed away. Her husband remained with her until the mortal breath had left her body, and so escaped the trials of his comrades.

---

* Wuddall in records. This is the William Wardwell whose daughter Frances married John Anthony, and was thus the fore-mother of Susan B. Anthony. This was a Quaker family, and afterwards lived at Portsmouth where there was a large Friends' settlement.

Gorton and ten others were taken to Massachusetts. They were tried on the charge of being "damnable heretics." They were convicted and sentenced to hard labor at Charlestown, Mass. The next year, 1644, this sentence was commuted to banishment. Surgeon John Greene was selected by the indignant Rhode Islanders to present their grievances to England. He got safely away in 1644, and made so favorable an impression in the mother country that he secured valuable concessions and privileges for R. I. While in England he married a former R. I. friend, the widow Alice Daniels, who had returned to her old home. She lived but a short time, and after his return to R. I. he married a third wife, Phillipa (or Phellix), who survived him. He died in 1759 at Warwick (Shawomet).* He was buried at Conanicut (or Connimicut) by the side of his faithful Joan. As has already been said, his children for many years held high official positions under the government. Nevertheless, after his death, John of Quidnessett was the leading Greene of Rhode Island, and stands out in a plain, clear light of his own.

I prepared a condensed genealogy of the Warwick Greenes, but find that it takes more space than can well be given it. I will only say, that but four of his children left issue, Mary Greene-Sweet, Deputy-Governor John, James and Thomas. Gen. Nathaniel Greene, the greatest of the Warwick Greenes, was the great-great-grandson of Surgeon John, [John[1], James[2], Jabez[3], Nathaniel[4] and General Nathaniel Greene[5].]

From thenceforth the line of John Greene of Quidnessett alone is traced.

---

* The spelling in Surgeon John Greene's will is calculated to excite a smile: "ffurthermore," "sonne," "akers," "lott," etc., are some of these queer spellings. The will closes thus:

"Signed by mee, John Greene, Senior.

A True Coppie as atests John Greene, Town Clarke.

per Ezekiel Hollyman, debety—"

CHAPTER IX

History of Richard Smith. His trading post. His Block House. Connection with John Greene. The Atherton Company and the Quidnessett land dispute. Trials of John Greene, the chief leader for Quidnessett. His quarrel with Awashuwett. His last days. His burial. Joan Greene and her character.

Pugnacious old John of Quidnessett! The author being twice descended from him, takes a relative's privilege of plain speaking. John Greene of Quidnessett was good to his women folks, as New Englanders say, and was as true as steel to his friends. The Quidnessett land dispute that lasted for twelve long years, would never have been won, as it eventually was, by the purchasers of the Atherton concession, had it not been for John of Quidnessett's grit and perseverance, and the stoutness with which he stood out for his own rights and his neighbors' rights as well. But with all his admirable qualities, we must confess that he looked to John Greene's comfort, John Greene's interest, and John Greene's pocket-book, and that he was a stormy character.

His history is so interwoven with Richard Smith's, that something of the latter's history must be given also.

Richard Smith was known as the Patriarch of Narragansett. He was among the first refugees in R. I., being then 40 years of age, and having a wife and four children. Although he came into this wild land for conscience's sake, he was not averse toward bettering his condition, when once he was there. He saw his opportunity in the neighboring Indian stronghold of Aquidnessett, or as the white men soon shortened it, Quidnessett.

In the History of Narragansett, Potter tells us that the Narragansett Indians occupied the present county of Washington, R. I. At this time their head sachem was Miantanomo. The tribe numbered 30,000 souls, of whom 5,000 were warriors. Most of the tribe were congregated in Aquidnessett, along the banks of the Cocumquissett and at Nancook. So that this region was very densely populated. Quidnessett extended from Potowomut River to Narragansett Bay, and its western boundary was the Pequot Path, (later called the Post Road,) that was the common thoroughfare between the tribes, and for all comers and goers to Massachusetts, Connecticut, or to the sea. The Pequot Path led to the sea by way of Cocumquissett Brook. Here, a mile and a half from the present Wickford, Smith decided to build a trading post.

Smith was politic enough to humor the Indian love of ceremony, and to gain their good will by formally asking their consent to locate among them. After some years, he purchased outright from them the land he had previously been using. After his death, when his son's title to the land was disputed, John Greene, who had been with him from the first, made this deposition, that throws a vivid light on Smith's early dealings with the Indians.

"King's Province in Narragansett 21 July, 1679.
To All Whom This May Concern :

I. John Greene, inhabiting in the Narragansett Country, called King's Province, I being a sworn Conservator of the Peace, do on my Oath affirme, that forty years and more ago, Mr. Richard Smith that I then lived with, did first begin and make a settlement in the Narragansett, and that by the consent and approbation of the Indian Princes and people, and did improve land mow meadows severall yeares before Warwick was settled by any English man ; and I, being present did see and heare all the Narragansett Princes being assembled together give by livery and seizing some hundreds of acres of land about a mile in length, and so down to the sea : this being about thirty years agoe, many hundred Indians being present, consenting thereunto.. . . . . .

This I certify to be true as I am in Publique office, on oath and under my hand.

John Greene."

Smith chose for the site of his trading post the spot already spoken of, near Cocumquissett Brook, and hard by the Pequot Path. Here he built a heavy and substantial block house or castle, as it was called. It was built of thick logs, brick and heavy timbers. The bricks, hardware and lumber used in constructing it were brought from Taunton, Mass., in boats. When the King Philip Indian War was on hand, Smith's castle became a fort. Forces assembled and marched from here. After the Great Swamp Fight, both the wounded and the dead were brought here ; 42 of the latter were buried in one grave near the house. This " Big Mound " can yet be identified. This noted landmark, the oldest building in this part of Rhode Island, is still standing. Richard Smith left it to his daughter, Mrs. Updike, and it is yet called the Updike House. It has been newly covered on the outside, but the old timbers and brick yet remain in it, and the interior is said to be very much as of old.

The Block House was at once home, fort, trading post and inn. All travelers, whether white men or Indians, were fed and lodged for as long a time as they chose to stay, free of all charge. Here Roger Williams was a visitor, staying days at a time, and preaching frequently. Some of his letters are dated from Smith's Block House. Smith was a shrewd trader. He sold the Indians glass beads, knives, hatchets, blankets and red cloth at extravagant prices, and took his pay in skins and furs at ridiculously low values. A plan a good many post traders have since followed in their dealings with the red man.

From the very first there was with him an Englishman, ten years his junior—John Greene of Quidnessett. This is one of the John Greenes already referred to as belonging to the English Gillingham Greenes. Born in 1606, he had come over in 1635, the year of the great exodus; he had made a brief stay in the West Indies, and had then joined the Massachusetts colony, only to push onward to R. I. the next year, disgusted with Massachusetts' illiberality in matters of religion. The year after that, 1637, found him the sole white man, save Smith himself, in the Indian settlement of Quidnessett.* Whether there was a relationship between the two men, or an old friendship in England, is now unknowable.

The relation between them at first was that of employer and employé. In time this is supposed to have become a partnership. Greene was a bachelor when he went to R. I., and was in no haste to change his condition. He lived in Smith's home as one of the family for years. There was the warmest possible friendship between the men and between their families. From various circumstances it is supposed that Greene married not far from 1642, when he was about 36 years of age. A good-sized family, mostly boys, grew up around them. The stirring times when England was convulsed in civil war, when Charles I was beheaded, and Oliver Cromwell was Lord Protector over England, were the quietest days of Early Rhode Island. Of the most of these years the records are absolutely silent as to John of Quidnessett. We know that he remained in business with Smith, and that all went well with him. Then came the great land muddle of Quidnessett, and John Greene at once became the most central figure on the canvas of that history.

Smith and Greene were for some years the only white settlers at Quidnesset. A Mr. Wilcox and Roger Williams purchased land there about 1643 or 1644. Williams, however, in the year 1651, sold his "trading house, two big guns and a small island for goats," to Richard Smith. Probably a few squatters were here and there, but practically it was still Indian territory up to June 11, 1659. On that date, Sachem Coquinaquant, on behalf of the Narragansetts, sold the entire region of Quidnessett to a company of land specu-

---

* The date of Smith settlement at Quidnessett is given by Daniel Gould Allen in his History of Quidnessett.

lators who were headed by Major Humphrey Atherton. There were a few R. I. parties in the company, notably the Patriarch, Richard Smith himself, but the most of them were Boston and Connecticut speculators.

Major Atherton talked the Narragansett tongue as fluently as an Indian himself. He had great influence with the chiefs. It is said that he paid but 16⅔ cents per acre for this land, which 40 years later sold in market at an increase of 1,000 per cent! Small wonder that the Atherton Purchase was backed by the then leading capitalists of the new world. John Greene of Quidnessett was not one of the original company, but became an early shareholder. Trouble at once sprang up. The settlers who came in, bought land as they knew, with a clouded title. But once having paid their money for it, they were determined to defend their title at all hazards. John Greene, by general consent, was the leader for the Atherton land purchasers.* He put up a hard and brave fight. He took abuse and arrest, insult and imprisonment; but he stuck to his claim with a bull dog grip, and in the end forced the R. I. Colony to aknowledge his title, and give himself and his companions peaceful possession of their lands.

It is impossible in a single paragraph to make clear why this Atherton land purchase had so shadowy a title   To begin with, Rhode Island, Massachusetts and Connecticut each claimed this region. Then R. I. had passed a law that no more land should be purchased from the Indians, without the Colony of Rhode Island's consent. Major Atherton paid no attention to this law, and R. I. at once proceeded to make things lively for the Quidnessett settlers. They were told they must purchase their property over from R. I., or she would not acknowledge their title, and she threatened them, if they claimed allegiance to Connecticut, that she would confiscate their property. The result was, the settlers banded together, and declared for Connecticut, which at once made R. I. their enemy.

But Connecticut was jealous also. She arrested John Greene, Thomas Gould and George Whitman, three very prominent men, and put them in jail at Hartford, because they had sent up a petition to the R. I. legislature for the release of their lands, thus acknowledging, as Connecticut thought, Rhode Island's claims.

In 1663 John Greene, Richard Smith and others petitioned to be under Connecticut jurisdiction. This made the R. I. officials very angry. In due time came this order :

---

*In a certain New England history it is stated that the second John Greene of Warwick—he who afterwards was known as Deputy-Gov. John—led the Quidnessett land fight. This is an error. When that gentleman was in England, he got the Atherton Co., then in the midst of their troubles, to concede their lands to the crown through him, in order to get a royal grant for the same. This lawyer service was the extent of his efforts. The mistake arose from the similarity of names, both being John Greene.

"Newport 1664, May 5.

Ordered, that a warrant goe from the Court to require **John Greene** Senior living at Narragansett, to come before this Court."

It is evident he did not go peacefully, for in the official records there is yet preserved this indignant letter written nine days later by John Greene's fast friend, Richard Smith :

"Wickford, 14 May, 1664.

Captain Hutchinson :

My kind respects unto you sir. This may give you to understand some late actions and proceedings of R. I. men, and if these actings of theyrs be not countermanded by the government of Conn., they will insult beyond measure. Three days since they came to John Greene's house at Aquidnessett with a warrant from theyre Court under the Governor's hand, and forceably fetched him away to Rhode Island where he yet remaynes. His goeing was also not known to any here.........

Rich. Smith, Sen'r."

There was a warm time at Newport. But the bluff old Indian trader stood his ground so sturdily that the authorities came to his terms, though none too graciously, as this official record shows :

"Newport, May 1664.

Ordered, that John Greene's petition shall be considered.

John Greene Sen'r, living at Narragansett or Aquidnessitt, having been called before the Court for to answer before the Court for his adhearing to the government of Conn. and having been examined consearning the premises, hee so answered as did give the Court just offence ; and upon the sence thereof, the sayd John Greene doth present his petition, praying the Court to pardon sayd offence in his adhearing to the government of Conn. and his answering to the same before the Court as hee did ; upon the real consideration of the aforesayd petition the Court doe pass by his offence, and doe promise to the aforesayd John Greene all lawful protection and doe declare that he is still looked on as a freeman of the Collony."

We all know the old rhyme,

"When the Devil was sick,
The Devil a saint would be :
When the Devil got well,
The d——l a saint was he !"

Stiff-headed old John of Quidnessett was a loyal "freeman of R. I." long enough to get home, and not much longer. For seven more years the struggle went on, then R. I. gave in. In May, 1671, a special court was held at Aquidnessett, and Greene and his comrades were assured of full possession of their lands, if they would acknowledge Rhode Island's jurisdiction. John Greene became a "freeman," as did his son Daniel upon the same day, May 20, 1671, and the 12-years land dispute was forever at an end.

The next year John of Quidnessett, with John Fones and five others, bought of Awashuwett, chief sachem of the Narragansett Indians, a large tract of land known as the Devil's Foot, or the Fones Purchase. This tract included a strip of country a long distance northwest of the Pequot Path from Devil's Foot Rock to Hunt's River.

When the King Philip War broke out, some three years later, Chief Awashuwett kept a sullen neutrality. About this time a dumb boy died under mysterious circumstances. There were not wanting whispers that the Indians had something to do with his death. Old John probably voiced the community's suspicion of the sachem's sincerity and of his conniving at the boy's death. A quarrel arose between them. After the war was over Awashuwett was tried by court martial in Newport for his treatment of John Greene. John Andrews, (into whose lines the Quidnessett Greenes afterwards married,) testified that Awashuwett had "laid hands" upon him. What the chief's punishment was we do not know. John of Quidnessett's sons, Captain Edward and Lieut. John, are believed to have won their titles in this Indian War. Possibly Lieut. James, a younger son, received his honors in the same war, though being barely of age when the war closed, this is not certain.

July 29, 1679, he, with 41 other leading Narragansett citizens, signed a petition to the King praying that he "would put an end to these differences about the government thereof, which has been so fatal to the prosperity of the place, animosity still arising in the people's minds, as they stand effected by this or that government."

Several times after this, John of Quidnessett's name appears on the records as a witness to the transfer of land, etc. March 24, 1682, he divided his land among some of his sons who remained in R. I. Beside these there were two or three sons who went to New Jersey, and a daughter or two. These other sons probably received their portion in money. As for the daughters, they did not count for much in those days, and received almost nothing from their fathers' estates. John Greene's wife was alive when these deeds were executed. There are three old and dilapidated graves in what was once a part of John of Quidnessett's land. Two of these rude head-stones bear the initials D. G. and R. G., and mark the graves of John of Quidnessett's son Daniel and his wife Rebecca. The other gravestone, the oldest of all, is marked I. G.* It is believed to mark the grave of Mrs. Joan Greene, wife of John of Quidnessett.

---

* Evidently intended for J. G. In olden times the two capital letters I and J were made almost exactly alike.

His grave does not appear beside hers. In Rhode Island they point out a grave some miles away, as that of John of Quidnessett. He is believed, from various things, to have died in 1695. Tradition says he was 96. He was really 89. Where Rhode Island people believe John Greene to have been buried is at the Old Field Graveyard, a mile west of Maple Root Church, that a hundred years later itself became a noted Rhode Island landmark. It is supposed that he left Quidnessett to live with his son John, and was buried where he died*.

John of Quidnessett's wife's name was Joan. There has been much idle conjecture as to whom she was. She was not the daughter of Surgeon John Greene, as some have claimed, for the Surgeon's daughter Joan died in childhood. Nor was she the daughter of Richard Smith, as others have insisted, for Joan Smith married a Mr. Newton. Gov. Bradford of Massachusetts, speaking of one held to be John of Quidnessett, uses this language: "One Greene who married the wife of one Beggarly." So his wife was a young widow, Mrs. Joan Beggarly, whom he probably married on one of his business trips to Massachusetts.

Whether she was handsome or plain-featured ; whether she was brilliant or dull, we do not know. But we do know she possessed a remarkably even, sweet temper that nothing could ruffle or disturb. After the then English custom, she had been baptized Joan, but was always called Jane. There is an old family superstition among the Quidnessett Greenes that all their Janes will be self-sacrificing women who will take special care of the sick, and tenderly care for the old and infirm among the relation. It is likely that this superstition dates from the life's record of this good, placid Jane herself.

Ever since this good dame's day there have appeared again and again among her descendants some of her own sunny tempered kind. They look through rose-colored spectacles, and keep up good heart and serene spirits whatever betide. This disposition is illustrated by the stock family story of one of these good-natured Greenes whose wife had a furious temper. The story goes that when she was pleasant, he always blandly spoke to her as "Wife." When she began to fret and scold, he would soothingly remonstrate,—"Come, come, Sister Greene, let's have no trouble;" but when the storm broke into a tantrum of rage and abuse, he would pick up his hat and beat a retreat, philosophically saying,—"Well! well! Mrs. Greene, have it your way! Have it your way!"

---

* There is tradition that sometime after the death of his wife Joan, the aged husband left the home place where his son Daniel lived, and took up his abode with his son Lieut. John, at Coventry, and when he died he was buried in the Old Field grave lot. Mrs. Hannah Howard says there are many graves there. Some are unmarked, and the head stones of part of the others are illegible. The head of the American line probably lies in one of these unmarked graves.

CHAPTER X

THE HUMAN SIDE OF THE STORY

The early Greenes as slave-holders and dram-drinkers   Their petty economies   Their superstitions and beliefs in witches and ghosts   Their freaks of conscience, and fear of education for women

Nor Right, nor Wrong? Who shall declare
When much depends upon the point
Of view   In justice, then, forbear
To judge these upright men of old
They did as seemed the Right to them,
And when two hundred years have rolled
Adown the stream of Time, our lives,
With taint of Wrong, may seem as fraught,
To those who follow us, as theirs——
These older ones——seem now.   Judge not
Our fathers, then   Their point of view
Was widely varient from our own,
Yet that they lived true, righteous lives,
And loved the Lord is clearly shown —A A S

It is with no small degree of complacency that the descendants of the early Greenes rehearse their foreparents' sacrifices for liberty of conscience They reckon them holy men and devout women, they speak approvingly of their thrift and prudence, they think of them as persons above petty superstition, and as having a bias toward learning and a liberal education in all things

But the truth is, our far-off fathers and mothers were as human as ourselves   They were not two or three centuries in advance of their age, nor were they saints   Perhaps it may bring the over-weening pride of family down, to consider some of their short-comings

The early Greenes were slave-holders   So were the Waites, Wardwells, Nichols, Coggeshalls, Tripps, Pierces, and almost every other family into which they married. Some of those old New Englanders made fortunes buying up West Indies' molasses and making it into rum. There was no tax on the rum, and in wholesales quantities it was supplied at sixpence a gallon. Some of the forefathers used to regularly load vessels with rum, take it to Africa and trade it for slaves and gold dust. They sold the rum dear, and bought the slaves cheap. So far from feeling guilty of a crime, some of those pious captains used to call all hands together for daily devotions, and, we are told, never failed to ask God's blessing on their slavery enterprise!

They were not hypocrites. In that day, no one thought it wrong to traffic in human flesh. Dr. McSparran, the noble old Episcopalian minister who baptized the children of the LaValley-Kings—a branch of the Quidnessett Greenes—owned no less than ten slaves. An eminent Massachusetts clergyman preached from the pulpit that Negroes, Indians and Quakers were the spoil of the righteous, i. e. given to their portion as slaves by an all-righteous Providence. As for drinking, it was only disgraceful to get drunk. Even then, the Deacon or the Elder himself might get a little "foxy" on Training Day or Christmas, without losing caste.

Again, the forefathers were undeniably thrifty; but we would be horrified to-day at their petty shifts and economies. A certain Massachusetts deacon used to blow out the light just before he commenced on his 20-minutes prayers so as to save the candle from wasting. It was a common thing to soak backlogs in water, so that they would burn slower and last longer. In summer, if the church was some distance away, the goodman and his dame, and their brood of Ezras, Ebenezers, Thomases and Josiahs, Pollys, Elizabeths and Susannahs, would carry their shoes and stockings in their hands until in sight of the church, and thus save the wear and tear on two-thirds of a dozen or so pairs of shoes. The daughters were taught to rub the bread dough so cleanly out of the rising-pan that the dish looked as though it had been washed and wiped. Rigid economy in those days of great families was indeed a cardinal virtue.

As to superstitions, the Greenes, like their neighbors, were chock full and running over with it. If a wart appeared on a girl's hand, she was told to steal a neighbor's dish-cloth, rub the wart with it, and then bury the rag ; they never doubted but what the wart would shrivel away as the dish-cloth decayed. If the son cut his foot, the "wise man" was called, and he stanched the blood by a mysterious muttered gibberish and by "touching" the patient. They saw "ha'nts," spooks and hob-goblins, and heard unearthly noises in graveyards. They suspected people of the Evil Eye, and as for witches, they firmly believed in them. It was not only in Salem that the witch excitement of 1692 ran high. All over Massachusetts, Connecticut and Rhode Island the witch craze spread. Hair-raising stories of witch doings and conjuring were told as gospel truth for generations after. The first family historian, Mrs. Nancy Nichols, collected several of these stories still handed down in her day, 1767–1820.* Unfortunately her recitals were verbal ones, and have become so dimmed in her descendants' memories that they cannot be given with any degree of accuracy.

The Greenes had many purely family superstitions. One of them was their dislike to have a picture made of themselves. Even as late as 1850, some of them would not permit a picture to be made of themselves under any circumstances. They believed that in every family there would be one daughter who would be her mother's double in looks, disposition and station in life. They were exceedingly superstitious as to names. But much of their belief in this has been lost. It is known that they thought each one of their Janes, whether born or married into the family, would be remarkably affectionate in her family, and would be exceedingly kind to the sick and the afflicted. It has already been told that one great branch of the Greenes adopted in England the custom of calling their Annes by the name of Welthian. After coming to the Colonies, they used the name of Welthian as both baptismal and given name; their Annes they now called Nancy, after the common custom of the day. The Greenes, one and all, firmly believed that their Nancys would have a strenuous life, full of cares, trials and vexations. They believed just as firmly that these Nancys would be extraordinary workers, and that somehow they would get through all their trials and be none the worse for them.

Several of these good ancestors were of so tender a conscience that they would leave the House of God rather than to stay and see it desecrated by people singing within its walls. A century later, other pious ancestors were shocked by the introduction of hymn tunes with printed notes; and also the introduction of instruments of music into the church. Plenty of them refused to let their daughters learn beyond the rudiments of reading, spelling, writing and arithmetic, from fear that education would " spile 'em."

Bless their dear, unreasonable, rigid and narrow old souls! If we were half as honest, industrious, and attentive to our own affairs as they were, we could more fittingly criticise them. Be assured they measured up to the requirements of honored ancestors better than we measure up to being their worthy descendants.

---

* Mrs. Nichols was a great-great-great-granddaughter of the emigrant John Greene of Quidnessett. She was a born historian. She was born in 1767, when parties were yet alive who could remember back into the first century of New England settlement. Owing to the prejudice of that day against literary women, her carefully collated history of family biography, ancestry, folk-lore and anecdotes was never written. She delighted in telling this to appreciative listeners, however. By an unusual stretch of generations she was my grandmother, although born ninety years before me. When a child I fortunately heard parts of this verbal history repeated by old people who had heard it from her own lips. Much of her history has perished, but from that that has come down to us, I obtained clues to interesting pages of family history that otherwise would have been forever lost.

PART TWO

GENEALOGY OF THE QUIDNESSETT GREENES

CHAPTER XI

THE FAMILY OF JOHN GREENE OF QUIDNESSETT

In preparing this genealogy over 1300 letters of inquiry have been written, family records hunted up, and gravestone inscriptions copied. Every author who could throw light on the subject has been consulted, and church and military records have been searched. In addition, the official town and state records of Rhode Island have been copied word for word, so far as they related to any of this family.*

There is no dispute as to the greater part of the Quidnessett Greenes' genealogy. In a few cases there are serious disagreements. As a man cannot possibly have but one correct pedigree, a disputed ancestry is a serious thing. In these cases I have taken a uniform course. The official records, being considered in law as upon their face documentary proof, are taken as the true statement, unless an error can be clearly proven in them. And to determine whether an error has been possible, all other evidence has been gathered together and weighed as impartially as may be.

Although the official records are received authority in law, a class of minor errors is bound to occur. Some of the town clerks were wretched penmen, and the early spelling was atrocious. In many cases the ink has faded so that it must be read under a glass. Hence arose such copyist's mistakes as Infield for Enfield, John for the abbreviation Jas., etc. Much care has been taken to correct these mis-readings.

Again, the records often abruptly cease, or perhaps skip a generation. The North Kingstown records that particularly concerned this family have been injured by fire, and partially destroyed.† It is in these cases that pri-

---

*The Vital Records of Rhode Island have been officially tabulated by James N. Arnold, who has given his life to genealogical studies. The R. I. legislature not only sanctioned his work, but made a liberal appropriation to cover the expense of the same. Subsequent legislatures have given it their approval and support. Mr. Arnold in person, loaned the author much that was invaluable to her work.

†The original name of this region was the Indian name of Aquidnessett, contracted to Quidnessett. In 1663, 't was incorporated as Wickford, and again in 1674 as King's Towne. In 1722, the southern part, originally called Pettequonscutt, was re-named South Kingstown, and the remainder was ever after known as North Kingstown.

vate records and family Bibles have played so important a part in bridging the gaps in the record.

One word more. To avoid confusion, the many early Johns and James are distinguished by some certain appellation. This is either some title to which they were entitled, or the nickname by which they were known during their life-time. Thus, the founder of this American line is John of Quidnessett; his son, Lieut. John of Coventry; and in the third generation it is John of Bristol, White Hat John, and Wealthy John.

John Greene[1] of Quidnessett did not marry until of middle age. It was a day of early marriages, which makes more noticeable the inclination of so many of the related Warwick and Quidnessett Greenes toward late marriages. Surgeon John Greene was thirty-four and his son, Deputy-Governor John, thirty, when they became Benedicts. The Surgeon's cousin, the John of Quidnessett of this history, was in the neighborhood of 36 when he took a wife. His son and namesake, Lieut. John, was 39, and another son, Daniel, was about the same age, when they married. Somewhere in the blood was a streak of unhaste to assume the ties of matrimony. But our dilatory ancestors were strong of physique and long-lived, and their crop of olive branches seemed in nowise lessened by their fathers' late start in "multiplying and replenishing the earth."

The date of John of Quidnessett's marriage can be nearly approximated. After living several years in Richard Smith's family, he married a young widow, Mrs. Joan Beggarly. It is Governor Winthrop of Massachusetts who gives her name. Therefore, she was doubtless a member of that Colony. Greene and Smith must have made many trips to Boston after goods for their Indian trading post. On one of these trips, Greene may have married the widow.

They raised a good-sized family. Like all the Gillingham Greenes they had more sons than daughters. As they had four sons old enough to be freemen in 1671, the date of their marriage was probably about 1642. Captain Edward was the oldest son, and born about 1643, as he had a grandson ten to twelve years of age, in 1695. Lieut. John* appears to have been the next son. He must have been near man's estate, in 1664, when in official records John of Quidnessett is styled John Greene, Senior. He is regarded as the "Son" in the tracts of land held by "John Greene and Son," in 1666, when he must have been of full legal age. Daniel and Henry were both "engaged" as R. I. freemen the same day with their father, the

---

*In nearly all R. I. histories, Lieut. John[2] of Coventry's birth is given as on June 16, 1651. This date is *not* that of Lieut. John's birth, but that of Lieut.-Governor John Greene of *Warwick*. The similarity of names and title has caused the confusion.

day of the great compromise of the Quidnessett land suit, May 20, 1671. So the younger of the two could not have been born later than 1650. A daughter is probably next; then came Robert, born in 1653, for he was a freeman in 1674. Huling gives James' birth year as 1655. There was a son Benjamin, supposed to be the youngest of them all. There was almost certainly a daughter Enfield, bearing that peculiar name that for five generations was handed down in the Quidnessett family. Probably there was a Welthian also. It was a Gillingham family name, and is found in the names of the brothers' daughters and granddaughters.

There were therefore eight children, and probably nine. Henry went to New Jersey, and Robert is supposed to have gone there also. No attempt is made to trace their lines or the daughters' families. The Quidnessett Greenes are therefore descended from one of these five brothers, Edward[2], John[2], Daniel[2], James[2] or Benjamin[2].

I have numbered the American generations from John Greene[1] of Quidnessett. He was fifteenth from Lord Alexander de Greene de Boketon, who received his title in 1202; ninth from Sir Henry Greene, beheaded in 1399, and sixth from John the Fugitive. His pedigree runs thus:

GREENE LINE. Sir Alexander[1]; his son[2] and grandson[3], whose names are lost; Sir Thomas[4]; Sir Thomas[5], who married Lady Lucie de la Zouch, descended from the royal Capetian line; Lord Chief-Justice Sir Henry[6]; the beheaded Sir Henry[7]; Thomas[8]; an unknown son[9]; John the Fugitive[10]; Robert of Gillingham[11]; John[12]; Henry[13]; Robert[14]; John of Quidnessett[15].

CAPETIAN LINE. Robert the Strong[1], made Duke de France in 861; Duke Robert[2]; Count Hugh the Great[3]; Hugh Capet[4], King of France; King Robert the Pious[5]; King Henry[6]; Hugh Magnus[7], Count de Vermandois; Lady Isabel[8], married to Earl of Leicester; Earl Robert[9], Lord Chief-Justice of England; Earl Robert[10]; Lady Margaret[11], married to Earl of Winchester; Earl Roger[12]; Lady Elene[13], married to Alan, Lord de la Zouch, Governor of Northampton; Lord Eudo de la Zouch[14]; Lady Lucie de la Zouch[15], who married the fifth Lord de Greene.

John of Quidnessett[1] was therefore twenty-fifth in descent from Robert the Strong; twenty-second from the king, Hugo Capet, and nineteenth from Hugh de Vermandois, the Great Crusader.

Those who like to get as far back as possible toward Noah, have only to count the generations between John of Quidnessett and themselves, and add to the above. This will show the number of generations in all, back to the fountain head.

Trace back along the line :
Acquaint you with the deeds
Of these old sires and dames,

And it shall prove, if needs,
The strongest reason why
  We, too, should do our best;
We, too, should live *our* lives—
  Those lives in comfort blest—
As suits the highest good,
  Nor heeds the Wrong's behest.

A. A. S.

CHAPTER XII

LINE OF CAPTAIN EDWARD GREENE[2]

Little is known of Captain Edward Greene[2], or of his line. He is supposed to have been the oldest son of John of Quidnessett, born about 1642. The clue to his age is that he deeded land in 1695 to his grandson, George Havens[4]. The lad to whom the land was given must have been ten to twelve years of age, as but a few years after himself and *wife* conveyed the same land to his great-uncle, Benjamin 2[2].

It is not known where he acquired his title, though most probably in the Indian wars. He was married young, his wife being Mary Tibbetts, daughter of Henry Tibbetts, an old settler of Quidnessett, who always followed John Greene's leadership in the land dispute, and was once imprisoned for resisting certain claims of jurisdiction. Lieut. John Greene[2], the next brother, is spoken of in a record of 1684 as of N. Y. It is supposed that Captain Edward and he went together to that then "far west" country. This must have been during the heat of the land dispute, as their names are not with their father's, brothers' and neighbors', who enrolled themselves as " engaged " to the R. I. side, at the day of the great compromise, May 20, 1671. Lieut. John returned after a few years. Captain Edward evidently did not. Four of the sons were given land by 1683, but he was not one. The records are silent for twelve years beyond that, to 1695, which was probably near the date of his return to R. I. This is when he gave his grandson a deed to a certain piece of land.

In 1695, he was enrolled as a freeman of North Kingstown, another proof that he had not been long a resident. In 1697, he sold 90 acres of land in East Greenwich, which is described in the deed as having been left to him by the will of his " honored father, lately deceased." There is a brief mention of Captain Edward Greene in the Council records of 1702. Again, Henry Tibbetts, in his will of 1713, left land to all his grandsons, excepting the sons of Edward Greene, " who are provided for." This is the last trace of Captain Edward[2] in the records.

As he lived in N. Y. twenty-five years or more, he probably left married

children behind him when he moved back to R. I.   He is not certainly
known to have had but three children.   The two older ones were both born
before 1680.   Their descendants are as follows:

——— Greene-Havens[3].   This daughter married into the Havens family who owned immense tracts of land in Southern Connecticut.   Her only
known descendant was George[4], to whom his grandfather deeded land.
Mary, Desire, Thomas, Jonathan and Robert Havens were all of proper age
to have been sisters and brothers to George Havens, but the records fail to
give their descent.

GEORGE GREENE[3].   He married Mary whose surname is believed
to have been Pierce, and thus she was related to his cousins, Peleg, Wealthy,
John and Usal Greenes' wives.   Her children and grandchildren have un-
doubted Pierce names, Bathsheba, Peleg, George, etc.

> ANNE GREENE[4] born 1702.
> SARAH GREENE[4].
> GEORGE GREENE[4] born 1704.
> > GEORGE GREENE[5], m. Ann ———.   They had WILLIAM, b. 1773, ESTHER
> > and SUSANNA.
> > BENJAMIN GREENE[6], b, 1750.
> > MARY GREENE[6], b. 1733.
> HENRY GREENE[4], m, HANNAH ———.   Had HENRY, born 1735 ; SARAH, GEORGE,
> JOHN, JONATHAN, BENJAMIN, JOSEPH and HANNAH.

George[3] is believed to have had a third daughter, Bathsheba[4], next
older than Henry[4].   She was a woman of great force of character, and her
descendants are proud to claim her as a fore-mother.   She married a widower,
William Bentley, and by him had five sons, William[5], born 1735 ; Thomas[5],
James[5], Greene M.[5] and Benjamin[5].   One of her step-sons having already
been named George, she named her fourth son Greene, after her father, and
this name, Greene, has been continued ever since in her line.   Her son
Greene[5] married Dinah Straight.   Their daughter Hannah[6] married Ephraim
Bennett.   The grandson of this last couple, Stephen B. Bennett[8], has written
a family history of much interest.   In it the descendants of Bathsheba
Greene-Bentley are traced in full.

Bathsheba's oldest son became an eminent Massachusetts divine, an intimate friend of the Adamses of that day.   Three of the others, Thomas[5],
Greene M.[5] and Benjamin[5] served in the Revolutionary War.   Eventually,
Benjamin settled at Sharon Center, Ohio, and Thomas and Greene M. Bentley in Pennsylvania, where they became prominent citizens.

Austin in his Genealogical Dictionary gives Robert[3] as a son of Edward.
There is a town record, "Robert of Robarth Greene, born 1741," that probably is of that man's son.   Robarth is a frequent spelling for Robert among
the Quidnessett Greenes.

1891.

A. A. Bennett

Author of "Bennett, Bentley and Beers Families"

There is yet another grandson of Captain Edward[2], who was Edward also, whether the son of George[3] or of Robert[3] is not clear. He married a daughter of William Tanner in 1739. He died before 1785, leaving, it is supposed, a son William[3]. Nothing more is known of the line of Captain Edward Greene.

It is reasonable that Captain Edward may have left a married son in N. Y. when he returned to R. I. There is a family of York State Greenes, who claim to be descended from the Quidnesset or Kingstown Greenes of R. I. These are probably of Captain Edward's line. They can give by name no ancestor farther back than Philarmon Greene, born after 1740. A partial continuance of this man's line is this:

> JOHN DAVIS GREENE of PHILARMON.
> WILLIAM GREENE,   "   "
> SAMUEL GREENE,   "   "
> ANDREW GREENE,   "   "
> ALONZO GREENE   "   "

These last would have been of about the seventh generation from John Greene of Quidnesset, if of Captain Edward's line, as he was the oldest child, and early married.

ADDENDA

Since Chapter XII was proofed considerable data has come to light about this line. Under A, B, C and D, these new facts are given:

(A.) OTHER N. Y. DESCENDANTS OF CAPT. EDWARD GREENE[2]. After a quarter of a century's pioneer experience in N. Y., Captain Edward Greene returned to R. I. A grown son or sons remained in N. Y. The Philarmon Greene branch has already been given. We now have records of a brother and sister who were almost beyond question grand-children of Capt. Edward.

Rachel Greene–De La Vergue[4], born in the lake or central regions of N. Y. in 1737. She married Louis, son of Dr. Nicholas de la Vergue, who came from France about 1630, during the last Huguenot persecution.

Jacob Greene[4]. Married Patience Sole. One of their children was Zophar[5], born Aug. 13, 1766. This son married in 1793, the half sister of his Aunt Rachel's husband; his wife being Susannah, the 13th child of Dr. de la Vergue. They had 10 children, Martha, Elizabeth, Mary, Husted, Patience, Amy, Julia, Susan, Catherine and Emeline.

Patience Greene[6], born Oct. 15, 1800, was married in 1820 to Job, son of John and Abigail Briggs. John was sixth in descent from John Briggs the contemporary of old John Greene at Quidnessett. He was doubly descended from the Spencers and Griffins and was sixth in descent from the head of the

Warwick Greenes, thus.   Surgeon John Greene[1], Mary Greene–Sweet[2], Benjamin[3], Welthian Sweet Briggs[4], John[5] and Job[6].   The line of Job Briggs' father, John[5], has been tabulated, and includes over 460 persons. I shall not attempt therefore to give the descendants of Job and Patience, but merely note that all their line have the blood of both Warwick and Quidnessett Greenes.

(B.) MORE OF BATHSHEBA GREENE'S LINE.   It has already been told that Bathsheba Greene[4] was first married to a Lewis.   Her date of birth is not recorded, but it appears to have followed that of George Greene[4], who was born in 1704.   These children were all close together, but little over a year between any of them, so that she was probably born in 1705.   She was then but about 15 when, as the justice carefully records it, she and Israel Lewis "Of ye towne of Westerly, according to ye Laws Custom and Usage of our Government are now this Day Lawfully Joyned together in the honerable state of matremony June ye 30, 1720." Israel Lewis died in the spring of 1732, making his wife executrix, and leaving her land and money. She had 7 Lewis children, Enoch, Israel, Ebenezer, Robert, Bathsheba, Elizabeth and Hannah.   Enoch, the oldest son, married Mary Kenyon and died at Westford, Conn., where his old home is yet a landmark of the region.   His heirs were Tacy, Mary, John, Israel, Bathsheba, Enoch, Elizabeth, Benedict and Joshua.   There are no records of the other Lewis children of Bathsheba's.

Bathsheba's second husband was much her senior, he having married the first time in 1703, two years before Bathsheba herself was born.   He had 8 children of his own, she had 7, and 5 more were born to them, making a family of fair size! Samuel Wilbour, J. P., records the marriage of "William Bentley, of William and Sarah, Westerly, R. I.," to the "Widow Lewis," Aug. 1, 1734.

(C.) Descendants of Hannah Bentley–Bennett[6] have been given. Greene M. Bentley[6], the Revolutionary soldier, and the eleventh child of Bathsheba Greene–Bentley, became the head of another numerous line by his daughter Sarah.   A full and careful history of this branch is being prepared by Dr. Frank H. Titus, U. S. A.   I shall give but two generations from Sarah, and leave fuller and meatier particulars to him.

Sarah Bentley[6] was married (probably in N. Y.) to Daniel Coryell. Her descendants still show one trait of Greene inheritance, one-sixth more sons being born to them than daughters.

Rachel, Sarah's oldest daughter, m. James Van Gorder, said to have been of a family originally from New Jersey.   They had 1 daughter and 4 sons.   Of these Sarah m. Matthew Neary and had 9 children. Henry m. Polly Shumway and had 2 daughters, and Louis m. Eliza Wilson and had 3 children.

Michael Coryell, Sarah's oldest son. m. Lydia Titus. They had 7 children. Of these Clarissa Ann m. Samuel Wallace, and had 3 children, and many grand-children; Matilda m. John Miller, and had 3 children and 24 grand-children; Samuel m. Esther Schofield and was the father of 4 children; Lydia m. George McNaughton, and was the mother of 5 sons and 3 daughters.

Sarah's next two sons, James[7] and Hiram Coryell[7], married respectively Ellen Wolf and Amanda Colegrove. To the latter was born 2 daughters. Jane Coryell[7], by her first husband, Horace Hungerford, had a daughter, Lucinda. Susan Coryell[7] m. Henry Hungerford, and had 5 sons and 1 daughter. Of Susan's children, James Hungerford[8] m. twice and had three children, and Julia A. Hungerford[8] m. twice, and had Lellie Nourse and George Flower, one by each husband. Daniel Coryell[7] m. Eliza Wood, and had 4 sons and 1 daughter.

Clarissa Coryell[7], 7th. child of Sarah Bentley–Coryell, and great-grand-daughter of Bathsheba Greene–Bentley[4], married Samuel Titus. They had 11 children, 7 sons and two daughters. Of these, Daniel[8] m. Eulalia Dodge, and had 5 sons and 3 daughters. Polly[8] m. Eli Shope and had 3 children. Greene Bentley[5] m. twice, and had 3 sons and 1 daughter. Jane[8] m. John Wigley and had 4 children by him. She then married Peter Magnet and had 4 more children. John[8] m. Mary Waldron and became the father of a dozen children.

Major Arthur Titus[8], was the fourth son of Clarissa Coryell[7] and Samuel Titus. He is a physician, and in the Civil War was Major and Regimental Surgeon in the 1st W. Va. Cavalry. He married Sophia Chabot. They had Frank, Samuel and Hattie.

Dr. Frank H. Titus[9] followed in his father's footsteps, and in the Spanish-American War was a Major and Brigade Surgeon. He is still connected with the Regular Army. He married Louise C. King, and has a daughter Louise[10].

(D.) Eunice[6], another daughter of Greene M. Bentley[5], was the second of this family to marry a Bennett. Over 300 descendants belong to her line. These live mostly in Ohio and Kentucky. Dr. Titus intends to include this line in his history also. I shall not attempt to give it.

CHAPTER XIII

In Rhode Island they have a strong tradition that this man was not the son of John of Quidnessett, or indeed at all John of London, as they call him, is held to have been John Clarke, a Regicide Judge who condemned King Charles to death in 1649, and who fled to America under the assumed named of Greene, and married Abigail Wardwell Without stopping to ask how he came to give Greene names to his children and how he came to own land that had been the elder John Greene's, we can show the groundlessness of the claim that he was John Clarke instead of John Greene, by comparing a few dates

To have been a Regicide Judge he would have been a middle-aged man in 1649, say 35 to 60 Now 19 year old Abigail married in 1684 He would have been 70 to 95 years old, a youthful bridegroom indeed! He would have lived 45 years longer, as this John certainly died Oct 6, 1729, by which time any of the Regicide Judges would have been 115 to 140 years old! The story is only a revamping of John of Quidnessett's reminiscences of his ancestor, John the Fugitive, with just enough changes to localize it. See Chapter V, where the question is discussed at some length.

John[2] is believed to have been born in 1645, The birthdate of June 16, 1651, usually given as his being of John[3] of the Warwick line He owned land with his father in 1666 But the land squabble so depreciated land that he became disgusted and went to N Y with his brother Edward Both were absent when the land suit was compromised, in May 1671 Edward remained away for 25 years or so But John, being a bachelor, and foot-loose, appears to have been part of the time in R. I and part of the time in N Y. The Greenes were famous walkers A 150 years later than this, it was nothing unusual for a Greene to walk from R I to N Y. and back, merely to see the country, or to pay a visit. It is quite probable that John came back during the Indian disturbance of 1675-6. It is thought he earned his title of Lieut in this King Philip's war

Lieut John, on some of his visits, had had his portion of his father's land set off to him. In March 1682, the elder John gave Benjamin, Daniel, and James their land, that joined the land already deeded to John. After his marriage in 1684, he decided to remain in R. I. However, when he moved to East Greenwich in 1685, and was enrolled as a freeman there, he was recorded even then as "Lieut. John Greene, Jr., of N. Y."

In 1684, being then 39 years old, he married a Massachusetts girl of less than half of his age, Abigail Wardwell. She was of the Lascelle–Wardwell family described in the Appendix. The love-smitten Lieutenant is supposed to have become acquainted with the young lady on the occasion of a visit paid by her to her many relatives, the Woddles (Wardwells), Pierces and Anthonys of Portsmouth, R. I. After her return to her home, at Ipswich, each visit required a trip of 250 miles or so, if he went by ship around Cape Cod. If he rode across country, he had a journey of 75 miles, along the Pequot Path and through the gloomy forests and sparse settlements of Rhode Island and Massachusetts.

A bachelor's courtship is proverbially an ardent one. Tradition tells us that after one of these lonely rides, he returned to Quidnessett with a comely young woman riding on a pillion behind him. This was bride Abigail Wardwell, or, as her intimates called her, Nabbie Woddle. Wardwell was a name that our ancestors pronounced a dozen different ways, but never by any chance as it was spelled.

Of Abigail herself we know little. She was of mixed English–Welsh–French stock. (William[1] of Richard Wardwell, who married Meribe[1] of Gershom Lascelle; Lascelle Wardwell[2], William Wardwell[3] and Alice, emigrants; Usel[4], their son, born 1639, married in 1664 to widow Mary Kinsman–Ringe, and Abigail, born Oct. 27, 1665.) The family had remarkable longevity. Her father, Usel, lived to be 93, and one of her sons lived to be 103. From the Huguenot side of the house came a brave, fearless, and venturesome disposition. They were a family of sailors, and those who remained on shore owned many slaves. Her own father was a slave holder. Nevertheless they were pious people. Probably from their Huguenot blood, they were a family that had a strong aversion to religious coercion or tyranny. Abigail's own grandfather had his freeman's privileges taken from him because he showed sympathy with those banished for heresy.

In 1685, soon after his marriage, Lieut. John moved to East Greenwich. Here he remained five years, and here two of his children, James and John, were born. In 1690 he moved to Coventry, built a sawmill which he is said to have put up with his own hands, and ran it there. He had been living there a couple of years when the word came that his wife's cousin had been hung in Massachusetts as a witch. Doubtless it was felt as a deep disgrace at the time.

Lieut. John was what is known as forehanded. He purchased a large tract of land in the township of Coventry, which was afterwards divided into many farms. It was all forest-land. He built his house at the foot of Harkney Hill.

Harkney Hill is a landmark. At one place there is a plain at the foot of the hill, watered by a small stream. Long before the white man's day this spot was a noted Indian camping place. A village of wigwams was usually sheltered under the great forest trees that stood on the banks of " the ringing brook," as a family poet phrases it. Greene cleared this land. Afterwards he took it for a family burying ground, and several generations lie sleeping there. Some of the graves are unmarked, and some have only common field stone markers at head and foot. At this late day it can never be determined who all are buried there. If, as is often claimed, Old John of Quidnessett spent his last days with his son John, he also lies there. This old, old burial place is even now known as the Old Field Cemetery.

It was about a mile away from this clearing, where afterwards he was to lie, that Lieut. John built his cabin. It was built in what was called the meadows, which lay at the foot of another part of Harkney Hill. Pioneers care little for architecture. Any kind of a shack will do them, so that it will shelter them. Usually a plain box-like house of logs is built, containing a single good-sized room, and a low loft above, reached by a steep ladder. As the family grows, a lean-to is built on, a summer kitchen added, rough porch and smoke-house built. The true pioneer was as happy in these narrow quarters as his favored sons in their 16-room mansions. It is all in the point of view. Well-to-do John and Abigail lived in that cabin the balance of their days.

Lieut. John died Oct. 6, 1729, at the good old age of 84, His brother James died the year before, and his brother Daniel the year after.

John and Abigail had 11 children, all of whom grew up. They were James, John, Jane, Usual, Ebenezer, Robert, William, Enfield, Mary, Hannah and Andrew. There is no further record of William or Andrew. The other nine were married and became heads of families.

The third child and oldest daughter was born at Coventry, Jan, 3. 1691. She was named Jane for her grandmother.* She married a man named Low. It was probably her daughter Alice who married Nathaniel Greene, in 1739, as Alice was a family name with the Wardwells.

Enfield Greene was the eighth child and second daughter. She was married March 21, 1719, to Samuel Cook. She evidently had much of her

---

* John of Quidnessett's wife invariably signed her name Joan, but was always called Jane. Her namesakes were all called Jane.

grandmother's sweet disposition, for her namesakes were plentiful for three generations in her brother's families. In those days a popular relative was always much named after. Mary, the third daughter, married —— Johnson. No attempt is made to give the lines of these daughters.

The remaining six children, James, John, Usual, Ebenezer, Robert and Hannah, became the heads of large families. Their lines will be next considered.

Two of this family, Robert and Hannah, married Andrews, the first of almost numberless marriages between these two early Rhode Island lines. The in-and-in marrying, so characteristic of the Greenes, was well exampled. John and Usual married two sisters, Ann and Susannah Hill, their distant cousins on their mother's side. If Ebenezer's wife was a Pierce, as from various circumstances seems likely, his wife was also a distant cousin both to himself and to the two sisters-in-law just named.

CHAPTER XIV

· *Descendants of James of Maroon Swamp*

James[3], [Lieut John[2], John[1],] was born at East Greenwich, R I, Aug. 18, 1685 He was the first-born of Lieutenant John and Abigail Wardwell–Greene He was married December 18, 1717, to Rebecca Cahoon He was 32, she barely 15 They had seven children, six of whom certainly married. James died in 1771, at the age of 86, and his wife survived him When she died in 1782, she divided the old homestead near Maroon Swamp by will among three of her six sons, James, Isaac and John Lieut John owned a large tract of land, all forest when he purchased it. This farm of his son James, near the Maroon Swamp, was part of the original tract

Rebecca Cahoon was the oldest daughter of Nathaniel Cahoon and his wife, Jane Jones, the daughter of Thomas Jones Properly the name should have been spelled Colquhoun The Colquhouns are an old Scottish family who pronounce their name Cahoon, but write it Colquhoun The Colquhouns had their own clan plaid, their clan pibroch or tune, and clan "flowers," the Bear-berry, Hazel and Dog-berry, a sprig of the foliage of which they wore in their " bonnets" in parades or in battle. And as might be expected, their descendants are also clannish in their ways

James and Rebecca had the usual Greene fortune,—more sons than daughters Their children were

        NATHANIEL, born June 4, 1718
        JAMES,   "   Nov 25 1720
        WARDWELL,   "   Jan 23, 1723
        ISAAC,   '   Nov 6, 1724
        PATIENCE,   "   April 7 1727
        CHARLES,   "   1729.
        OTHNIEL

A wing of the Rebecca and Jane Greene-Andrews line claim these two women were also daughters of James and Rebecca Cahoon. If so, they must have been born after 1730 There is no official record of them

Of Othniel we have only the birth record Two of the sons, James and Wardwell, married cousins, two Greene girls. Nathaniel married Alice Low, who is supposed to have been his aunt Jane Greene-Low's daughter. So that half the family married relatives. Patience married Benjamin Andrews, Aug. 10, 1746. So far as can be traced, the descendants of Maroon Swamp James are as follows:

"SQUIRE" NATHANIEL GREENE.[4] [James[3], John[2], John[1].] He was born June 4, 1718, and died Sept. 2, 1809, in his 92nd year. He was usually called Esquire or Squire Nathaniel. He was married March 8, 1739, in his 21st year, to Alice Low, daughter of John Low. He married (2) Mary ———.

Not far from where Lieut. John of Coventry had his unpretentious home, Squire Nathaniel built a gambrel-roofed house. This house was in the meadow, and still standing not half a century ago. Some of the Squire's great-grandchildren were born there. He never recorded his family. All that we certainly know of his family by his first wife is that he had a daughter Alice, (Alcy,) who married Jonathan Bennett, May 12, 1765. All that we know of his second family is that he had

NATHANIEL GREENE, JR.[5] born June 27, 1765. Like his father, he lived to be old, dying April 1855, nearly 90. He it was who built the Greene House upon Harkney Hill, a landmark of the region.

Nathaniel Jr. married his third cousin, Patience Matteson, still remembered as a sprightly little old lady, wearing a white lace cap. She was the daughter of Jonathan and Elizabeth Matteson. [Jonathan[5] Martha Green-Matteson[4], John Greene[3], James[2], John[1].] Through Martha Greene-Matteson, she was descended from Elder Obediah Holmes, who for his Baptist doctrines was so cruelly whipped by the Boston authorities (1651) that he could not stand. They had seven children.

Paris M. Greene[6]. [Nath[5]., Nath[4]., James[3].. John[2], John[1].] He was born July 2, 1790, died Dec. 20, 1817. His first wife was Hannah, daughter of Joseph Wicks, and the second was her sister Elizabeth.

Hannah Wicks Greene-Howard[7], b. Jan. 12, 1812; d. July 26, 1877. She was named for her young mother, who died when she was four months old. Hannah married Ephraim Howard. See Chapter XXVII.

Benjamin Greene[7], b. 1814; d. 1832.

Mary E. Greene-Weaver[7]. [Paris[6], Nath[5]., Nath[4]., Jas[3]., John[2], John[1].] She was born Sept. 9, 1815; d. Feb. 25, 1892. M. 1836 to Jason Weaver. They afterwards removed to Conn. They were much esteemed people.

William P. Weaver[8], b. Feb. 20, 1838. M. Angie Brown. They live in Canterbury, Conn.

Lucius Edward Weaver[8], b. Jan. 13, 1874, m. Ruth T. Champlin. They live in Willimantic, Conn. They have one daughter,

Doris Lilian Champlin[9].

Mary Elizabeth Weaver-Potter[8], b. Nov. 8, 1842; m. March 27, 1862, to George W. Potter. No children. She has been a widow since 1901.

Edward Francis Weaver[8], b. Sept. 19, 1851; m. Melissa M. Burgess. One son.

Harry Francis Burgess[9].

Jennie Maria Weaver-Harris[8], b. Dec 31, 1852; m. Lyman W. Harris. Is now a widow. One son living.

Clarence Walter Harris[9].

George B. Weaver[8], b. Jan 4, 1855.-Unmarried. Lives in Brooklyn, Conn.

Alice Emma Weaver-Bass[8], b. March 3, 1858 ; m. Edwin Bass in 1886. No children.

Paris Greene,[7] b. 1817 ; d. 1822.

AARON GREENE[6]. [Nathaniel[5], Nathaniel[4], James[3], John[2], John[1].] He was born June 15, 1792, and died March 15, 1841, aged 49 years. He was never married, but the bans of marriage had been published between he and Cynthia Johnson. She afterwards made her home with his father, as an own daughter would have done, and on the death of her betrothed's father and brother, she received a large sum of money in token of their appreciation of her homekeeping for them so many years.

GEORGE W. GREENE[6], next brother to the above, b. Jan. 4 1794; d. Nov. 28, 1878, in his 85th year, unmarried. He built a considerable addition to his father's house, and opened up a store in one wing and the basement. The innovation succeeded, and he amassed in this country store $60,000. He had a pride in the Greene family. He erected several monuments to forefathers of his line.

WATERMAN GREENE[6], [Nathaniel[5], Nathaniel[4], James[3], John[2], John[1].] He died in Massachusetts, which had been his home for many years. He married Violata ——.

Orris Greene[7].

SARAH GREENE-JOHNSON[6], sixth child of Nathaniel Jr., was born May 16, 1802, and died July 19, 1864.

John Francis Johnson[7] died in the Civil War, Aug. 22, 1863, in his 24th year.

SYBIL GREENE-MILLER[6], next daughter of Nathaniel, Jr., m. to John P Miller of Coventry. No records.

DAMARIS GREENE-GREENE[6], youngest daughter of Nathaniel, Jr., was born March 2, 1807, and died Aug. 2, 1861. She married Lawton Greene, son of Elijah.

Nathaniel C. Greene[7], b. in 1841 ; d.; 1864, in Andersonville Prison, Georgia, during the Civil War.

JAMES GREENE[4]. [James[3], John[2], John[1].] Born Nov, 20, 1720. First wife was Mary, daughter of Increase Allen. Second wife and mother of his two youngest children was his second cousin, Humility Greene[4]. [Henry[3], Benjamin[2], John[1].]

INCREASE GREENE[5], b. Aug. 30, 1740 ; m. Comfort Weaver.

James Greene[6], b. in 1742.

Comfort Greene[6], b. in 1765.

THOMAS GREENE[5], b. March 24, 1743 ; m. Sarah Corey.

Matteson Greene[6], b. March 25, 1772.

Waity Greene-Cahoon[7], m. Wm. Cahoon, Jr.

Wanton Greene[7], m. Susan A. Cornell.

JEDEDIAH GREENE[5], b. April 13, 1747 ; m. Waitstill Bates, 1769.

Olive Greene-Potter[6], m. to William Potter.

Rhoda Greene-King[6], m. to Randall King of Coventry.

JONATHAN GREENE[5], b, Feb. 20. 1748; m. Lydia Nichols.

HENRY GREENE[5], b. July 28, 1754 ; m. Mercy Corey. Henry was a Revolutionary soldier.

Job[6], 1778 ; Cyril[6], 1779; Spicer[6], 1781 ; Whipple[6], 1782 ; Cynthia[6], 1786 ; Humility[6], 1789. All that is known of them.

Hannah Greene-Johnson,[6] b. 1784 ; m. Reuben Johnson.

Cynthia Johnson[7]. See paragraph of Aaron Greene.

REBECCA GREENE[5], b. May 22, 1756.

WARDWELL GREENE[4]. [James[3], John[2], John[1].] Born Jan. 23, 1723.; m. Oct. 7, 1748, to his 16-year old cousin Ann (Nancy) Greene[4].

[Robert², John², John¹.] Their family was divided after the usual Greene proportion, six sons to two daughters. Catharine was born 1748 ; Edmund, May 12, 1752 ; Robert, Nov. 10, 1755 ; Ann, 1763 ; and Benjamite, March 7, 1771. No further records of these.

WARDWELL GREENE⁵, b. Sept. 2, 1760; m. ———— Johnson. He lived to be 90. Wardwell removed to Richland, N. Y. During the Revolutionary War he was shot through the neck and left for dead upon the field. The Captain sent men back after the body, and they found him pressing each opening together with his hands, thus stanching the blood. When restored to his family, his Quaker mother said, ———— "Thee should be thankful to the good Lord for the preservation of thy life." To which he replied, ———— "Rather to the Captain and the volunteers who brought me away !"

Vedare Greene⁵. A celebrated N. Y. lawyer in his day.

RATHBUN GREENE⁵, b. 1787. Married Feb. 25, 1810, to Jane, dau. of Capt. Samuel Millard. He moved with wife and 5 children to Otsego Co., N. Y. in 1820. They had 13 children. I have these records. Wardwell, b. July 3, 1812 ; Samuel, b. Jan. 9, 1814 ; Olive, 1815 ;–1870 m. to Charles Georgia ; Hannah, m. Joseph Wilson ; John R. died in Brooklyn ; Job lived in N. Dakota ; Orpha m. Benjamin Mackey ; George moved West ; Mary m. Chancellor Houghtaling, of Union, N. Y. Dexter died in Civil War ; Albert lived in Central N. Y. ; Eliza became the wife of Belden Allen.

Almanzo Johnson Greene⁶, oldest son of Rathbun Greene, of above paragraph, was born April 1810. His first wife was Vilette Johnson. They had 11 children, of whom the second is John W. Greene, M. D., who was born in 1836.

James Greene⁶, b. April 25, 1768.

Wardwell Greene⁷ [Jas.⁶, Wardwell⁵, Wardwell⁴, Jas³., John³. John¹.] He m. (1) Eunice Short, and (2) Polly Peabody. All but Leland and Ann of his children were by the last wife. Wardwell lived at Farmington, Mich. 11 children.

Leland, Ann, Emily, Wardwell, Sidney, Betsey, Maria, Seneca, and Helen, name records only.

Lucinda Greene–Webster⁷, m. G. Webster of Farmington, Mich.

Jarvis Greene,⁸ leading citizen at Pontiac, Mich.

Champlin Greene⁷.[Jas⁶., Wardwell⁵, Wardwell⁴, Jas³., John², John.¹] He m. Fanny Hazen and lived at Farmington, Mich. His children were Warren, Mariette, Amanda, George W., Ann, Theodosia, Caroline and Edward

Leland Greene⁷, [Jas.⁶ Wardwell⁵, Wardwell⁴, Jas³., John³, John¹.] He m. Nancy Wilmarth, and lived at Farmington, Mich. His children were Dexter, Adelia and Amelia, Wesley and Thomas.

Luther Greene⁷. Brother to the above. He m. Mary Ann Lee. He also lived at Farmington, Mich. He had two children, Dr. Marshall and Caroline Greene.

Calvin Greene,⁷ brother to the preceeding. He m. Louise Baldwin. They had Addison, Ray, Mary, Lucy and Avis.

Chauncey Greene⁷, younger son of James⁶, of Wardwell⁵, etc. Born about 1816 ; m. Cornelia Henry. He was a well-known agricultural writer. There were four children, Florence, Edith, Ida and Meredith.

COL. ISAAC GREENE⁴. [Jas³, John², John¹.] Born Nov. 6, 1724; m. Mary Weaver in 1754. One child died young. Only birth records of Mehitable and Joseph. Abigail m. Oliver Wicks, and James m. Genevieve Case. One son alone leaves traceable line.

JUDGE BENJAMIN GREENE⁵. Born Feb., 1760 or 1764. Died Jan. 4. or Jan. 14, 1842. (Records vary.) First wife, Sarah Brayton. By her he had Caleb, who m. Phebe Matteson, Hannah and Isaac. By second wife, Henriette, he had Sarah, Barbara and Hiram.

Hiram Greene⁶, son of Judge Benjamin and grandson of Col. Isaac. His first wife's only son died at manhood. His second wife was Abigail Johnson of Greene descent. [Abigail⁶ Daniel⁵, Abigail Greene–Johnson⁴, Usal Greene³, John² John¹] By her he had Tryphena and Benjamin. Hiram died, aged but 23, though twice married and the father of three children.

Tryphena Greene–Johnson⁷, daughter of Hiram, m. her second cousin, Philip Johnson. [Philip⁷, Philip⁶, Ezekiel³, Elizabeth Greene–Johnson⁴, Usal Greene³, John², John¹.] Their children have five strains of Greene blood.

Harty Johnson–Whitford⁸, m. Carmi Whitford.

Philip R. Johnson⁸. Has a son and a daughter.

Tryphena Johnson–Howard⁸, m. George P. Howard. [George⁸, Hannah W Greene–Howard⁷, Paris M. Greene⁶. Nath. Jr.,⁵ Nath⁴., Jas³., John², John¹.] See Chapter XXVII.

Edna Priscilla Johnson–Shippee⁸, wife of Henry Shippee,

Patience Jane Johnson–Batty⁸, m. Lauriston Batty; d. in 1882.

Zilpha Johnson–Foster⁸.

CHARLES GREENE⁴. [Jas³, John², John¹.] Born July 28, 1729.

Othniel Greene⁵.

Lois Greene,⁶ b. 1770.

Charles Greene⁵. This may possibly be a son of Othniel, but is thought to be his younger brother.

Charles Greene⁶, b. Oct. 4, 1798.

William Greene⁶, b. in 1799.

Paul Allen Greene⁶, b. Oct. 26, 1808.

CHAPTER XV

Descendants of Wealthy John[3]

John Greene[3], who is here designated as Wealthy John, was born in East Greenwich, April 9, 1688 He was the second son and child of Lieut John[2] and Abigail Wardwell-Greene Nov. 30, 1713, when in his twenty-sixth year, he married Ann Nancy Hill The knot was tied by John Spencer, Justice Here the Puritan cropped to the surface In rebelling against England's ecclesiasticism, the Puritans, almost to a man, refused to have a clergyman marry them, so insistent were they on an entire separation of church and state The Quidnessett Greenes stuck to this rule until the Revolutionary War

Though his wife's name was always written as Ann, after the custom of the day, she was familiarly called Nancy. She was a distant cousin of her husband She belonged to a branch of that ultra-Puritan family, the Lascelle-Wardwells, for a fuller account of which see Appendix She was the daughter of Henry Hill, the first of his line in Rhode Island [Richard Wardwell[1], William[2], in to Meribe, dau of Gershom Lascelle, Rosanna Wardwell-Waite[3]; Mehitable Waite-Hill[4], John[5], Jonathan[6], Henry[7], Ann[8]]

Wealthy John's pedigree on his mother's side ran thus. Richard Wardwell[1], William[2], who m Meribe Lascelle, Lascelle[3], William[4], Usal[5]; Abigail Wardwell-Greene[6], John[7] So the children of John and Ann, (Nancy,) had two strains of this Lascelle-Wardwell blood, and a strain each of the Waite and Hill blood

It is known that Ann or Nancy Greene was extremely young at the time of her marriage, scarcely more than a child, in fact Her life was not a bed of roses She had eleven children in a little over sixteen years, and had the hardships of a half-settled country to endure in addition to that

We can imagine this busy Nancy caring for her brood of little ones. We can think of her washing and ironing, spinning, carding and weaving, milking and churning, scrubbing, soap-making, sewing, cooking and quilting, caring for her sick, and knitting stockings for her baker's dozen of people each year. A light dawns upon us then as to how the family superstition arose as to our Nancies always being over-crowded with work and responsibility, and how, stirring, bustling, and moving on, they always get through with it with great credit to themselves. This was the first Nancy among the Quidnessett Greenes. Doubtless, she was the typical Nancy that the others are supposed to pattern after,—particularly so, after one or two of them happened to lead a life as strenuous and yet as successful as her own.

Wealthy John knew well how to hold on to all that came into his hands. His wife, by her thrift and industry, helped him along. He went to West Greenwich, then rather a new region,* and opened up a large farm. Nancy (Ann) died, and he married Mary ———— for his second wife. He himself died in the autumn of 1756, aged 68. Beside his land, and the two farms he gave his sons Silas and John, he left personal property that was inventoried at £3,212, 5s., 7d., or about $15,200. As the purchasing power of a dollar was as great as three or four dollars is now, such a sum was equal to about $50,000 at the present day. A plain farmer who possessed this much personal property, and land beside, was held in those days to be a very wealthy man indeed.

There is a good deal in heredity. Nathan[4], the youngest son of Wealthy John, had a son Jabez[5] who went to N. Y. and became the head of an important line. It is safe to say that there are more men of great wealth in the Jabez Greene line than in any other Greene branch whatever.

The fifth child, Elizabeth, is supposed to have died young, as she is not mentioned in her father's will. Of the ten remaining children, three married Mattesons, for these two clannish families were particularly drawn together. The oldest son, Silas, married Humility Greene, his second cousin, the granddaughter of his great-uncle, Benjamin.

The descendants of Ann, Enfield, Silas, Mary, John, Margaret, Timothy, Samuel, Esther and Nathan are as follows :

ANN GREENE–NICHOLS[4]. She was the oldest child, and was born December 1, 1714. She was married to John Nichols, Jr., March 22, 1733. The marriage must have been quite a family affair. Five years before, the young man's uncle, William Nichols, married Ann's aunt, Mary Hill; a couple of years after that, his father's cousin, John Nichols, married Ann's aunt, Esther Hill; some time after, his own cousin, Hannah Nichols, married Ann's nephew, Captain Ebenezer Hill. All of which transactions are a fair sample of the way early Rhode Island families are crossed and recrossed with each other in marriage.

* It was made into a town or township in 1741.

As many who read this are descended from this couple, the bride-groom's pedigree is given at some length. The family of Nichols descend from Nicholas, (or Nigell, or Nichol), de Albine. He came to England from Normandy, and was advanced into the favor of Edward the Confessor, 1042–1066. He was the stem-father of this family. All the English Nicholses had a pheon as a device on their coat-of-arms. A pheon is the head of a javelin or dart; it is called the Broad R, or broad arrow, because used to mark Crown property. Originally the king's sergeant-at-arms carried this device before his majesty in royal parades. By this it is supposed that an early ancestor, probably Robert Fitz–Nigell, son of Nicholas de Albine, and high in power, held this office under either William the Conqueror, or his son. There was a large and wealthy branch of the family in Glamorganshire, Wales, from which particular line John Nichols, Jr., was descended. He was fourth in descent from Hon. Thomas Nichols,* of Newport. Thomas came from Wales. He was married about 1569 to Hannah Griffin, born 1642. They came to Newport, where he became prominent. He is spoken of as having been Deputy † for twenty years, from 1678 to 1698. He was one of the 48 grantees to whom, in 1677, the township of East Greenwich was originally deeded. He died in 1708 at East Greenwich. His sons were men of influence, Captain Benjamin being Deputy-Governor for some years, the highest office in the colony.

The second son and third child of Hon. Thomas was "Aristocratic John," born April 16, 1666, and died 1725 at East Greenwich. The mother of his children was his first wife, Hannah Forman. His name frequently appears in the records. Evidently he was a stirring, energetic man. Tradition says he was a proud man, quite inclined to think himself above the common herd. His tastes were those of a gentleman. He possessed much land, and left personal property valued at £573, 11s., ($2,850), equivalent to nearly $10,000 at the present day. This was esteemed a comfortable fortune in those days. His silver plate, pictures and books are spoken of as of something considerable in the inventory, the silver plate alone being valued at £55, 17s., 6d.

His oldest son was John, born in 1689. His father left him one-fourth of his East Greenwich real estate. The oldest son of the third John was this John, who married Ann Greene. Family tradition asserts that he was fully as aristocratic as his grandfather, and that he liked to live in good style.

---

* Additional Nichols matter was received after this chapter was in the publisher's hands. It will be found in Appendix.

† Mitchell, in his History of Bridgewater, says this is the old term for a Representative to the Colonial Assembly. (Legislature.)

In fact, the whole line are what is known as "good livers." This John lived for a time at East Greenwich, then removed to Providence, it is said. He was miserably careless about recording his children's names. There are three children supposed to have been his, though there is a certainty only as to two of them, Enfield and Job.

> ENFIELD, born March 4, 1734.
> ANN (Probably). Married about 1763.
> JOB. He married Susanna King,* a daughter of that Huguenot couple, Magdalen and Marie La Valley-King. Her line is traced in Chapter XXII.

It is strange how long a feeling of ill-will is handed down in old families. In 1687, a few years after East Greenwich was thrown open for settlement, a number of Huguenots fled from religious persecution in France, and came to R. I., settling at what is now Frenchtown in the township of Warwick, which is not far from the East Greenwich line. Hay was a valuable commodity. Leading East Greenwich men, working in agreement with each other, put up large quantities of hay on the unfenced East Greenwich "meadows." The Frenchmen saw an opportunity to turn a pretty penny for themselves, so they began to cut and cure hay without leave or permission from anyone. This provoked words and much wrangling. The quarrel became too warm for the Deputy-Governor of the Colony, so it was referred to the chief officer of the Crown in America, Governor Andros of Massachusetts. Andros professed to be greatly moved by pity for the newcomers, who unless favored would doubtless suffer for necessities. But Andros was usually at loggerheads with the colonists, and there may have been some truth in what the colonists thought, that he sided against them to "even up" matters with them.

Andros ordered two Justices of the Peace to divide the stacks of hay into two even lots. The one lot was given outright to the Frenchmen. The other was divided into eleven shares and given to eleven men. Among these were John Nichols, Giles Pierce, George Vaughan, John Andrews and John Sweet, with whose lines the Greenes afterward much intermarried. Aristocratic John was particularly angered at what he considered an outrage, and the very sight of a swarthy-faced Frenchman roused his ire. He passed his Frenchiphobia—to coin a word—on to his line. Great, therefore, was John's anger when his son Job fell in love with a black-eyed French girl, and married her. It is said that he never fully forgave his son, and never overcame his dislike to his foreign daughter-in-law.

Job[5] was as careless as his father in neglecting to record his family. We know that he lived in Providence, and that he had more than one son

---

* She was born in France, and named Suzanné, which in America became Anglicized into Susannah and Susan.

in the Revolutionary War. He had a son John, and a daughter Almira, who died at 23. Beside these was a son David, born in 1763. David enlisted June 14, 1778, in Captain Philip Traffarn's company of Col. John Topham's regiment, and served as a bugler in the Revolutionary War. He was less than sixteen years of age. The company was disbanded March 16, 1779, but he enlisted again. David married Nancy King. She was doubly related to him, being of Greene descent on her mother's side, and a niece of David's mother on the father's side. Part III of this book is almost wholly taken up in tracing the descendants of this couple. To these chapters those interested are referred.

ENFIELD GREENE–MATTESON.[4] She was the second child of Wealthy John Greene. She was born March 31, 1716, and was married to James Matteson, March 3, 1738. He was the son of Capt. Henry, the son of Henry Matteson. Six and seven years later, Enfield's brother John and sister Margaret, married two Mattesons, sister and brother, who were niece and nephew of this James Matteson who married Enfield. Fully one-third of the Quidnessett Greenes have Matteson blood. The affinity of the two families for each other is something remarkable. The Mattesons have an old and romantic family history. It is given at length in the Appendix.

James Matteson[5] and his wife moved to Foster, R. I. They had these children, beside two who died in infancy:

URIAH[6], born Jan. 23, 1739.
SILAS[6], b. Dec. 10, 1740.
ANN[6], b. Feb. 8, 1742.
ENFIELD[6], b. Sept. 23, 1750.

SILAS GREENE[4] was born Sept. 29, 1717. He was the oldest son. He was married about 1743 to his second cousin, Humility Greene[4], [Benjamin[3], Benjamin[2], John[1]] who was one year his senior. There has been great confusion in family biographies between this man's wife and the wife of his cousin James, [James[3], John[2], John[1]] whose wife was Humility Greene also. As accurate and painstaking histographer as Frank L. Greene, A. M., says that Silas married Humility, daughter of Henry Greene. *That* Humility, on the contrary, married James, as his second wife. The two Humilities were the children of brothers, Henry and Benjamin, sons of Benjamin.[2] Each named a daughter after his mother, Humility Coggeshall–Greene. Benjamin's Humility was a few years the elder. Her father's home was in Westerly. When James Greene took his second wife, to show certainly which Humility he married, it was added on the records, "of West Greenwich." West Greenwich was the home of Henry Greene, and therefore Silas married the other Humility. Beside, James was not born until near the close of 1720. Had he married Benjamin's Humility she would have been between four and five years his senior, itself improbable.

OBEDIAH[5], b. 1744.

ANNE[5], b. Aug. 6. 1745 ; m. Jan. 24, 1768, to Joseph King of Coventry.

ELIZABETH[5], b. 1746.

MARGARET[5].

HENRY[5] (?) Not on some lists. Doubtful if of this family.

MARY[5], b. March 17, 1751. Perhaps m. Rufus Collins. 1771.

MARY GREENE–JOHNSON.[4] She was born Jan. 31, 1719, and m.
Bartholomew Johnson, Jan. 14, 1741. No further trace of her line.

JOHN GREENE.[4] He was born May 31, 1722. He m. Ruth Matteson, the niece of his brother-in-law, James Matteson, in 1745. [Ruth[4],
Henry[3], Capt. Henry[2], Henry[1].] They had these children :

ELIZABETH[5], b. Aug. 20, 1746.

CALEB[5],   b. July 8. 1748; m. Mary ——— . Lived in E. Greenwich.

LUCY[5],   b. June 28. 1750; m. Stephen Briggs, 1767.

SILAS[5],   b. July 26, 1752.

FEAR[5],   b. Oct. 2, 1754.

JOHN[5],   b. Dec. 17, 1756; m. Catherine ——— .

CLARKE[5],   b. Jan. 31, 1759.

MARGARET GREENE–MATTESON[4]. She was born Jan. 27,
1724, and was married to Henry Matteson of West Greenwich, in Sept.,
1743. He was a brother to her brother John's wife. Their children that
lived were these :

RHODA[5].

CALEB[5], b. Sept. 2, 1751.

JOSHUA[5], b. Aug. 17, 1753.

FEAR[5].

JAMES[5], b. July 20, 1757.

HENRY[5], b. June 18, 1760.

TIMOTHY GREENE[4]. He was born July 14, 1725; married Silence
Burlingame, who in one record is called Mrs. Silence Burlingame, and was
probably a young widow. He was well known, his fame continuing even
until this day. He is usually spoken of as Elder Timothy. He was the
first pastor of the famous Maple Root Six Principle Baptist Church, and
served them from 1763 to 1770. He was married in West Greenwich, but
resided mostly in Coventry. He died about 1780. His oldest son, Peleg,
has been much confused with another Peleg Greene, born four years earlier,
the son of George Greene, and grandson of Edward.[2] A careful comparison
of records convinces me that Timothy's son Peleg has the record here given :

PELEG GREENE[5], b. April 1752; m. Freelove Crawford in 1779. Had these children: Russell, Allen, Ellen, Warren, Sarah, Peleg and Benjamin Franklin. Nothing of their lines is
recorded, save that Sarah m. a Mr. Bill, and their daughter, Ann Eliza, m. Pulaski Greene,
son of David.

ENFIELD[5], b. May 15. 1754.

HULDAH[5], b. Dec. 21, 1757; m. Caleb Wood of Coventry, 1789.

LEVI[5],   b. June 6, 1759. He had 11 children. Huldah m. Godfrey Slocum; Fanny
m. Orange Chaplain; Eunice m. David Crippin; Aurilla m. a Mr. Chappel; Sophia m. David
Curtis; Emma m. Abner Beardsley; late in life, they moved to Minn., where she died;

Waterman died single; Horace m. Diantha Powell; Zephaniah m. Zerilla Gould; Speedy m. Gerothman McDonald and Laura m. Sheldon Wilcox.

 MARY⁵, b. May 5, 1760. Was possibly she who m. David Nicholas and had daughter, Priscilla, b. 1785.

 SILENCE⁵, b. April 14, 1762.

 ROWLAND⁵, b. April 12, 1766.

  Lester⁶.

  George⁶.

 ELIZABETH⁵, b. May 9, 1768.

 SAMUEL GREENE⁴. He was born May 29, 1727. Probably it is he who m. Hannah Weaver of West Greenwich, March 31, 1751.

 ESTHER GREENE-WEEKS⁴. She probably m. John Weeks or Wicks, of W. Greenwich, Dec. 21, 1747.

 NATHAN GREENE⁴. He was born May 9, 1731; m. Huldah Bowen, Sept. 24, 1756. The name of Richard Bowen, (spelled in the old records Bowin, Bowyn, Bowyng, etc.,) has been borne in this same family since 1600. Several brothers, Richard, Thomas and Obediah, were early and leading residents of Rehoboth, Massachusetts. It is not clear which of these was the father of Richard³, though his grandfather was certainly Richard Bowen, Senior, who died in Feb., 1674. Richard Bowen³ was married to Mercy (Mercye) Titus, Jan. 9, 1783. The fifth child of this union was Jabez⁴, born Oct. 19, 1696. On the 30th of January, 1718, he married Huldah Hunt, herself of the third generation of the Rehoboth Hunts. One of their daughters, Huldah Bowen⁵, married this Nathan Greene of Rhode Island. Evidently, she was exceedingly popular in her husband's family, as she had many namesakes. After her death her husband married Ruth ———— and named the only child of this marriage Huldah, after the wife of his youth. Nathan had six children by his first wife, and one by the last.

 ESTHER⁵, b. 1756.

 BOWEN⁵, b. 1758. Served as Revolutionary soldier, 1776, in Col. Topham's regiment.

 CHAFFEE⁵, b. 1760. Served in the Revolutionary War, 1776, under Col. Topham.

 JABEZ⁵, b. Dec. 14, 1762. Revo. sol. See paragraph below.

 DANIEL⁵, b. 1765.

 NATHAN⁵, b. March 4, 1768.

 HULDAH⁵, born May 2, 1774 ; child of the last wife.

 Jabez⁵ became the head of a numerous, wealthy and important line. The history of this branch has been written by Myron W. Greene, himself a descendant of Jabez. Mr. Greene has given me full permission to use his work. I have therefore condensed it into a single chapter, and have made my own comments. But the data is nearly all Myron Greene's.

CHAPTER XVI

LINE OF JABEZ GREEN[5] *

Fifth in Descent from John of Quidnessett

And Jabez was more honorable than his brethren   And Jabez called on the
Lord of Israel, saying, ' O ' That Thou wouldst bless me indeed, and enlarge my coast,
and that I hy hand might be with me, and that Thou wouldst keep me from evil, that it may
not grieve me,'   And God granted him that which he requested '
—*I Chronicles, Chap IV, 9-10 v*

The line of Jabez Green[5] has held more public offices and acquired greater wealth than any other branch of the Quidnessett Greenes. Jabez's descent was this   Nathan[4], John[3], John[2], John[1]. The particulars of his descent are given in former chapters   Jabez[5] was the middle child in his father's family, Esther, Bowen and Chaffee being older, and Daniel, Nathan and Huldah,—the last a half-sister—being younger   He was born Dec 19, 1762.

When the Revolutionary War was fairly begun this family of brothers were determined to take part in it   And the records show that in 1776, when Bowen, the oldest brother, was but 18, Chaffee but 16, and Jabez lacking a few months of 14, all three enlisted in Col. John Topham's regiment, in which were already nearly a dozen of their cousins   Bowen saw service for a time in Col Lippitt's regiment also   The others remained with their original brigade, which saw active service for several years   It is probable that Jabez, from his tender years, was at first a drummer boy or bugler, as boys under military age were accepted for this service   We know that two years later Jabez's own cousin, David Nichols, a lad of fifteen, joined this same Topham's regiment as a bugler, being considered too young to bear arms

This regiment saw hard service in the state of New York   It is a curious coincidence that, after the Revolutionary War was over, one by one these cousins found their way back to N Y, until by 1801, seven of the

---

Most of this branch drop the final e

90

dozen cousins in that regiment were living in the Empire State. The war seems to have led to a general upheaval and moving about. A large number of R. I. people moved to Massachusetts. About the close of the century a western fever struck them, and nearly all of them again moved on, this time to the state of New York.

Jabez Green was one of this family colony. He lived for a time at Lanesborough, Berkshire County, Mass. He moved to Scipio, N. Y., in 1798, with wife and seven children. His wife was Abigail Wilcox, whom he married October 7, 1784.

Jabez acquired a large amount of land, and in the half of a dozen years that he lived in his new home he had already become a well-known citizen. He was the Crier of the U. S. District Court at Aurora, N. Y., and was there in the discharge of his duties when he died suddenly at Court, Sept. 19, 1804, in his forty-second year. He left his widow with eight children, the youngest a baby five months old. She was a mother that looked well after her children's interests, and she gave them a superior education for that time and age.

There had been nine children born to Jabez and Abigail, but Esther died young, and Sarah died in 1814 at the age of twenty-six. Nathaniel[6], the oldest son, born 1786, married Delia Greene of the Warwick line, but died childless at Rush, N. Y., in 1857. The descendants of Jabez's line are therefore from one of the three brothers, Archibald Harper[6], Abner[6], or Nathan Green[6], or from one of the three sisters, Huldah Green–West[6], Laura Green–Brainard[6], or Jerusha Green–Green[6]. Three of the seven children who lived to marry, Nathaniel, Nathan and Jerusha, married a brother and two sisters, Delia, Maria and John Green, who were of the Warwick Greene line.

HULDAH GREEN–WEST[6]. [Jabez[5], Nathan[4], John[3], John[2], John[1].] She was born Feb. 8, 1791, and was married in her twenty-seventh year to Pelatiah West, Nov. 27, 1817. She died May 23, 1867. To her were born nine children. She lost two children in infancy, both named Edgar Nathaniel. Three adult children, Samuel Shepherd, Ira Brainard and George Peletiah, died single at various ages from nineteen to forty-three. Another daughter, Abigail Maria West[7], born March 11, 1827, became a foreign missionary. At twenty-six she went to Constantinople, Turkey, and became the Principal of a missionary boarding and training school for Armenian girls. For thirty-five years she was either in the active missionary work in Turkey and Armenia, or traveling in the interest of missions in England and America. She returned from the mission field in 1888. Miss West wrote much on missionary themes. Her "Romance of Missions" passed through many editions. She died June 21, 1894.

HENRY TRACY WEST[7], [Huldah[6], Jabez[5], Nathan[4], John[3], John[2], John[1],] the only son of Huldah Green—West that lived to marry, was born Oct. 17, 1824, in Rochester, N. Y. He early began a stirring career, having taught in both the public schools and the academy at Palmyra, N. Y., before his marriage, and he was not yet 21 when, on June 10, 1845, he married Mary Olivia Sears, the daughter of Rev. John Sears. The next day the youthful couple started for Lake Co., Illinois, where for a time he divided his time between farming and teaching. Then he engaged in the drug business, living in different states, and rising until he was the general western agent for several patent medicine firms, and lastly one of the firm of wholesale druggists, Burnhams & Van Schaack, of Chicago.

He went to Colorado in 1870, as one of the Committee which located the city of Greeley for the Union Colony of Colorado. He was first Secretary, and then President of the Colony, and started the first bank in Greeley. In 1878 his fortune was swept away by an unfortunate coal-mining investment. He again worked his way up, only to lose all fourteen years later by the failure of a company in which he had invested. For the third time he began at the foot of the ladder, taking up book-keeping, insurance, etc., with the zeal of a young man. Mr. West has risen to very high rank in the Masonic order. He joined the order in 1851, and rose to be a Knight Templar, having filled no less than thirty-one distinct offices in that time, including that of Grand High Priest, Eminent Commander, and Captain General.

Henry T. and Mary O. West had five children, of whom Walter and an infant son are dead. Their other children are these:

George Henry West[8], b. Jan. 29, 1850. He has been m. twice. The first wife was Mary Caroline Wheeler. He has been twice Mayor of Greeley and is the Secretary of The Colorado Farm and Live Stock Company, an important business firm of Denver, Colorado. His children were all born in Greeley.

Edna Wheeler West[9], b. Feb. 15, 1873.

Amy Treadwell West[9], 1876–1889.

George Henry West[9], 1878–1879.

Olive Caroline West[9], b. Nov. 14, 1882.

Paul Sears West[9], b. July 26, 1885.

John Roylance West[9], b. Sept. 29, 1888.

Lina M. West-Gipson[8], b. Aug. 20, 1852. She m. Albert E Gipson, of Caldwell, Idaho. He is now the publisher of the Gem State Rural. He is Secretary of the State Board of Horticulture, and was formerly a prominent attorney. Their children are

Mary Florence L. Gipson-Stalker[9], wife of Dr. W. C. Stalker.

Albert W. Gipson[9].

Ruth Gipson[9].

Lawrence H. Gipson[9].

Alice Gipson[9].

James H. Gipson[9].

Margaret Gipson[9].

Edgar V. Gipson[9].

Harry T. West[8], b. Dec. 18, 1857, in Kenosha, Wis. He was a lumber and commission merchant of Denver, Col.

SARAH ELIZABETH WEST-GRASSIE[7], [Huldah[6], Jabez[5], Nathan[4], John[3], John[2], John[1].] She was born April, 27, 1820. She was a Foreign Missionary for seven years, returning in 1862. The next year she married Rev. William Grassie, D. D. Their home is in Meadville, Pa.

Jessie Duncan Grassie[8], b. June 15, 1864.

Edna Maria Grassie[8], b Sept. 3, 1867, d. July 31, 1870.

Annie Eaton Grassie[8], b. July 23, 1869, d. Sept. 20, 1887.

William Schauffler Grassie[8], b. Jan. 28, 1872, m. Katherine Mellinger, Sept. 12, 1899. They have Sara Fearnis and Marie Mellinger.

HENRY T. WEST

ARCHIBALD HARPER GREEN[6]. [Jabez[5], Nathan[4], John[3], John[2], John[1].] He was born May 31, 1794, in N. Y. He married (1) Esther Tupper, Jan. 16. 1818. She was the mother of his children. She died in 1830, and the next year he married Elnora Parker. He moved to Michigan in 1828, and died at Adrian, in that state, April 7, 1887, aged 93 years. Farmer, blacksmith and insurance agent. He was a strong Abolitionist, associating himself with such anti-slavery leaders as Gerrit Smith, Wendell Phillips and William Lloyd Garrison. He had three children:

BETSEY ANN GREEN[7]. She was born Nov. 17, 1818. She m. (1) Norman Rowley, Dec. 29, 1836; (2) Benjamin Weldon, in 1855; (3) William D. Conat, in 1868. She had five children, all but one by the first husband.

John Tupper Rowley[8], b. June 5, 1838
Esther Anna Rowley[8], b. Dec. 9, 1840.
Sarah Hannah Rowley[8], b. Feb. 11, 1844
Alfred Brainard Rowley[8], b. April 17, 1854; d. 1854.
Albert C. Weldon[8], b. Sept. 7, 1856. Is living at Ransom City, Dakota.

HELEN ANTIONETTE GREEN-SMITH[7]. [Archibald Harper[6], Jabez[5], Nathan[4], John[3], John[2], John[1].] She was born Oct. 12, 1823. Married Nathan Smith in 1842. They have two children;

Alfred N. Smith[8], b. June 22, 1843; d. 1863.
Elmer D. Smith[8], b. Nov. 20, 1854; m. Carrie L. Bailey, 1886.

JOHN WEST GREEN[7]. [Archibald Harper[6], Jabez[5], Nathan[4], John[3], John[2], John[1].] He was born April 9, 1828, at Rush, N. Y M. Helen D. Moore, Oct. 22, 1854. He led a life of much responsibility. His fidelity to every trust, and the absolute integrity of his life, left a record of which any man might be proud. He had the courage of his convictions and dared to be an out-spoken anti-slavery man and at a time when it cost something to take such a stand.

John West Green lived in Michigan, Tenn., Washington, D. C. and California. He was successively clerk, telegraph operator, book-keeper, business manager of a city paper, and rail-road constructor, all in the space of 13 years. Then in 1862 he accepted a position in the Post Office Department, Washington. D. C. Soon after he was appointed to a position in the Treasury Department, where he remained nine years. Secretary of the Treasury, John Sherman, paid him the high compliment of appointing him, in 1877, one of the three Commissioners to go to England in charge of $18,950,000, in U. S. bonds to be refunded by the Rothschilds. Afterwards, he was made Chief Inspector of the P. O. Department. In all he served continuously 21 years in trusted government positions. After removing to California, he was for a time Cashier of the Southern Pacific R. R. He was twice appointed Postmaster of the city of Los Angeles, dying in office, Aug. 3, 1891. To him and his wife was born one son

Charles Earnest Green[8], b. Oct. 31, 1855. He is m. to Mary Elizabeth Eldridge, daughter of John Oscar and Elizabeth Risdon Eldridge, of Springfield, Mass. He was connected with the Southern and Central Pacific Railroad Companies of California in various capacities, from 1875 to 1898. At present he is the Manager of the Crocker Estate Company and Vice-President of the Crocker-Woolworth National Bank of San Francisco. He is a member of the Masonic Fraternity, being a Knight Templar and 33° Scottish Rite Mason. He has the usual Greene luck, his children being sons.

Eldridge Green[9], b. Nov. 3, 1883.
Allan Lee Green[9], b. Jan. 14, 1886.
Charles Arthur Green[9], b. July 16, 1887.

LAURA M. GREEN–BRAINARD[6]. [Jabez[5], Nathan[4], John[3], John[2], John[1].] She was born Aug. 14, 1796, and married to Hezekiah Brainard in 1820. She died in 1835, aged 39 years, and was buried at Rush, N. Y.

ORRIN NATHAN BRAINARD[7], b. 1821 ; lives at Carbondale, Illinois.

AUGUSTUS BROCKWAY BRAINARD[7], b. 1824 ; lives in Grand Rapids, Michigan.

BYRON STRONG BRAINARD[7], b. Aug. 31, 1826 ; lives in Ogden, Utah.

ABNER GREEN[6]. [Jabez[5], Nathan[4], John[3], John[2], John[1].] He was

ABNER GREEN

born in Lanesborough, Mass., Sept. 17, 1798. Came as a babe to N. Y., where he lived and died. March 27, 1825, he married Nancy Ketchum. He was a strong, robust man, and lived to his 94th year, dying April 17, 1892.

Abner Green was every inch a typical Greene. He had the square, heavy-set frame, the broad forehead and kindly mouth of the family. He was a farmer, and a liberal supporter of what he esteemed worthy enterprises. He contributed toward the endowment of the Genesee Wesleyan Seminary in 1832, not waiting, as some rich men do, to will away in gifts what they can no longer use. Of his seven children, Henry Granville and Abner Baxter died in early childhood, and a daughter, Ellen L., died in her 20th year. The families of the other four children are as follows :

MORTIMER H. GREEN[7], [Abner[6], Jabez[5], Nathan[4], John[3], John[2], John[1].] B. March 7, 1826. He m. Ellen M. Flinn, Jan. 6, 1848. He was successively farmer, postmaster and banker. He died Sept. 14, 1879, and was buried at Rush, N. Y.

Azalia Ethelwyn Green–Weaver[8], b Nov. 25, 1848 ; m. Lucius E. Weaver Dec. 13, 1871.

Paul Weaver[9], b. May 8, 1873.

Margaret Ethelwyn Weaver[9], b. April 16, 1877.

Abner Green[8], d. young.

Marion Keeler Green–Peet[8], b. Dec. 6, 1856 ; m. to James Clinton Peet, Jan. 14, 1880.

Mortimer Silas Peet[9], b May 15, 1881.

Azalia Emma Peet[9], b. Sept. 3, 1887.

Nelson Rusk Peet[9], b. May 17, 1889.

Aurora Matilda Green–Baldwin[8], b. Jan. 30, 1860 ; m. to Le Grand M. Baldwin, Dec. 15, 1884.

Pierre Baldwin[9], b. Jan. 4, 1886.

Myron Harley Baldwin[9], b. April 23, 1889.

MARVIN JABEZ GREEN[7], [Abner[6], Jabez[5], Nathan[4], John[3], John[2], John[1],] born Jan. 11, 1829, at Brighton, N. Y. He married Cornelia Gillman, Dec. 28, 1853. He was a banker

HOME OF CHARLES A. GREENE, NEAR HIGHLAND PARK, ROCHESTER, N. Y.

in Cuba, N. Y., at the breaking out of the Civil War. He entered the army, and became First Paymaster. Afterwards he was appointed Brigade Commissary. After the war, he was engaged in the banking business at Rochester until his death, May 22. 1870. Three children.

    Delfred Green[8]. Died young.

    Geraldine Green–Mudge[8]. b. Jan. 20, 1859 ; m. to Charles Mudge, Dec. 13, 1883.

        Winifred Mudge[9]. b. Nov. 17, 1884.

        Helen Louise Mudge[9]. b. Aug. 26, 1887.

        Geraldine Mudge[9]. b. Nov. 26, 1888.

    William Sprague Green[8]. b. Oct. 31. 1861 ; m. Virginia Reynolds, April 24, 1883. He is a farmer.

        Edward Randolph Green[9]. b. May 30, 1884, at Sodus, N. Y.

  MARY E. GREEN–BROWN[7]. [Abner[6], Jabez[5], Nathan[4], John[3], John[2], Jonn[1].] She was born Dec. 1, 1830, and was married to James Douglas Brown, Dec. 16, 1858. Her husband is a lawyer, and their home is in Brooklyn, N. Y.

    Ellen Ethlyn Brown[8]. b. and d. in 1860.

    Baxter Lamont Brown[8]. b. Jan. 20, 1864. m. Cora Cowgill, Feb. 26, 1889. He is a Civil Engineer, and lives at Pineville, Kentucky.

        Clarence Cowgill Brown[9]. b. Nov. 24, 1889, in Lawrence, Kansas

    Maritza Brown[8]. b. Jan. 17. 1875.

  CHARLES A. GREEN[7]. [Abner[6], Jabez[5], Nathan[4], John[3], John[2], John[1].] He was the youngest child of Abner Green, and was born in Rush, N. Y., Aug. 1, 1843. He married Jennie C. Hale, of Rochester, N. Y., on Sept. 3. 1873. He was with his brother Marvin Jabez in a bank in Cuba, N. Y., until the dark days of the Civil War, during which time he became a Commissary clerk at Washington, D. C. After the war he engaged in the banking business until the panic of 1873 compelled him to suspend. It was a fortunate thing for him. He had inherited that seven-centuries love of the Greenes for horticultural and land-scape art, for trees and fruit and flowers ; for broad acres kept in apple-pie trim, and for a park-like setting about the home. He bought an old homestead at Clifton, N. Y., and began farming, and the propagation of plants. He soon became one of the leading nursery-men of America. His firm is known as the Green Nursery Co., of Rochester, N. Y. He publishes Green's Fruit Grower, and has written several helpful horticultural works that have had a wide circulation. As an author his style is clear and unaffected, and he is entirely free of the fault of writing over people's heads. The struggle of his first horticultural efforts is amusingly told in the book,——"How I Made the Old Farm Pay." He and his wife have three children.

    Mildred E. Green–Burleigh[8], wife of Robert E. Burleigh, b. Sep. 3, 1875.

        Onnolee M. Burleigh[9]. b. Aug. 22, 1899.

        Kenneth E. Burleigh[9]. b. Sep. 24. 1901.

        Robert Green Burleigh[9]. b. Sep. 21. 1903.

    Marion E. Green[8]. b. Jan. 24, 1882 at Clifton.

    Marvin H. Green[8]. b. Aug. 8, 1884. " "

JERUSHA GREEN–GREEN[6]. [Jabez[5], Nathan[4], John[3], John[2], John[1].] She was born Sept. 6, 1800, in Scipio, N. Y. She married her sister-in-law's brother, John Green, of Balston, N. Y. She died June 30, 1861. She had seven children, of whom all but the oldest died young. Jerusha's husband is claimed to have belonged to the Warwick branch of the Greenes, and was therefore about her sixth cousin.

    JAMES A. GREEN[7]. b. Jan. 8, 1838, in Rush, N. Y. He m. (1) Susan Margaret Smith, in 1860 ; (2) Kate Monroe of Toledo, Ohio, June 18. 1884. He is proprietor of the Union Transfer & Storage Co., Detroit, Michigan.

        Edith G. Green[8]. d. young.

        Vincent V. Green[8]. b. March 31, 1874.

CHARLES A. GREENE

Publisher of "Greene's Fruit Grower," and author of
various practical agricultural works

1864-1904

[signature]

Author of " Jabez Greene and His Descendants "

NATHAN GREEN[6]. [Jabez[5], Nathan[4], John[3], John[2], John[1].] He was born April 5, 1804, at Scipio, N. Y., but five months before his father's death. He married Maria Green of Balston, July 1, 1827, making the third marriage between Jabez Green's children and that particular Balston family of Greenes. After her death he married Rachel Perry, of the celebrated Perry family, from which came Commodore Oliver Hazard Perry, the hero of Lake Erie, and Commodore Mathew Perry, who unlocked the gates of Japan to the civilized world. Her father, Elnathan Perry, was in the Revolutionary War battles of Bennington, Saratoga, Monmouth, Trenton, Eutaw Springs and Yorktown, and was an eye-witness to the surrender of both Burgoyne and Cornwallis.

Nathan Green was a public-spirited man. He owned much land. He gave the building sites free for two schools and two churches, and in many other ways gave a helping hand to worthy causes. His family of six children, five sons and one daughter, all lived to become heads of families.

JONATHAN H. GREEN[7], [Nathan[6], Jabez[5], Nathan[4], John[3], John[2], John[1].] was born Sept. 19, 1828. He m. Jane Cornelius, Oct. 17, 1849. He removed to Michigan, where for 18 years he filled various government positions, such as being Deputy Marshal, U. S. Court Bailiff, etc. He retired from active life in 1881. Has three children.

Addie Green-Graves[8], b. March 5, 1851, m. to M. M. Graves, Dec. 20, 1870.

Chauncey Graves[9], b. June 3, 1873.

Mabel Graves[9], b. Sept. 11, 187-.

Olive J. Graves[9], b. Jan. 1, 1883.

Alice Green-Barker[8], b. May 14, 1856; m. to David Barker, Nov. 1, 1863.

Anna E. Barker[9], b. March 26, 1887; d. 1889.

Addie E. Barker[9], b. March 26, 1887

Arthur C. Green[8], b. May 21, 1864; m. Sarah Hunt of Macon, Michigan, Nov. 19, 1885. He is a farmer, and lives at Adrian, Michigan.

Florence E. Green[9], b. Feb. 13, 1888.

IRA WESLEY GREENE[7], [Nathan[6], Jabez[5], Nathan[4], John[3], John[2], John[1].] He was born May 2, 1832, and has been twice married, (1) to Hester A. Ruliffson, Dec. 26, 1855; (2) to Ellen Maria Williams, Dec. 26, 1866. He was a banker for a time, then turned his attention to farming, and particularly to the growing of choice field seed crops. This is an important industry in the state of New York, as so many city seedsmen and florists must have their high grade seeds raised for them. Ira Wesley Greene had three children by each marriage.

DeLos Ruliffson Greene[8], b. Feb. 26, 1858, in Rush, N. Y. Married Ella Jane Colburn, 1882. He died Sept. 10, 1887. He was a farmer and Superintendent of the State Experimental Station.

Hattie Maria Greene[8], b. Feb. 3, 1861. She is a graduate of Rochester City Hospital Training School.

Myron Wesley Greene[8], b. Nov. 26, 1864, at Rush, N. Y. He is a graduate of Genesee Wesleyan Seminary, 1887, and Williams College, class of 1890. Myron W. m. Nancy Laura Lancaster, of Leadville, Col., April 27, 1900, and has two sons, Lancaster Myron, b. Feb. 21, 1901, and Norvin Ruliffson, b. Sept. 13, 1902, and a daughter, Zeta Priscilla Greene, born March 2, 1904. He is a private banker and dealer in government, municipal and corporation bonds, in Rochester, N. Y.

Myron W. Greene is the author of "Jabez Greene and his Descendants," published in Jan. 1891. It is a business man's book, short, to the point, and without clap-trap or spread-eagleism. He started out to tell who Jabez Greene's posterity are, where they live, and what they are doing. With a few exceptions, he is my authority for all statements made in this chapter.

By his last wife, Ira Wesley Greene[7] had these children :

Chester Pollard Greene[8], b. Nov. 4, 1869, m. Elizabeth Smith.

Carrie E. Greene-Hawley[8], b. June, 30, 1872, wife of H. Hawley.

Albert Ira Greene[8], b. Nov. 30, 1874.

THEODORE DE LOS GREEN[7], [Nathan[6], Jabez[5], Nathan[4], John[3], John[2], John[1].] He was born in Rush, N. Y., June 16, 1834, and married Eliza Harris, Oct. 24, 1860.

Leroy Homer Green[8], b. Sept. 30. 1874 ; d. 189—.

JEROME MARION GREEN[7], [Nathan[6], Jabez[5], Nathan[4], John[3], John[2], John[1].] He was born Jan. 23, 1841, and married Emily Barker, Oct. 15, 1863. He was a farmer at Adrian, Michigan. D. March 26, 1901.

Carrie M. Green[8], b. 1865 ; d. 1877.

HORACE M. GREEN[7], [Nathan[6], Jabez[5], Nathan[4], John[3], John[2], John[1].] He was born Sept. 3, 1842, in Rush, N. Y. He married Julia H. Granger, Oct. 4, 1871.

Florence Green[8], b. Jan. 5, 1873.

ELLEN O. E. GREEN-DARROHN[7], [Nathan[6], Jabez[5], Nathan[4], John[3], John[2], John[1].] She was born Oct. 16, 1847, and married to Maurice R. Darrohn, Oct. 26, 1871. Seven children.

Everett Green Darrohn[8], b. July 21, 1872.

Perry Simpson Darrohn[8], b. March 31, 1874.

Eva May Darrohn[8], b. Nov. 9, 1875.

Maurice Donald Darrohn[8], b. Dec. 30, 1877.

Joseph C. Darrohn[8], b. March 31, 1879.

Clara Ellen Darrohn[8], b. April 24, 1883.

Anna Mabel Darrohn[8], b. Nov. 7, 1884.

CHAPTER XVII

LIEUT. JOHN[2] OF COVENTRY'S LINE

Descendants of Usal, Ebenezer and Robert Greene

Usal Greene[3] must have been sorry a thousand times that his great-great-great-great-grandfather was a Frenchman with a French name that English tongues could not speak   Old Gershom Lascelle's daughter must needs name her son Lascelle after her father   By the time this name had reached this Lascelle Wardwell's grandson, born on American soil in 1639, no pretence was made of retaining the old pronunciation   And, as the town recorders spelled "by ear," there arose that remarkable putting down of a name that caused Savage to annote it, "Usal, Usual, Uzal, Usewell, Uzell or other outlandish name " *

Abigail Greene was the Massachusetts Usal's daughter, and she had the temerity to name her third son after her father. I have retained the spelling of Usal or Usual, as the simplest form of the name. But R I records give it in these different ways   Usal, Uzal, Uzall, Youzell, Yousiel, and even Usualell ! This Usual of the unusual name led an unusually long life and left an unusually tangled family record behind him   His children's births are some of them given as at three different dates   He is said to have been 98 years, 100 or 101 years, or 104, or as tradition says, 110 years old when he died   One writer puts his death on Oct 14, 1794, one in 1795. But James N Arnold in his Vital Records quotes a notice from a contemporaneous R. I. newspaper at the time of his death, which states that "Usall Greene" died at Coventry, Oct 24, 1797   His birth records show him to have been born Jan 23, 1694, so that he was 103 years, 9 months and 1 day old at his death   The Wardwell blood ever showed in remarkable longevity, but Usal Greene broke the record for the R I branch of the family

Usal Greene spent his long life in Coventry   His first four children were recorded in Warwick   After the readjustment of the townships and

---

* See Savage's Genealogical and Historical Dictionary of New England.

the making of a new one, he recorded these same four children and two that were born afterwards, in Coventry. I have a third record that gives these same six children. These are the only authentic, at-the-time compiled records, and only these six children are certainly his. There is a group of names, Timothy, Jonathan and Jane, that some authorities call Uzal's, but there are no official records for them.

USUAL GREENE[4]. (Written also Usal, Yousiel and Youzel.) [Usal[3], John[2], John[1].] Born March 22, 1729, or March 22, 1730. He married a Conn. lady, Mrs. Martha Polit, Sept. 14, 1753. He lived in Coventry. He joined the 6-principle Baptist church of Maple Root in 1785. No other documentary record of him.

HENRY GREENE[4]. Born Feb. 20, 1730, Feb. 20, 1731, or 1732.

ABIGAIL GREENE–JOHNSON[4]. [Usal[3], John[2], John[1].] She was born Feb. 9, 1732, Feb. 9, 1733 or 1734. According to official records she married Elisha Johnson, Jr., Nov., 1750. Private records give the name as Ezekiel.

> DANIEL JOHNSON[5]. In two private records he is given, once as the son of Abigail, and once as her sister, Elizabeth Greene-Johnson's son. Probably Abigail's son.
>
> Abigail Johnson–Greene[6], m. Hiram Greene[6], [Benjamin[5], Isaac[4], James[3], John[2], John[1],] her third cousin. Line given in Chapter XIV.
>
> Ezekiel Johnson[6]. Perhaps he who m. Sarah Matteson, 1787.
>
> Huldah Johnson[6].

ELIZABETH GREENE–JOHNSON[4]. [Usal[3], John[2], John[1].] She was born Jan. 28, 1735, or Jan. 28, 1736. Almost certainly married Ezekiel Johnson, brother or cousin to Abigail Greene's husband.

> EZEKIEL JOHNSON[5], m. Ruth, daughter of Joseph Matteson. Had Phebe, Catherine, Ruth, Betsey, Nancy, Caleb, Philip, Rufus, Joseph and Ezekiel.
>
> Philip Johnson[6], of above, m. Priscilla, daughter of David and Mary Greene–Nichols. Their children were:
>
>> Hiram N. Johnson[7], b. Aug. 17, 1808.
>>> Zina Johnson[8], living in Phenix, R. I.
>> Alexander Johnson[7], b. April 25, 1810.
>> William G. Johnson[7], b. May, 1815.
>> Caleb Johnson[7], b. Jan. 28, 1818.
>> Philip Johnson[7], b. March 30, 1822. He m. Tryphena H. Greene, his second cousin. He is particularly versed in family history, and is considered good authority on disputed points. See Chapter XIV.

ROBERT GREENE[4]. Born April 4, 1738.

PHILIP GREENE[4]. Born May 24, or 26, 1740.

Ebenezer Greene[3], [John[2], John[1],] was the fifth child of Lieut. John Greene. He lived in Coventry. His wife's family is unknown, although certain considerations point to her having been a Pierce, and therefore a distant relative on his mother's side, as the Pierces were a branch of the Wardwells. He, too, is claimed as the father of Rebecca and Jane Greene-

Andrews. His children are twice recorded, both in Warwick and Coventry. Two daughters are among the number, but no Jane nor Rebecca. He had six sons and two daughters.

JOHN GREENE[4]. [Ebenezer[3], John[2], John[1].] He was born April 15, 1732. Married Abigail ————.

    DANIEL GREENE[5], b. Dec. 19, 1762 ; m. Lucenia Matteson, his third cousin. [Lucenia[6], Wm.[5], Martha Green-Matteson[4], John Greene[3], James[2], John[1].]

      Clark Greene[6], m. Susannah Westcott.

        Lawton Greene[7], m. Sarah A. Card.

          William Ray Greene[8], m. Lilian Andrews. He is considered uncommonly well versed in family history.

    Wanton Greene[6], (of Daniel, grandson of Ebenezer), m. Mercy Sweet, daughter of Burton and Rachel Matteson-Sweet. Burton Sweet was the grandson of the Huguenots of Chapter XXI, Magdalen and Marie La Valley-King.

      Ray Greene[7], m. ———— Coggeshall.

        Laura Greene-Sweet[8]. Lives in Providence, R. I.

  SILAS GREENE[5]. (of John[4] of Ebenezer[3].)

EBENEZER GREENE[4]. [Ebenezer[3], John[2], John[1].] Born Feb. 13, 1737. Tradition says he was an old bachelor when he married. He presented each of his namesakes with a solid silver spoon of dessert size, with the request that it be passed on to an Ebenezer among their sons. One of these spoons is now in the possession of his sister Olive's great-grandson, E. C. Pierce, of Wolcottville, Indiana. This is supposed to be the Ebenezer who m. Betsey Briggs and had

    WELTHIAN GREENE[5], b. either in Dec. 1791 or Sept. 16, 1792. The first date is probably intended for his marriage date.

    EBENEZER GREENE[5]. Married Sally Ann Vickery. 5 children.

ROBERT GREENE[4]. [Ebenezer[3], John[2], John[1].] Born April 14, 1739. He married Welthian Greene, his Uncle Robert's youngest daughter, March 10, 1762. Had these children :

    PELEG GREENE[5], b. June 25, 1762.

    MARY GREENE[5], b. July 23, 1764.

    AUDREY GREENE[5], b. Nov. 1, 1766.

    STEPHEN C. GREENE[5], b. April 11, 1768.

    JOB GREENE[5], b. June 15, 17—. M. Ann Brown. **Not on one record.**

      Harriet Caroline Greene[6], b. 1819.

    ENFIELD GREENE[5], b. June 25, 1742.

ELISHA GREENE[4]. [Ebenezer[3], John[2], John[1].] Born March 24, or March 14 by another record, 1745. He married the widow Priscilla Matteson in 1775.

    JOSEPH GREENE[5], b. June 23, 1776.

STEPHEN GREENE[4]. [Ebenezer[3], John[2], John[1].] Born April 6, 1748. He served in the Revolutionary War, and in 1835 was yet alive. He lived near Centerville, where his family is buried. His daughter, Freelove, fell into the wheel-pit of the mill there and was drowned, March 6, 1839, aged 47 years.

SENECA GREENE⁵, (probably,) b. Nov. 14. 1782.
AUGUSTUS GREENE⁵, (probably); m. Mary Andrews, 1806.
STEPHEN GREENE⁵, (probably); m. Mary Darish, 1816.

OLIVE GREENE–PIERCE⁴. [Ebenezer³, John², John¹.] She was born July 1, 1751. M. Samuel Pierce. Line traced in Chapter XXIV.

JOSEPH GREENE⁴. Born April 29, 1755.

Robert * Greene³. [John², John¹.] He was married Nov. 19, 1730, at East Greenwich, to Mary Andrews. He lived for a time in Coventry, but at the time of his second marriage was living in Canterbury. He had seven children by the first wife, and one by the last, who was Susannah White of Canterbury. One son died young. Of the twins, Robert and Andrew, born 1734, and Persolloe and Mary, born in 1736 and 1739, we have birth records only. Of Benjamite, born Feb. 23, 1741, we have only the further notice that his wife's name was Sarah. The two remaining daughters both married cousins, as below :

ANN GREENE–GREENE⁴. Born Feb. 5, 1732, m. her Uncle James' son, Wardwell Greene. Her line is traced in Chapter XIV. Ann was a Quaker in faith.

WELTHIAN GREENE–GREENE⁴. Daughter of Robert Greene by his last wife, Susannah White. She married Robert, the son of her Uncle Ebenezer. See Robert.

---

* Robert Greene is frequently entered on the records as Robarth

CHAPTER XVIII

Descendants of Hannah Greene–Andrews[3]

This chapter is a difficult one In the main I follow Miss Hattie James' work, "The Andrews Genealogy." This lady inherited an aptitude for genealogical work from both her father and grandmother. She was born in an Andrews community, and personally knew the half dozen old gentlemen of 85 and 90, who were looked up to as authority on the intricate family relationship She interviewed all of these, solicited family records from branch after branch, and made a careful study of the old books and records. After years of labor and expense, just as she was getting it into shape for publication, grievous bodily affliction befell her She finished it lying upon her back, and writing with benumbed, half-paralyzed hands The *Gleaner* of Phenix, R I , ran it as a serial for something over a year A friend tells us that this invaluable work has netted its author not a penny When her years of suffering are over, too late it will be realized by this family that a historian was in their midst, and they appreciated her not.

Hannah, tenth child and fourth daughter of Lieut John[2] and Abigail Wardwell-Greene, was born not far from 1706, and married about 1727. Her marriage is recorded in the town records. but is so illegibly written that the last name can hardly be deciphered. Huling and Arnold thought the name Arnold, but Miss James positively identifies her as the wife of John Andrews.

The Andrews are an important R I family The founder was John Andrews, variously called in his day, Andrace, McAndrews, McAndros, Andrus and Andrew Originally from Scotland, or of Scottish descent, he came to the New World for religious peace. He settled first at the Barbadoes, then at Boston, and next at Cape Cod Because of the Massachusetts authorities' rigid stand against heresy, he removed to Rhode Island, casting in his fortunes with old John Greene of Quidnessett and his companions. He it was who testified after King Philip's war of seeing Chief Awashuwett lay hands upon John Greene. He was one of the six with Greene, Capt. Fones and four others, to buy Fones' Purchase from the chief sachem of the Narragansetts in 1672. His son, John Andrews, Jun., was one of those concerned in the hay dispute with a band of Huguenot refugees, (spoken of in Chapter XV,) which waxed so serious that Governor Andros had to decide it.

The senior John Andrews had a son William², and William² had this son John³, who married Hannah Greene³. John Andrews³ was born March 23, 1702. He died May 18, 1795, in his 94th year. He came from Frenchtown, in Warwick, and settled in Conventry at Maple Root Plains. When the church was established that afterwards became known far and near as the celebrated Six Principle Baptist Church of Maple Root, he and his wife were among the charter members. They had four children. Anne, the oldest, became Mrs. Weaver, but died childless; Hannah, the next child, never married. The two sons, Elnathan and William, married sisters, Jane and Rebecca Greene, their mother's nieces or great-nieces. We know no more of Hannah Greene-Andrews' life.

There is a sharp dispute in the family as to whose line Jane and Rebecca Andrews belong. All agree that they were descended from Lieut. John Greene and his wife Abigail, that they were sisters, and that Jane was Elnathan's wife, and Rebecca was William's wife. Usal³, James³ and Ebenezer³, three sons of Lieut. John, are each claimed as their father, while yet another wing of the family holds their father was Squire Nathaniel Greene, the oldest son of James. Every one of these positions is vouched for by certain old heads, who claim to know the family from A to Z.

Usal's claim is to be at once rejected. Jane was married in 1757, and Rebecca, by the latest, was married by the year after. Usal's youngest recorded child was born in 1740. Allowing two years between births, had these two children followed that son, they could have been but 15 and 14 at time of their marriages. Altogether improbable.

Ebenezer and James each recorded their children, including daughters. The official records give neither a Jane nor a Rebecca among them. James' youngest recorded child was born after 1729. Ebenezer has a list of eight children, from 1732 to 1755. Those who think the daughters his, point to a gap of five years in one place between children's ages. That they are left out of the records is the hard thing to get over, with both the James and Ebenezer claim. Nathaniel⁴, son of James³, was married early in 1739. He failed to record any of his children. If his oldest were these two daughters, they could easily have been 17 and 16 at time of marriage. Young indeed, but not unusual in those days. This claim has the least difficulties, but it is least accepted by the family themselves. They were certainly grand-daughters or great-grand-daughters of Lieut. John, Miss James at first thought the sisters were of the line of James. Afterwards, she placed them as of the line of Ebenezer.

Elnathan Andrews[1] was born on the same day as General Washington, Feb. 22, 1732. He was married at 25 to his cousin Jane Greene, June 21, 1757. They went to housekeeping within a quarter of a mile of his father's. They were parents of five children, Waity, Bethana, Timothy, John and Rebecca. Elnathan outlived Jane, and married a second wife, Mrs. Ezekiel Johnson. Miss James says Elnathan died June 20, 1824, in his 93rd year.

William and Rebecca Andrews had twice as many children as the other family. They had James, William, Ellen, Abigail, Elnathan, Elcy (Alice), Hannah, Timothy, Rebecca and Isaac.

These Andrews were all highly respected people. They were clannish in their ways and their marriages, and they are largely so to this day. A large proportion of the last five generations have belonged to the Six-Principle Baptist Church. This is a branch of the Church that is little known outside of Rhode Island. It takes its name because it claims to be founded on the first and second verses of the sixth chapter of Hebrews, and holds as cardinal doctrines the six principles there enumerated, viz.: repentance, faith, baptism, laying on of hands, resurrection of the dead, and eternal judgment.*

In 1762 this Maple Root Church was organized with 26 members. A church was built in the country, in the middle of a sandy plain, where four highways met. It was about one-and-a-third miles from the Old Field Cemetery, where slept Hannah Greene-Andrews' father and mother and kindred, and, as many think, old John of Quidnessett himself. It was almost a family church, and as such remained, the Andrews name always predominating above all others. Its first pastor, 1765–1770, was Rev. Timothy Greene, a nephew of Hannah Greene-Andrews.

This church of small beginnings grew to have a continent-wide fame. It had, at one time, the largest membership of any country church in the United States, and at stated times has yet a congregation that any city church might be proud of. The first church building was outgrown, and sold in 1797. Elnathan Andrews gave a lot across the road from the old church, and donated timber for a new building. This church is as unlike an ordinary church building as can be imagined. There is no ornamentation about it. It is built on the style of a plain two-story dwelling house.

By 1821 the church had *460 members!* Elnathan Andrews, one of its first members 59 years before, and the donor of its church home, was yet living. Those were its palmy days. Afterwards branch churches were es-

---

* The Six Principle Baptists claim to particularly represent the teachings of Roger Williams.

MAPLE ROOT CHURCH. R. I.
THE MOST FAMOUS COUNTRY CHURCH IN AMERICA

tablished at other places that cut its membership down to its present number, about 140 persons.   But on the first Sunday in June it is the custom for
historic old Maple Root Church to open wide its doors to its children far
and near.   On that day the crowd is so great that only the early comers can
get within its walls.   The pond where the converts are baptized is a half-
mile away.   There is always one special tune that is sung on the long march
to the water, and there is one room on the Gorton place that for over 70
years was used as a dressing room for those who were immersed.   Incidents
like these show that Rhode Island, as well as Connecticut, might have the
name, "The land of steady habits."

Before giving a synopsis of the branching out of these two families, a
brief reference to the families with which they so much intermarried may be
of interest.   The Briggses were descended from John Briggs, who lived three
miles from old John Greene of Quidnessett, and was one of old John's followers.   Briggs was associated with Greene, John Andrews and three others
in making the great Fornes' Purchase of land from the Chief, Awashuwett,
in 1672, the year after the great land dispute was settled.   Naturally, the
intimacy of the fathers continued between the families.

The Sweets were descended from John Sweet of Dedham, Mass., who went with Roger Williams to Providence in 1636. He died the next year, leaving a widow and two little sons, John and James. The year after this his widow married Ezekiel Holyman, who has gone down to fame as the man who performed the irregular baptism of Roger Williams, late in 1638. Williams came to believe only immersion was valid baptism. He could not get a clergyman to immerse him, so Ezekiel Holyman baptized him, and then Roger Williams turned immediately around and baptized Holyman, and after that the others, including Holyman's recent bride. The young Sweets were old enough to remember this scene, and doubtless it had its influence in making the first generations of the family such strong. Baptists. Those who intermarried with the Andrews were from John Sweet[2].

As for the Mattesons, who intermarried with the Andrews, as they did with the Greenes, their history is specially given in the Appendix Chapter.

Elnathan Andrews' descendants are outlined as follows. For a fuller account I refer those interested to Miss James' "Andrews Genealogy."

WAITY ANDREWS–GREENE[3]. M. Charles Greene, and died, leaving a son Charles. The next sister, Bethana, married the widower. No record of any children.

TIMOTHY ANDREWS[5]. B. Nov. 22, 1762. He married a distant cousin, Russelle Matteson. On her father's side she was of the James Greene line, [Russelle[6], William[5], Martha Greene-Matteson[4], John Greene[3], James[2], John[1].] The mother was Sarah, daughter of Henry and Rachel Greene. Miss James speaks of Rachel as of the "same Greenes." Thus four strains of Quidnessett Greene blood flowed in their children's veins. Of their 12 children, 11 married, and 5 of these married Sweets of La Valley-King descent.

BETHANA ANDREWS-SWEET[6], M. Caleb Sweet of Burton and Rachel Sweet. Line traced in Magdalen King Chapter.

FREELOVE ANDREWS-VICKERY[6]. M. Benjamin Vickery of Dighton, Mass. Those who continued the line were George Vickery, who m. Priscilla, dau. of Elijah Greene ; Sally, who m. Ebenezer, son of Ebenezer Greene ; and Miranda, who m. Varnum James Tefft.

PELEG ANDREWS[6]. M. Mercy, dau. of Joseph and Elizabeth Greene–James. She was descended from the Warwick Greenes. 4 children.

JANE ANDREWS–JAMES–WAITE[6]. She first married her sister-in-law Mercy's brother, Perry Greene James. They had four children. She afterwards married Sheffield Waite, son of that Revolutionary patriot, Major Yelverton Waite. The Waites were a good family. Miss James gives a telling word picture of the old colonial home, the generous manner of living, and the courtly old people. Mrs. Waite was an expert in family genealogy.

Phebe A. James--Sweet[7], m. Abel M. Sweet, son of William. She died in Conn.
Adeline Frances Sweet--Andrews[8], m. Thos. Tillinghast Andrews. Four children.

Joseph James[7], b. 1812 ; d. 1872. M. Almira Kimball. Had Caroline, Sarah, Mary Ann, Henry M., Almira K., Anna J. and Cora P.

Albert Greene James[7], b. July 21, 1819 ; m Mary Ann Bowen, of Thomas and

Phebe Bowen. Nine children, Thomas Bowen, Phebe B., Mary Eliza, Harriet Frances, Charles Henry, Joseph, Frederick B., William Greene and John Walter James.

Harriet Frances of the above is the Miss James who wrote the Andrews genealogy. She was left a motherless girl while her younger brothers were small. She was ever after her father's housekeeper, and brought the younger ones up with faithful care. Though since 1888 an invalid, she has done good work with her pen, and her patience and cheerfulness have been the admiration of all. She has helped me much by personal notes.

Maria James--Matteson[7], b. Sept. 27, 1822. M. Thomas of Rufus and Lucy Spink Matteson. Five children.

SALLIE ANDREWS-SWEET[6], b. 1794, m. William, son of Burton and Rachel Sweet. Nine children. See Magdalen King Chapter.

GEORGE ANDREWS[6], b. Aug. 7, 1797; m. Esther Barnes. D. in Noank, Conn., April 7, 1872. Five children, Benjamin Franklin, Ezra Barnes, Sabrina E., Charles Beaumont and an unnamed infant.

MATTESON ANDREWS[6], b. 1799; m. Lucy Sweet. D. in Natick, R. I., Jan. 27, 1852. Nine children.

JONATHAN ANDREWS[6], b. Oct. 5. 1801; m. in 1825 to Roby Sweet of Burton and Rachel Sweet. He d. in Minnesota in 1868. These children:

Burton Sweet Andrews[7], b. May 10, 1827. Living in Tennessee. M. Phebe Capwell. Children.

Bethana Andrews--Pendleton[7], b. 1829; m. to Joseph Pendleton. Five children.

Charles Waldo Andrews[7], b. May 31, 1837; m. Mary Eliza Halliday. Two sons, Walter C. and Jonathan J.

Joanna Andrews--Williams[7], b. 1804; d. 1879. M. to Senaca Williams of Conn. Four children.

JOHN ANDREWS[6], b. July 4. 1806; m. Antha Sweet of William and Elcy (Alice,) Sweet. Antha was of La Valley-King descent, her grandmother being Sarah King. This has been a leading family. They have a John Andrews' Branch reunion and clam-bake, each summer. John and Antha had eleven children. For fuller particulars, see Miss James' Genealogy.

Timothy Andrews[7], b. Nov. 30, 1828; m. Eunice, dau. of Asa Matteson. No children.

William Andrews[7], b. 1830; m, (1) Abbie Woodmansee, and (2) Mystilla Tarbox. Eight children, Millard Fillmore, Mary Josephine and Abbie Frances, by the first wife; and Edwin, Bernice, Edward, Mabel Devona, and Annice Maria, by the last wife.

Elsie Andrews--Matteson[7], b. April 15, 1832; m. in 1847 to Deacon John Matteson of Asa and Meribah Potter--Matteson. Like his wife, John Matteson had the blood of all the clan families, including La Valley and King descent. Of their nine children, one died young. Of the other eight, all but one married relatives, making a line so complex this chapter has not space to unfold it. It is probably the most tangled case of relationship in this book. The children who married are Elihu R., m. to Roby E. Andrews; Phebe Josephine, wife of Oliver H. Greene; Charles James, m. to Mary Amanda Matteson; Mary Jane, wife of Edward C Capwell; Eunice Margaret, m. to George Warren Andrews; John Titus, m. to Amanda M. Greene; Cynthia Lily, wife of William Briggs; and Clara L., the wife of John P. Perkins.

Mary Ann Andrews--Barber[7], m. to Samuel Hoxsie Barber. Children, Beethoven, Fernando A., Harriet T., and Mary A.

Hon. J. Titus Andrews[7], b. July 31, 1836; m. in 1857 to Mary Ann Sweet, dau. of Amos and Ruth Sweet. No children. He was state senator several years, and is a prominent man,

Abbie Francis Andrews--Harrington[7], m. to Job Whitman Harrington. Her children are Orville F., Antha Jane, Bernard Auff, Edward B., and William Harris Harrington.

John Francis Andrews[7], b. May 21, 1845; m. Dec. 25, 1866, to Mary E. Howard, dau. of Ephraim. Two children. Line given in Howard Chapter.

Lois A. Andrews--Cahoon[7], m. to Edward Cahoon. No children.

Nelson Andrews[7], m. Phebe E. Spencer. His son is Leon D.

Frederick Tillinghast Andrews[7], m. Clara J. Vaughn. No children.

Jane Andrews--Briggs[7], m. to Halsey James Briggs. Their children are Fred Delos, Frank Garfield and Arthur T.

NELSON ANDREWS[6], b. 1808; d. 1882. M. Meribah W. Harrington. Both were leaders in their community. Their children who grew up, were these:

Thomas T. Andrews[7], b. 1836; d. 1870; m. Adeline Francis Sweet. Their children are Taney Grant, Hortense Virginia and Isabel Francis.

Ebenezer Edwin Andrews[7], b. 1837; d. 1862; m. Maria Arnold. Had Henry Edgar and Elmer Andrews.

George Jastrom Andrews[7], m. Lucy Jane Matteson. No children.

JOHN ANDREWS[5] } [Elnathan[4] and Jane[4], John[3] and Hannah[3],
REBECCA ANDREWS[5] } John Greene[2], John Greene[1].] I have no records of either of these lines.

William Andrews[4] and his wife Rebecca Greene-Andrews had ten children. Their fourth and sixth children, Abigail Andrews-Mott and Elcy Andrews-Matteson, left no issue. Two of their sons, Elnathan and Timothy, died when young men. James, William, Ellen, Hannah, Isaac and Rebecca, each left families.

JAMES ANDREWS[5]. He married Elcy (Alice) Rice of Coventry. They had ten children. Their five younger children died young.

STEPHEN ANDREWS[6], m. Anice Spink. 9 children; 62 grand-children. His sons were Perry, Sheffield, Benjamin, Stephen, James and Wheaton. Daughters were Mrs. Polly Greene, and Mrs. Mary Ann Place.

TIMOTHY ANDREWS[6], m. Freelove Warner. One son, James, m. Eliza Clark. His dau. Cynthia m. Jeremiah Matteson.

ZILPHA ANDREWS-SWEET[6], m. James W. Sweet.

Abigail Sweet-Bentley[7], m. Benj. Bentley. Had Allen, Albert and Andrew.

Rev. Philip Sweet[7], b. Sept. 28, 1811; d. June 13, 1897; m. Louise M. Colvin. He was considered one of the family authorities on their history.

Philip Allen Sweet[8], m. Julia Colvin.

Josephine Sweet-Briggs[9], wife of Charles Briggs. Died at birth of her first child.

Philip Sylvester Sweet[9], b. 1867.

William Henry Sweet[8], m. Margaret Kettelle.

Henry Almon C. Sweet[9], b. 1869.

Ellen Sweet-Battey[8], m. to George W. Battey.

Ellen Louise Battey[9], b. 1869.

Henry Battey[9], b. 1870.

Mary Ann Sweet[7], b. in 1822.

James Wilber Sweet[7], m. Mercy Matteson. No. children.

ELIZABETH ANDREWS-BARTLETT[6], m. Seneca Bartlett. 4 children.

HANNAH ANDREWS-FISH[5]. B. in 1763; d. 1853; m. Ichabod Fish. This was a large family, and one that has intermarried with all the clan families. Ichabod was of King–La Valley blood. I do not attempt to give them in full. Their sons were Joshua, Ichabod, George W. and Wilson Fish. The daughters were Rebecca, who was (1) Mrs. Capwell, and (2) Mrs. Abel Matteson; and Sarah, who became Mrs. Ebenezer Matteson.

ISAAC ANDREWS[5]. A twin of Rebecca. He married Remittie, or Submittie Matteson, the daughter of Joseph and Annis Blanchard-Matteson. Three of their children died young, and their daughter, Mrs. Rebecca Matteson, left no heirs.

GEORGE WASHINGTON ANDREWS[6], m. (1) Esther Barber, mother of his two older children; (2) Mary Ann Essex. His daughters, Susan and Eliza, married, but left no children.

Burrill Andrews[7], m. Hannah Anstress Clark. Children were Esther, Devillan E., William Clark, John Hoxie, Amy, Mary Duritta, Hannah Almira, George Burrill, Oscar Oatley and Stephen Bowen Andrews.

ESTHER ANDREWS-FAIRMAN[6], wife of Erastus D. Fairman. Five children.

HON. ISAAC CLAY ANDREWS[6], b. 1832; d. 1897; m. Olive Miranda Whitman. He was a member of the State legislature, and a leading man in many ways. Had these children: Byron B., George, Stephen W., Mrs. Lidia Fish, Isaac Palmer and Eliphalet.

Asher Robbins Andrews, m. Susan Ella Barber. Three children, Carlton, Mary and Susan.

Richard William Andrews, m. Mary A. Burlingame. Had Elmer M., the present Superintendent of the Arkwright Mills.

HANNAH ANDREWS-SWEET[6], b. 1804; d. 1846. She m. William Chauncey Sweet, son of Rev. Pentacost Sweet. She died at birth of her second child.

William Leon Sweet[7], b. Jan. 16, 1844. He fitted himself for a physician, but but his health failing he became a druggist in Boston. He married a Miss Ida Thayer. No children. He served in the Civil War, and was injured at Belle Plains, Va.

Hannah Sweet-Howard[7], b. Oct. 19, 1846. Before her marriage, she was for some years a graduate trained nurse. She married John W. Howard, July 12, 1887, and now resides near Washington, R. I. Mrs. Howard has been a tireless helper in collecting information for me, and also assisted Miss James in her genealogy. She takes a keen interest in matters historical, and possesses a ready pen, corresponding for the best papers in the state. See Howard Chapter.

WILLIAM ANDREWS[6], b. 1805; d. 1882; m. Diana Potter. Three children died unmarried; William, Jr., and Ella Andrews-Carpenter died leaving no living issue. Mary Andrews Capwell, m. Beverly Capwell of Pa. Has William E., Harmon B., Phebe (m. to Wm. Packard), Ella M., Clarence J., Diana, Bianche and Frank Capwell.

Henry Potter Andrews, m. Bertha Weed. No children.

POTTER ROBERT ANDREWS[6], b. in 1807; d. 1881; m. Ursula James. Six children lived to marry, Dyer Edward, Abbie Francis, Hannah M., Sarah A., Diana, and James A.

ANN MARIA ANDREWS-MATTESON[6], b. 1810; d. 1841; m to Philip, son of Peleg and Mary James-Matteson. See Appendix.

David Matteson[7] is her only living son. He m. Maryett Brown and now lives in Abilene, Kansas, where he and his sons are leading citizens.

Charles David Matteson[8], m. Frances A. Ethering. They have Carrie Maude, Alta May, Roy H., Harry Ray, Ralph A. and Faye Bessie.

Hattie Amelia Matteson-Laney[8], b. 1865, m. Joseph Laney. They live in Kansas. Their children are Myrtle M., Leroy D., Stuart Everett, and Iola E.

William Avery Matteson[8], b 1871.

Henry E Matteson[8] b. 1878

Nellie A Matteson[8], b 1880

ISAAC WEEDON ANDREWS[6], m Mary A Hoxsie

Mary Eliza Andrews-Greene-Chaffee She m. (1) Charles A Greene, and had one child , m (2) George Chaffee, and had five children by him

REBECCA ANDREWS–WAITE[5]. Twin to Isaac. B. May 24, 1773; m. to Sheffield Waite, son of Major Yelverton Waite The Waites have a family tree of their own, of which they are justly proud They are also of Lascelle descent. [Sheffield[7], Yelverton[6], Joseph[5], Joseph[4], Samuel[3], Samuel[2], Thomas[1], third in descent from Gershom Lascelle.] See Appendix Chapter Of this particular family it has been said, " No praise was too high for them, and none were more universally respected " After Rebecca's death her husband married Mrs. Jane Andrews-James, the first wife's cousin

Rebecca and Sheffield's children were Phebe, wife of Rev Pardon Tillinghast, and mother of 13 children , Stephen, with 2 children , Zipporah, wife of Daniel Bowen, and mother of 11 children , Sheffield, with 2 children, and Martha, wife of Resolved Harvey, with 2 children

Phebe[6], wife of Rev Pardon Tillinghast, had a daughter Phebe[7], who married Reynolds Waite They had

Reynolds L Waite[8] He m Eunice Matteson, [Eunice[6], Benoni[5] David[4], David[3], Josiah[2], Henry[1].] whose grandmother, Dorcas Matteson, was herself a Waite

Mabel E A Waite-O'Niel[9] She was a teacher for some years in the Elmwood Grammar School of Providence, She was married Sept 18 1902, to Mr O Neil of Providence, R I. She has assisted this work by furnishing records and memoranda collected by her deceased aunt, Miss Dorcas Matteson

CHAPTER XIX

Daniel Greene[2] was the third or fourth son of John Greene of Quidnessett and his wife Joan   If he was the third son, he was born about 1647, if the fourth, about two years later.   He is known to have been regarded as a substantial citizen, yet the records of him are meager enough.   After the older brothers had gone to N Y, and several of the younger sons had shown a roving disposition, his old father came to consider him as his own right arm   With his brother Henry he became a freeman of R I Colony, May 20, 1671, the day of the great compromise over the 12-year land suit of Quidnessett.   As soon as their father gave his allegiance, they followed his example

March 24, 1682, his father gave several of his children a deed to land. This land was part of the first John's Quidnessett purchase, and to Daniel was given the home place of 120 acres   There was a clause in the deed, as there was in those of the others also, that he was to pay 30 shillings a year, as long as either of his parents lived   This is not far from $7 50, reckoned in our money.   Its purchasing power, however, was several times greater then than now   These several small annuities, in that day of simple habits, and with their quiet tastes, sufficed doubtless to keep the old couple in spending money

Unquestionably, Daniel[2] lived on at the old home with his father and mother.   His mother may have died about the time he married, 1689   Old John is said to have spent the last years of his life at Coventry, with his son Lieut John[2], and to have died there

Like so many of his family, Daniel was slow to marry, being 40 or 42 years of age at the time. He was married July 16, 1689, to Rebecca Barrow She is believed to have been related to Henry Barrow, the Martyr.

The Puritans or Congregationalists were called at first Brownists or Barrowists, after two of their first leaders   Henry Barrow, Barrowes or Barrowe, was an uncompromising foe to formality or ceremony in religious services   He published in London two books, in 1590 and a little later   One was entitled "A Brief Discoverie of the False Church; as is the Mother, so is the Daughter." The other was "Platform which may serve as a Preparation to drive way Prelatism." It served, however, to enrage the church authorities. He was arrested, tried for "writing and publishing sundry seditious books and pamphlets tending to the slander of the Queen and government," and was executed at Tyburn, London, April 6, 1592, or as some say, 1593. Many of his congregation fled to Amsterdam, Holland, for safety. In 1616 some of his friends reorganized a church in the suburbs of London. In 1632 the government imprisoned 42 of this church for heresy. So oppressive were the authorities that in 1634 no less than 30 of the church, including some of Barrow's own kindred, came to America. Rebecca was almost certainly descended from this family.

Daniel and Rebecca had 7 children, of whom two died while young. Daniel's will was proved June 9, 1730, so that he was 81 or 83 years of age at death. His wife survived him. He left his farm of 120 acres to Daniel, Jr. The rough and discolored headstones of this couple are still standing near Allen's Harbor, togther with another rude stone, marked I. G., which tradition says marks the grave of Joan Greene, capitals I and J being used interchangeably in those days.

PELEG GREENE[3]. According to one account; oldest son, born in 1690. Married Mary Pierce, Dec. 8, 1715, in Kingstown. The records have been badly damaged by fire. As near as can be made out, there were Elisha, Lidye, Peleg, Mary, and twins, Phebe and Ann. Dates all burned. Mary, the wife, must have died, also one of the twins, as a little after, in the same book, three children are recorded to Peleg and Dinah Greene, viz.:

> Hope Greene[4], b. May 22, 1725.
> Rachel Greene[4], b. June 27, 1726.
> Ann Greene[4], b Sept. 30, 1728.

DANIEL GREENE[3]. According to one account he was born Aug. 9, 1690, and Peleg in 1692. I believe the true date is Oct. 8, 1692. He married Dec. 23, 1721, when already something of a bachelor, his uncle Benjamin Greene's daughter, Catherine[3]. The wife was born about 1700, and died about 1736. She was the mother of all of Daniel's children, Benjamin, Joshua, John (or Jonathan.) After Catherine's death Daniel married Mary Ralph. He was a stirring business man, and much esteemed, and added largely to his estate. His will was proven July 24, 1770. In it he gave the home farm to his son John, and commended his step-mother to his care.

> Benjamin Greene[4], born —— 12, 1722, m. Jan. 5. 1744, to Anne Utter of Warwick. He died a few years after, leaving a daughter Catherine, whose grandfather, Daniel Greene, acted as her guardian.
> Joshua Greene[4], m. Dinah Carpenter, Feb. 12. 1746. By her he had Mary, Catherine, Abigail, Daniel, Elizabeth, Fones, and Susannah. He married (2) Alice Potter of Waite descent, June 1, 1771, and by her he had a son Joshua.

JOHN GREENE[4]. Little is known of him, although he lived on the home farm. It is thought by some that he made an early marriage, and by that wife had Gideon, who married Mercy Howland, 1769, and had Hannah, Howland, Judith, Lloyd, Philadelphia, Luciana, John, Gideon and Daniel. There is no proof one way or the other. He certainly married Sarah, dau. of John and Hannah Carpenter Spink, Dec. 24, 1758, and by her had 5 children. In advanced life he moved to N. Y. and died there, 1802.

Ruth Greene–Huling[5], b. July 1759, m. Andrew Huling   Her great-grandson, Prof. Ray Greene Huling, is a noted educator, in charge of the Cambridge, Mass., Schools. He takes a deep interest in genealogy, and his History of the Greenes of Quidnessett, published in the Narragansett Historical Register, is widely known and often quoted from. He placed the manuscript copy of the same in my hand together with copious notes.

Hannah Greene–Spencer[5], b. Nov. 1760, m. Peleg Spencer.

Sarah Greene–Huling[5], m. Augustus Huling, brother of Andrew.

Patience (Patty,) Greene–Kenyon[5], said to have m. Judge Kenyon of N. Y.

John Greene[5], b. 1772, m. Waity Kenyon. Moved to N. Y. Died at Penn Yan, N. Y., Oct. 21, 1857. He sold the old Greene farm, so long in the family, to Silas Allen, Oct. 7, 1797, signing the deed as John Greene, Jr. of Penn Yan, N. Y. This was the last foothold of the Greenes upon their original Quidnessett soil, and as there has been controversy as to the date, and the seller, this is given in full to settle the matter. This John Greene was noted for his fun and good nature. His children were Daniel, Benjamin, Richard, John R., of Kansas, Sarah, who m. —— Strowbridge of Pa., and three other daughters.

REBECCA GREENE[3], b. April 12, 1696. No further record.

RACHEL GREENE–AYLESWORTH[3], b. May 6, 1698; m. Philip Aylesworth, the son of Emigrant Arthur Aylesworth and Mary Brown, the granddaughter of Rev. Chad Brown of Providence, R. I., who succeeded Roger Williams as minister at Providence. They had seven children who lived to marry, Job, Philip, Sarah, Phebe, Martha and Elizabeth. Also

CAPTAIN ARTHUR AYLESWORTH[4], 1721–1801. He m. Freelove, daughter of Edward Dyer. Edward was of the Dyer line that according to The New England Genealogical and Historical Register was descended from the Quaker Martyr, Mary Dyer, who was hung in Boston, in 1660, as a " pestilent heretic." She was the wife of William Dyer, for many years Secretary of Providence Plantations. Mary Dyer was one of the three leaders who started the Friend's first Society in R. I. Captain Arthur's and Freelove's descendants therefore count among their ancestors two who suffered martyrdom for Christ within 70 years,— Henry Barrow and Mary Dyer.

Captain Arthur had nine children, of whom the fourth was Arthur Aylesworth, Jr[5], 1763–1834. He m. Abigail Dyer, dau. of Col. Charles Dyer. They had six children, of whom the oldest was.

Mary Aylesworth–Reynolds[6], 1780–1832. M. to John B. Reynolds. They had 13 children, of whom the ninth was.

Ann Greene Reynolds–Hull[7], m. to Edward C. Hull. Had these children. Sarah E., Mary who m. Charles H. Pierce, and Charlotte.

Sarah E. Hull[8], of above, m. in 1901 to John Flavel Greene[8] of Warwick line. [John Flavel[8], James[7], William[6], Abraham[5], James[4], Jabez[3], James[2], Surgeon John[1].]

John Flavel Greene[8] is a church officer in the historic First Baptist Church of Providence, founded in 1638, and of which it is thought Surgeon John and his wife Joan were constituent members. Eight generations, and yet the same family is represented in the same church !

RAY GREENE HULING, SC. D.

Author of " The Greenes of Quidnessett "

Daniel had a son Jonathan[3], the youngest of his children. He married Susanna Buers in March, 1733. D. 6 years after, leaving Ebenezer[4], born Nov. 4, 1738. Probably he who moved to N. Y. and had Ebenezer and Benjamin, killed by Indians and tories in Revolutionary War, and Joseph, born in 1767, volunteered in 1779, at 12 years of age, the youngest soldier in the Revolutionary War. This Joseph had Daniel, Ebenezer and Benjamin.

CHAPTER XX

The whole of Part Third of this book is given to the descendants of Deborah[5], great-granddaughter of Lieut. James Greene. The history of this line up to her day, as well as the pedigree of the rest of the family, is given in this chapter.

Lieut. James Greene[2] is believed to have been the seventh child and sixth son of John Greene of Quidnessett and his wife Joan Beggarly. Huling gives his birth as in 1655. In the North Kingstown records of March, 1698, he is designated as Lieut. James. He was 20 years old when King Philip's War opened, and a scion of the most prominent family at Quidnessett. He may have received his military title then, or have later been an officer in the colonial militia, which in those days of frequent Indian disturbances had their regular training days, and their regular officers. They were Minute Men, i. e. soldiers allowed to disperse and go about their usual avocations in time of peace, but had to be ready at the bugle's blast to fall into line and fight for the colony.

His first wife was Elizabeth ——————, and he married early. In a North Kingstown record of March 7, 1698, he is called James Greene, Senior, showing that his son James was then a man grown. When old John of Quidnessett divided up land among certain of his sons, March 24, 1682, there fell to James' share 60 acres bordering on Allen's Harbor. His will was probated Sept. 10, 1728. In it he mentions his second wife, Ann, and his two sons, John and James.

The line of the son James is utterly unknown. The records have been badly burned, and there is now no trace of him.

John, the other son, lived at both Bristol and at Quidnessett. His wife was Elizabeth. It is handed down in the family, and names, circumstances and family anecdotes entirely confirm it, that Elizabeth was the granddaughter on the one side of Hugh Parsons, and on the other of Elder Obediah Holmes.*

---

* To forestall criticism the author will say she is herself a Congregationalist, and not a Baptist. It may be taken for granted that she has made the case out no worse than it was on her Congregational brethren, the Mass. authorities.

Parton tells us something of Elder Holmes. At Lynn, Mass., was an aged man who was secretly a Baptist. He sent word to the Newport Church, 70 miles away, asking some of the brethren to come and see him before he died. Rev. John Clarke, the minister, and two elders of his church, Obediah Holmes and John Crandall, made the trip, arriving at Lynn on Saturday. The next day Rev. Clarke began to preach to the family of his host. Two constables arrested him and his two companions as "erroneous persons," and carried them to Boston. Rev. John Cotton severely declared that they ought to be hung for they were "soul-murderers." Governor Endicott was more lenient.

"You deserve to die," said he, "but this we have agreed upon. Mr. Clarke shall pay £20 fine; Obediah Holmes, £30; and John Crandall, £5 . . . . or else they are to be well whipped."

Holmes refused to pay his fine, as did they all. Friends paid the others out against their will. Holmes received " 30 lashes with a three-corded whip from the public executioner, so that for many days he could take no rest except by supporting himself on his elbows and knees." [Arnold.]

From Seekonk, 50 miles away, an old man by the name of Hazel or Hazell—(a member of the Lascelle family, it often being pronounced and written Hazell and Uzell,)—came to visit his friend Holmes and sympathize with him. He came in time to see his brutal punishment. When the barbarous ordeal was over, he went up to Holmes and shook his hand. For this he was arrested, and sentenced to be fined or whipped. He was so affected that he died, a martyr to his friendship.

Obediah Holmes has namesakes for six generations in this John Greene family.

Hugh Parsons, the other ancestor of Elizabeth, was born in 1613, in Great Torrington, England. This is the town that has been called the " hot-bed of Puritanism," and from which the Hills, the Westcotts, and some of the Waites also came. He came to Massachusetts in 1630 and lived there for 20 years. His first wife and first wife's children all died. He married (2) Elizabeth England, the young widow of William England. Their oldest daughter was Hannah, who married Henry Matteson, and became the foremother of all the Mattesons. The Westcotts and Parsons were already related by marriage in England. Hannah's marriage to Henry Matteson brought in an intimacy with that family also. The clan feeling is plainly seen in the several Westcott and Matteson marriages entered into by this John Greene of Bristol branch.

Mrs. Elizabeth Greene was the namesake of her grandmother, Elizabeth Parsons. She was also the second consin of Stukeley Westcott's children, and he was one of the pillars of Roger Williams' church. One of her children married a wife of Westcott blood ; one married a Matteson ; and two of her grandchildren married Mattesons also.

We do not know all of John Greene of Bristol's children, owing to the burning of the North Kingstown records. They had James, Thomas, Martha, Enfield, Sarah, and perhaps others. Order of birth unknown.

THOMAS GREENE⁴. He married Elizabeth ———— and had Thomas, Hannah, Nathaniel, Mary and Benjamin.

ENFIELD GREENE–PHILLIPS⁴.

> MARTHA PHILLIPS-MATTESON⁵. Married John Matteson⁴, [John³, Francis², Henry¹.] her third cousin. They had Joshua, Susanna, Enfield, Hannah, John and Elizabeth.
> FREELOVE PHILLIPS-MATTESON⁵. Married Abraham Matteson⁵, [Abraham³, Hezekiah², Henry¹.] He was related to her twice over, as his mother was a Westcott. They had Margaret, Elizabeth, Lydia, John, Abraham, Daniel and Thomas.

JAMES GREENE⁴. He was married May 18, 1727, by Thomas Spencer, Justice of the Peace, to Elizabeth, oldest daughter of John and Rosanna Westcott-Smith-Straight, a distant relative. Elizabeth's father had this pedigree : Captain Thomas Straight, who probably acquired the title in the Pequot War of 1637, married Mary Long, daughter of Joseph and Mary Long. By this wife he had Henry Straight, born in Watertown, Mass., in 1651. Henry came to R. I. and married Hannah Torman. They had two sons, Henry and John, and John, born March 1, 1678, married the young widow of Daniel Smith, who had been Rose or Rosanna Westcott.

The descent of Rose, (Rosanna,) wife of John Straight, was this : * About 1565, Meribe, of Gershom and Meribe Lascelle, early French Huguenots, was married in England to William Wardwell, son of Richard and Mary Ithell-Wardwell. A daughter of this couple, Rosanna, married a Waite, and Mehitable Waite of the next generation married Richard Hill. Among other children these Hills had John, the head of the line of Hills from which Usal and "Wealthy" John Greene afterwards took wives, and Rose or Rosanna, born in 1613. All of the last mentioned parties came to America. Their home in England had been at Great Torrington, in Devonshire.

The Westcotts were of Great Torrington also. Richard Westcott had married Mary Parsons in 1611. Their son Stukeley Westcott, came to Mass. about 1635, the same year Rose Hill came over. They were nearly the same age, and old friends, and it is all but certain they married. All through their line the unusual name of Rosanna has gone down. Up to 1750 the name never occurred in R. I. records but what a relationship could be traced straight back to this Stukeley Westcott and wife.

Their oldest son was Amos Westcott. He married two sisters, the

---

* The trans-Atlantic records that apply are scant, but I believe this to be substantially correct. It is the result of much research.

youngest, Deborah Stafford, marrying him June 9, 1670. Rosanna was their daughter. She married Daniel Smith, and after his death, John Straight, by whom she had nine children Elizabeth was the oldest, and was born Oct 8, 1705

The Westcotts were the most uncompromising of Baptist families. They were exceedingly proud of having, through Stukeley Westcott and his wife, a hand in the historic first Baptist Church in America. The tradition of this has come straight down to the present generation of Rose's descendants, and for the first few generations one of them who dared join some other church was held to have almost put himself outside of the pale of the family Elizabeth impressed her Baptist principles as strongly on her family, as her mother, Rose, had done on hers And that is all we really know of those two generations, except the names of their children

James Greene[1] and Elizabeth had Sarah, born in 1728, Ann, Benjamin, Jeremiah, Dinah, Abel and Deborah

BENJAMIN GREENE[2] [James[1] John[3] James[2], John[1],] born Aug 28 1734 in East Greenwich Married May 25, 1760, to Comfort Carr, who was also of Lasceile descent His home was in West Greenwich Of his children, James, Anstress and Benjamin, there are only birth records

Caleb Greene[6], 1764—1823 Had a son Samuel

Virtue Greene-Matteson[6], b May 3 1767, m Edmund Matteson her distant cousin Virtue was a second wife All of Edmund's children that are known to be hers, were Virtue, who married her mother's cousin John Greene (Abel[5] James[4], etc), Lydia, who married Stephen King, and Stukeley, who had Ira, John and Stukeley of his own

JEREMIAH GREENE[2], b June 1, 1736, m Freelove Hopkins, 1760 They had Russell Barbara, Gardiner, Waite Jeremiah, Abial and Ann Jeremiah was a Revolutionary soldier

DINAH GREENE-KITTLE[3], b Feb 5 1739, m Edward Kittle, March 27, 1762 The name is now written Kittelle or Kettelle

Asa Kittelle[6] 1770—1849 M in his 50th year to Eunice Pendock, whose father came from France She was 19 She died at 38 the mother of 14 or 15 children Of these, Freelove became Mrs John Sheldon, Lydia m Isaac Peck, Lois m Robert Pierce, Mary m Benjamin Arnold All these had children Albert F m Sara E Matteson his cousin's daughter No children See Kittelle Chapter

Elizabeth Kittelle-Brown[6], m Nicholas Brown

Amos Kittelle[6] d Oct 10, 1849, m his relative Thankful Straight They had Lucy A who m John Waite, Isaiah, who m Susan Geer, and Caroline, who m Albert Baker All these had children

Rufus Kittelle[6], m (1) Susan Greene (2) Lydia Rogers His children were Senaca, James Thomas, Rufus Noel, Caleb and three daughters

Samuel Kittelle[6] Children were Mrs Celinda Spencer, Mrs Ruth Bates, and Benjamin

Silas Kittelle[6] He m a Tarbox and had a son Samuel

Ephraim Kittelle[6], m July 21, 1799, Newie (Renewed) Briggs of King blood [Renewed[4], Sarah King[3], Magdalen[2], John[1]] One of their daughters married her cousin Gideon Hopkins Their daughter Dinah m Joshua Fish of Ichabod and Hannah Andrews-Fish, and had Isaac, Rebecca, Joshua, Ichabod, Lydia, Susan and George W Ephraim and Newie had also sons George Othniel, William and Peleg Kittelle, and a dau Almira, who m. Philip Davis

James Kittelle[6]. Married his cousin, Elizabeth King. See Kittelle Chapter.

ABEL GREENE[5], b. Oct. 14, 1741 ; d. 1828 ; m. Ann (Nancy) King, 1764. Abel was a Revolutionary soldier. He and his sons had a grist-mill and a saw-mill. His wife was of the La Valley-King family. They had nine children, seven of them sons. Obediah, Abel Jr., and John, Greene all moved to Susquehanna Co., Pa. Of Samuel, Mary, Elizabeth, Obediah, Paul and Jeremiah, there are only birth records.

Nathan Greene[6], b. Aug. 12, 1766, m. Abigail, and had Welcome, b. 1795.

John Greene[6], m. in 1803 to his cousin, Virtue Matteson, dau. of Edmund. [Edmund[4], Eben.[3], Hen.[2], Hen.[1]] They lived in Pa,.

Nathan Greene[7], son of John, etc., m. Lovica Haverly, and had by her Simon, Ellen and Lonise. M. (2) Mary A. ———— and had Harrison, Elmer and Finley. One of the daughters became Mrs. Crawford, and left a son, Nathan Crawford[9].

William Greene[7], m. Phebe Haverly.

       Emily Greene-Beninger[8]. She had sons Punderson and George.

       E. M. Greene-Ford[8].

       Mary Greene-Bennett[8].

Mercy Greene-Gregory[7], wife of Taylor Gregory. One dau., Mrs. Lydia Place.

Lydia Green-Whitcome,[7] wife of John Whitcome. Children, Amanda, Virtue and Scott.

Sarah Greene-Matteson[7], m. her cousin, Reuben Matteson. They had Stillman, Beninger, Byron, John, Abbie. Syce and Nicholas Matteson.

Job Greene[7], m. Eunice Doolittle. Had James, John and Charles.

James Greene[6]. [Abel[5], James[4], John[3], James[2], John[1].] He married (1) Mary Brown in 1797, the mother of all his children but one. James[7] was by the last wife. Two of his children, Dinah Greene-Johnson and Nathan Greene, left no children.

Comfort Greene--Davis-Harrington[7], 1799--1872 ; m. (1) George Davis. Their daughter Mary m. George Arnold and had four children, and their son William m. his second cousin, Sarah, daughter of Gideon Hopkins. They have four children. Comfort m. (2) Daniel Harrington.

Nancy Greene--Potter[7], 1801--1872. She was the last one of three sisters to die within a month and 12 days. She married Benjamin Potter. Her daughter Mahala m. Thos. Sprague, and Zilpah m. Frederick Tibbetts. Both have children.

Alice Greene--Greene[7], 1803--1872 She m. Horace Greene of Coventry. Two children died. Of Buriel and Nathan there is no record ; of Edwin and Oscar nothing beyond that they are married. Louise Greene--Greene died without issue ; Cynthia m. Joab Whaley and Oliver m. Phebe, daughter of John Matteson.

Abel Greene[7], m. Sarah Olin. Moved to Illinois, and left unknown descendants.

James Greene,[7] 1812--1877. Half-brother to the others. M. Nathan's widow, Lois Pollock--Greene.

DEBORAH GREENE[5]. Born Sept. 23, 1744 ; d. in 1812. Married her brother Abel's brother-in-law, Samuel King, April 15, 1766. Part III of this book is given entirely to her line.

MARTHA GREENE–MATTESON[4]. She was married 10 days before her brother, James Greene, being married to Joseph Matteson May 8, 1727. He was her mother's first cousin, and had at that time a grown son by his first marriage. Had nine children. Of Obediah, Elizabeth, Thomas and Eunice I have no records. Martha's line is a most extensive one, and cannot be given as fully as I would wish, from lack of space.

ALICE MATTESON--WHITFORD[5], wife of Thomas Whitford, her cousin. Line intermarried with the Tarbox branch later.

JONATHAN MATTESON[5], m. Elizabeth Hackstone. Miss James, the historian, and the line of Benjamin Greene, including many of the Howards, are from Jonathan through marriages of his daughter and grand-children.

EZEKIEL MATTESON[5]. [Martha Greene[4], John[3], James[2], John[1].] This is a most important branch. He married Rosanna Matteson, daughter of Josiah and Mercy Nichols-Matteson, grand-daughter of Josiah and Rosanna Westcott--Matteson, and great-grand-daughter of Henry and Hannah Parson--Matteson. Ezekiel and Rosanna were twice over fourth cousins, and once third cousins. The fourth cousinship came in through the English Parsons--Westcott marriage, first on Ezekiel's mother's side, and again on Rosanna's grandmother's side. [Rosanna[5], wife of Josiah Matteson, Senior, Zerubabel[4], Robert[3], Stukeley[2], son of Richard and Mary Parsons--Westcott[1].] Ezekiel was born in 1743 and married, Feb., 1774, in West Greenwich. Six children lived to marry. Of Thomas and Josiah, I have no lists.

Martha Matteson--Hopkins[6], m. Daniel Hopkins, descended from Stephen Hopkins of the Mayflower, and Regicide Judge Theophilus Whaley. See Chapter XXVIII. She had a son Greene Hopkins. A daughter Mercy m. George Harrington, and their dau. Betsey m. Wm. E. Gilmore.

Meribah Matteson--King[6], wife of George King. See Chapter XXVI.

Esther Matteson--King[6], wife of Joel King. See Chapter XXX.

Joseph Madison[6], born March 2, 1791, m. Celia Fowler, and d. Aug. 9, 1887, in his 97th year. His branch adopted the spelling of Madison, about the time of President Madison's election. Six children, only three of whom left heirs.

Joseph Warren Madison[7], [Matteson line, Joseph[6], Ezekiel[5], Joseph[6], Henry[1].] 1820--1900. He married Maria, dau. of Alfred U. and Ann Allen--Smith. The wife was descended from John Greene's firm, friend, the Indian trader Richard Smith. [Alfred[8], Silas[7], Christopher[6], Thomas[5], John[4], William[3], James[2], Richard Smith[1].] They had these children who married:

George Warren Madison[8], m. Fannie L. Spink. Their children are Warren, Harold L., Ralph, Louise, Francis S. and George M.

Celia Maria Madison-Mathewson[8], b. March 11, 1857; m. Nov. 8, 1881, to her second cousin-german, Thomas Mathewson. [Thomas[7], Syria Wilbur[6], Wilbur[5], Russell[4], Josiah[3], Josiah[2], Henry Matteson[1].] The form of Mathewson was adopted by Wilbur, and followed by his descendants. Thomas Mathewson's line is well worth tracing. He is the oldest living son of Syria Wilbur Mathewson, the well-known proprietor of that beautiful summer resort at Narragansett Pier, the Mathewson House. He has Westcott blood through the wife of the first Josiah, [Rosanna[5], Zerubabel[4], Robert[3], Stukeley[2], Richard[1].] Through the mother, who was a Hill, he has Lascelle-Wardwell and Westcott blood, and is also lineally descended from Roger Williams. His mother was also of the Warwick Greenes, and of the Allens of Prudence Island. [Thomas[6], Amma Eliza Hill-Mathewson[7], Lucy Ann Allen-Hill[6], Hon. John Allen[5], Patience Greene-Allen[4], David Greene[3], James[2], Surgeon John Greene[1].] The Hon. John Allen of this line was the brave but rash man who made so caustic a reply to the British officers who offered him gold for provender for the British Army, that Wallace, in anger, burned every house, barn and haystack on the island, and drove Allen's family out in their night clothes, while the flames licked up the home that had been the pride of the island. See Chapter XXIV.

Thomas and Celia Mathewson have two children, Anna M. and George Hill.

John Harris Madison[7], brother of Joseph Warren ; 1828–1887. Son, Joseph Slocum.

Thomas Edwin Madison[7], 1830–1885 ; m. Emily Havens. Had George Edwin and Thomas Edward.

JOHN MATTESON[5]. [Martha Greene-Matteson[4], John Greene[3], James[2], John[1].] He married Elizabeth King of the La Valley-King family, Oct. 1, 1761. Deacon John Matteson of Nooseneck, R. I., was said to have been descended from him.

LOIS MATTESON-TARBOX[5]. M. Samuel Tarbox, Sep. 1, 1761. The Tarbox family is an old English one. The curious name, once written Tarbocke and Torbock, commemorates the Danish invasion of England, more than twelve centuries ago. It was originally Thor's bock or beck, i. e. the god Thor's brook. The stream still runs by the old Tarbox Hall, six miles from Liverpool. Some of Lois Matteson's descendants have the coat-of-arms, an elaborate escutcheon with two full length figures as supporters at the sides. The motto's meaning is, "Destiny Separates, but Inclination Unites."

John Tarbox came to Lynn, Mass., by 1630. He was one of the first iron-workers, and turned out the first kettles ever made in America. After John[1], came John[2], who came to East Greenwich about 1695. During the French and Indian War he was captured at Oswego. Again at the Crown Point expedition, he was made a prisoner, and remained so a year, dying on the coast of Africa in 1759. Samuel, his son, was then a grown young man, and married Lois three years after his patriotic father's death.

Of their large family of children, John, Whipple, Benjamin, Margaret and Welthian all married and moved to other parts, and their children are unknown. David's son Anthony left three daughters. Samuel had two children, John and Edith, but their children are unknown.

Curnell Carpenter Tarbox[6], [Lois[5], Martha Greene-Matteson[4], John[3], James[2], John[1],] 1776–1862. M. Sally Adams. She was a lineal descendant of John Adams who came to Mass. in 1630, and it is said of Richard Warren of the Mayflower, also. She was related to the two Presidents Adams. Her father, Philemon Adams, was a Revolutionary soldier. Curnell and Sally's son, Eliphalet, left an unknown heir. Their dau., Sally Maria, m. her cousin Daniel, and line is traced with his. Wealthy m. Enos L. Preston, her children all died but three, George H., Augustus and Frank T.

Hiram Tarbox[7], 1819–1878; M. his cousin Eunice ; six children lived. Of Alfred, no records ; Eunice m. Joseph Prentice ; Ann A. m. her cousin, Anthony Spencer ; and Isabelle m. Stephen Cleveland. All left children.

George W. Tarbox[8], 1827–1902. He lived in New York City. He m. Caroline Lewis, descended from the Mayflower families of Gov. Bradford, Rogers, Alden and Mullins, as well as Col. Gallup, Thos. Stanton, the first Indian interpreter, Rev. James Noyes, the founder of Yale College, and half a dozen other old colonial families. Mrs. Tarbox is also descended from John Greene of Quidnessett through Eleanor Greene-Lewis[6]. See line of Benjamin[3], Chapter XXI. The children of Geo. W. Tarbox are Ida, Kate and George.

William B. Tarbox[8], 1835–1897. M. Sarah Bingham.

Carrie E. Tarbox-Smith[9], wife of Russell Smith.

Joseph Tarbox[6], m. Esther Whitford. Eight children lived to marry. Eunice m. her cousin Hiram, and line is traced with his.

Matteson Tarbox[7], 1791–1859. M. Phebe Bailey. They had William H., unmarried ; Daniel, who m. Mary Clark and has Jesse and Clarence ; Ann, wife of William Andrews, and mother of Edwin, Bernice, Edward, Mabel and Annie ; Charles A., who m. Mary Shippee, and has a son Fred ; Joseph, who left no issue ? and Phebe Maria, wife of

George C. Goodwin, and mother of Florence Goodwin.

Fones W. Tarbox[7], [Joseph[6], Lois Matteson-Tarbox[5], Martha Greene-Matteson[4], John[3], James[2], John[1],] 1794-1867. M. Sarah Spencer. 14 children, of whom 10 married. No record of Franklin's family.

Hiram Tarbox[8], b. June 15 1817. Living in 1904 in full mental vigor. He is called the "Patriarch of Tremont," a part of Greater New York, where he has lived since 1851. He was postmaster there for 20 years. Like most of the Tarboxes, he is a man of substantial qualities and high standing in the community. He furnished the Tarbox names and dates for this chapter. His wife was Mary Clark. She died in 1879. Their children are Mary C. born 1840; Hiram T. born 1842; Sarah E., widow of Joseph H. Lee; and Charles W., married to Margaret Behrens. They have one daughter, Elsa.

David Tarbox[8], 1819-1892. M. (1) Amanda King, and (2) Mrs. Sally Jackson. His dau. Abbie is the wife of Hiram Peck, and Sarah is wife of Robert Jackson. By the last wife he had Oscar, Orville, Otho, Osman, Fones, John and Ella, the wife of Clinton Hopkins. Most of these children have families.

Caleb Tarbox[8], m. Maria Clark, and had Egbert, Agnes and Edgar, all of whom married.

Robert Tarbox[8], m. Harriet Wells. Their son Abijah J. d. unmarried. John, Fones, Laura, Charles, Ralph, Isabel, Byron and Hattie are all married.

William Tarbox[8], 1826-1898. M. Mary E. Bennett. Of their children, Wm. Spencer and Ulysses are unmarried. Mary Ellen, Gerome, Lydia, Napoleon, Wealthy and Ida are all married.

Horace Tarbox[8], by first wife, Adeline Mitchell, had these children who lived to marry: Adeline, Benjamin, Huldah and Ella. By his second wife, Catherine Cavanagh, he had Horace and William.

Orrin Tarbox[8], m. Sarah Bennett. They have Eunice, Edward, Herbert, Hattie, Sarah, and Mary. Their son Edward has 7 children, and their dau. Mary has one child.

Sarah Tarbox-Hall[8], m. Emery H. Hall. They have Benj. E., Charles A., Remus, Hannah and Mary. All but Charles and Remus are married.

Edward Tarbox[8], m. Susan Cleveland. They have one living daughter, Mrs. Bertha M. Wilcox. She has also one daughter.

Roby Tarbox-Spencer[7], [Joseph[6], Lois Matteson-Tarbox[5], Martha Greene-Matteson[4], John Greene[3], James[2], John[1].] M. Richard Spencer. He was a descendant of Randall Holden, one of the proprietors of Warwick, and one who suffered imprisonment at the hands of the Mass. authorities for his heresies. Richard was also descended from the Warwick Greenes, thus: [Richard[7], John[6], Wm.[5], Wm.[4], Audrey Greene-Spencer[3], John Greene[2], Surgeon John[1].] Roby and Richard had six children marry, Anthony, who m. Ann Tarbox, and had one child; Audrey, who m. her cousin, Benjamin Spencer, and had 10 children; Joseph, who m. Celinda Kettelle, and had 10 children; Augustus, who m. Mary E. Harrington; Huldah, who m. Daniel C. Bailey, and had three children; and E. Amanda, who m. Job Briggs. Mrs. Briggs is an expert on family genealogy, and has supplied many difficult links for these pages.

Hannah Tarbox-Carpenter[7], 1800-1866. She m. Curnell Carpenter. They had Curnell John, who m. Huldah Blanchard; Sarah J., who m. Sylvester Stone; Esther M., who m. Charles Shippee; Lydia, who m. Stephen Brown; Hannah, who m. George W. Braymon; and Mary G., who m. Horace E. Chadwick.

Jane Tarbox-Shippee[7], 1803-1868. One son, Chas. R. He has 3 children.

Daniel Tarbox[7], [Joseph[6], Lois Matteson-Tarbox[5], Martha Greene-Matteson[4], John Greene[3], Jas.[2], John[1].] 1805-1896. Like the other brothers in this family, he stood very high in public estimation. He spent several years in business in Europe. By first wife, his cousin Sally Maria Tarbox, he had Curnell, who m. Harriet Ransford ; Louis Perret, who m. Ann Eliza Grant ; and Wealthy Maria, who m. George T. Brown.

By his last wife, Lucelia Verrington, he had Daniel, killed in the Civil War; Lucelia ; Anna ; and Effie L., who m. David O. Cargill.

David Tarbox[7], [Joseph[6], Lois[5], Martha[4]. John[3], Jas.[2], John[1],] 1808-1892. M. Mary Spencer, a niece of Richard Spencer, his sister Roby's husband. She was of the line of Randall Holden and the Warwick Greenes. They had 14 children, only two of whom married. Wealthian is single ; Oliver Cromwell m. Ann Maria Watson ; and Annie E. m. Alvin A. Briggs.

CHAPTER XXI

THE TRIBE OF BENJAMIN

I head this chapter, The Tribe of Benjamin, for tribe it is. It is the most prolific house of the many prolific ones we are studying. 12, 14 and 15 were a common number of children in a family. Captain Amos of this line was the father of 19 children. Amy Knowles-Greene, wife of Amos, a son of " White Hat " John Greene, was able to boast that at the age of 89 she had four generations of posterity, and 364 descendants ! So impressed with the importance of having many olive branches was one of this tribe, Charles Greene, a great-grandson of " White Hat " John Greene, that not content with his own modest supply of 13 children, he raised 22 more, making a lively brood of 35 youngsters brought up under one roof-tree !

Frank L. Greene, A. M., B. A., has written a careful history of the family of Benjamin Greene.* It is a large volume, and even then he failed to get all of them. I shall refer those interested to his work. In this chapter only the first generations will be traced, as a rule, although in certain cases the genealogy is brought down to the present time, as where Mr. Greene has failed to list them, or where new evidence clears up a former tangle or dispute.

Benjamin Greene[2] was the youngest son of John Greene of Quidnessett and his wife Joan. He married Humility Coggeshall. Her grandfather was John Coggeshall, the first President of Providence Plantations, who died in office, Nov. 27, 1648. Her parents were Joshua and Joan West-Coggeshall.† Her father, Joshua Coggeshall, together with Mary Dyer, the Martyr, and Daniel Gould, founded the first Friends' Society in R. I. Private records give her birth in 1671, but the official record places it in Jan., 1670.

Benjamin Greene's name is frequent in the records. His land joined that of his brother, James Greene, at Quidnessett. He also bought part of his brother Edward's estate, and seems to have owned considerable real es-

---

* The Greene Family, by Frank L. Greene, A. M. Price, $8.00. Mr. Greene at present is Principal of Grammar School, No. 9 Stirling Place, Brooklyn, N. Y.

† Joan West was probably the daughter of Francis West, who was in Duxbury, Mass., by 1640.

tate beside. In 1704–5 he was involved in lawsuits over this land. The next year he sold out and moved to East Greenwich, where he died early in 1719—not in 1716, as some have it. He helped to lay out the Path Road, that followed the old Pequot Indian trail from the Bay.

Benjamin and Humility had 12 children, having five sons in succession, and then seven daughters. Caleb died in 1727, and there are only birth records of Sarah and Dinah ; Mary married Thomas Spencer ; Catherine married her cousin, Daniel Greene³ of North Kingstown ; Ann married Daniel Tennant; Phebe married Thomas Wells of Westerley ; and Deborah married William Reynolds of East Greenwich. This leaves the lines of four sons, John, Benjamin, Henry and Joshua. Four things are noticeable of this confederation of families : (1) Their numbers. (2) The many soldiers sent to the French-and-Indian and Revolutionary Wars. (3) Their religious bias, by which a great majority became Seventh-Day Baptists. (4) The overflow of the middle generation to New York State, and of the later generations to Minnesota and other western states.

"WHITE HAT" JOHN GREENE³. Frank L. Greene thinks he was born about 1688; I should put it two years earlier, reckoning from the other children's ages. He was Lieut. John, an officer of the home militia or Minute Men ; but as his uncle, Lieutenant John, is always spoken of by that title, I shall not use it. There were, beside the uncle, two cousins of his, all named John Greene, and a half dozen Warwick John Greenes in the next township. Two nicknames served to distinguish this John of Benjamin from the others. One was "Lord John," perhaps from a haughty or consequential air. The other was "White Hat John," which shows he had a few eccentricities, and is the more human to us because of it. He bought land in West Greenwich in 1733, eight years before it was set off into a town (township) by itself, so he was something of a pioneer.

About 1709 he married. Some histories say Oct 13, 1726, but that was the date he receipted for his wife's portion of her father's estate. His wife was Mary, daughter of Arthur and Mary (Brown) Aylesworth. She was a sister to Arthur Aylesworth, who married Rachel Greene, daughter of Daniel, and a cousin to Elizabeth, John Greene of Bristol's wife. She was a granddaughter of Rev. Chad Brown, the first regular minister at Providence, (if Roger Williams is not counted), and also a granddaughter of Elder Obediah Holmes, of whom more is told in Chapter XX. She was the mother of 15 children, three of whom died young. After she died "White Hat" John married Mrs. Priscilla Bowen, Aug. 7, 1741. He died in 1756, leaving a good estate. 12 children, 2 daughters and 10 sons, lived to marry: Thomas, Philip, Benjamin, Elizabeth, Ruth, William, Josiah, Amos, Jonathan, Caleb, Joseph and Joshua.

THOMAS GREENE[4]. Born about 1710. Married Sarah ———, 1730. Six children, John, Stephen, Mary, Sylvester, Elizabeth and Lowest or Lois. Allen[6], son of John[5], was a Revolutionary soldier, and head of a considerable line.

PHILIP GREENE[4]. Born about 1712. Married (1) to Theodosia Spencer, daughter of Capt. Robert Spencer; and (2) to Mrs. Mary Reynolds-Sweet. He lived in West Greenwich, R. I. His children were by the first wife. There were 11, of whom seven were sons. Two died young. Of George (1738) and Sarah (1745) there are only birth records. Zilpha married ——— Noxon, and Rhoda m. Nathaniel Brown.

Eleazer Greene[5], b. July 22, 1735. M. at 19 to Sarah Carpenter. Lived in W. Greenwich. Two sons, Philip, b. March 10, 1755, and Oliver, b. Feb. 8, 1757.

Job Greene[5], b. March 10, 1737. Married March 6, 1760, to Christian Greene, his great-uncle Henry's daughter. [Christian[4], Henry[3], Benjamin[2], John[1].] They had a son Solomon.

Elder Elisha Greene[5], [Philip[4], "White Hat" John[3], etc.], b. July 14, 1740. At 18 he married Edith Stafford of Warwick. She was probably of Westcott blood, and certainly was related to Rosanna Straight, whose daughter married James Greene of John of Bristol. They lived at West Greenwich, and had but three children. Lucy m. Solomon Lewis of Conn. Lodowick was a Revolutionary soldier, and the head of almost an army of descendants, mostly in N. Y. I give Stafford's line alone.

Elder Stafford Greene[6], [Elisha[5], Phil.[4], John[3], Benj.[2], John[1].] b. Jan. 19, 1726. M. Lydia Brown.

Amos Greene[7], m. Hannah Nichols. Had six children, Stafford, Almon, Edith. Also

Mervyl Greene-Hiscox[8], wife of Otis Hiscox. Has Lydia, Edna and Irving.

Eunice Greene-Morehouse[8].

Lydia Greene-Brown[8], wife of Ambrose Brown.

Horatio Brown[9], of Pawtucket, R. I.

Seth Greene[7], m. Welthean Greene, his second cousin. [She of Gideon[6], Caleb[5], Benj.[4], etc.]

George Greene[8], m. Maria Lewis.

Ann Greene-Allen[9], m. John Allen. She has Lula (Mrs. Chas. S. Greene), Grace (Mrs. Walter Riley), Milton and John.

Elisha Greene[9], m. Louise Congdon.

Elisha Greene[8], m. Susan Tillinghast. One son, John B.

Allen Greene[8], m. Celia M. Carpenter. They had Chas. A., and Roxana (Mrs. John B. Sheldon). This Chas. A. Greene[9], born Sept 6, 1849, m. Mary E. Andrews, and has a son Walter[10], and and a grandson, Walter[11]. Chas. A. Greene[9] has the historical turn of so many of this family. He prepared an abridgement of Ray Greene Huling's "Greenes of Quidnessett," which ran as a series in the *Gleaner* of Phenix, R. I., and had a wide circulation.

Mary Greene-Lillibridge[8], m. Jesse R. Lillibridge. They had Herbert, Seth, Mary (Mrs. Elmer Cole), and Byron.

Eunice Greene-Carpenter[8], m. Christopher Carpenter. They have Mrs. Nettie Haven, Mrs. Annie Higgins, and Mrs. Eva McCabe.

Josiah Greene[7], [Stafford[6], Elisha[5], Phil.[4], John[3], Benj[2]., John[1],] born April 22, 1789; m. Elizabeth Lewis, Feb. 4 1810. Had 6 children. Varnum and Lydia married, but left no living heirs.

Stafford Greene[8], b. Aug. 11, 1813; m. Amy Hazard Lewis.

Harriet J. Greene-Witter[9], wife of Jonah Witter.

Has Eva L., Henry J. and Chas. A.

Alice A. Greene-Matteson[9], b. July 3, 1843; m. to David Edwin Matteson. [Matteson line, David Edwin[7], Peleg[6], Peleg[5], David[4], David[3], Josiah[2], Henry[1].] He is also of Westcott, and Lascelle-Waite descent. They have two children living, Edwin Stanley and Walter Marshall.

Josiah Greene[9], m. Mary Alice Walker. One son, Chas. H. They live in Alameda, California.

Alma Greene-Gorton[5], wife of Benj. Tillinghast Gorton. He is a descendant of Samuel Gorton, imprisoned by the Mass. authorities for heresy. They have Abbie, Jason and Henry, all married.

Sabra Greene-Hazard[5], m. James Hazard. One son, Chas. L.

Betsey Greene-Nichols[5], m. Giles M. Nichols. They have a daughter, Angie E.

Lucy Greene-Lewis[5], (of Stafford[6], Elisha[5], etc.), m. Thomas Lewis. Had Stafford, Wellington, Seth, Palmer, Lydia, Lucy, Amy, Dennison and Stephen.

Caleb Greene[5], [of Phil.[4], "White Hat" John[3], etc.] b. Dec. 1, 1748. Married Mary ——. Lived in W. Greenwich. They had David (1771), Job (1776), Sarah, Spencer (1781), and Russell (1796).

John Greene[5]. Died before 1755. Said to have left a son Solomon.

Captain William Greene[4]. ["White Hat" John[3], Benjamin[2], John[1].] M. Judith Rathbone. Lived at Westerly. Many of his descendants moved to N. Y. It would take two chapters the size of this to enumerate his posterity. This is an honorable and leading branch. Frank L. Greene's book gives the full line. Wm. Rathbone, Benjamin and Pardon were the leading ones of his family.

Josiah Greene[4], b. about 1715; m. to Hannah Mowry. Lived in Charleston, R. I. Had 10 children, and descendants innumerable. Two of his sons, Benjamin and John, served in both the French-and-Indian and Revolutionary Wars. For gallantry at Monmouth, John was made a Captain.

Amos Greene[4], b. April 17, 1717. Lived at Charleston. M. Amy Knowles, who counted 364 descendants when she was 89 years old. She lived to be over 100. One son, Capt. Amos, had 19 children. The chiefs of this house were Amos, William, Thomas, Jaffrey and Henry. Frank L. Greene's book gives them in full.

Benjamin Greene[4], [John[3], Benj.[2], John[1],] born 1719. M. (1) Mercy Rogers, Feb. 7, 1741; and (2) Mrs. Anna Greene-Sweet, his cousin. Mercy Rogers was the daughter of Samuel Rogers, and was, it is claimed, a lineal descendant of Thomas Rogers of the Mayflower. The Rogers family is an ancient one. The original name was Hruod or Hrother in the Frankish tongue, and meant fame or glory, or according to another rendering, "one whose word is reliable." The first Rogers was Norman-French. The earliest ancestor of the American branch, that can be substantiated, was Aaron Rogers, a native of Rome, Italy, who came to London in the year 1300. He was a merchant, and became enormously wealthy. His great-grandson was John Rogers, who was prebendary (member of the Cathedral Chapter, a sort of secular clergyman,) of St. Paul's Cathedral. For his stanch adherence to the Protestant faith, Queen Mary had him burned at the stake at Smithfield, London, Feb. 4, 1555. He was the first martyr of her reign. There is an old, old Bible, burned, and a few pages missing, that is preserved in Alfred University, Alfred, N. Y., where so many of Mercy Rogers-Greene's descendants live. It is claimed that this Bible went to the stake with its owner, but was only partially destroyed. James Rogers, one of the earliest settlers in America, brought this Bible with him. He had such a superstitious faith in it that when in peril in the wilderness he slept with it under his head to protect him from the Indians.

The Rogerses in some way are connected with the Lascelles. They probably married into the family, the generation following the martyr, John Rogers. They are remarkably long-lived, eight at least of the American-born Rogerses reaching the century mark before 1800. They have a beautiful coat-of-arms. In the upper part of the shield is a conventionalized fleur-de-lis, "the lilies of France," and in the lower part is a five-pointed star. The crest is sometimes a helmet, and sometimes a fleur-de-lis. The motto is, "Nos Nostraque Deo,"—"Ourselves and our possessions to God." Surely an appropriate motto for a family, one of whom went to the stake for his religion, and others crossed the ocean to find a home in the wilderness where they might worship God in freedom.

Mercy Rogers bequeathed this goodly inheritance of blood to all but the youngest of Benjamin Greene's children, Mary being by the last wife. As Frank L. Greene gives a score or so of pages to this branch, I shall only carry out the pedigree of those imperfectly traced by him, and of the youngest daughter, a tangle in whose ancestry the family desire straightened.

Simeon Greene[5], b. Dec. 13, 1742.

Caleb Greene[5], b. Aug. 2, 1744; m. (1) to Sarah Brown, and (2) to Welthan Ellis, the mother of his children. They had Sarah, Thomas, Gideon, Lydia, Mercy, Eunice, Lois and Simeon. I give the line of the third of these, Gideon.

Gideon Greene[6], [Caleb[5], Benj.[4], John[3], Benj.[2], John[1],] b. March 7, 1777; m. Mary Tillinghast on Christmas, 1795. 14 children; 2 died young; 3 never married; and 2 left no heirs.

Phebe Greene-Andrews[7], m. Geo. Andrews. Had Gideon, Robert, James, Hannah, Elizabeth and Phebe.

John T. Greene[7], m. Fanny Sheldon. His dau. Lydia[8] m. Burrill Waite; Caroline[8] m. Jonathan Word, and had Mrs. Jane Word-Capwell, John Word, and Mrs. Caroline Word-Parker. The son, John A. Greene[8] m. Mary Holland.

Welthean Greene-Greene[7], m. Seth Greene. See under that heading, this chapter.

Benjamin Greene[7], m. Mary Bennett. They had Maximilian, Lucretia and Caleb; Alpheus[8], who m. Sarah Scott and had Byron, Ella, Emma, Angie, Edwin and Mary; Amos[8], who m. Angeline Scott and has two children; Melissa[9], wife of James Dennison; who has one child; and Caroline[9], wife of Chas. Tyler, who has three children.

Gideon Greene[7], [Gideon[6], Caleb[5], Benj[4]., John[3], Benj[2]., John[1].] 1814-1876. M. Sally Fry, dau. of Samuel and Phebe Fry.

Phebe Greene—Henry—Payson[8], b. July 2, 1837; m. (1) to Harris E. Henry, and (2) to Willis H. Payson.

Ida E. Henry-Page[9], m. Dr. Warren Ellis Page, 1885. No children.

Anna B. Henry-Page[9], m. in 1886 to Elmer Ellsworth Page, brother of her sister's husband. Their children are Edith E., Lester C., Raymond H., Dorothy G. and Frank W.

Mary G. Henry-Howard[9], m. in 1884 to Charles T. Howard, son of Henry and Catherine Greene-Harris-Howard. She died Oct. 26, 1893, leaving one living child, Frederick N.

Frank G. Payson[9], m. Lavinia May Drake in 1890 One child, Lillian H.

Gertrude H. Payson-Howard[9], m. in 1897 to Charles T. Howard. They have a son Henry by this marriage. Their home is in Providence, R. I.

Of most of the other children of Benjamin, Frank L. Greene's book gives full information. Jonathan[5] married Margaret Budlong, and three of his sons married Budlongs also. He was a Revolutionary soldier, and left numerous posterity. Clark[5] m. Mehitable, daughter of Henry and Mehitable Waite-Reynolds. They lived in West Greenwich and had 11 children. Clark was born Aug. 2, 1751, and was married at 33. Elizabeth[5] m. Joseph James, an officer in the Revolutionary War, in Col. Lippitt's Reg't. Their son, Rev. Henry James, was a well-known writer and Swedenborgian minister, and *his* son, Henry James, Jr., is the popular novelist. Lois[5], born 1755, m. her cousin, Sergeant Luke Greene[5], [Joseph[4], John[3], Benj[2]., John[1].] They had 10 children. This was one of the important N. Y. lines. These, with the children already enumerated, complete the list of Mercy Rogers, the first wife's children.

There yet remains a daughter Mary by Benjamin's last wife. Her posterity have been much bothered as to where she belongs. D. Byron Waite, the Waite family historian, thought her a second cousin of Gen. Nathaniel Greene, and the daughter of Benjamin Greene of Warwick. But the Benjamin of Warwick he gives had no Mary among his children.* His wife, Mary Fry-Gould, was a rich young widow with two children when he married her. One of these was indeed a Mary—Mary Gould—but she married the very John Allen spoken of in Chapter XX, the man who angered the British so that they burned the whole of Prudence Island in retaliation.

The official records give Benjamin Greene's second marriage to Mrs. Anna Sweet. And to them was born Mary, March 24, 1766. Cross records of the Henry Greene family show that a daughter, Anna Greene, was the wife of a Greene. The descendants of this Mary, born March 24, 1766, are positive that her mother was the daughter of Henry and Margaret Rathbun Greene. They are also positive as to this Mary having a brother Clark, and a sister, Mrs. Elizabeth James. Besides this she named a daughter Mercy, after her father's first wife, and another daughter Lois, after her half-sister. This identifies this Mary beyond question as the daughter of Benjamin, son of "White Hat" John, and his last wife, Mrs. Anna Greene-Sweet-Greene. By her first husband Mrs. Sweet had a son. She had also a daughter Alice, whom the Waites think to have been a full sister to Mary Greene-Waite. I feel positive that she was a Sweet, and therefore a half-sister. Alice became Mrs. Budlong. Her son, Dr. Caleb Budlong, was a celebrated physician in his day.

Mary Greene married Peleg Waite, Christmas, 1783. As pointed out in the Appendix, Thomas Waite was a great-grandson of the old Huguenot, Gershom Lascelle. Peleg was descended from Thomas thus: Thomas[1], Reuben[2], Thomas[3], Thomas[4], and Peleg[5]. The Waite ancestry itself was honorable and ancient. It will be found in the Appendix. Mary Waite out-lived her husband, almost completing her 96th year, and was a remarkably bright, alert old lady. She and her husband moved to Petersburgh, N. Y., when their oldest child was a baby, and lived and died there. They had 10 children, Greene, Clarke G., Mercy, Thomas, Benjamin G., Alice, Tabitha, Mary, Lois and Laura. D. Byron Waite's book is almost entirely given to this family. I shall therefore only attempt to give the line of three descendants in whom I am particularly interested.

Elvaton Waite[7], was the second child of Clark G.[6], the son of Mary Greene-Waite[5]. He was m. (1) to Abigail Roble and (2) to Elizabeth Benway. He is yet living in 1904, over 90 years of age. His children are Elvaton E., Mansir K., Malden C., Josephine, Emma, Sarah E., Merton B. and Martha.

Josephine Waite-Barker[8] of above m. Frank Barker of Rochelle, Ill., and has three sons, Frank, Perry and Malden. She is a student of history, and particularly interested in genealogy. The author acknowledges her indebtedness to her on several points.

*See Allen's History of Quidnessett, which is exceedingly full as to this Benjamin and family.

Mrs. McCrossen[7]'s lineage is this: Mary Greene-Waite was her grandmother. Her father was Thomas Waite[6], born May 1, 1791, and her mother was Chloe Roblee. They had six children, of whom only one left any issue. That one was Mary G. Waite, who married Dr. David McCrossen of Michigan. She is a widow. Her only daughter is Medora, wife of William N. Perkins of grand Rapids, Mich. They have one son, Benjamin McCrossen Perkins[9].

D. Byron Waite[7], the historian of this Waite family, is also a grandson of Mary Greene Waite[5]. His father was Benjamin G. Waite[6] of N. Y., who married Mary Odell, a sister of Mrs. Lydia Baxter, the poet. Benjamin had six children. The daughters were Mrs. Mary Ball and Mrs. Augusta Burton; 2 sons died unmarried; Edwin was Secretary of State for California, when he died in 1894. He left daughters only. D. Byron Waite, therefore, alone perpetuates the name of all this family. He was a leap-

AUTHOR OF " WAITE GENEALOGY."

year son, born Feb. 29, 1828. By his first wife, Harriet Merinda Brown, he has B. Audubon, of British Columbia; Buretta, who was Mrs. Drayton Muchler, and died at 21, leaving a son Percival; and Percival Waite, of Kettle Falls, Washington. Byron Waite's present wife was Amanda Colvin.

Mr. Waite had his history in mind about forty years, and spent two years of labor upon it, getting Old World records and early New England entries, etc. He found, according to his friends, that after all his pains, a few grumblers were ready to raise a hornet's nest about his ears—the usual reward of a genealogy hunter. He lives at Springwater, N. Y.

JONATHAN[4] AND CALEB GREENE[4]. Little is known of them. Their descendants are supposed to be mostly in N. Y.

JOSEPH GREENE[4], of "White Hat" John[3], Benj[2]., John[1]. M. Margaret Greenman. He was head of another tremendous line, most of which reside in N. Y. Five of his sons were in the Revolutionary War, John, Edward, Perry, Serg't. Luke, and Lieut. Charles, and all were in Lieut.-Col. Van Rensselaer's Regiment of N. Y. Three of Joseph Greene's sons, Perry, John and Joseph, married three sisters, Sarah, Catherine and Hannah, daughters of Jonathan and Hannah Godfrey-Nichols, and lineally descended from Deputy Governor Benjamin Nichols of early days. Judge Edward Greene, one of Joseph's sons, was the great-grandfather of Frank L. Greene, A. M., author of the valuable family history already mentioned.

JOSHUA GREENE[4], ["White Hat" John[3], Benjamin[2], John[1].] He was the youngest of this large family. His line has been hard to trace because the whole family have been careless about recording themselves. Joshua lived in Charleston, R. I. His wife was Mary Max.

son, whom he married about 1755. There were at least 8 children, and perhaps more. Frank L. Greene gives the lines of Samuel, Edward, Maxson and Mary. I give the families of John and Caleb, sons whose lines have hitherto not been recorded in family histories. All of Joshua's descendants, so far as known, went to N. Y.

John Greene[5]. Born not far from 1761, and died in 1843. His family records were burned, but family names, inter-marriages, and corroborative circumstances show conclusively that he was Joshua's son. He went to New York City, but left before the close of the Revolutionary War, as unwilling to stay where the British were in possession. In 1789, he located at Waterloo, N. Y. His wife was Mrs. Sally (Beadle) Taylor. Of their children, Hannah m. William Norris ; Helania m. Albert Vredenburg, and Sally m. (1) a Wells, (2) Samuel Crandall.

John Green[6], m. Caroline Hutchinson or Jefferson ; 2 children.

William Greene[6], m. his cousin, Elizabeth Beadle.

David Green[6], m. ——— Mosher.

Samuel Greene[6], the fifth child, was b. June 23, 1811. His wife was Melinda Haskins. Their son, Lorenzo[7], lives at Spencer, N. Y. Himself of the good old Greene stock, and his wife, Mrs. M. A. Greene, descended from the Hunts and Cooks of early Plymouth, the Bowens of Rehoboth, the Huguenot family of Luce and the Quaker family of Fish, they naturally take a deep interest in genealogy and colonial history.

Caleb Greene[5]. M. Martha Spicer, Aug. 17, 1799. She was born in 1778, and he is thought to have been at least 5 years her senior. They lived in N. Y. Their children were these :

William Greene[6], 1800–1855. Dau. is Mrs. C. A. Wells.

Richard Greene[6], 1802–18—. Married Lora Church, and in 1844 moved to La Grange Co., Indiana. A noted abolitionist, a noble, generous soul that did honor to his ancient name. No children. The author is a namesake of his wife.

Thompson Greene[6], b. 1804. D. in Alleghany, N. Y.

Levi Greene[6], b. 1807. D. in Ottawa Co., Ill.

Eldridge Greene[6]. Died in Oceana Co., Mich.

George A. Greene[6], 1809–1889. M. in 1832 to Julia Daboll. Had Mary, Richard and Martha. Mary is Mrs. Woods of N. Y. Richard is living on his estate of Greenhurst, Nampa, Idaho.

To return to the other sons of Benjamin :

BENJAMIN GREENE[3], [Benjamin[2], John[1].] He married Eleanor, daughter of Matthew and Eleanor Randall, March 19, 1714. They lived at Westerly, R. I., and nearly all the line have been Seventh Day Baptists. They have been people most highly respected.

SARAH GREENE-HISCOX[4], 1715-1753. M. Josiah Hiscox.

HUMILITY GREENE-GREENE[4], b. Feb. 6, 1717. Frank L. Greene says she married Ichabod Randall. If so, she was left a widow so soon that she was spoken of by her maiden name, for she is certainly the Humility Greene that the official records say was married in 1743 to Silas Greene. [John[3], John[2], John[1].] Her line is given with her husband's in Chapter XV. See remarks in this chapter on Humility, dau. of Henry Greene[3].

ELEANOR GREENE-LEWIS[4], [Benjamin[3], Benjamin[2], John[1].] B. March 2-, 1718 ; m. Amos Lewis, who was thus descended from the first R. I. Lewis of Westerly : Amos[4], Joseph[3], John[2], John[1]. It is supposed that either they or Amy Greene-Lewis and husband were the grandparents of the Lewises who so freely intermarried with the line of Philip Greene, Eleanor and Amy's own cousin. The probabilities are all in favor of their descent from Eleanor.

Matthew Lewis[5], m. Sept. 18, 1760, to Susannah Philips.

Elizabeth Lewis-Paddock[6], m. to Thomas Paddock.

Rev. Benjamin Greene Paddock[7]. His dau., Delia A., became the wife of Dr. Horace Lathrop.

William Lewis[5]. Almost beyond question Eleanor's son.* The only doubt is whether he was her son, or her sister Amy Greene-Lewis's. He was named for her cousin, Captain William Greene, of Westerly also. This William Lewis m. Abigail Middleton in 1760.

William Lewis[6] was a Revolutionary soldier when very young. Also was in the War of 1812. He m. Elizabeth Noyes. Her descent was this : Eliz.[6], Wm.[5], Deacon John[4], Rev. James[3] (one of the founders of Yale College), Rev. James[3], Rev. Wm. Noyes[1], Rector at Salisbury, England, in 1602. Elizabeth did not lack for pedigree. She was a great-great-great-grand-daughter of the Washington family itself, and was also a lineal descendant of the Mayflower families of Alden, Mullins, Rogers and Governor Bradford.

William Lewis[7], m. Esther Sisson, descended from Richard Sisson, an early R. I. pioneer, thus : Esther[7], Gilbert[6], Wm.[5], Wm.[4], Thos.[3], Geo.[2], Rich[1]. His daughter Caroline m. G. W. Tarbox, and has her record with his, in Chapter XX. Another daughter m. A. H. Watkins of Cooperstown, N. Y. Their daughter is Carrie L. Watkins.

Elizabeth Lewis-Grant[7], married into the famous Emigrant Matthew Grant family, from which General U. S. Grant also sprang. Her only child is Mrs. R. H. White of Cooperstown, N. Y., a leading D. A. R.

Henry Lewis[6], Veteran of War of 1812. Married Mollie Cheeseborough.

Nathaniel Lewis[6], Veteran of War of 1812. M. Hannah Cheeseborough.

Phineas Lewis[6], m. Margaret McKenney.

Priscilla Lewis--Lewis[6]. She m. Charles Lewis. Her great-grandson is Carl A. Lewis[9], the genealogist and publisher of Lewisiana, of Guilford, Conn.

BENJAMIN GREENE[4], (Benj[3]., Benj[2]., John[1],] b. March 2, 1720. It is supposed that he married Niobe Paul, 1742-3, at Newport. If so, he had Thomas, Penelope, Deborah, Anne, Nathaniel, John, Mary and Elizabeth. I believe these to have been his, although if it be true, as one reports it, that he died at 33, this could not be, as last four children were born after that date.

Thomas Greene[5], b. 1743 ; m. Sarah Matteson about 1763. They had Phebe, Ruth, Joseph, b. 1768 ; Matteson, b. 1772, and Mercy.

MATTHEW GREENE[4], is the way the official records give it ; John Matthew, the private records have it ; 1722-1757 ; m. Judith Maxson in 1749. Three daughters and one son.

Benjamin Greene[5], m. Grace Rogers, 1781. Had Matthew, Benjamin, David, Amos, Esther, Lucy, Henry Paris, Thos. Rogers, and Paul. This is a large family and one that deserves more space given to it.

MARY GREENE-BRIGGS[4], b. May 18, 1726. By a peculiar error the town clerk of East Greenwich recorded both Mary and her next younger sister, Amy, as children of Henry and Margaret Rathbun Greene. Cross records and private lists which have fortunately been preserved, agree in calling them Benjamin[3]'s children. Amy, indeed, is actually recorded in the official records as belonging to both brothers. I have proof that both daughters belonged where I now place them, as the sixth and seventh children of Benjamin and Eleanor Randall-Greene.

Mary became the head of an important line. She was married at 22 to Captain Thomas Briggs. Pioneer John Briggs was his great-grandfather. Richard Briggs, his grandfather,

---

*Carl Lewis, the Genealogist, differs from the author. He says there is as yet no real proof as to who was the mother of William.[5]

married Susannah Spencer, daughter of John and Susannah Griffin-Spencer. See Appendix for particulars as to the Briggs and Spencer forefathers.   One of the sons of Richard and Susannah was Francis, who married a daughter of Thomas[2] and Martha Shippee-Matteson.   Capt. Thomas, a son of Francis and Mercy Briggs, was therefore a lineal descendant of five of the oldest R. I. families.

The Captain was a sea-faring man of venturesome disposition.   His shipwrecks, escapes and trying experiences are still a matter of tradition in the family. Capt. Thomas and Mary had eight children.   Their descendants have been almost a family of teachers.   Many of the sons have followed the sea, or their country's flag, or explored strange lands.   Several of the daughters have been poets.

Their immediate family embraced Caleb, b. 1749, Cary, b. 1751, Rachel, b. 1753, Francis, b. 1755, Martha, b. 1757, Christopher, b. 1760, Humility, b. 1763, and Mercy, b. 1765. Of Humility and Christopher I have no record.   Francis, called "Laut" or "Kip," married Marberry Jones at 20.   He died, probably but a young man, in England.

Caleb Briggs[5], b. June 19, 1749, d. Nov. 14, 1828.   When a young man he went to Dutchess County, N. Y., where were many families of R. I. extraction. Here he married Abigail Ryder, daughter of John and Freelove Hill--Ryder.   Abigail's mother, Freelove Hill, was the daughter of Joshua and Judith Tucker--Hill.   This Hill family were certainly of Lascelle--Wardwell descent.   See Appendix. Joshua Hill was probably the grandson of Jonathan Hill, who went to R. I. in an early day.   As to Abigail's Ryder blood, see under foot notes relating to Jacob Baldwin.

Caleb Briggs could not depart enough from his Quaker blood to bear arms during the Revolutionary War.   However, his conscience allowed him to hire a substitute, and to make himself so active in various ways that the British made several attempts to capture him.   Once his wife seized a gun and held a party of red-coats at bay until her husband escaped.   They had six sons, Jonathan, Robert, Elias, Cary, Caleb and Solomon.

Jonathan[6], the oldest son, m. a Knapp.   His daughters were Mrs. Abigail Mosher, Mrs. Polly Buckram, and Sally, who married a relative, Enoch, son of John Briggs.   This last daughter had John, Pheba A. (Mrs. Stacey), Sarah A., Enoch, Eliza (Mrs. Barton), Mary (Mrs. Snyder), Frank and Virgil.   Jonathan's only son is Caleb Thomas Briggs, b. March 17, 1820, still living in 1904, and an entertaining correspondent.   He has two living children, Mrs. Harriet Willis, and Alfred Martin Briggs, who has a family of 7 children.   His dau. Elnora left a daughter, Inez Randall[9], and another daughter, Josephine, left a son, Amos Seymour[9].

Robert[6], the second son, moved to Canada.   He had Caleb and Jonathan.

Cary[6], m. a Knapp.   He had two daughters, one of whom was Mrs. Adsit.

Caleb[6], m. Matilda Parks.   They had several daughters and a son George.

Solomon[6], m. Betsey Buckbee.   Eight children lived to marry.   I have records of these.

Jane Ann Briggs-Cook[7], 1827-1876; m. Theodore A. Cook.   He was of Quaker stock, and German descent, the name originally being Cookingham.   A son of Jane A. is A. T. Cook (Augustus Theodore), the well known seedsman and flower-grower of Hyde Park, N. Y.

Catherine Briggs-Eckert[7], m. Nelson Eckert of Greene descent. Their married children are William H. Eckert, and Mrs. Sarah E. Smith of Brooklyn.   Both have children.

Henry Jonathan Briggs[7], m. Mariette Underhill.   One son, Henry S.

Abigail Briggs-Cookingham[7], m. George W. Cookingham.

Elias N. Briggs[7].   Had one daughter, Mrs. Imogene Butts.

Isaac Briggs[7].   Children, Thomas, Elizabeth and Sarah.

Elias Briggs[6], third and remaining son of Caleb and Abigail, was b. Aug. 10, 1775; d. March 3, 1837.   His wife was Catherine Campbell Livingston

LIEUT.-COL. ELIAS BRIGGS BALDWIN
b. June 17, 1834, eldest son of Jacob and Abigail
(Briggs) Baldwin and gt.-grandson
of Mary (Greene) Briggs

ABIGAIL (BRIGGS) BALDWIN
1812-1888, great-granddaughter of Mary
(Greene) Briggs

COLOR-BEARER DANIEL P. BALDWIN
1841-1864, son of Jacob and Abigail (Briggs)
Baldwin and gt.-gt.-grandson of
Mary (Greene) Briggs

of Scotch descent on her mother's side. Her father was lineally descended from the fifth Lord Livingston, a guardian over Mary, Queen of Scots. This Lord's grandson, Rev. John, was a Cromwell sympathizer. Charles II accordingly banished him in 1663. His son Robert, b. 1654, while yet a lad came with Holland neighbors to N. Y. He bought of the Indians 160,000 acres of land on the Hudson River, which George I confirmed in a grant. The American members of the family have ever been noted for their brain power. Elias Briggs was an extensive land owner. It is quite probable that some of this land came by his wife, as the Livingstons had lands and to spare. She is said to have exhibited the family talent and sterling worth.

Elias and Catherine had 11 children. William and Robert never married. Walter settled in Ohio. Nancy became (1) Mrs. Jonathan Evans, and (2) Mrs. Daniel L. Halsey. She had 7 children. Athaline m. John Collins, and was the mother of 5 children. Amy m. Orville Sackett, and had 13 children, two of whom died in the Civil War. Sarah m. David Crego, and had two sons. Catherine m. David Duncan, and had 3 children. Melissa m. Hiram Shaw. Dr. Caleb C. Briggs, b. 1827, was the youngest of all. He was a surgeon in the Union army, and at one time on duty on S. S. "Northern Light."

Abigail Briggs[7] was the fourth child of this large family. She was a woman of strong personality, public spirited and high-minded. The Baldwin sons took much of their ambition from her. She married in 1806, Jacob Baldwin, son of Elisha Baldwin, Jr. and Jemina Ryder.* Abigail was the mother of 15 children 2 of whom died young. Philetus, Charles and Sarah M. never married. Her son Daniel P., was color-bearer in Co. C., 36th Ill. Infantry. He was killed at the battle of Resaca, Ga., May 14, 1864.

The second son of this family, Elisha Jacob Baldwin, m. Rhoda Rix. They had Frank H. and Eugene W. Charlotte J. Baldwin m. Eldad Hall, and has many descendants, mostly in Illinois. Frances J. became Mrs. Z. Bruyn, and the mother of Melissa A. and Hattie B. Miletus O. Baldwin has a family

*The Baldwin descent is supposed to be from George Baldwin, in R. I. before 1653, and later living in Yorkshire, (now in the neighborhood of Hempstead,) L. I. From George, through Thomas, the line runs through James to Elisha, Senior, a Revolutionary soldier. This Elisha's son, Elisha, Jr., m. Jemima Ryder. Their son was Jacob who married Abigail Briggs.

It is remarkable in how many respects the early history of the Ryders parallels the early history of the de Greenes. Osmond, companion of Rollo the Norseman, who gained Normandy, A. D. 912, was the head of a noble house. Several of this line were with William the Conqueror in the conquest of England, 1066. They bore the surname of Foliot. Before 1165, Jordan Foliot, a second son, had the good fortune to gain title and an estate. He at once assumed the name of de Rither, which probably denotes that he held the office of King's Rither, of Chief Forester, and through the King's personal favor enjoyed his sudden rise in the world. The name became corrupted into Ryder.

Sir William de Bythre was a Crusader under the same Prince, Edward "Longshanks," 1271, as the unfortunate third Lord de Greene, who died in Palestine that same year. Sir William's emblem was a blue banner bearing a device of three golden crescents. It has ever since been borne on the coat-of-arms of the family. Sir William, like the fourth Lord de Greene, accompanied Edward I in his war against Scotland. Sir William, through his mother, was of close blood kin to Lady Lucia de la Zouche, ancestress of all the Warwick and Quidnessett Greenes, as both were descended from Eudo and Alan, Earl of Little Britain.

A dozen generations after this crusader Sir William came Thomas Ryder, who came to Mass. in 1636. His son—or grandson—John[2] lived at L. I. and New York. A neighbor of his at Newtown, L. I., was a former Dutch ship-carpenter, Hereks Siboutszen Krankheyt, who had received a large grant of land. To him and his wife, Wyntie Theunis de Kay, were born 14 children. John Ryder[3] married one of the daughters, Adriantie Hereks, in the Reformed Dutch Church of New York, June 27, 1690. Several Holland keepsakes are now in possession of the Briggs family, and are much prized.

Then came Hercules[4], Jacob[5], Rev. Joshua[6], and then Jemima[7], mother of Jacob[8] Baldwin, who married Abigail Briggs.

of 12. Noah A. married Nancy Buchanan, a relative of President Buchanan, and has a family of 5. George W. m. Albina Regan. They have 3 daughters. Hattie M. became Mrs George Durand, and has one son, William Arthur. Arthur E. Baldwin is an attorney at Omaha. He married Edith Langdon, and has two daughters.

The remaining one of the 15 children is the eldest of them all. Lieut.-Col. Elias Briggs Baldwin[8], was b. June 17, 1834. He took an active part in the Civil War, being first, Captain of Co. C., 36th Ill. Inf., then Quartermaster, and lastly Lieut.-Col. in the 8th Mo. Cavalry. His first wife was Julia Cornelia Crampton, dau. of Nathaniel and Lucy Hart (Dudley) Crampton, of Conn. His present wife was Lydia A. Gibbs, of Bridgton, Me.

Lieut.-Col. Baldwin's first wife was a distant relative of his, she being twice descended from William Spencer, the early emigrant who was their common ancestor. Miss Crampton traced her descent from a dozen leading Colonial families of Conn., including a lineage from Stephen Hopkins of the Mayflower. Her sons were Evelyn B., Milton Nathenial, and Burton Lincoln. The last wife's children were Edwin Miles and Mrs. Julia Anna Ball, of Oswego, Kansas,

Milton Nathaniel Baldwin[9], b. Dec. 24, 1863; m. Lucy, dau. of Arthur and Libby (Hughes) Bryant, a grand-niece of the poet William Cullen Bryant. Children: Edith Cornelia, and Lydia Briggs, descended from Stephen Hopkins, paternally, and from Wm. Mullins, John and Priscilla Alden, and Francis Cooke, maternally, of the Mayflower.

Burton Lincoln Baldwin[9], b. Sept. 23, 1865; m. Minnie May, dau. of John Rhodes. Children: Walter Burton, Julia May, and Genevieve Cowles.

Edwin Miles Baldwin[9], 1868-1890. Died in his 22d year. Deputy Clerk of the District Court, Labette Co., Kansas.

Julia Anna Baldwin-Ball[9], b. Aug. 15, 1870. M. to Ollie W., son of Aaron Ball. Children: Charles Edwin and Geraldine.

Evelyn Briggs Baldwin[9], the eldest of Lieut.-Col. Baldwin's family, was born at Springfield, Mo., July 22, 1862. He is sixth in line from Capt. Briggs, still remembered for his hazardous voyages. No doubt in his case, from his Hill-Ryder blood, there has been an out-cropping also of the old adventuresome Hugenot blood, once so plainly shown in the Pierce and King mariners and Buccaneers. Mr. Baldwin is a member of the National Geographical Society and of the New York Yacht Club.

In 1893-4 he was with Peary's North Greenland Exposition as 1st Meteorologist. In 1897 he visited Spitzbergen, as a volunteer to accompany Andree in his voyage toward the North Pole, but the unfortunate Andree and his two comrades taking advantage of a favorable wind, got away shortly before Mr. Baldwin's arrival at the balloon station. In 1898-9 he was second in command of Wellman Expedition, Franz-Josef Land, and in 1901 he organized and commanded the Baldwin-Ziegler Expedition. Mr. Baldwin has written a book of his experience, "Life in the Great White World," and has lectured extensively on Arctic life and Polar problems. He has a fine collection of mounted Arctic animals, Eskimo furs and implements, models of sledges, canoes, etc.

Evelyn B. Baldwin is unmarried, and therefore free to give his life to

EVELYN BRIGGS BALDWIN, (ARCTIC EXPLORER)

his chosen work, the search for the North Pole. With the ambition and energy of youth still his; with the possession of a scientific training and years of real experience to aid him, and an enduring physique behind all, the world may expect to hear more of him in the years to come.

Captain Cary Briggs[5], [Mary Greene-Briggs[4], Benj. Greene[3], Benj.[2], John[1],] b Aug. 19, 1751. He was m. in 1771 to Elizabeth, dau. of Josiah Jones. He served in the Revolutionary War, and after followed the sea for several years. He died in 1839. Of his children, Sarah never married; Gideon m. Nancy Morey, and settled in Canada; Lucy and Polly married two brothers, Holden and John Moon, and left descendants.

Benoni Briggs[6], [Cary[5], Mary[4], etc.] His first wife was Mercy, dau. of Judge Rowland Hall of N. Stephentown, N. Y. By her he had these : Alma, who m. Josiah Whittemore of Erie Co., N. Y. She has descendants. Alvin Briggs[7] had no children. Rowland H. Briggs[7] m. Mercy Maria Bull, and had three daughters, Alma O., the poetess ; Electra M., who m. her father's sec ond cousin, Gideon S. Hall ; and Caroline, who died unmarried.

By his last wife, Mrs. Lydia (Morey) Hall, Benoni[6] had Benoni Jay, who m. (1) his third cousin, Alice M. Arnold, by whom he had Clarence and George D. Briggs, and (2) Lizzie McMahon, by whom he had Beatrice.

Rachel Briggs--Hall,[5] [of Mary Greene--Briggs[4], etc.,] b. March 21, 1753. M George Hall, a Revolutionary soldier, and a lineal descendant of Edward Hall, who came to Mass. in 1636. Some of their sons moved to Canada. Their daughters were Alice and Betsey. I have records of these sons :

Reuben T. Hall[6], m. Lydia Whitman. His son, Rhodes Whitman Hall, has a daughter, Mrs. D. L. Ashdown, and perhaps other children. Reuben[6] was the father also of Sally (Mrs. Patrick Collins), Rachel, Phebe (Mrs. George Hackett, of Ill.), Polly Ann (Mrs. Nathaniel Haskins, of Mass.), and Reuben T. Hall, Jr. of Pa. The latter had 8 children, one of whom is Mrs. Edith Butts of Farmington Hill, Pa.

Caleb Hall[6], m. Lydia Morey. He had two sons. Caleb, Jr., and Gideon S. The latter m. the daughter of Rowland Hall Briggs.

Gideon Hall[6]. Had a large family. Moved "West."

Martha Briggs--Babcock[5], [of Mary Greene--Briggs[4], etc.], b. May 11, 1757. Married a Babcock. Her descendants are mostly in N. Y. Her son Silas' dau. Malina m. Elijah Arnold, and their dau. Alice m. Benoni Jay Briggs[5].

Mercy Briggs-Horton[5], [of Mary Greene-Briggs[4], etc.,] b. Aug. 3, 1765. She m. John Horton and lived on Black River, near Stephentown, N. Y. A dau. married Josiah Roberts.

AMY GREENE-LEWIS[4], [Benjamin[3], Benj.[2], John[1],] b. Sept. 10, 1727. Married Elisha Lewis, probably a brother to Amos.

CALEB GREENE[4], b. March 21, 1729.

Matthew Greene[5], had son Squire[6] with numerous offspring.

Benjamin Greene[5], 1769–1834 ; m. Bridget Wheeler in 1796. He had Benjamin, George, and daughters.

REV. JOSEPH GREENE[4], [Benj.[3], Benj.[2], John[1],] 1731–1796 : m. Hannah Thurston. He was so faithful a minister that his church at Leyden, Mass., erected a monument to his memory. His children were Paul, m. to Deborah Clarke, and line living mostly in N. Y.; Keziah, wife of Dennis Taylor, 12 children ; Mary ; Benjamin, who m. ———— Chapin in 1797, and from whom an influential line has sprung. Many of these are in Pa.

HENRY GREENE[3], [Benjamin[2], John[1].] He was of North Kingstown (Quidnessett), R. I. May 15, 1724, he married Margaret, daughter of Joseph and Mary Mosher-Rathbone. She was fifth in descent from Richard

Rathbun or Rathbone, [Margaret[5], Joseph[4], John[3], John[2], Richard[1].] He lived mostly in E. Greenwich, but died in W. Greenwich. Beside his land, he left a thrifty fortune of £2,667, over $13,000, or according to present values, about $40,000.

It is generally held that the official records of this family are not trustworthy. I have several authentic private and cross records, and can say with positiveness that the supposed errors arise from two things : (1) Confused record lines which make it hard to tell which birth date fits which child or who married who. (2) An error by which 3 children belonging to a brother and a cousin were recorded as Henry's. Cross records of related lines, and private records have corrected all this, save that there is room for doubt as to the exact birth dates of some of the daughters. Henry and his wife had eight children. The 3 children recorded, that were not his, were Mary, born 1726, and Amy, born 1727, his brother Benjamin's children ; and Nathan, born 1731, his cousin, Wealthy John's son.

HUMILITY GREENE-GREENE[1], [Henry[3], Benj.[2], John[1],] married her second cousin, James Greene, son of Maroon Swamp James. Austin, Huling and Frank L. Greene all three say she married Silas Greene, the son of Wealthy John. But Silas married her *cousin* Humility. The two brothers, Henry and Benjamin Greene, each had a daughter Humility. Benjamin lived in Westerly, and Henry in the territory set off in 1741 as West Greenwich. Benjamin's Humility, had she married James Greene, would have been more than four years older than he—an improbable difference in that day. When James Greene[4], [James[3], John[2], John[1],] married his second wife, she is expressly mentioned as Humility Greene of *West Greenwich*, i. e. the daughter of Henry, who lived in that township. She was born Feb. 12, 1725. Her line is traced with her husband's, in Chapter XIV.

BENJAMIN GREENE[4], [Henry[3], Benj.[2], John[1],] b. July 17, 1729. He married Mehitable, dau. of Job Tripp, lineally descended from John Tripp of Portsmouth, of the early colony. He died at Exeter, R. I., after 1804. They had 10 children who lived beyond infancy : Eunice, Waite (Mrs. George Moore), Henry, Margaret, Joseph, who m. Mary Lewis, Sarah, Benjamin Jr., Mary, Duty and William.

Benjamin Greene[5], of above, was the eight child of Benjamin and Mehitable. He was b. Aug. 13, 1764, and d. April 22, 1855, at Benton, Pa., in his 91st year. He was m. at 23 to Joanna, dau. of Captain Robert and Eunice Waite-Reynolds, Joanna was sixth from Thomas Waite of Portsmouth. [Eunice[5], John[4], Sam.[3], Sam.[2], Thos[1].] See Appendix. They had 12 children : 3 died young or never married. The others were Henry ; Sarah (Mrs. Hallstead); Mary (Mrs. Raymond); Robert, m. to Melissa Rice ; William, m. to Celinda Capwell ; Hiram, m. to Eliza Dean ; Lyman, m. (1) to Almira Capwell, and (2) to Mary Chase ; Nancy (Mrs. Dean) ; and Alanson B., m. to Sybyl Dean.

Dr. Henry Greene[6], of above, was the oldest son. He was b. Jan. 8, 1788, at Exeter, R. I., and d. Nov. 28, 1825, at Factoryville, Pa. He was married in his 19th year to a young widow, Mrs. Almira Gardner, dau. of Samuel and Content (Calkin) Rice. Dr. Henry was esteemed a superior physician and surgeon. He served in the latter capacity during the War of 1812.

Norval Douglas Greene[7], [Dr. Henry[6], Benj[5]., Benj[4]., Henry[3], etc.,] b. Sept., 1808, d. Jan. 17, 1901, in his 93d year. He m. (1) Ann Eliza, dau. of Isaac and Nancy Tripp--Vaughn. M. (2) Charlotte, dau. of Albert and Mindwell (Schultz) Felts. He was a merchant, starting into business for himself before he was 21. He was widely known

DOUGLAS N. GREENE
SYRACUSE, N. Y.

throughout northeastern Pennsylvania, and bore a high reputation for ability and unswerving integrity. By his first wife he was the father of six children, all of whom are now deceased. By his last wife he had three children, only one of whom is alive.

Ellen Greene[8], 1831-1846. Died at 15.

Caroline Greene[8], 1833-1851. D. at 18.

Emily Greene–Warner[8], 1835-1877. M. Lewis B. Warner. She had one son, Norval Douglas, b. 1859.

Henry Greene[8], 1837-1364. M. Sarah Knapp, and was the father of Alma I. (deceased), Henry I., and Clarence O. He was a member of a Pennsylvania Regiment, and died during the Civil War.

Louise Greene–Van Buskirk[8], 1839-1884. She m. Clarence Van Buskirk, and had Stella and Maud Louise.

Ann Eliza Greene[8], 1841-1884.

Douglas N. Greene[8], only surviving son of Norval Douglas and Charlotte Greene, was born Oct. 8, 1844, at Scranton, Pa. He served in a volunteer Penn. Reg't during the Gettysburg campaign. He has his father's keen business acumen. Before he was 20 he entered the employ of the Delaware, Lackawanna and Western R. R. Co., in Coal Department, at Scranton, Pa. In less than six years he was Secretary and Treasurer, as well as director, of the Northern Coal and Iron Co. He has stuck to the coal business and is now one of a firm that has offices in several large cities for the sale of coal in the state of New York, and in Canada. Beside this he is identified with many other business interests. He is a bank director, Vice-President of McMillan Book Co., and is an officer and stockholder in various large business concerns in Syracuse, N. Y., his present home. He is Vice-President of the Syracuse Chamber of Commerce, a member of various clubs and patriotic organizations, an Elder in the Presbyterian Church, and director and treasurer of various charitable institutions. Evidently there is small chance for time to hang heavy upon his hands! Mr. Greene was married Oct. 21, 1869, at Scranton, Pa., to Emma Christie, dau. of Joseph J. and Susan H. (Barton) Posten.

Annie Posten Greene[9], b. Feb. 3, 1872; d. at 1 month.

Joseph Douglas Greene[9], b. Feb. 3, 1874.

Albert Henry Greene[9], b. Nov. 13, 1875; d. at 11 months.

William Cullen Greene[7], [of Dr. Henry[6], Benj[5]., Benj[4]., Henry[3], etc.], 1810-1847. M. (1) Aurelia Stone, and (2) Sabra Stone, sister of the first wife. By his first wife he had Maria L. (Mrs. Dean), Benjamin Marshall, and Josephine A. (Mrs. Smith). By the second wife he had Hortense B. (Mrs. Kennely) and Rhoda A. (Mrs. Bailey).

Emily Greene–Miller[7], 1813-1835. M. Joseph B. Miller. Left one son, Jerome G., a successful lawyer. He m. Emily Hollenback, and has 3 children, George H., Walter G. and John B.

Marie Louise Greene–Stone[7], 1815-1842. M. Jeremiah Stone. She left two daughters, Mrs. Almira Northup and Mrs. Emily Perry.

Leonidas Rice Greene[7], 1818-1881. M. Emily D. Leighton. They had 2 children, both of whom died before their father.

MARY GREENE-PIERCE[4], [Henry[3], Benj.[2], John[1].] Most probable date of birth, Jan. 6, 1733. Given also as 1731. She was married in 1753 to George Pierce, son of Giles and Comfort Nichols-Pierce, and had quite a family.

ANNA GREENE-SWEET-GREENE[4], [Henry[3], Benj.[2], John[1].] Two dates of birth given, but supposed to be Nov. 4, 1736. She married (1) Peleg (?) Sweet, and had a son Peleg, and it is thought a daughter Alice, who married a Budlong. When a widow, she married her cousin Benjamin, ["White Hat" John[3], Benjamin[2], John[1].] This marriage is given both in official and private records, the discovery of which clears up a one-time tangle. Benjamin and Anna's one daughter was Mary Greene-Waite[5], whose line is given elsewhere in this same chapter.

JOB GREENE[4], [Henry[3], Benj.[2], John[1],] b. March 2, 1735. M. Meribah Carr of remote Lascelle-Wardwell blood. They had Eunice, Sarah, Henry, Margaret, Job, Nathan, Susannah, Meriba, Humility, Gardner, Polly and Amey or Amos. A large line. See Frank L. Greene's History.

CATHERINE GREENE-PIERCE[4], b. May 15, 1738. M. in 1760 to her sister Mary's brother-in-law, William Pierce, son of Giles and Comfort Pierce.

CHRISTIAN GREENE-GREENE[4], b. 1740. This is one of the confused records. Cross records prove her to have married Job Greene[5], [Philip[4], "White Hat" John[3], Benj.[2], John[1].] her cousin's son. They had a son Solomon.

JEREMIAH GREENE[4], b. April 11, 1743. Probably married Deborah Campbell, July 20, 1765.

JOSHUA GREENE[3], [Benj.[2], John[1].] He d. 1795. His wife was **Mahitable** ———. I have no official records of his descendants, but it is probable that these are of his line.

HOPE GREENE-THORNTON, m. Borden Thornton, 1797.

SAMUEL GREENE, b. 1758 ; m. Mehitable Thornton, 1783. M. twice after that.

William Greene, m. Phebe Brown, 1808. Had Samuel, Ruth, Duty, Benjamin, James, and Allen. By second wife had Mehitable, Mary and Sarah.

By Abigail, the second wife, Samuel Greene had these : Joshua Hospard, James A., Frederick Smith, and Peter Castoff. By third wife, Sarah, he had Samuel Towle and Randall Eldred. Of his sons, James A., b. 1796, had John Herman, b. 1823, and William Omen, b. 1832.

PART THREE

RELATING TO DESCENDANTS OF

DEBORAH GREENE–KING AND SAMUEL KING

Some may think an undue amount of space has been given to this house   I would say that my first intention was to confine myself exclusively to Samuel and Deborah Greene-King's posterity   In presenting this I am giving what I first planned, but setting it off by itself so that those who take no interest in it can see at a glance what field it covers, and pass it by.

Part Three has been laboriously searched out.   Knowing that this section would meet the severest criticism, whether deserved or not, I have submitted the full text of the Joel, Stephen, George, David and Cynthia King chapters, as well as that of the Barnes, Bradley, Lamson and Pierce, and the Henry, Richmond, George and Nelson Nichols' chapters to the heads of their lines, and have their full approval   From lack of time, it has not been done with the others, but the data has been furnished by those supposed to be most expert in their particular family history.

CHAPTER XXII

THE UNION OF THE GREENE AND LA VALLEY-KING LINES, THROUGH DEBORAH GREENE'S MARRIAGE TO SAMUEL KING

Deborah Greene³ was the daughter of James Greene, grand-daughter of John Greene of Bristol, great-grand-daughter of Lieut. James, and great-great-grand-daughter of John Greene of Quidnessett, the emigrant. Old John of Quidnessett had 800 years of certified pedigree behind him. It is given in chapter XI. This descendant, Deborah, born 49 years after his death, was the fore-mother of a great host. She took a new departure,—married outside of her family, and outside of the coterie of old Rhode Island families into which alone the Quidnessett Greenes seemed to feel a right to marry. Before we take up the personal history of her family, let us study the history of the two houses from which Samuel King sprang,—the Kings* and La Valleys.

———————

THE KINGS. There are in R. I. the Coventry Kings and the West Greenwich Kings. This is an English name, yet the West Greenwich Kings have always been credited with having come from France, not England. Traditions spring up in long settled communities like toadstools in dank ground. One story is that two brothers came from France, and settled; the one in Coventry, the other in West Greenwich. Another is that at the time so many Frenchmen fled to R. I. for religious refuge, 1685-1700, that a Huguenot ancestor, Jean (John) La Baighn or La Quien came to Quidnessett, and that his name became corrupted into Kant, Kane and King. In addition, the West Greenwich family have a half dozen versions of a half-Cid, half-Robinson Crusoe sort of an ancestor, who bore a charmed existence, and had as many lives as a cat.

The true story is this : King is an old English name. There were no

———————

*At the beginning of my researches, I absolutely rejected all I had ever heard of John King, though it rested on the excellent authority of Mrs. Nancy Nichols, the first family historian. She heard it from the lips of her grandfather, own son of King, the Buccaneer. Nevertheless, it was so highly spiced a romance as to seem entirely improbable. I faithfully ran all evidence down, and have to admit the truth of the story, almost word for word as I heard it at first. This is an instance where truth is stranger than fiction.

lords, or dukes, or marquises in their ranks. They were of the middle class, husbandmen and tradesmen. The first ones were lucky enough to be patronized by some king. Just as at the present day, English shop-keepers put on their signs, "Hatter to his Majesty," or "Tailor to the King," so these ancestors paraded their royal patronage until their neighbors called them King's men (Kingmen). In time the name was shortened into King.

Not far from London there lived a family of Kings. They became connected by marriage about 1600 or a little earlier with the semi-Huguenot family of Lascelle-Wardwells. (See Appendix.) Records are scant and obscure. But apparently after 1565 a Lascelle girl married a Pierce, and their daughter married a King. The main point is that this infusion of Huguenot blood gave an adventursome, roaming disposition, and a spirit of resistance to religious coercion. It is not strange, therefore, that in the great anti-Laud emigration in 1635, that several of this family came to the New World. These were Michael, Thomas, William and John. It is not my purpose to trace the dispersion of these men. The Massachusetts Kings seem mostly from John, who with his wife Mary settled at Weymouth in 1639. His descendants for a long time were nearly all seamen. It is probable that he was the uncle to whom his namesake was consigned 26 years later. Emigrant William's son William is believed to be the one of that name that in 165— received 15 lashes on the bare back from a cat-o-nine-tails, because he had accepted Quaker doctrines.

Thomas King of those mentioned, was 21 when he crossed the ocean in 1635. To him and his wife Ann was probably born Clement,* Clement who married and came to R. I., where we get the first notice of him at the birth of one of his children in 1682. He was the head of the Coventry Kings, with whom we have nothing more to do.

A King brother remained in England. He lived in London and was a man of means. One of his younger children was born in 1654, and named John. He was a puny mite of a child, that gave small promise of growing up. When he was eleven years old, the plague struck the city of London. This was the Black Death that made the year of 1665 memorable. The disease began with a chill and giddiness; great boil-like swellings and livid spots like bruises appeared upon the body, followed by violent vomiting, convulsions and death.

The country was wild with terror. Cordons of troops were thrown around the city, and not a soul permitted to leave it. The ships were not allowed to leave the quay. London became a charnel house. Though lime was sprinkled in every house, and great fires keep burning at the crossings of the streets, the very air was putrid. 70,000 people died. Men were crazed

---

* Circumstantial evidence—not official records.

through fear. Others committed suicide to escape the loathsome death of the plague. Each day the dread cry resounded along the streets,—" Bring out your dead ! " Sometimes there were none to answer, for only festering corpses remained within.

Whole families died, and their bodies were flung without ceremony into the horrid plague trenches of Bone Hill. The Black Death reached the home of this King. It took the father, the mother, the sons and daughters, all save one, and he the poor weakling. When the plague ceased, a friend of the child's father hunted up a sea captain about to sail for Massachusetts. Little John stood by and saw this good friend pay the captain the passage money for the child, and heard him charge him to deliver the boy to his uncle in the colony.

On the voyage the captain changed his plans and sailed to Providence, R. I., instead. Arriving there, he claimed the lad was a waif and owed him for his fare. To recompense (?) himself he bound the boy out until he should be 21, and pocketed the money for his indenture. The boy was so small that the captain passed him off for seven, so that he had 14 years to serve as a bound boy. However, he was kindly treated, and fortunately grew strong and robust. He became a seaman, and an expert one. He was a bachelor, with no ties to bind him to the shore.* His excitement-loving Huguenot blood was strong within him. It was the palmy days of the Buccaneers, and John King became one of them. The Buccaneer of that day stood in relation to the common sailor as Roosevelt's Rough Riders stood with the common soldiers of the Spanish-American War. His calling was legitimate enough, but there was dare-deviltry enough mixed up with it to attract alike romantic men of morals, dashing adventurers and cool-headed criminals.

If there were incarnate fiends among them, like Captains Teach and Blackbeard, there were other captains who regularly held morning devotions with their crew. There were Buccaneers who used to read their Greek Testaments for pastime, and not a few who rose high in honor in the king's service. The only requirement was that every man should live up to Sir John Hawkins' motto, " Hate the Don † like the Devil's limb," and be ready to take his life in his hand to revenge himself on them.

Spain's treachery and cruelty began the trouble, which lasted over 100 years. She had rich possessions then in the West Indies and South America. Her enemies fitted out privateers against her. Whenever they could capture a Spanish ship they took her and her cargo for their own. When-

---

* In after years he said that never but once in his life did he meet a kinsman after he left England at 11 years of age. That one was one of his Massachusetts sailor cousins.

† Don, a cant term for the Spaniard.

ever they could capture a Spanish town they did so, and burned and looted the place. There was bloodshed and cruelty on both sides. Admiral Blake, Sir John Hawkins, Prince Rupert, Prince Maurice, and other titled men were in this desultory warfare. Buccaneers, filibusters and freebooters were some of the names they were called. The Spanish called them Sea Devils, Wankers and Cobras of the Sea. Their names for themselves were Sea Rovers and Brethren of the Coast, and they called their bloody work "Singeing the Spaniard's beard."

In John King's day Holland, France and England were all united against Spain. There was great rivalry among them for adventure. Some of their ships sailed around the world. They doubled Cape Horn, they explored the Pacific, they touched China, they cruised around Africa. Adventures, shipwrecks, fighting, looting and hardships fell to the lot of all. Now they were half starved, and now again rolling in riches. Damphier, a Buccaneer, one of the first to sail around the world, had at one time 1,000 captured slaves on his ships. Cavendish, after a rich haul, sailed into London, his sails damask, his top sail cloth of gold, and all his sailors clothed in silk. John King himself used to say in after years that it was "a hard life and wicked life, but a merry one."

Tradition says John King commanded a Buccaneer ship. There is no proof of this. What we do know is that for some years he was one of the crew, probably an under officer of the ship commanded by Captain Robert Kidd.* Kidd was a celebrated Buccaneer, noted for his cool, nervy daring, and for his many hard tussels with the Spaniards in the West Indies.

A few years before the close of the century treaties were made, and England withdrew her privateers. Henceforth, to rob Spanish ships would be piracy and not reprisal. Not a few who had followed that calling for years failed to make the fine distinction, and kept on in the old way. Spain complained. The English government then commissioned Capt. Kidd, in 1695, to clear the West Indies of all piratical craft. For a time he did this. But the life was too tame for him. Leaving New York in 1697 with a crew of 155 men, he coolly turned pirate himself, and was not particular as to the nationality of the ships he robbed, at that.

One of the first ships that surrendered to his guns had John King on

---

* Legally, he was William Kidd, and commissioned as such. However, he was always called Robert. There is an old, old song extant, beginning.
> "My name was Robert Kidd.
> As I sailed, as I sailed.
> My name was Robert Kidd,
> As I sailed."

Kidd was superstitious. Believing he could succeed as a pirate only by the favor of the Evil One, it is said that before he unfurled his black flag he buried his Bible in the sand, in the presence of his crew. It is also said that each chest of his treasure was buried with blasphemous incantations to the Devil to protect his own.

board as a seaman. Kidd promptly invited (?) his old crony to join the crew. The penalty of refusal would have been to have walked the plank into the ocean, or to have been marooned on some uninhabited island.* King had no relish for either. He joined the crew. Kidd mistrusted his sincerity, however, and watched him so closely that it was months before an opportunity to escape came to him.

The *Adventure*, the pirates' craft, crossed the ocean. Kidd went first to Madeira, then down the African coast, and around the Cape of Good Hope to Malabar and into the Red Sea. He captured several Moorish vessels, and had a hot fight with a Portuguese ship, in which he was worsted and glad enough to get away. Afterwards he captured two rich ships. He took his crew into one of these, the *Quedagh Merchant*, and at Madagascar, on his way back, burned the badly riddled *Adventure*. He came back along the African coast.

Here the official records for a time cease. From King's own narrative, Kidd ventured through the Straits of Gibraltar, then not owned by the English, and less closely guarded than now. The Algerines were notorious and savage pirates. Doubtless he wished to recruit his numbers there, for the records show that he at once crossed the ocean afterwards to the New World. It was at the close of this return trip that Kidd is said to have buried the immense treasures that have been searched for so unavailingly. He was captured in 1699, tried and executed in 1700.

It was in Algiers that King's opportunity came to escape. The French were on particularly friendly footing in Algeria, and ships plied constantly between Algeris in Northern Africa and the city of Marseilles on the Mediterranean coast in Southern France. King had learned to speak French from the French Buccaneers. He passed himself off for a Frenchman, managed to get on board a French ship, and crossed over to Marseilles.

Where he went from Marseilles is conjecture. We only know that he lived and died in South France. He escaped in 1698. He was then an old bachelor of 44. He became smitten with the charms of a French woman, and in 1699 married her. There are reasons to believe that but one child was born of this marriage. This was a son, Magdalen, born Aug. 23, 1702.

Magdalen's feminine name has puzzled many. It is a French fashion, if the god-mother of a child is of a superior rank, to compliment her by christening the child after her. Thus one of the Duc de Montmorencies was Anne, because his god-mother was the French queen, Anne of Austria.

* Alexander Selkirk was a marooned Buccaneer. In 1719 he was rescued from the island of Juan Fernandez, where he lived for years in solitude. De Foe took Alexander Selkirk's experience as the foundation of his famous Robinson Crusoe.

Many other instances could be given. Magdalene was a favorite name in Southern France, because it was believed that the Mary Magdalene of the gospels, fleeing from religious persecution, came to Southern France and died there. Mediterranean France was honeycombed with Protestantism, particularly the nobility. Some high-born Magdalene, that John King and his wife were particularly proud of being favored by, became their only son's sponsor. In her honor they named him Magdalene. He always wrote it, however, without the final e.

It is supposed that John King lived until about 1740, being not far from 86 at his death. Escaping as he did, he saved but one memento of his many years upon the deep. This was an object neither valuable nor rare. It was a large conch shell, with the apex bored out so that it could be blown as a horn. It was a particularly good one, with a peculiar deep boom that could be heard a long distance. Whether as a trusty he carried it with him as he left the ship at Algiers, to call the boats to him if he found recruits, or food supplies, or whatever he was sent on shore to obtain, or whether, sailor-like, he regarded it as a mascot, from some incident connected with it, and carried it with him for good luck, will never now be known. His son Magdalen brought it with him to America, and gave it to his middle son, Samuel. Samuel King, in 1814, on a visit to his daughter in N. Y., gave it to her youngest child, Nelson Nichols, then a child but 2 years old. It is now in the possession of V. D. Nichols, of San Jose, California.

The only other thing known of John King is that he suffered from gout, brought on by the wine-drinking carousals of his Buccaneer days. Some of his descendants are the most rigid of abstainers, but when the rheumatism or the gout gets hold of them they have a practical reminder that the sins of the fathers are yet visited upon the children.

As his son married a La Valley, the history of that house will next be given.

THE LA VALLEYS. After the Roman Empire fell, more than a dozen centuries ago, Gaul (France) was then conquered by the Franks. Their chiefs were counts, petty kings in all but name, making their own laws, waging private wars, and coining their own money. Very proud, haughty, and over-bearing were these heads of Frankish houses. One of the proudest was the house of de la Vallé, once the second most powerful family in all France.

They were the autocrats of the valley of the Loire, the chief river of France. Not at all modestly they chose their surname, de la Vallé. as though they alone were *the* family of that great water-way from the inland mountains of France to her ocean line, 600 miles away. A thousand years has brought many changes to the name. It is variously Vallé, Vallee, de la Val, de la Valan, La Valliere, Le Valley and La Valley. The name became della Valle in Italian, De Laveleye in Belgian, and De Ovalle and de Ovaglie in Spanish. But always, from the great dukes to the poorest untitled one of the name, they were proud of their old blood, and of the special privileges that France granted them up to 1792, when in the Reign or Terror all these were abolished and their records burned.

The present Queen of Holland and Emperor William of Germany are both proud, it is said, of having the blood of this house in their veins. It came to them through their famous ancestor, William of Orange, who married Louise, daughter of Admiral de Coligny and his wife, Charlotte de la Val. No brighter name is on the page of France's heroes. He owed his fame as the dauntless leader of the oppressed Huguenots solely to his wife's influence. In the presence of the whole village she arose and, with deep emotion, declared her belief in the reformed faith; and that though it might cost her wealth, position and life itself, she would cast in her lot with the people of God. He was so moved he followed her example. At once he became a leader. For 12 terrible years he fought at the cannon's mouth to win a right for the people to worship God after their own conscience. Tricked by a false truce into Paris, he was one of the first of the 30,000 victims slain in the massacre of Saint Bartholomew's Day, Aug. 24, 1572.

The spirit that animated this old family is seen in the motto of Admiral Andre de Lavel. His coat-of-arms represented a burning, flaming oar, with this motto underneath: " Pour un Aultre Non!" A poet thus interprets its meaning :

> " . . . .When I give, I give my all,
> For her my love, for him my friend,
> My steel, my gold, my life I spend ;
> My sword shall flash, my blood shall flow
> For these. *But for another, No!*
>
> " Show me but cause for quarrel strong,
> . . . .
> Then through the wave I winged will fly,
> Will cleave with oars the yielding sky,
> Will flame through ocean, float through air,
> Will all things suffer, do, and dare,
> For friend I love, for cause I know,
> I fight ! *But for aught other, No!* "
>
> —*Dora Greenwell.*

Most of us have thought Bluebeard a nursery myth, but the tale is only an exaggerated libel of one of this family. Giles de Laval, Lord of Raiz, and Marshal of France in 1429, was nicknamed Bluebeard by his soldiers, because of his thick beard, so inky black as to be really blue-black. He was brave but cruel, and his men hated him. The Duke of Brittany, his rival, wanted him out of his way. Getting him in his power, the Duke lent a willing ear to the most absurd charges. Testimony was given that Laval practiced sorcery, and that he killed children to use their blood in his incantations. He was therefore burned at Nantes, in 1440, in punishment for these murders it was pretended he had committed, and for crimes against the state.

Only two years after brave Coligny was assassinated, Geoffroi Vallee wrote a sarcastic infidel work, "*La Beatitudes des Crestiens.*" He was tried for the offense, condemned, and hung in Paris, Feb. 9, 1574. Afterwards his dead body was burned.

So if any one is unduly elated over his 12-centuries transmitted La Valley blood, let him think of Geoffroi Vallee and Bluebeard, and restrain his ardor.

The greatest of houses cannot have all its members wealthy or titled. Some of them must gravitate toward the middle classes. Thus it happened that Magdalen King, without a title, and without a fortune, yet married a wife of the proud La Valley stock.

———

Magdalen King was born Aug. 23, 1702, in Southern France. He had a slight infusion of Huguenot blood on his father's side, while his mother was wholly French. He was tall, fair, and blue-eyed. Magdalen was a most devoted son, and to the day of his death, he never tired of rehearsing John King's many adventures. At about 25 he married Marie La Valley, of a protestant family of that name.

Her father, Peter La Valley or La Vallais, had several grown children by 1725, so that his own birth must have been not far from 1675. His wife's name was Suzanné. This was a favorite name with the French of that day. From the story in the Apocrypha of Susannah and the Elders, they took Suzanné to represent the persecuted church. Nearly every French religious family had a Suzanné in it. Mrs. La Valley appears to have died in France many years before her husband. Peter's family consisted of at least three sons and his daughter Marie.

Marie La Valley was a woman of remarkable individuality. Across the gulf of nearly two hundred years she stands out before us, a sharply distinct personality. We know how she looked. We know her disposition. We even know of her headaches, and of the puddings she used to make.

She had plenty of the family pride, though she had too much sense to parade it. Her conversation was witty, brilliant and sparkling, yet beneath it ran the family reserve. She locked her private affairs and her heart's secrets from outsiders, and kept her plans to herself.

Marie La Valley was energy personified. She was steam and electricity in human form. She never knew she was tired until she was rested again ; never knew she was sick until she got well ; and never knew she had a hard or discouraging thing to do until it was over with. What she undertook she carried through, and no opposition or obstacles ever stopped her. She kept more irons in the fire than half a dozen ordinary women, but none of them ever burned. She bore 10 children and raised them. She kept her house in apple-pie order, and another such a famous cook the annals of the family do not record. To this day her cream biscuits, her roly-poly puddings, her dried beef, shaved into wafer thinness, cooked in cream, and served with split biscuits, are handed down in memory.

Very proud of his stirring, bustling, quick-stepping wife was Magdalen. Very proud her descendants have been of her. But this woman of intense, high-strung organization, though she lived to extreme old age, salted her whole line with weak hearts, headaches and nervous disorders. A little less steam pressure would have been better for them.

Marie La Valley was of medium height. She was dark, and had expressive black eyes. She had the mobile countenance of a true French woman, her face lighting up and reflecting every emotion or animation as she talked. She had several descendants that resembled her, and two that in looks were herself over again. Those who have a curiosity to see how she looked will please turn to the frontispiece, for the author is one of the two.*

Six of Magdalen and Marie's large family were born in France. These were Grace, Suzanné, Elizabeth, John, Mary and Sarah. The La Valleys were strong in their religious convictions. There had been a few years' lull in Huguenot persecutions, but now trouble began again. In 1724 Louis XV issued a severe edict against all protestants. They were not allowed to assemble for worship, to have their marriages celebrated, children baptized, or dead put away by the rites of their church. This edict was a little slow in making itself felt where the protestants were strong. Gradually it was enforced more and more, and caused much distress to all godly minded Huguenots.

Many of them took refuge in other lands. Two of Peter's sons, Peter Jr. and David, went to the American colonies. We find them both at Marblehead, Mass., by 1727. Both were ship-masters. Peter Vallais,—for so he wrote his name,—became an intimate friend of Peter Faneuil, who built

---

* Nothing ever caused me more annoyance in my childhood than the frequent exclamation of old people—" She is the image over of Aunt C., and everyone said she was the dead picture of the French-woman."

famous Faneuil Hall and presented it to Boston. He was not only Faneuil's ship-master, but was considerably trusted by him in important commercial transactions.

The other La Valleys remained in France. John King was old, and wanted to end his days there. His son would not leave him. Peter would not leave his daughter. But the heathenish way in which they had to bring up their children was a sore trial to them. Grace, the oldest child, was baptized. None of the rest of them had been churched. When once Magdalen's father had paid the debt of nature,—which is supposed to have been in 1740,—La Valley, now getting to be an old man, his son-in-law's family, and a son or two of his own, set sail for America, probably in one of the ships that were in charge of his ship-master sons. The family came straight to Marblehead. Neither Peter La Valley nor Magdalen King liked it there. There was a new exodus.

One of La Valley's sons, possibly that Peter or David that had been so long in Massachusetts, but more probably a younger one newly from France, went to what was known as the Royal Grant. This was in Vermont, and was a new region just being opened up. He remained there, and the Vermont line of Le Valleys still continues. Peter, together with Magdalen's family, and a younger son, went south to Warwick, R. I., where at Frenchtown there was a good-sized Huguenot settlement. They arrived there in 1741. Here Magdalen stayed for 12 years, and here Peter La Valley died.

At a part of Warwick called Cowesit, Rev. Dr. James McSparran, a noted Episcopal minister, had established a mission church. Nearly all Huguenots affiliated with either the Episcopalians or the Presbyterians. Dr. McSparran thought it a promising opening. The wealthy church at Newport gave him their first church building, a substantial and sightly edifice. It was taken to pieces, loaded on sloops, and carried to Cowesit, then rebuilt. It proved a great disappointment to the good doctor, who could never build up much of a following. He saw more results with the newcomers than with any of the other French settlers. These last gladly availed themselves of church privileges.

July 16, 1741, Dr. McSparran baptized all the children but Grace. She had been baptized in France. Four times more in the next ten years, he records another child baptized, as Ann, Samuel, Margaret, and Paul were added to Magdalen's family.*

---

*From records of St. Paul's Church, Narragansett, R. I., Dr. McSparran's own writing.
"Baptisms by Dr. James McSparran, Episcopal Missionary of the Venerable Society of England, for the Propagation of the Gospel in Foreign parts.
      King.
   Susannah of Magdalane at Coesit, July 12, 1741
   Eliza. of Magdalane at Coesit, July 12, 1741

THE MAGDALEN—KING CEMETERY

(Photographed by George W. King)

The genial doctor, a cultured and brainy man, became a warm friend of Peter La Valley, and remained so until the latter's death in 1756. The old Frenchman was buried in the mission graveyard at Warwick. The next year Dr. McSparran died, and the mission was given up. The church was once more torn down and carried on sloops to the shore of another town, preparatory to being again built up. A terrible storm arose, and when it had spent its fury, it was found that every stick of timber had been swept into the ocean. Such was the end of the old church in which all but one of Magdalen King's children were baptized. The Kings grew up and found other church homes. None of them were ever connected again with this church in whose faith their grandfather died.

The name of the son of Peter La Valley that remained at Warwick, I do not know. This son was married in France, and had Peter, Michael, and John, born in France. His other children, Stephen, Marietta, Susan and Christopher, were probably all born in R. I. No attempt is made to trace this line beyond the first generation. His line all write their name Le Valley.

Three years before Peter La Valley died, his daughter's family moved a few miles away from Warwick. Magdalen purchased a 200-acre tract of land in West Greenwich Township, about a mile from the East Greenwich line. It was on what was called the Division Road, or the Providence and New London Turnpike, near what was known as Webster's Gate. Magdalen built what was considered a large and good house in those days. He cleared the farm up in good shape, excepting a few rough, rocky points. One of these was Rocky Hill woods. In one place there was a flat ledge known as the Threshing Rocks, because for years the farmers in the vicinity brought their grain here and threshed it out with flails upon the rocks.

At another point in the same woods were the Indian Rocks. Before the white man's day, the Indians used to come here and hold their feasts. The rocks rise abruptly 30 or 40 feet high. A shelving rock overhangs the base in one place, making a fine shelter from storms. It is a shady nook, and the ground is carpeted with pine needles. Here the last Thursday in August, the Magdalen King clan annually meet, and hold a clam-bake.

Magdalen King died in 1775, the year that the Revolutionary War began. He was buried on a slight rise of ground on his farm. In time two

---

John of Magdalane received in church at Cocsit, July 12, 1741.
Mary   "   "   "   "   "   "   "   "   "   "
Sarah "   "   "   "   "   "   "   "   "   "
Ann   "   "   "   "   "   "   "   Aug. 22, 1742.
Samuel of "   "   "   "   "   "   April 21, 1745.
Margaret of "   "   "   "   "   "   Oct. 16, 1748.
Paul   "   "   "   "   "   "   "   May 19, 1751
     Grandchildren of Mr. La Valley."

or three generations were buried there. About 1850 the cemetery was enclosed by a faced and capped wall, and an iron gate placed at the entrance. It is kept in presentable shape by the kindred. The farm passed out of the family's possession in 1839. The house was burned soon after. The premises are now one of the typical deserted New England farms, grown up to scrub oak and pitch pine. The old Threshing Rocks are used as a quarry, and many factories have been built from them.

Magdalen's son Samuel always lived on the home place. His mother outlived her husband 17 years, dying between 85 and 90 years of age, in the year 1792. The order of births of Magdalen's older children is mostly unknown.

GRACE KING[3], oldest child of Magdalen and Marie, married an Englishman and moved to Canada. The last ever heard from her she wrote to her sister and brother-in-law, Susan and Job Nichols, lamenting that her sons were all in the British army, fighting against her brother and nephews in the Revolutionary War.

SUSAN KING–NICHOLS[3]. Born in France. Named Suzanné for her grandmother La Valley. The name was later anglicized into Susan. She married Job Nichols. See Chapter XV. On his father's side he had this descent: Hon. Thomas Nichols[1], John[2] (b. 1666), John[3] (b. 1689), John[4], father to Job. On his mother's side he had Wardwell, Hill and Greene blood, the last line running thus: John Greene of Quidnessett[1], Lieut. John[2], Wealthy John[3], and Ann Greene-Nichols[4], who was his mother.

We know little of this couple. They lived in Providence. Susan was said to have had the French talent for fine cooking. Her family inherited this gift, even her sons excelling in that art. Job and Susan had more than one son in the Revolutionary War. Their son David married Nancy, his uncle Samuel's daughter. His line is traced with hers, among her mother, Deborah Greene-King's descendants. See Chapter XXXIII.

JOHN KING[3]. Born in France. Married March 30, 1758, to Deliverance Spink. Deliverance was born April 9, 1735. She was descended from Robert Spink, one of the early Quidnessett settlers. Robert and Alice had Capt. Ishmael, who was born in 1680, and was exceedingly well known in his day. His wife was Deliverance. They had Benjamin, who was the father of Deliverance who married John King. All of John King's line have been money-makers.

WILLIAM KING[4], b. March 22, 1759.

RACHEL KING[4], March 16, 1761.

PAUL KING[4], m. Dinah ———. They had Mary, b. 1790, and Philip, b. 1792. I think it very probable that this record belongs to his uncle Paul. See last page of this chapter.

WANTON KING[4], m. Sarah Matteson, a most saintly woman. They are believed to have moved to Pompey, N. Y. They had Ward, b. 1800; Phebe, 1802; Thomas M., b. 1803; Susannah, b. 1805; and a Winton or Wonton, a few years later.

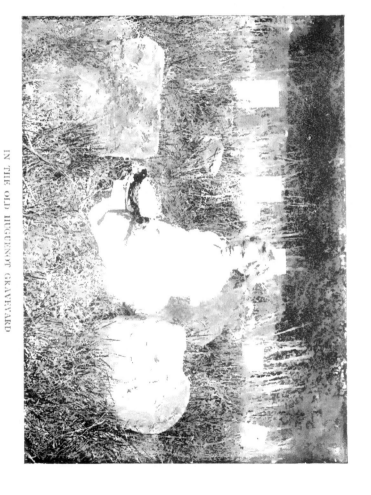

IN THE OLD HUGUENOT GRAVEYARD

Sarah King is sitting between her great-great-great-grandparents' graves

JOB KING[4]. He moved to N. Y. Married Eunice Albro. They had Job, Paul and Henry. For her descent from "Quaker John" Albro, see Chapter XXXV. Their son Paul moved to Ohio. Paul's son John lives in Chicago and is worth $2,000,000. Paul probably had sons Volney and Lorraine also. Job, Jr., also moved to Ohio. Henry married Cynthia Nichols, his second cousin. His line is traced with hers, in Chapter XXXV.

ELIZABETH KING–MATTESON[3].

Born in France. Married Oct. 1, 1761, by Rev. Preserved Hall to John Matteson, son of Martha Greene-Matteson, and grandson of John Greene of Bristol. They had a son Philip. His son was Asa, who m. Meribe Potter, and had Clark, James and John Matteson.

JOHN MATTESON was a prominent man. He was deacon for many years in Maple Root Church. He died about 1902. In 1847 he m. Elsie Andrews, [Elsie[7], John[6], who m. Antha Sweet of King-La Valley descent, Timothy[5], Elnathan[4], who m. Jane Greene, Hannah Greene--Andrews[3], Lieut. John Greene[2], John Greene of Quidnessett[1].] She was related to him five times over. They had 9 children, one of whom died at 14.

Elihu Matteson, b. 1849; m. a cousin, Roby Ellen Andrews. They have Annie, Gertrude, Byron L. and George A.

Phebe Josephine Matteson-Greene, b. 1861. Wife of Oliver, of Horace and Alice Greene--Greene. [Alice[7], Jas[6]., Abel[5], Jas[4]., John of Bristol[3], Lieut. James[2], John of Quidnessett[1].] Their dau., Mariette is Mrs. Rhodes Allen, and has a child, Maud Hazel. Their son is Lowell James, and their younger daughter, Elsie, is Mrs. Charles Andrews, and has one son, Charles, Jr.

Charles James Matteson, b. 1853; m. Mary Amanda of Eben, and Susan Fish--Matteson, thrice related to him, and herself of King--La Valley descent. Their oldest son, Frederick, m. Bertha Jane Harrington, and has Mary, Charles, John Lee and an infant. The next child, Susan, m. William Harrington, and has a daughter, Cora May. The next children, Everett Earl and Erving Dell, are twins, born in 1881.

Mary Jane Matteson-Capwell, b. 1855; m. Edwin C. Capwell. They have Frank Herbert, who m. Ella Capwell, and had 1 child, Merle Belle;—and Luther Lee.

Eunice M. Matteson-Andrews, b. 1858; m. Geo. Warren Andrews. They have Lula Belle, Gertrude M., Eva L., George Lester and Grace M.

John Titus Matteson, b. 1860; m. Amanda Melvina Greene of Wm. and Sarah. Their oldest daughter, Nettie E., is wife of Walter Andrews. The other children are Arthur C., Charles James, Frances W., Henry and Willard.

Cynthia Lily Matteson-Briggs, b. 1867; m. Wm. Briggs. She d. Sept. 1, 1895, leaving a son, Frederick D.

Clara L. Matteson-Perkins, b. 1869; m. John P. Perkins. She d. 1892, leaving two sons, Frank and Walter.

SARAH KING-BRIGGS-SWEET[3].

Born in France. She married Burton Briggs, Sept. 26, 1754. He was the youngest son of Robert and Renewed Briggs, and grandson or great-grandson of Job Briggs, an early pioneer, one of the purchasers, with John Greene of Quidnessett, of the Fones Purchase, in 1672. Burton and Sarah had two children. He died, and his widow married, May 3, 1761, William Sweet. He was descended from John Sweet, who followed Roger Williams to R. I., in June, 1636, and died the same year. [John[1], John[2], William[3], William Sweet[4].] He was called by the nickname of William Wickeboxet, to distinguish him from other William Sweets. They had two children.

JOHN BRIGGS[4], b. March 28, 1755. He m. Eunice Stone. He was called Handkerchief John, from always wearing a handkerchief about his head.

> Sarah Briggs--Briggs[5], m. her second cousin John Briggs, Jr., and had Nathan, Hannah, Tanner, Deborah, John Stone, Maglin King, (intended for Magdalen,) and Sarah.
>
> Burton Briggs[5]. m. Waity Arnold. 1812.

RENEWED BRIGGS--KITTELLE[4], b. Dec. 26, 1756. She was always known as Newie. She m. Ephraim Kittelle, and her line is given with his in Chapter XX.

BURTON SWEET[4], oldest child of second marriage. He m. Rachel Matteson. They had 9 children, and their children's children have increased until it is utterly impossible to attempt to list them in this chapter. The whole line has married and intermarried with the Andrews line. I give but the heads of Burton and Rachel's descendants, and refer those interested to Miss James' "Andrews Genealogy." Caleb, William and Roby Sweet married three Andrews, Sally, Bethana, and Jonathan, their brother.

> William Sweet[5], m. (1) Elcy Weaver. Had by her Antha and Abel. Antha m.
>
> John Andrews, and became the fore-mother of a particularly great tribe. William Sweet m. (2) Sallie Andrews and had Francis, Enos, Stukeley, William Rhodes, Amos (called California Amos), Caleb, Charles, Amy and Alice.
>
> Caleb Sweet[5], m. Bethana Andrews. Had Phebe, Burton, Amos..
>
> Francis Sweet[5], m. Betsey Tarbox.
>
> Sally Sweet--Matteson[5], m. Philip, son of John and Elizabeth King--Matteson. See elsewhere in this Chapter.
>
> Mollie Sweet--Vaughan[5], m. James Vaughan, who was descended from John Vaughan born before 1630. They had John, Clark and George.
>
> Mercy Sweet--Greene[5], Had a son Ray Greene.
>
> Thankful Sweet[5], Had son David.
>
> Roby Sweet--Andrews[5], m. Jonathan Andrews. They went to Tenn., and had a large family. See Miss James' work.

THANKFUL SWEET--MATTESON[4], (of Sarah King--Sweet), m. Thos. Matteson, and went to Vermont.

MARY KING[3]. Born in France. Married, but name not known.

NANCY (ANNA) KING--GREENE[3]. Born in R. I., 1742. She was the first of her family to be born in America. M. in 1764 to Abel Greene, son of James, and grandson of John Greene of Bristol. See Chapter XX. Her brother Samuel married Abel's sister Deborah. The families were always intimate with each other. Abel was a Revolutionary soldier, and delighted in story telling and reminiscences. He died in 1829. He ran a saw-mill and gristmill for many years. They had a large family, some of whom moved to Pa. For list of Nancy and Abel's children, see Chapter XX.

SAMUEL KING[3], b. in Feb., 1745. Died in 1829. He was married April 15, 1766, to Deborah Greene, his sister Nancy's sister-in-law. Deborah's lineage is fully given in Chapter XX. She was great-great-grand-daughter of John Greene of Quidnessett. She was her husband's senior by five months, having been born Sept. 23, 1744. She died in 1812. Deborah King was one of the "good-natured Greenes," as that placid, never-get-angry type used to be called by the family. She was a woman of fine mental powers. Samuel brought her as a bride to the old home, and it is said that the affection between Marie La Valley and Deborah was like that between Naomi and Ruth in Bible days. A large family were born to Samuel and Deborah. They were Nancy, Sarah, Mary, Elizabeth, George, Hannah, Dinah, David, Paul, Joel and Stephen. Paul died a bachelor. All the others are traced in separate chapters.

Samuel King was an expert mill-wright. He built mills all over R. I., cider mills, woolen mills, cloth mills, fulling mills, saw mills and grist mills. He was a man who thoroughly understood the business and put up good, honest constructions. Three great-grandsons, S. K. Matteson, Riley Barnes and George Nichols, were all noted mill-wrights, and all inherited this special aptitude from Samuel King.

He served in the R. I. Militia during the Revolutionary War. Several have asked for a record of this fact. Rhode Island's Revolutionary records are not complete. Only a fragment of a payroll, made at the close of a little "brush" with the enemy, contains his name. It proves his regular connection with the Militia, however, and entitles his descendants to join the Sons or Daughters of the Revolution. The following explains itself:

> "Record & Pension Office, Washington, D. C.
> "July 1, 1901.

"Record No. 658329.

"It is shown by the records that Samuel King rank not stated, served in Capt. Samuel Wilber's Company of Rhode Island Militia, Revolutionary War. His name appears on a pay abstract of that organization, dated April 6, 1777, with remarks.—

> "'Marched Mch. 13–1777. Discharged Mch. 30th. Days in service, 17. No further information relative to his service has been found on record.

> "By authority of Secretary of War."

MARGARET KING–EDWARDS[3], baptized Oct. 16, 1748. She was married Aug. 15, 1770, to Peleg Edwards, son of Christopher. She was his second wife. They had Christopher, b. 1771; Jacob, b. 1774; Perry, b. 1776; Sarah, b. 1778; and Mercy, who married Chas. Andrews in 1816.

There is a large line of Edwardses in R. I. who have more or less considered themselves as descended from Margaret. Possibly they are from a son of Peleg Edwards by his first wife, but they are not Margaret's line. These Edwardses trace back to Richard Edwards who married Mary Howard, (sister of Capt. Howard who married Hannah King, Margaret's niece). But Mary Howard was born in 1770. Margaret's children are accounted for nearly ten years beyond that date. Mary Howard would not have married a man that much her junior.

PAUL KING[3], baptized May 19, 1751. He married Dinah Matteson Dec. 22, 1789. See note in list of John King's children. The children there credited to his nephew Paul are much more likely to have been his.

CHAPTER XXIII

DESCENDANTS OF SARAH KING–HATHAWAY[6]

FAMILY TREES. For the pedigree of the English Greenes, and their relationship to the Capet Kings of France, see Chapter XI. For the Greene descent from John of Quidnessett, together with the allied lines of Straight, Holmes, Westcott and Parsons, see Chapter XX. For King and La Valley lineage see Chapter XXII.

Sarah King-Hathaway[6] was the second child and daughter of Samuel and Deborah Greene-King. She was born about 1769, and married Nathan Hathaway, whose first wife was her cousin Mercy Le Valley. To Mrs. Sara E. Kittelle I am indebted for all the data as to her children. She had but three children, all daughters, Nancy, Susan and Betsey. All her descendants are from Nancy, as the other daughters never married.

NANCY HATHAWAY-SUNDERLAND[7], b. May 17, 1807. She became the wife of John Sunderland, son of George, and grandson of William Sunderland. Her family was the reverse of her mother's, all seven being sons.

NATHAN SUNDERLAND[8]. He m. Adeline Johnson, in 1835. 8 children. Emily, b. 1836, d. at 35 ; William N., d. at 38 ; Henry at 23, and Adelaide at 1. The records o the others are as follows :

    Francis Luther Sunderland[9]. Had two children, Willett and Charles.

    Herbert C. Sunderland[9], b. Sept. 15, 1847 ; m. Harriet Mitchell. They had an infant that died, and a son, Fred C., b. Jan. 1, 1879.

    Charles E. Sunderland[9], b. July, 1849 ; m. Harriet Brown in 1869. They have William, b. in 1870, and Lily.

STEPHEN SUNDERLAND[8], b. Nov. 4, 1810, d. 1853. His wife was Eliza G. Sherman. 8 children, of whom 3 died in infancy. There is only birth date for Amy A. Dorcas died at 17, and William at 26, unmarried. This leaves only these:

    Stephen W. Sunderland[9], b. March 3, 1847 ; m. Mary Meilhenry in 1875.

    Eliza A. Sunderland-Cook[9], b. May 16, 1852 ; m. George W. Cook of Warwick, R. I. They had Arthur, who died at 21, Georgiana M., wife of Fred Place, and Howard L.

JOHN SUNDERLAND[8].

WILLIAM SUNDERLAND[8]. He married Anna Kenyon of Coventry, R. I. They had one daughter, Bertha, m. to Robert Everett.

HENRY SUNDERLAND[8]. [Nancy[7], Sarah Hathaway[6], Deborah Greene-King[5], etc.,] b.

March 18. 1816, d. Feb. 11, 1887 ; m. in 1842 to Marcelia, dau. of Rufus King. She was of the Coventry Kings, not of the Huguenot Kings, from which her husband came. 6 children.

Ann Maria Sunderland-Field[9], b. Jan. 18, 1844. Wife of Harrison Field. They have Leonard, b. 1871 ; Maud, 1873 ; Mabel, 1876 ; and Lyman, 1882.

John H. Sunderland[9]. D. in 1875, aged 29.

Nancy Emma Sunderland-Le Valley[9], b. Aug. 26, 1850, d. March 14, 1890 ; m. Wm. F. Le Valley, son of Robert, in 1873. He was of the same La Valley stock as herself, through one of the sons of Peter La Valley who died in 1756.

Mary E. Le Valley-Northup[10], wife of Alonzo Northup. They have Gladys I and Harriet F.

William F. Le Valley[10], b. May 24, 1881.

George Sunderland[9], b. Dec. 1, 1852 ; m. Mary Hopkins in 1883. They have Lena, b. 1884 ; Wallace, 1888 ; and George, b. 1891.

Augustus H. Sunderland[9], b. May 11, 1856 ; m. Carrie B. Johnson in 1881. They have Alice, b. 1883 ; Ethel, 1884 ; Herbert, (dead); Norma, b. 1890 ; and Maud, b. 1893.

Idella F. Sunderland-Burnham[9], twin to Augustus H. M. in 1874 to Alfred D. Burnham. They had Edith, who died at 10, and Alfred T. b. 1888.

ALFRED SUNDERLAND[8], (of Nancy[7], of Sarah H.[6], etc.)

THOMAS SUNDERLAND[8], [Nancy[7], Sarah Hathaway[6], Deborah Greene-King[5], etc.] He

CHAPTER XXIV

THE PIERCE FAMILY

LINE OF SANFORD AND MARY KING–PIERCE

Mary, the third daughter of Samuel and Deborah Greene-King, [Mary, Deborah⁵, James⁴, John³, James², John¹,] married Sanford Pierce⁶, the son of Olive Greene-Pierce⁵, [Samuel⁶, Olive⁵, Ebenezer⁴, Ebenezer³, John²,John¹.] The Greene descent of both has been traced, and also the La Valley-King descent of Mary. The Pierce family also has its history, interwoven in part with others, and will be given here, before the personal story of Mary and Sanford is begun. I have confidence in the pedigree as here given. It is the result of *close* comparison and study of very old records, which are, however, as I am free to admit, brief and sometimes confused.

The name was originally Norman French, and was then St. Pierre—(Saint Peter.) The first name-bearer was a devotee of Saint Peter, who had taken, it is supposed, some special vow or obligation before the shrine of the saint. The family were of noble blood. Their coat-of-arms showed two bend sable. It is an old escutcheon, showing some variation in different lines. They came to England at the Conquest, or soon after, and there the name quickly corrupted itself into Pierce or Pirce, written at first Piers or Perres. The descendants of the younger sons of the family became reduced to the common rank. It is perhaps but a coincidence, yet it is worth noting, that William Langland who wrote the famous poem of "Piers the Plowman," about 1362, locates his Piers of the remarkable visions in the Malvern Hills, on the Welsh border. The first glimpse we get of the line of Pierces we are trying to trace, is in North Wales, about one hundred years after the date of the poem.*

---

*There is a tradition, as Mrs. Belle Pierce-Estabrook tells us, that this family have royal Stuart blood. If so, it was in the same way and in the same sense in which Cromwell had royal Stuart blood; i. e., there is a strain in the blood of descent from the Norman Baron Alan, whose son was made Lord Steward to the Scotch King David. From the Lord Steward's family the royal Stuarts sprang in meteoric career, only to sink into ruin so pathetic that it has made their memory immortal. Many old Welsh families had a cross of this Baron Alan blood.

It is only justice to Mrs. Estabrook to state she does not accept the old records that I quote. She believes that the Pierces "are of Royal Stuart blood, and went to France after the overthrow of the royal house, taking the name meaning a stone or rock."

In the Appendix it is told that a young woman of this Welsh Pierce family, prior to 1500, married an Ithell. Their son, Pierce Ithell, had a daughter Mary who married an Englishman, Richard Wardwell. One of the Wardwells' sons married a Huguenot refugee's daughter, Meribé Lascelle.

The heads of this Huguenot family, Gershom and Meribé Lascelle, had another daughter whose name, as near as we can get at the original form, was Anterés, which would be pronounced An-te-rees, or An-te-race, with the accent on the last syllable. The name was handed down in the Pierce family for several generations, under the forms of Antrace, Antires, Anterace, or Ansutrass, and particularly as Antress and Anstress. This daughter with the odd name married a Pierce, whose baptismal name is unknown to us. We do know that he belonged to the same branch whose blood was in the Wardwell line into which Meribé (Maribah,) the sister of Anterés, married.

The French blood thus brought into the Pierce family has markedly shown itself. The romantic and spectacular side of the Gallic character has tinged the whole blood of this line. An instance is the act of old Robert the Emigrant, who brought bread with him from England, bread that is yet preserved in his family, a memento as sacred as the Jewish shew bread of the altar itself. The Pierce of to-day has a Frenchy, imaginative, sentimental and reminiscent side to his character, however practical he may be in other ways. Every pathetic or romantic episode in their history has been preserved, until their chronicler suffers from embarrassment of riches, so many and so varied are these anecdotes. The Lascelles, like so many French families, delighted in mellifluous and high-sounding names. More than any other branch of the family, the Pierces have preserved this peculiarity. In studying 200 years of early New England records, the Pierces led any other family whatever in original, peculiar and poetical names. Pardon, Preserved, Myell, Suthcote, Val, Backus and Clothier, Bashabee, Barsha, Squier, and Lewis-Desabaye-Besayade are a few of these names that now occur to me. To this day the Pierces largely choose sentimental names for their offspring.

Anterés Pierce had quite a family. Almost certainly she had an Ebenezer, Thomas, Michael and Azrikam, and probably an Edward and a Stephen. One of her younger children was a daughter who married ———— King. This daughter's descendants continued the names of Thomas, Michael, Ebenezer and Edward for several generations. Her sons Thomas, William, John and Michael King came to America in 1635, and a great-grandson, John King the Buccaneer, came to R. I. in 1665, a child of 11 years. Buccaneer John was the great-grandfather of Mary King-Pierce herself. So that by her and Sanford Pierce's marriage were united her remote Pierce-

Ithell and Lascelle-Wardwell blood, and his Pierce and equally remote infusion of Lascelle blood. Each was of course of Greene blood also. So these several small trickles from the parent streams, re-united, became something of a current itself.

In the next generation a large number of allied families, Waites, Hills, Wardwells, Lazells (Lascelles), Slocums, Brownells, Kings and Pierces came to the Colonies, seeking religious freedom. From the early records, General Ebenezer Pierce's careful Pierce genealogy, and from the New England Historical and Genealogical Register, it appears that the Pierces among these may be subdivided into several groups of presumable brothers, the first descendants in each group cousins to those of the others, and all of course grandchildren to Anterés Pierce and her husband. Only one group concerns this history, save that Thomas Pierce of Woburn deserves mention as being the ancestor of President Pierce.

The group in which we are interested consists of four brothers—so the best authorities consider them—John the Patentee, Robert, Capt. William and Capt. Michael. Three of these were men of distinction in their day. They were grandsons of Anterés Pierce, and sons of Azrikam Pierce and his wife Martha.* Besides these are three, evidently closely related to them, and believed to be a brother's children. These are John the Emigrant, of Watertown, Daniel of Watertown and Newbury, and Richard of Rhode Island. It is thought these three were the sons of a Jeremiah, but of his name there is no absolute certainty.

Before passing on to Richard of Rhode Island's line, let us glance at the history of his three then-famous uncles. John the Patentee, (who may have been an uncle instead of a brother to the others,) was a merchant of London. He was the owner of the historic Mayflower. An association of merchants, with John Pierce at their head, secured a patent in 1620 from the Virginia Company for the use of the Mayflower colonists, who then expected to settle in Virginia. When the Mayflower returned in the spring of 1621, with the news of the change of base, John Pierce obtained a new grant or patent to Plymouth Colony, dated June 1, 1621. He himself started for the new world in the ship Paragon, but it proved unseaworthy and put back. He then sent the patent on in the ship Good Fortune, which reached Plymouth Nov. 11, 1621. He remained in London,† but used his means and ships in building up the colony.

---

* Those two names, Azrikam, (frequently Ezrikam, Eliakim, Azrakin and Azra in the records,) and Martha, are repeated over and over in their descendants names, as only an ancestor's name would be. Azrikam is never met with outside of this branch.

† So say all authorities but one, I find no trace of him in America.

He put his brother—so Gen. Ebenezer Pierce styles him—Captain William Pierce as master of first one and another of his ships. A year from the time he first visited Plymouth Colony, Captain William owned 13 slaves. Doubtless he owned many more as his fortunes increased. In a letter of 1638, which has been preserved, is this language: "The ship Desire, Capt. William Pierce, returned from the West Indies after a 7-month's voyage. He brought cotton, tobacco and negroes from Providence, [one of the West Indies' islands,] and salt from Tortugas." And yet a historian of those days speaks of him as "A godly man, and a most expert mariner!" Doubtless he was a good man, for these things did not trouble men's consciences then.

Pope in his history says that up to 1640 Capt. William crossed the ocean oftener than any other man then living. He made many voyages between England and Virginia or to the West Indies. Twice he essayed to go to Plymouth, but each time had to put back because of a leaky vessel. This was in 1621 and 1622. In 1623 he came in the Ann, in the Charity in 1624, in an unregistered ship in 1625, in the Mayflower in 1629, and in the Lyon or Lyon's Whelp in 1630, 1631 and 1632, making seven voyages to Plymouth within ten years. He brought a great many of his kindred over in his ships, also Rev. Cotton, Roger Williams and other eminent men.

At first he lived in Virginia, where he had a plantation of 200 acres at James City. Here his first wife, Mrs. Jone (Jane) Pierce, died. She left a daughter Jane, who married John Rolfe, the widower of Pocahontas, the Indian princess who saved Capt. John Smith's life. In 1632 he removed to Boston. Here he was of great influence, and made for them their first Almanac in 1639. In 1641 he attempted to land a ship-load of colonists on the Island of Providence, one of the Bahamas. The inhabitants resisted the intrusion, and in the battle that followed he was shot, the 13th of May, 1641.

Captain Michael Pierce, the third prominent one of the brothers, was an Ensign under Captain Miles Standish. In 1669 he was made Captain. He was easily the greatest Indian fighter of the King Philip War. But close to Rehoboth, Mass., near the Pawtucket River, he was hemmed in by a host of red men, on March 26, 1676. He had only 52 white men with him and 11 friendly Indians. In the fearful massacre that followed only three of the sixty-three escaped. Thus dearly he sold his life on that Sabbath day's fight, so long ago. The family of Richard (his nephew) have this battle handed down in their memories, and tradition could be no more positive than theirs that they are nearly related to him. Richard Pierce's line was exceedingly proud of their near relationship to Captain Michael, and named after him for five generations.

Richard[5] the Emigrant*, [Jeremiah[4], Azrikam[3], Anterés Lascelle-Pierce[2], Gershom Lascelle[1],] came to Massachusetts, probably about 1635. His wife was Elizabeth————. Richard was one of those who thought the Massachusetts authorities exercised tyranny in religious matters. He accordingly went to Portsmouth, R. I., and became a Friend or Quaker. His descendants of the particular line we are tracing, went to Prudence Island, or Chippacursett, as the Indians called it. Together with the Hills, who were relatives, the Allens and Sanfords, they were the leading families of that island, until the Revolutionary War. The British in vain tried to buy hay or provision from the Prudence Island farmers. They were so stanch a band of patriots that not one would part with provender for the British army, even at double price.

An English officer attempted to overcome the scruples of Hon. John Allen, of this island. The Hon. John, who was hot-headed, exploded with wrath, and refused in a taunting way to have anything to do with the redcoats. Wallace, the British officer in command, in reprisal for the insult, sent troops with orders to burn every house, barn and haystack on the island, from end to end. The order was carried out to the letter. Allen's family were thrust out in their night clothes, and of their household possessions saved only some silver teaspoons that Mrs. Allen snatched up as the soldiers drove her out. and thrust into her bosom. Samuel Pierce, Senior, great-grandson of Richard the Emigrant, and grandfather of the Sanford we are tracing, was turned out of doors also, his house, barn and hay burned, and his cattle taken. He left the island at once, and none of the family ever returned. He saved a few small articles in his flight, and they are yet kept as heirlooms, including some of the garments, and a teapot with the date of its making, 1746, stamped upon it.

Richard the Emigrant's line were mostly seamen. In a hundred years' time no less than six were sea captains, and as many were drowned at sea. They were all slave-holders. The records would indicate that, next to the Tripps, they were collectively the largest slave-holders in the colony. One reason was that many sailors habitually made trips to Africa, trading New England products for slaves and gold dust. These slaves cost them but a trifle, and they could afford to own plenty of them. Some of the family died on the African coast, on slaving expeditions. The brother of Captain Daniel in our tracing line being one of them.

The close of the seventeenth century were the palmy days of the Buc-

---

*Some of the family hold that this Richard was Capt. William's son. He indeed had a son Richard by Bridget, his second wife. The Milton. Mass., church records show that Richard of Capt. William was baptized Jan. 23. 1636. then a small child. Richard of Portsmouth had children born before 1650. so could not have been the same.

caneers, those sea rovers who made it a matter of conscience to despoil
Spanish possessions, and take the booty captured for their own.   Spain was
a hated nation.   So far from considering themselves pirates, those free-boot-
ing ancestors thought it a feather in their cap to board Spanish vessels, and
to take Spanish towns in the West Indies.   The Prudence Island Pierces
had their full share in all this.

The family soon lost their Quakerism.   During the Revolutionary War
48 Pierces of R. I., nearly all lineal descendants of Richard, Senior, enlisted
in the army.   Not a few of them were officers.

Richard's son, Richard Jr.[7], had by his first wife, Joyce, a son Daniel[8].*
This Daniel was married in 1708 to Patience (Patty) Hill, a distant cousin.
Patience was the daughter of Jonathan Hill, the uncle of Ann and Susanna
Hill who married " Wealthy " John Greene and Usal Greene.   One of the
oldest sons of Daniel and Patience Pierce was Samuel, Senior, whose house
was burned by the British.   In 1744 this Samuel married Hester or Esther
Wiley.   (The name is written both ways.)   Their third son, Samuel, Jr.,
was born April 13, 1752.   He married Olive Greene[5], [Ebenezer[4], Ebenezer[3],
John[2], John[1].]   As her grandmother was probably a Pierce, she was a cousin
on the Pierce side, and a very distant one on the Lascelle-Wardwell side.

Samuel and Olive lived mostly at Bristol, R. I.   Here she died, July
14, 1786, in child-bed, at 35 years of age.   The solid silver " name " spoon,
an heirloom in the family, was doubtless presented to an Ebenezer Caleb of
this family, who died young.   It was presented by Ebenezer Greene and
Caleb Hill, the one the brother of Olive, the other Samuel's great-uncle.   It
must always descend to an E. C. Pierce.   The only sons that survived were
Daniel, Caleb and Sanford.   The last was evidently named for their fast
friends, the Sanfords of Prudence Island.   Sanford married his distant
cousin, Molly King[6].   [Deborah Greene-King[5], James Greene[4], John[3], James[2],
John[1].]

Sanford[9] was the oldest child of Samuel Jr. and Olive Pierce.   He was
born May 10, 1773.   His wife, Molly King-Pierce, was two years his senior,
having been born June 29, 1771.   They were married in West Greenwich,
R. I., which was her home, probably about 1797.   What was known as the
Military Tracts of Northern New York had been thrown open to settlement
on advantageous terms.   After living in Mass. for about a year they went to
this region and settled in Onondaga County, in that part of Pompey afterwards called Fabius.   It had only been surveyed in 1794, and bears, panthers

---

* In some Indian uprising Daniel did service. He held the rank of Captain, and was noted for his
valor and successful stratagems against his wily foe. He was usually called Captain Daniel or Fighting
Captain Daniel. It is known that he followed the sea a part of his life, and the sobriquet of " Bo'sen
Dan'el" (Boatswain Daniel) was also much used of him.

and wolves abounded. Deer were so plentiful that the settlers had venison as commonly as we now have beef. Here they remained for 24 years, then removed to a new settlement just being made at Palermo, in Otsego County. Ebenezer, their " home son," having moved to Northern Indiana in 1837, Sanford and his wife went to him, and died at his home,—Mary (Molly) Sept. 9, 1838, and Sanford June 29, 1849.

Mary, the wife, was a slender, petite woman, with a fair, expressive face and beautiful eyes. She had the quick wit and bright way of her French grandmother, Marie La Valley-King. She had her supersensitive, nervous organization as well. A shock left a mental cloud for some years upon her in the latter part of her life.

Sanford and Mary had five children, all of whom lived to marry. Catherine remained in N. Y. The others all moved to La Grange Co., Indiana, and died there.

MARGARET PIERCE–MUNGER[7]. She was born in 1798, and married when but 16. Her husband was hunting, and while chasing a deer over Oneida Lake broke through the ice and was drowned, leaving Margaret a widow at 17. She was later married to Allen Munger. She died at Wolcottville, Indiana, in the " sickly year," Oct. 4, 1838, aged 40 years. Beside her own children she brought up Nancy Matteson, who married Ira Nichols.[7]

BETSEY MUNGER[8], m. Hiram Roberts.

Melissa Roberts—Smith[9], wife of John Smith. One daughter.

ALFRED MUNGER[8].

CATHERINE MUNGER[8], m. Sanderson Eastlake.

SAMUEL PIERCE[7]. There is not a sadder page in this book, than of this man's history. He was a young man of promise, good-looking, upright, and exceedingly ambitious and proud. He married a young and pretty girl, Mary Andrews. Before her oldest son was born, she sank into a mental imbecility that lasted her life. People did not understand the laws of heredity in those days, or realize the curse in her blood to the offspring of an unfit mother. The children kept coming until there were six, every one of whom was a degenerate. Samuel Pierce never held up his head again. He lost all ambition or care to live. He died in 1857, aged 57.

EBENEZER PIERCE[7]. He was born Oct. 19, 1801. He taught school at Pompey Hill, the winter he was 19. The next spring the family moved to what is now Palermo, then an unbroken forest.* Dec. 29, 1821, he was one of the principals to a double wedding, when Rachel McQueen became his wife, and his sister Catherine became the wife of Ephraim McQueen. Four children were born to them in their little cabin in the clearing, Polly (Mary),

* His mother, Mrs. Pierce, rode on horseback, with a feather bed tied on behind her and carrying a baby in her arms. It was hardly as stylish a mode of traveling as a modern automobile jaunt, but it answered all purposes then.

Seymour, Atelia and Clark. Mrs. Rachel Pierce died Sept. 15, 1832, in her 31st year.

His second wife was Julia Arabella Collins, who was born May 26, 1816, in Windham Co., Vermont. She outlived her husband nearly thirty-eight years, dying in Saratoga Springs, N. Y., Oct. 26, 1902, in her 87th year. She was more than an ordinarily capable woman, level-headed and energetic always. She was a capital hand at rehearsing stories of pioneer life. It was as good as a novel to hear her relate, when the western fever attacked her husband, how in 1837 they made the overland trip from N. Y. to Northern Indiana, with some other families. They were seven weeks on the road. There were twenty-six in the company, three of them babes under three months old. On the way, sixteen of the twenty-six came down with the measles, to say nothing of a score of other haps and ills.

A log house was hastily built in the deep woods. Here this girlish wife watched over the brood of six little ones, and quaked in her shoes each time an Indian showed his dusky face. One time Schomack, the old Pottowatamie Chief, grunted and patted Mrs. Julia on the shoulder, patronizingly complimenting her to her husband by repeating, " Nice squaw ! nice squaw ! "

Once when Eben—the name her husband usually was called—was away from home, six Indians stalked into the house. They helped themselves to the bread in the bake-oven, and as they were not given anything else one of them shook his fist in the young wife's face. She expected to be killed, but he made signs they would leave if she would give them what they took to be a piece of dried venison. She gave it to them. The first to taste it made a horrible face, while the others burst forth into derisive hoots. The supposed venison was dried beef's gall, about the bitterest thing on the face of the earth.

Eben Pierce was a man of sound judgment and irreproachable life. He died of small-pox Jan. 20, 1865, at his home near Wolcottville, Indiana. His descendants by his first wife are these:

POLLY PIERCE-JENNINGS[8]. Born Feb. 16, 1824, in N. Y. Died in Indiana, March 4, 1853. She was married to Orville Jennings, Oct. 8, 1848.

H. Seymour Jennings[9].

H. SEYMOUR PIERCE[8]. Born Sept. 19, 1828, and died Aug. 15, 1838.

ATELIA PIERCE-WATSON[8]. Born July 26, 1830 ; m. March, 1852, to Anthony Watson. She died in Indiana, Dec. 17, 1854, aged 24.

EBENEZER CLARK PIERCE[8]. He is always called Clark. No one stands higher in the community than he. Like all of his family, he is a Baptist. He is a successful man, has been a farmer, but now lives in Wolcottville, Indiana. He was born Nov. 15, 1831, at Palermo, N. Y. He was married March 2, 1856, to Christine Raber, who was born in Summit Co., Ohio. By her he had five children. She died May 13, 1370. His second wife was Mrs. Margaret Lukins, who lived but a few months after their marriage. Aug. 4, 1874, he married Sarah Jane Snyder, who was born in Wayne Co., Ohio, in 1845. They have had seven children :

Frank H. Pierce[9], b. Dec. 22, 1856; m. in 1886 to Florence Selby. They live in N. D. and have one daughter, Arabelle.

Ida O. Pierce[9], b. July 31, 1859; d. Feb. 17, 1864.

Atelia M. Pierce-Diggins[9], (called Tillie), b. Feb. 10, 1862: m. to William Diggins, Oct., 1886.

Frank Diggins[10].

Harold Diggins[10].

Owen E. C. Pierce[9], b. June 15, 1865; m. Maria Weatherwax, Dec., 1887.

Claud Pierce[10].

Elsie A. Pierce[9], b. July 20, 1867; d. Sept. 19, 1870.

By his last wife Clark has these children:

Merritt Pierce[9], b. May 21, 1875.   He m. his third cousin, Emma E. Nichols July 29, 1896.   He is a teacher, as was also his wife.

Marjorie Elide Pierce[10], b. ——— 1897.

Jay Pierce[9], b. Jan. 3, 1877; m. Ella Lamp, Nov., 1900.

Harold Pierce[10].

Winnafred Pierce[10].

Flora Belle Pierce-Diggins[9], b. March 9, 1879; m. to Geo. F. Diggins, Dec. 18, 1901.

Lora Dell Pierce[9], twin of Flora.   M. to Chas. Myers, March 18, 1903.

Charles Pierce[9], b. Feb. 24, 1881; d. March 23, 1883.

Frederick Pierce[9], b. March 17, 1885; d. Sept., 1887.

Pansy Pierce[9], b. April 6, 1887.

By his second wife, Julia A. Collins, Eben Pierce had these children:

JOSEPH ANSEL PIERCE[8], usually called by his second name, was born Nov. 24, 1833. He was married (1) in 1856 to Eliza J. Hoard, who died in 1870. M. (2) to Lucy Shafner, in 1878, and (3) to Lucinda Stockwell, in 1893. He is now living at Fowler, Ill.

Emily L. Pierce[9], b. Nov. 25, 1857. D. at 7.

Charlotte E. Pierce-Dossa[9], b. Nov. 23, 1859.   Married Frank O. Dossa in Dec. 1875. They have Florence, Lafayette, Ansel and Dota.

William Wallace Pierce[9], b. June 5, 1862.   Married Rose Ette Fleharty, May 12, 1883.   He is in the real estate and insurance business at Wetumka, Ind. Territory.

Myrtle Belle Pierce[10], b. Oct. 13, 1884; d. at 5 years.

Flossie Dell Pierce[10], b. Aug. 26, 1886; d. in her fourth year.

Bertha Floyce Pierce[10], b. Aug. 30, 1895.

Wallace Ross Pierce[10], b. Aug. 10, 1900.

George L. Pierce[9], b. Aug. 9, 1865.   Married April, 1887, to Belle Squires. Their son, Vernon L., was born in Jan. 1889. George L. the father, d. Nov. 30, 1900, and his wife died the next month.

Belle M. Pierce-Aron[9], b. Oct. 1867; m. to Chas. Aron, July, 1888.   They have 4 children.

Florence O. Pierce-Morrell[9], b. Oct., 1869.   She m. Frank Morrell in Sept., 1901. She died in April, 1903. No children.

By the second wife were these children:

Oliver W. Pierce[9], b. Feb. 24, 1879.

Loretta U. Pierce-Harger[9], b. March 1, 1882, and m. in Feb., 1901, to Howard Harger. She has 2 daughters.

Daisy O. Pierce-Sawyer[9], b. Aug. 11, 1883, and m. to Noah Sawyer in June, 1900. She has 2 sons.

By the third wife there was another son Loron L. Pierce[9], born Aug. 30, 1895. The wife died 5 months after, Jan. 17, 1896.

REV. FRANCIS EDWIN PIERCE[8].   He was born March 3, 1837, in N. Y. He was married to Eliza Maria Nash, Jan. 5, 1860, at Kendallville, Ind. Miss Nash was the daughter of Col. John and Catherine Wolcott--Nash, and was born in Middleburg, Ohio, Aug. 5, 1840. She was lineally descended from the two famous Connecticut governors, Roger and Oliver Wolcott, and from Oliver Wolcott, Senior, a Signer of the Declaration of Independence. To Frank and Eliza were born eight children. Mrs. Eliza Pierce died in Benton County, Indiana, Nov. 3, 1884.

Rev. Frank Pierce was married secondly to Eliza Lardner, daughter of John and Eliza Ralph-Lardner. She was born in London, England, Feb. 16, 1849, and came with her parents to the United States in 1850.

Rev. Frank was ordained a Baptist minister in 1869, and preached for some years in Indiana and Vermont. Is not now in charge of any work, although he occasionally preaches. His home is at Ellendale, North Dakota. None of his children live there. "It almost takes a state for a child," as their father says, as they are scattered in Indiana, Ohio, Iowa, Minn., and S. Dakota. His children are :

Infant son[9], b. Nov. 22, 1860, and died Dec. 11, 1860.

Lida Adell Pierce-Rank[9], b. Sept. 22, 1864. She was married to H. C. Rank Aug. 27, 1885. He is the County Auditor of Benton Co., Indiana.

> Edith Lucile Rank[10], b. June 24, 1889 ; d. 1894
>
> Helen Mignon Rank[10], b. June 24, 1894.
>
> Harold Leo Rank[10], b. Sept. 17. 1898.

Flora Emma Pierce-Graves[9], b. Jan. 22, 1867 ; m. to Rev. James Wesley Graves, July 25, 1892. He is the pastor of the First Baptist Church of Waverly, Iowa.

> Ruth Vivian Graves,[10], b. Nov. 27, 1893.
>
> Esther Bernice Graves[10], b. Sept. 16, 1896.
>
> Thelma Blanche Graves[10], b. Sept. 14, 1897.

Clark Edwin Pierce[9], b. June 24, 1869 ; and m. to Etta M. Young, Feb. 19, 1891. He is a farmer, and lives near Wentworth, S. Dakota.

> Rexford Vernon Pierce[10], b. Oct. 8, 1892.
>
> Raymond Ralph Pierce[10], b. March 1, 1896.
>
> Ethel Muriel Pierce[10], b. Sept. 2, 1897
>
> Melvin Leo Pierce[10], b. April 19, 1899 ; d. April 11, 1900.
>
> Francis Milton Pierce[10], b. Sept. 5, 1901.
>
> Ruth Mildred Pierce[10], b Dec. 17, 1902.

Fannie Ina Pierce-Hard[9], b. May 24, 1871 ; m. to A. C. Hard M. D., Feb. 25, 1893. They reside at Worthington, Minn.

> Walter Hard[10], b. Jan., 1896, d. at two months.
>
> Arthur Hard[10], b. July, 1902.

Ruth Eveline Pierce-Crigler[9], b. May 10, 1873 ; m. to Le Roy Crigler. April 27, 1896. He is an artist and printer at Columbus, O.

Francis Elbert Pierce[9], b. Dec. 5, 1877 ; m. Edith May Constable, Nov. 29, 1892. He is a graduate pharmacist, located at Goodland, Indiana.

Bernice Ethel Pierce-Wedgewood[9], b. April 24, 1881 ; m. to Eugene Howard Wedgewood, Feb. 14, 1901. He is a farmer, living near Trent, South Dakota.

FLORA A. FIDELIA PIERCE-LEONARD–HARRIS[8]. She was born near Wolcottville, Indiana, Sept. 30, 1841. At 20 she was married to David Pitt Leonard, Nov. 9, 1861, and immediately went to West Dover, Vermont, where they lived for 24 years. Pitt Leonard was the son of Rev. Daniel and Sally Maria Leonard. He was universally well spoken of, and was a leader in his community. He died in 188-. Two children were born to this union. Flora married for her second husband, Elder Clark Harris, an elderly gentleman of the highest standing. He had been an acceptable officer of the M. E. Church for over 40 years. After this marriage they resided in Saratoga Springs, N. Y., where he had capital invested in city real estate. He died April 10, 1898, aged 84 years. The widow yet lives in Saratoga, a quiet unassuming woman of real worth and kindliness of heart.

Francis Pierce Leonard[9], b. Nov. 3, 1862. At 16 he entered the Wilmington (Vt.) Savings Bank. He was for three years Manager of the State Life Insurance Co. of

Chicago. He also graduated from the Law School of the State University of Minnesota. With the exception of those years, he has spent all his life in the banking business. He has been for many years the Receiving Teller of the Farmers and Mechanics Savings Bank of Minneapolis, Minn., said to have the largest capital of any bank west of Rochester, N. Y. He resides at 3300 Tenth Avenue, S. Minneapolis. He married Emogene Perry of West Wardsboro, Vt., Nov. 16, 1886.

F. Perry Leonard[10], b. Sept. 18, 1887.

Gladys Leonard[10], b. Nov. 15, 1888.

Faith Leonard[10], b. March 11, 1890.

Harry Wentworth Leonard[9], b. Aug. 2, 1867, in West Dover, Vt. March 16, 1893 he married in Albany, N. Y., Mae Agnes Lantz, the daughter of Levi S. and Sarah J. Leinbach-Lantz, who was born in Burlington, Michigan. They live in Saratoga Springs, N. Y., but his place of business is in Schenectady, N. Y. He is a member of the firm of Van Voast & Leonard, General Insurance Agents, and is a successful business man.

FAYETTE JUDSON PIERCE[8]. B. Dec. 22, 1845, and d. Jan. 1, 1846.

MARIA E. PIERCE[8]. Born Feb. 6, 1850; d. Aug. 8, 1851. She was accidentally killed by being dropped from the arms of a playmate who was visiting the older children.

SOPHIA ARABELLA PIERCE-ESTABROOK[8]. She is known in the family as Belle. She was born Nov. 9, 1853, near Wolcottville, Indiana. The Pierce daughters were usually belles. None more so than this youngest child of Ebenezer's, vivacious, witty, and gifted in music and song. She married Taylor S. Estabrook, Aug. 22, 1871, at Wilmington, Vt.

Taylor Snead Estabrook was born May 31, 1847, in West Dover, Vermont. His family is an old New England one, and he himself was a lineal descendant from one of the minute men killed at Lexington, April 19, 1775. Few men made as many friends and as few enemies. All his life he was a man who dared to reach out. At nineteen, he learned the baker's trade in Baltimore, Maryland, and in a year's time was conducting for himself the largest wholesale bakery in the city. After various experiences in 1881, he came to Saratoga Springs. At this fashionable summer resort he kept a summer hotel. During the winter season he conducted college halls where hundreds of students were cared for, first at Trinity College, Hartford, Conn., and then at Cornell University, Ithica, N. Y. Mr. Estabrook always had crowded houses, although he never sacrificed for one moment his Christian principles. He never attended the races, never allowed a bar in one of his houses, and never suffered wine or brandy to be used in his kitchens in sauces or other cooking. He died Oct. 4, 1903, and is buried in Greenridge Cemetery, Saratoga Springs, N. Y.

Mrs. Estabrook takes a deep interest in historical and genealogical matters, and helped to prepare the Estabrook Genealogy. She has supplied much data for this chapter, and I regret that her well-written "Sketches of Pioneer Life and Pioneer Experiences," describing the early days of the family, could not appear because of lack of room.

Lula Belle Estabrook,- b. in Wolcottville Indiana, Aug. 31, 1873. She is an artist in oils, pastel and water colors, and also teaches in the city schools.

Harold Pitt Estabrook[9], b. in West Dover, Vt., June 29, 1876. He is an electrical draughtsman, and also an artist in crayon. Lives with his mother at Saratoga Spring, N. Y.

Leo Taylor Estabrook[9], b. at Saratoga, N. Y. Jan. 13, 1884. Is now in the Baltimore Medical College, preparing himself for his specialty of surgery.

CATHERINE PIERCE–McQUEEN[7]. She was born at Fabius, N. Y., March 24, 1805. She was married to Ephraim McQueen, Dec. 29, 1821, at Palermo, N. Y., at the same time that her brother Eben married Rachel McQueen, sister of Ephraim. This was a most happy marriage. Her husband never tired of telling of his courtship. Ephraim, son of James McQueen, came among the very first to the new lands thrown open to settlement. There was clearing and everything to do at once, and no time to build even a log cabin. He built a shack of boughs, or a brush wigwam. There was no door nor window, and to keep the wolves from coming in at the opening a fire of logs was kept burning all night. He was standing at the front of this shack, almost unmanned by homesickness, when a party of movers passed by. There was a trim-built, comely girl among them, this very Catherine, so petite that she weighed but 90 pounds. As she passed the forlorn figure by the shack she gave him an arch smile, and he fell in love with her on the spot. No more homesickness then. The Pierces located two miles away, and he made his way often through the gloomy woods to her father's door. One night he was followed by a wild beast, a bear or panther, nearly the whole distance.

Eight children were born to this pioneer couple. The household increased, in fact, faster than their table lengthened, and there came a time when they all had to stand up to their meals to get around the table, and their elbows touched. The farm, opened up under such difficulties, became a good possession eventually. Catherine was all energy. She was an expert weaver, and sold much cloth, sometimes 200 yards at a time of her own weaving. She delighted in old keepsakes, and to her was given the china of her grandmother, Olive Pierce, and the teapot that was purchased for her great-grandmother, Hester Pierce, in 1746. Doubtless Hester was proud of it. When the British burned their homes over their heads she saved this teapot. The dress and bonnet she wore were also preserved, and fell to Catherine's share of keepsakes. They are treasured highly by her descendants. Catherine died April 30, 1870. Her husband held the rank of Captain in the State militia. He died Aug. 22, 1883.

STEPHEN PIERCE McQUEEN[8]. Born April 29, 1825 ; d. Jan. 8. 1826.

MARGARET McQUEEN[8]. Born August 5, 1827; d. Sept. 11, 1829.

SANFORD McQUEEN[8]. Born Oct. 5, 1830. The 10th of May, 1863, he married Mrs. Lucy Jennings. His wife died July 7, 1873. Sanford is a farmer, and lives on the old homestead.

EMERY WILSON McQUEEN[8]. Born Aug. 16, 1833. He married Emma J. Thomas, Feb. 19, 1873. He is living at Obi, N. Y.

Lida May McQueen-Lewis[9], b. July 4. 1874, and m. to Linn A. Lewis, Nov. 11, 1891. They live at Obi, N. Y.

Burdette Wilson Lewis[10], b. June 3, 1894 ; d. at 9 months.

Leo Lyle Lewis[10], b. Aug. 16, 1897.

Clifford Leroy Lewis[10], b. Nov. 16, 1899.

Orla Seymour McQueen[9], b. Jan. 11, 1886.

Leon Ephraim McQueen[8], b. Nov. 28, 1891.

JAMES McQUEEN[8]. Born Nov. 5, 1836. Married Mary E. Preston, March 28, 1872. Enlisted in the 136th N. Y. Volunteers in the Civil War, but was rejected because of lung trouble.

Howard Preston McQueen[9]. b. Nov. 3, 1877 ; d. 1901.

Jennie Lilian McQueen-Burdick[9], b. June 17, 1884 ; m. to Horace Burdick, Sept. 25, 1901, at Palermo, N. Y.

Ella Marion Burdick[10], b. Jan. 18, 1903.

CATHERINE McQUEEN-SCUDDER-WELLWOOD[8]. She was born July 30, 1838. Married Orrillus Scudder, June 9, 1861. He served three years in Co. E., 110th Regiment, N. Y. Volunteers, in the Civil War. He died May 16, 1861. She married (2) Dr. James J. Wellwood, and lives at Wellwood, N. Y. She is again a widow.

OSCAR McQUEEN[8], Born June 14, 1841 He married Mrs. Harriet Storer-Jennings, the window of Mashall Jennings, Nov. 28. 1871. He is now living on the old homestead. Oscar enlisted in Co. F., 147th Reg't, N. Y. Volunteers, Aug. 23, 1862. He was taken ill while helping to defend Washington, and after being in the hospital for months, was discharged Feb. 6, 1863, for physical disability.

Frederick Ephraim McQueen[9], b. Feb. 27, 1873. He was married to Luna A. Whitney, Oct. 16, 1895. He lives at Syracuse, N. Y., and is a R. R. Postal Clerk on the N. Y. Central.

George Oscar McQueen[10], b. Oct. 30, 1897.

Lida Ellen McQueen[10], b. Feb. 12, 1901.

Clara Jane McQueen-Sheldon[9], b. Sept. 28, 1876. She was married to Burke J. Sheldon, March 17, 1897. Living at Schroepple, N. Y., on a farm.

Harold Sheldon[10], b. May 30, 1899.

Fred Josiah Sheldon[10], b. July 9, 1901.

Frank Pierce Sheldon[10], b. Aug. 3, 1903.

HENRY SEYMOUR McQUEEN[8]. Born April 21, 1844. He married Almira Hoyt, April 2, 1873. He is a farmer and lives in Palermo, N. Y.

CAPTAIN STEPHEN KING PIERCE[7]. He was born July 21, 1807, near old Pompey, N. Y. He was of a peculiar temperament, dreamy and retrospective. Yet as a young man he showed the full fire and vivacity of his race. He was a dashing young Lieutenant in one of the Indian wars. While doing garrison duty, in an emergency he performed a high officer's part, and for this act was promoted to a captaincy. His sword that he carried at that time is now in possession of his son Amasa.

Stephen's first wife was Mehitable Bellows. She was of a delicate, blonde type, sweet and gentle in all her ways. Stephen simply worshiped his fragile little wife. When the doctor told him that the only chance for her life was a change of climate, he started with her to Northern Indiana, that had then just been thrown open for settlement. A log cabin was hastily built. It was forty miles to the nearest pane of glass, or even a nail. The cabin had neither window or door that winter. An aperture in the the logs admitted light, and a heavy blanket was hung over the opening left for a door.

Late in the winter the wife took to her bed. The author's own father, Nelson Nichols, sat up with her one night until late. He started homeward, carrying his gun with him on account of the danger of panthers or wild-cats. A pack of wolves took after him, and though he made all possible speed, were soon snarling at his heels. He used up all his shots, and brained the next wolf to reach him with the butt of his gun. He had given himself up for lost, when a light blazed out, and the wolves sulked away. His young wife, hearing the shots, threw aside the blanket that darkened the door, and the

REV. DE WITT M. PIERCE AND WIFE
OF NESBIT, OKLAHOMA

sudden blaze of light was all that saved him. Such were the perils of those early days.

Mehitable died May 20, 1837, aged 25 years. All the neighborhood for miles around attended the funeral, and they numbered just—seven—adults! Hers was the first white person's death in what is now LaGrange County, Indiana. She was buried on her husband's farm, in what was afterwards the Pierce Cemetery. Her death was a blow from which Stephen never rallied. He was a changed man ever after. On his wedding day he had worn a fine broadcloth suit, and a tall, bell-crowned beaver hat, then considered the height of elegance. He declared that this suit and hat, that he had first worn on the happiest day of his life, he would always wear as his Sunday's best, in honor of his wife's memory. Forty-two years he kept that vow. I can remember seeing him, with his patriarchal white locks covered by the quaint high hat, and his spare form clothed by the carefully preserved suit of antiquated cut. He asked to be buried in those clothes, and his wish was granted. He died April 2, 1880, in his seventy-third year.

Stephen's second wife was Pamelia Burr Olds. They were married in 1838. She was the type of a strong, courageous New England woman, conscientious and hardworking. She could never, however, overcome his melancholy. She died in 1890, aged 76.

Stephen had one son by his first wife, Fernando C. He was romantic and headstrong, and ran away in boyhood to see more of the world. In 1865 he suddenly appeared, quite as the hero of the old novel used to do, with gold in his purse, and a belt of gold around his waist, and a story of years spent in Central America and on the Pacific Coast. He had just sold a mine in Idaho for the gold he brought with him. He spent his money generously, enjoyed a visit with the home friends, then passed on to Missouri. He made bad investments, and in seven years time was working as a day laborer. His wife, Emma Johnson of Missouri, died leaving him two children, Viola Maud and Julian Stephen. Fernando then went to California, and from that time to this has never been heard from.

The children and grandchildren of Stephen and Pamelia Pierce are as follows :

REV. DeWITT M. PIERCE[8]. He was born Nov. 27, 1843, and married Christina Bassler in November, 1867. Mrs. Pierce was born in Germany in 1850, and came to America when three years old. The father and mother always lived with DeWitt. Sometime after his father's death he went west, and entered the ministry. He is now located near Kingfisher, Oklahoma, where he owns a quarter section of land. He takes a great interest in genealogy, and has helped much in data for this chapter.

Gertrude Evalinda Pierce-Hays[9], b. Oct. 4, 1868. Her husband is William Hays. They live in Kingman, Kansas.

Walter Scott Pierce[9], b. Aug. 20, 1870. M. Maud Collins. They live in Kansas City, Mo.

Wellington Gladstone Pierce[10], b. Oct. 4, 1898.

Hortense Imogen Pierce-Cochrane[9], b. July 18, 1872. She is the wife of William Cochrane, and their home is at Kingfisher, Oklahoma.

Dwight Upton Cochrane[10], b. April 26, 1900.

Carl Jay Pierce[9], b. in July, 1874. Married Minnie E. Snodgrass, Sept. 3, 1902.

Lura Viola Pierce-Hollar[9], b. Jan. 9, 1877. M. to Charles B. Hollar, of Claude, Oklahoma.

Hays Hollar[10], b. Dec. 6, 1898.

Christine Hollar[10], b. Aug. 9, 1900.

Marian Jane Pierce-Dahe[9], b. March 8, 1879. M. to Henry H. Dahe, of Okeene, Oklahoma. Mr. Dahe is a native of Germany.

Paul Arthur Dahe[10], b. Aug. 1, 1899 ; d. young.

Clarence Russell Dahe[10], b. Feb. 9, 1901.

Earl Adella Pierce[9], b. Feb. 27, 1881.

John Stephen Pierce[9], b. March 3, 1884.

Ralph Clay Pierce[9], b. Sept. 11, 1887.

Olive Elsie Pierce[9], b. Dec 11, 1889 ; d. young.

Elmer Le Roy Pierce[9], b. May 7, 1891.

ORRIL PIERCE--SCHOFIELD[8]. She was born near Wolcottville, Indiana, in 1845, and married to Joseph Schofield, May 12, 1870. Her home is in Hammond, Indiana. She has had 8 children, all of whom are living.

Minnie May Schofield--Ray[9], b. Feb. 18, 1871 ; m. to Thomas Ray, July 3, 1891.

Alvin Ray[10], b. July 26, 1894.

Walter Ray[10], b. March 20, 1897.

Leon Ray[10], Oct. 17, 1900 ; d. Feb. 3, 1902.

John Pierce Schofield[9], b. May 16, 1873.

Charles Henry Schofield[9], b. March 20, 1875 ; m. Annie Custy, Jan. 11, 1902.

Clara Jane Schofield--Rhodes[9], b. April 27, 1877; m. to Peter Rhodes, Dec. 31, 1899

Ralph Emerson Rhodes[10], b. Sept. 16, 1900.

Roy Cecil Rhodes[10], b. June 11, 1902.

Bertha Victoria Schofield-Veach[9], b. Aug. 3 1879 ; m. to Henry Veach, Jan. 22, 1903.

Grace Myrtle Schofield[9] b. Aug. 7, 1881.

George Washington Schofield[9], b. Dec. 20, 1883.

Elmer Ellsworth Schofield[9], b. April 1, 1887.

AMOS PIERCE[8], a twin. Born July 3, 1848. He served in the Civil War. Is married and living somewhere in Missouri. He is said to be doing well.

AMASA PIERCE[8], a twin brother to Amos. He went to Minnesota about 1876. July 3, 1877, he married Martha, the daughter of Henry and Lucinda Stanley-McKibben. Two of her double cousins married relatives of Amasa's. Martha is of the Jennings-Stanley family of Illinois, from which William Jennings Bryan also sprang. They live at Butler, Minnesota.

Evangeline J. Pierce-Thompson[9], b. June 5, 1878 , m. to Persia B. Thompson, Oct. 13, 1898.

Jefferson Thompson[10], b. Sept. 10, 1901.

Leona M. Pierce[9], b. 1886 ; d. 1888.

Elna M. Pierce-Reeser[9], b. Oct. 11, 1881 ; m. to William Reeser.

Pamelia Lucinda Pierce[9], b. Nov. 29, 1883. Is a teacher.

Archibald J. Pierce[9], b. Oct. 11, 1885.

Elsie M. Pierce[9], b. Oct. 20, 1887.

Minnie V. Pierce[9], b. Sept. 18, 1889.

Infant son, still-born, July 29, 1891.

Stella L. Pierce[9], b. Nov. 5, 1892.

Frank S. Pierce[9], b. Dec. 18, 1896.

CHAPTER XXV

DESCENDANTS OF ELIZABETH KING–KITTELLE[6]

FAMILY TREES   For descent from the first Lord de Greene de Boke-ton, A. D. 1202, and from the Capet royal line, A D 861, see Chapter XI.

For their lineage from John Greene of Quidnessett, together with that from Capt Straight, Elder Obediah Holmes, Stukeley Westcott and Hugh Parsons, see Chapter XX.

For their descent from John King and Peter La Valley, see Chapter XXII

Elizabeth King-Kittelle[6] was the fourth daughter of Samuel and Deborah Greene-King[5]. She was born about the close of the year 1771 and married about 1800 to her cousin, her aunt Dinah Greene-Kittle's son, James Kittle The family now write it Kittelle or Kettelle.   The name is an old British one   It is a place name, denoting that the first name-bearer lived by a river kittle, i. e , a wier or fish-trap   The family tradition is that the family came from England after 1700   But I find this peculiar name before 1650 among the Massachusetts colonists.   It is probably the same family.   It is usual for a few generations to be dropped in traditions.

We know little of these cousins   James was a farmer   His wife Eliza-beth is yet remembered for her serenity and goodness   They had five child-ren   Their daughter Roby never married, nor did their only son, Anthony. Their descendants are all from Hannah, Olive, or Deborah   Elizabeth died Dec. 10, 1838, and her husband some 13 years later

HANNAH KITTELLE-HARRINGTON[7], b Oct 11, 1801 , d Dec. 27, 1843   She m Daniel Harrington, who outlived her 29 years   He was born Dec. 28, 1801, and was the son of Job and Mereba Harrington, and grandson of Job Harrington, Senior, an old friend and next neighbor of Magdalen King's in West Greenwich. Job Harrington, Senior, was himself the son of a still older Job   The Harringtons are from a centuries-old English family, the heads of which bore high titles.   Hannah and Daniel lost two small children who are not enumerated

CARMI HARRINGTON[8], b. Nov. 23, 1822; d. June 17, 1887. He m. Lydia Coggeshall of Middleton. The Coggeshalls came for religious liberty to R. I. at the time Mrs. Anne Hutchinson was expelled from Mass. for heresy. They helped to found Portsmouth in 1638. One of this family, John Coggeshall, the first President of the Colony, died in office in 1648 ; and Joshua, his son, was one of the three founders of the Friends in R. I.

     John L. C. Harrington[9], b. July 22, 1858 ; m. in 1880 to Ella Borden of Middletown. The Bordens were cotemporaries of the Coggeshalls, and very prominent people indeed in the pioneer days of R. I. John and Ella have Erma Rebecca, born June 12, 1881, and lost a son, John William, who was younger.

NANCY HARRINGTON–ALBRO[8], b. Aug. 22, 1824 ; d. March 8, 1866. She m. H. Green Albro. He was descended from " Quaker" John Alborough or Albro, one of the earliest R. I. refugees for religious faith.

     Alanson Albro[9],* m. his fourth cousin, Eva Capwell, daughter of Searles and Susan Capwell. [Eva[9], Susan[8], of James Greene[7], James[6], Abel[5], James[4], John of Bristol[3], Lieut. James[2], John Greene of Quidnessett[1].] They have 6 children.
     Stephen Albro[9].

DANIEL HARRINGTON[8] b. Sept. 27 1834 ; d. Oct. 14, 1895. He m. Sarah A. Spink, Oct. 10, 1852. She was descended from Robert Spink, first of Allerton and later of Quidnessett, more than 200 years ago. Daniel and Sarah had a large family, four of whom were born dead, and two others of whom died before they were grown. I give the adult children only. This family lived for some years in Pa. then removed to Kansas.

     Ida Harrington–Stauffer[9], b. Nov. 7, 1855 ; m. Robert Stauffer in 1880. No children.
     Hannah Harrington–Sharits[9], b. June 13, 1858 ; m. William Sharits in 1886. They have Kika, Oakley Brown, and Bonnie.
     Nellie E. Harrington–Smith[9], b. June 13, 1863 ; m. James Smith in 1886. They have a son, Roscoe Lectis.
     Lucia Harrington–Mercer[9], b. Aug. 2. 1866 ; m. Joseph Mercer in 1885. They have Robert Earl, William Dwight, Gladys, Burnett, Margaret and Joseph Daniel.
     Addie A. Harrington–Grubb[9], b. Jan. 24, 1868 ; m. Charles Grubb in 1887. Their son is Albert Roy.
     William D. Harrington[9], b. Jan. 2. 1873 ; m. Emily H. Lee in 1896. They have Raymond, Rosa Pearl and Lawrence Edwin.

ANTHONY KITTELLE[7], the only son of James and Elizabeth, died unmarried.

ROBY KITTELLE[7], b. April 11, 1807; died at 72, unmarried.

OLIVE KITTELLE–MATTESON[7], b. Aug. 16, 1810; d. Feb. 20, 1857. She married her cousin's son, John Weaver Matteson[8]. His mother was Ruth Howard–Matteson[7]. Her line merges with his, and will be found in Chapter XXVII.

DEBORAH KITTELLE-FIELD[7], of James and Elizabeth Kittelle, b. July 27, 1812 ; d. in 1878. She was the wife of Albert S. Field, of Providence, R. I.

     SARAH W. FIELD[8], 1841-1855. Died at 14.
     ALFRED F. Field[8]. b. Aug. 11, 1842 ; m. Mary E. Kenyon. They had Sara, who d. at 25 ; Minnie G., who d. at 23 ; and Albert K., who d. at 2 ; besides these :
         Marion Deborah Field-Hobart[9], b. April 21, 1871, wife of William H. Hobart, Their child is Helen Marion.
         Albert Searles Field[9], b. June 25, 1875.

This is given also as Alphonse.

JENNIE E. FIELD—JOHNSON[8], of Deborah[7]. Wife of Thomas J. Johnson of Dwight, Ill. She is now a widow. Mr. and Mrs. Johnson lost their first child, Byron Love, at four. Other children came to them until there were five, filling the house with their happy play and laughter. Dec. 1882, scarlet fever—that dread disease, of which the bare mention of the name makes a parent shudder—entered that home. Eight year old Herbert died on Dec. 12 ; 7-year old Byron on Dec. 20 ; little 4-years old Roscoe on Dec. 24 ; and 10-year old Irving, the oldest child, on Dec. 26. Every boy they had perished in two weeks, leaving only their little sister, Viola, born July 31, 1880.

CHAPTER XXVI

DESCENDANTS OF GEORGE KING[6]

FAMILY TREES. For the descent from Sir Alexander, first Lord de Greene de Boketon, A. D. 1202, and the descent from Robert the Strong, Duke de France, A. D. 861, see Chapter XI.

For their lineage from John Greene of Quidnessett, through James Greene[4], by their father, and through Martha Greene[4], by their mother; also their lineage from Capt. Thomas Straight, Stukeley Westcott, Elder Obediah Holmes and Hugh Parsons, see Chapter XX.

For their descent from John King and Peter La Valley, see Chapter XXII. For the mediaeval history of the Mattesons, see Appendix.

George King[6] was the fifth child and first son of Samuel and Deborah Greene-King[5]. He was born May 21, 1774, and died in 1833. He married his second cousin, Meriba Matteson, who was born April 25, 1779, and died in 1847. Meriba was of Greene descent, and also doubly descended from Henry Matteson, the Emigrant. Her Greene blood was of the same line as her husband's. His grandfather, James Greene[4], and her grandmother, Martha Greene[4], were brother and sister, children of John of Bristol, grandchildren of Lieut. James, and great-grandchildren of John Greene of Quidnessett.

Meriba's grandmother, Martha Greene[4], married Joseph Matteson, (see Chapter XX,) the son of Emigrant James Matteson. Their son was Ezekiel[5], and two of his daughters, this Meriba and her sister Esther, married sons of Samuel King. Their father, Ezekiel, married a wife of his own name, Rosanna Matteson, and her line was this: James, the father of the Mattesons, married Hannah, daughter of Hugh Parsons. Their next to the youngest son was Josiah, who married Rosanna, daughter of Zerubabel, granddaughter of Robert and great-grand-daughter of Stukeley Westcott, of whom Chapter VII tells. Their son, Josiah Jr., married Mercy Nichols, of Stephen Nichols. Their daughter Rosanna, named for her Westcott grandmother, married Ezekiel Matteson[5], and was the mother of Meriba.

178

Now as it happened, the Kings' grandfather, James Greene[4], married Elizabeth Straight, whose mother had been a Rosanna Westcott also, a daughter of Amos, and grand-daughter of Stukeley Westcott. So on that side George and Meribah were again related, being about fourth cousins to each other. They were again twice-over fourth cousins through their descent from Hugh Parsons. John Greene of Bristol's wife was a grand-daughter of his, and Joseph and Josiah Matteson, sons of the Emigrant, were grandsons also. Nothing pleases a Rhode Islander like being mixed up in a tangled relationship. These four-different-ways-related young people were considered as having done quite the proper thing to have made another cross in the relationship, to hand down to their children.

The peculiar name of Meribah was for a long time confined strictly to families descended from the Huguenot family of Lascelle, (see Appendix) whose foremother was Meribé. It was a favorite name with the Waites, Carrs, etc., of that blood. Meribah Matteson–King was a namesake of some of these, and so the quaint, centuries-old name became grafted into this family tree, to reappear in her namesakes.

George King lived and died at West Greenwich, on a farm adjoining that of the old family homestead, the Magdalen King farm where his father, Samuel King lived. They had seven children, 4 sons and 3 daughters. Celia's line went west ; Caleb's went to N. Y. The others remained in R. I.

DAVID KING[7], born July 23, 1802. He married his first cousin, Thankful Hopkins, the third child of Christopher and Dinah King–Hopkins[6]. She was born April 17, 1802. They were each about 20 when married. They had nine children, 4 sons and 5 daughters. They had few grand-children or great-grand-children. The name of King entirely lapsed in their successors.

SALLY A. KING–SWEET[8], b. April 29, 1823. M. Wm. Rhodes Sweet. Had 3 daughters and 2 sons. Mary became Mrs. George Brown. She is dead. John Sweet was twice married, and has two children, Mamie and Emma ; Eliza m. Lewis M. Hawkins. Both are dead, leaving no children.

DEBORAH KING[8]. Died young.

JOHN KING[8], b. Feb. 24, 1826. Died at 24.

AMANDA KING–TARBOX[8], b. March 29, 1828, m. David Tarbox, a distant relative. [David[8], Fones[7], Joseph[6], Lois Matteson–Tarbox[5], Martha Greene–Matteson[4], John Greene[3] of Bristol, Lieut. James[2], John Greene[1] of Quidnessett.] She died July 5, 1853, leaving Abbie A., who m. Hiram Peck, and had Sarah and Dora ; and Sarah J., who m. Robert Jackson, and had Grace, Thomas and Almyra, that lived.

ABBIE A. KING[8], b. July 3, 1829 ; d. single.

GEORGE KING[8]. Died young.

ANN ELIZA KING–FRANKLIN[8], b. April 21, 1834. M. Clark Franklin. Their son, John C. Franklin[9], m. his third cousin, Annie E. Howard. [Annie[9], John W[8], Ephraim[7], Hannah King–Howard[6], Deborah Greene–King[5] etc.] Mr. Franklin is a teacher.

Sarah Franklin[10], b. April 27, 1888.

Charles Sheldon Franklin[10], b. July 29, 1889.

CHARLES C. KING[8], born July, 1836. Died single.

RHODES A. KING[8], 1839-1892. M. Mary A. Hughes. No children.

JOHN KING[7]. Died young.

MARCY (MERCY) KING-BROMLEY[7] of George[6] of Deborah Greene–King[5]. She was born April 10, 1807; d. June 17, 1846. Married Roger Bromley in 1825. A few years after they were married, they lived for a time in N. Y. Bromley P. O. in that state is named after Mercy's husband. The first child died in infancy. The records of the others are as follows:

WILLIAM BROMLEY[8], b. 1831. He lives in Michigan. Nov. 25, 1855, he m. Caroline Latham, and has Lillian, b. in 1856, and Frank b. 1866.

MARY A. BROMLEY-HOWARD[8], b. 1835, and m. in 1855 to Charles D. Howard, of Mass. descent. His first American ancestor, John Howard, or Haward, or Hayward, as they spelled the name then, was a prôtege of Captain Miles Standish. The Howard family is a very old one, and was honorably distinguished more than 1,000 years ago. This branch of the family have a beautiful coat-of-arms. Mrs. Howard is a wide-awake woman, that takes an interest in the questions and reforms of the day. She is the mother of 8 children. Her home is in Pawtucket, R. I.

George B. Howard[9], b. 1856. Died young.

Charles W. Howard[9], b. July 24, 1858. He m. Hannah Greenhalgh. 1 daughter. Nellie E., b. July 31, 1884.

Julia Ida Howard--Redford[9], b. Oct. 26, 1864; married John Redford, Oct. 18, 1892. They have Grace H., b. 1894; Alice E., 1896; Ethel M., 1899; and twins, Bertha and Lucy, born Dec. 31, 1902.

Clara A. Howard--Marcroft[9], b. Oct. 12, 1863. She married Samuel Marcroft Nov. 1894. They have Howard K., b. 1896; the twins, Samuel D., and Charles D., 1898; Hazel, 1900; and Roy, 1901.

Mary Emma Howard[9], born March 10, 1860; Jennie F., born March 29, 1870; William Henry, b. March 12, 1872; and Franklin B. Howard, b. May 21, 1876, are none of them married in 1904.

JAMES BROMLEY[8], of Marcy King--Bromley[7], of George King[6], was born in 1837. He lives in Minnesota.

SARAH BROMLEY-ESTERBROOKS[8], (Marcy[7], George[6].). Wife of Edward Esterbrooks. 2 children, Nancy, born 1860, and Mary, born in 1864.

CHARLES BROMLEY[8], b. 1841. Married, but no children. Lives in Wisconsin.

ALONZO BROMLEY[8], b. 1843. He lives in Michigan. He has one son, Leslie, born in 1876.

JULIA BROMLEY-WHITTEMORE[8], 1845-1875. Wife of Gilbert Whittemore. No children.

SARAH KING-WINSOR[7], of George[6] of Deborah Greene–King[5]. B. May 9, 1811; d. in May, 1897. She m. Joseph Winsor in May, 1830. She was the mother of 7 children, 5 of whom died in infancy.

GEORGE E. WINSOR[8], b. May 2, 1831; m. Emeline A. Eddy in 1850. Their son Charles E., born 1851, and their daughter, Minnie A., born in 1864, never married. Their dau., Anna Cora, was born in 1862. She is the wife of Edward Gee, and has two children, Ethel and Helen.

SARAH WINSOR-ESTEN[8], b. Aug. 25, 1834; m. Leprelett Esten in 1855. 2 children, Charles and Florence died in childhood. Leprelett W., b. in 1856; m. Alice D. Bradford. No children. Walter K. Esten, b. 1868; m. Alice L. Whitehead. One child, Florence Gertrude, born 1903; Bertha F. Esten, born in 1871; m. William F. Marshall. They have Clinton E., born in 1892, and Helen E., in 1895.

WHIPPLE KING[7], of George[6], of Deborah Greene–King[5]. He was born June 9, 1813, and died Aug 29, 1903, in his 91st year. 3600 years ago,

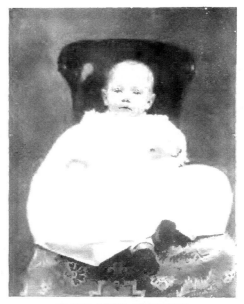

OF THE TENTH GENERATION
DAUGHTER OF WALTER K. AND ALICE ESTEN
B. SEP. 12, 1903

THE SITE OF THE OLD MAGDALEN-KING HOME, WHERE
GEORGE KING WAS BORN

FOUR GENERATIONS OF ONE FAMILY

Whipple King, b. June 9, 1813; J. W. P. King, his son, b.
Feb. 24, 1847; George W. King, grandson, b. May 19, 1867,
and George W. King, Jr., great-grandson, b. Feb. 25, 1899.

Joseph brought his father Jacob before Pharaoh. As that haughty king looked upon that head, blossomed white with time, and beheld his venerable countenance, he was moved, and said, "How old art thou?" There is indeed a gracious old age that singles out its possessor from other men.

No higher compliment can be paid to Whipple King than to say that he so shaped his life that 90 slow-rolling years but brought serenity to his countenance and fortitude to his soul. He was the patriarch of his clan, and the revered father-deacon of his church. His son's children's children looked up to "Big Grandpa" as their grown-up playmate. His son and his grandson looked to him for counsel. To the last he retained his interest in the world about him. He took much interest in The Greene Tree and its Branches, that he was destined never to see in print. Several times he dictated letters embodying his almost century-long recollections, and sent it to me to help over difficult portions of the book. He passed peacefully away after a short illness, on Aug 29th, 1903.

Whipple King was a farmer. He for a time lived in Onondaga Co., N. Y., and in Griswold, Conn. Afterwards he lived on what is known as the Passaquisett Brook Farm, not far from Kenyon, R. I. It was here that he died. He married Elizabeth, daughter of Luke Clark, of Richmond, R. I. She was 17 months younger than himself, but died some years first. They had but one son.

JOHN W. P. KING[8] was born Feb. 24, 1847. His wife was Harriet E. Tefft, daughter of Sprague and Eliza M. Tefft, whom he married in Griswold, Conn., Dec 7, 1865. She was born Jan. 31, 1845. They have three children. J. W. P. King taught school for 20 years. He is a director in two banks, but resides on his Passaquissett Brook farm, and considers himself first of all a farmer. Both he and his wife take a great interest in temperance work. He has been for years one of the State Prohibition Committeemen, and was their last candidate for State Treasurer. There was not the shadow of a chance of this party being elected, but he received a highly complimentary vote of over 1,600.

George Whipple King[9], of J. W. P. King[8], of Whipple[7], of George[6], b. May 19, 1867. He married Martha E., daughter of Capt. Thomas Saunders, Aug. 13, 1891. After his graduation, George King was for some years in the government service among the Indians. He is now an officer at the R. I. Reform School, at Howard, R. I. He is an expert amateur photographer. He photographed for this work the Huguenot graves in the old Magdalen King Cemetery. The little girl sitting between her great-great-great-great-grandparents' graves is Sarah, his second daughter.

Frances Elizabeth King[10], b. Aug. 9, 1892, at Klamath Indian Agency, Oregon.

Sarah Saunders King[10], b. June 9, 1895.

George W. King, Jr.[10], b. Feb. 25, 1899.

Ruth Elizabeth King–Earnshaw[9]. B. Feb. 19, 1872; dau. of J. W. P. King. She was married Aug. 1, 1896, to Oscar E. Earnshaw.

Eldred King Earnshaw[10], b. Oct. 1, 1898.

Joanna Reynolds King–Clark[9]. B. Sept. 28, 1873. She m. Thomas G. Clark, April 25, 1895.

Leon Whipple Clark[10], b. March 19, 1898.

Edith May Clark[10], b. March 16, 1899.

CELIA KING–KING[7], of George[6]. She married her double cousin, Thomas Matteson King[7], son of Joel and Esther Matteson–King. Her line is therefore merged into his. **See Chapter XXX.**

CALEB KING[7], of George[6], of Deborah Greene–King[5]. He was born Feb. 21, 1820. D. Feb. 22, 1863, aged 43. His son gives this biography: " In the month of Feb., 1838, Caleb King left his birthplace in West Greenwich, R. I., traveling 300 miles in mid-winter, with a horse drawing a sled made from green sapling poles. On his eighteenth birthday he arrived at his Uncle Joel King's in Pompey, N. Y." He married Elizabeth Bonat, or Bennett, as it is more commonly called. Her grandfather was John Bonat, who came from Germany. Her father, Peter Bonat, was a pioneer at Tully, N. Y. Peter's wife and Elizabeth's mother was a Van Patten of Holland extraction. They were long-lived, Elizabeth's grandmother Van Patten living to be 99. Caleb died on his farm near Tully. His wife outlived him ten years. They were Baptists, and gave liberally toward the erection of the Church at Vesper, N. Y. Five children lived to be grown.

GEORGE KING[8], of Caleb[7] of George[6], etc. B. April 27, 1846. He is a merchant at Borodino, N. Y., and at one time was Postmaster. Nov. 13, 1873, he married Dora S. Wright of Manlius, N. Y. They have one son, Wright R. King, who was born Sept. 24 1874. Wright was married in 1896 to Gertrude Taylor of Spafford, N. Y. They have no children. He is now engaged with his father in the mercantile business.

PETER B. KING[8], b. May 11, 1848; d. Dec. 6, 1870, aged 22 years.

JOEL KING[8], b. Jan. 31, 1850. Dec. 6, 1871, he m. Diana Evans of Cicero, N. Y They had Albert, Henry and Bertha E. This wife died in 1880. Joel m. (2) Mary E Northway, Dec. 3, 1881. They have William R., born March 29, 1883, and Grace E. b. Sept. 25, 1888.

Bertha E. King–Talmadge[9], b. Dec. 26, 1874, m. to Clarence Talmadge, June 24 1896. They live at Davenport Center, N. Y., and have Emие K., Clarence L. Mary Bernice, Clara Grace and Diana L.

SARAH M. KING–PARKERSON[8], of Caleb[7] of George[6]. She was born March 6, 1852. married Oct. 29, 1868, to Francis Marion Parkerson, and has been a widow since 1891. 7 children, all of whom live in N. Y.

Henry Marion Parkerson[9], b. July 30, 1870.

Emma Louise Parkerson–Holmes[9], b. Nov. 16, 1872. Is the widow of Leon V. Holmes. No children.

George Bennett Parkerson[9], b. Jan. 10, 1875, m. Edith E. Clark. Their children are Bernie Rosette and Marion Orson.

Maud Elizabeth Parkerson–Hughes[9], b. Dec. 28, 1877. Wife of Wm. James Hughes. They have one child Harold K.

Anna May Parkerson[9], b. May 15. 1879.

Arlie Starr Parkerson[9], b. Aug. 11. 1887.

Elsie Marion Parkerson[9], b. April 21, 1891, just one week before her father's death.

CALEB E. KING[8], of Caleb[7], of George[6], etc. He was b. Feb. 23, 1863. On his 24th birthday he married Mary E. Landphier of Scott, N. Y. She is descended from the Huguenot family of Lanphears of R. I., who came to the colony a few years prior to 1700, to escape religious persecution. He was a man much esteemed. He was a merchant at Borodino, N. Y., and served several years on the Board of Supervisors of Onondaga Co. He died suddenly while sitting in his office, April 2, 1901. Their son Clarence died in 1888, a small babe. Their other child, Ruth Elizabeth, was b. May 11, 1893.

CALEB E. KING. 1863–1902

Reproduced by permission from Supervisors' Journal for 1900. He was a member of the Board of Supervisors at his death

CHAPTER XXVII

FAMILY TREES. For descent from the first Lord de Greene de Boketon, A. D. 1202, and descent from the royal Capet line of France, A. D. 861, see Chapter XI.

For lineage from John Greene of Quidnessett, and from Capt. Straight, Stukeley Westcott, Elder Obediah Holmes and Hugh Parsons, see Chapter XX.

For descent from John King and Peter La Valley, see Chapter XXII.

Hannah King—Howard[9] was the sixth child and fifth daughter of Samuel and Deborah Greene-King[5]. She was born June 25, 1777, and d. April 6, 1831. Her husband, Capt. John Howard, was born July 27, 1773, and outlived her 14 years, dying May 28, 1845. In 1794, when he was 21 and she 17, they were married. In August of that year he bought a farm of his mother, and on this farm, a few miles out from Washington, R. I., they lived and died.

The Howards are a very old family. The family themselves are fond of claiming Hereward, the brave Saxon who took his stand on the Island of Ely, and was the last to surrender to William the Conqueror (1073), holding out seven years against him, as their ancestor. But he was only one of this tribe, not the founder. The Howards held the hereditary office of Hog Warden under the Saxon kings, who took pride and found profit in immense herds of swine that fattened on the acorn mast of the king's forest. These swine had to be herded, marked and ringed, killed and cured, and the meats disposed of. The officer who had the oversight of all this ranked high at the King's Court, the office itself corresponding somewhat to our President's Secretary of the Interior.

The English tongue of a thousand years ago made short work of Hog Warden. It became Ho-warden, then Hayward, and last of all, Howard. Historians write it Howard, as pronounced, but common usage in England, that even yet lingers in the "tight little isle," is to *spell* it Hereward, Hayward and Haward, but to speak of it as Howard. It is the survival of the spelling of the name when is was yet called Haward and Hayward. Some families used all three spellings, at the fancy of the individual members. During the Conquest all titles were taken from the Saxons. The Howards were almost the first family to whom title was restored. The blood of the Howards flows in half a dozen ducal families in England. Almost alone, of English families of noble or gentle blood, they are of Saxon, and not of Norman descent.

The first Howards that came to the colonies were Lieut. Thomas Hayward and Ensign John Haward, who came about 1638. They settled first at Duxbury, and later at Bridgewater, Mass. Nahum Mitchell, the celebrated antiquarian, was himself born at Bridgewater. He says these two men were related, and both called themselves Howard, being distinguished as Hayward of the Plain, and Haward of the Hill. The coat-of-arms of the American branch of the family has been authenticated.

Its shield is divided by a *bend*, a broad band passing diagonally across it. The upper and lower fields thus separated, each bear as charges three *cross-crosslets fitchee*, i. e., crosses, with the lower part pointed, as though sharpened to drive in the ground, while the top and side arms, that make the familiar " cross," are themselves each crossed by a bar, making a cross or crosslet of each point. The crest above the shield is a crowned lion, denoting that some of the family have intermarried with royalty. The motto is *Virtus Sola Invicta*——Virtue alone is invincible.

Capt. Howard descended from Lieut. Thomas Hayward the Emigrant. He himself adopted Howard as the spelling of his name, but his mother in her deed to him in 1794 is called Elizabeth Hayward. Emigrant Thomas was a Deputy, or as we now say, Representative to the Old Plymouth Assembly. Two of his sons fought in King Philip's War. A daughter, Dorothy, was captured with others, by the Indians in 1675. She had once shown a special kindness to an Indian boy. Her captors put her companions to death, but treated her kindly because of the past, and finally sent her back to her family.

This incident illustrates a family trait. Great kindliness of heart belonged to them. They were a quiet family, talking but little, and never pushing themselves forward. Nevertheless, their substantial qualities always brought them to the fore. The prevailing disposition of the family is yet of this type.

Lieut. Thomas had a son Deacon Josiah. One of the Deacon's sons was Joseph, born 1673. He moved to Wraynham, Mass., and his sons again scattered, so as to be difficult to trace.

It is thought that one of his sons was Ephraim, **born 1716**, who lived

VIRTUS SOLA INVICTA.

Howard.

for a time at Braintree, Mass., and from there, still a young man, came to R. I.

Ephraim married Tabitha Hill,* thus bringing in a strain of Lascelle–Wardwell, Waite and Hill blood, for which see Appendix. Ephraim's wife died when he was 33. He died 10 years later, Aug. 9, 1759, leaving Ephraim, Jr., and two other sons.

Ephraim, Junior, m. Elizabeth Myers, April 12, 1764. They had 5 children, of whom the youngest was our Capt. John who married Elizabeth King. His family have always been very proud of him. He was a man of rectitude and influence, and was honored in many ways. He was commissioned a Captain in the State Militia in 1806, and was ever afterwards called by that title. To him and his wife were born nine children, one of whom died at birth, and is not named in my list. Three adults of this family never married.

OLIVER HOWARD[7], [Elizabeth[6], Deborah Greene-King[5], James Greene[4], John of Bristol[3], Lieut. James[2], John of Quidnessett[1].] He was b. April 5, 1795, and was a twin. He died in Sept., 1868. Oliver's wife was Sarah Tefft. They had a family of 10 children, not one of whom died in infancy. By a strange fatality his line, nevertheless, almost died out, being continued in a small way by but one son.

George W., the oldest son, d. in 1844, at 22; Palmer G., the next son, died the next year, aged 21; Alfreda, Hannah and Sarah died in '52, '53 and '56, aged respectively 18, 21 and 17 years. Amy died in 1897, unmarried, at the age of 67; Abbie F., born in 1837, never married; Elizabeth became Mrs. Oliver R. Matteson, and Tryphena became Mrs. Henry A. Harkness. No record given of any issue to either of them. This leaves one son alone:

OLIVER C. HOWARD[8], b. Oct. 6, 1844. Married at 33 to Maria L. Burton.

Charles Howard[9], b. July 6, 1878; died when 3 years old.

Henry Howard[9], b. Sept. 24, 1880.

Mary M. Howard[9], b. July 23, 1887.

RUTH HOWARD-MATTESON[7], [Hannah[6], Deborah Green-King[5], etc.,] b. Feb. 22, 1796. She married Levi Matteson. His Matteson lineage was this: Henry the Emigrant m. Hannah Parsons. Their oldest son, Capt. Henry, m. Judith Weaver. Their son, Jonathan, Senior, married for his second wife Meriba Waite. Jonathan, Junior, of the next generation, married his cousin, Dinah Matteson of Henry[3], Henry[2], Henry[1]. And their son Aaron, who married Dorcas Weaver, was the father of Levi who married Ruth Howard. Levi gave to his children, therefore, two strains of Matteson, and a strain of Parsons and Lascelle-Wardwell-Waite blood. Levi and

---

* Some of the family have it that his wife was Tabitha Nichols. His grand-daughter, Tabitha Howard married Christopher Nichols. Hence arose the confusion.

Ruth's line have married back into the relationship on every side, making a tangle hard to unravel.

JOHN WEAVER MATTESON[8], b. Feb. 17, 1820. At 22 he married his mother's cousin, Olive Kittle, who was some 9 years his senior. He was drowned in Narragansett Bay, by the capsizing of his boat in squall, leaving her with four small children. She died when the youngest was 10 years old, having literally worn herself out to provide for them and keep them together.

Infant son b. and d. in 1843.

Henry C. Matteson[9], b. Jan. 3, 1844. He was a natural mathematical genius, giving the answers to abstruse problems, like a flash,—one of those cases that defy ordinary mental laws. He entered the Civil War, and died soon after.

Charles E. Matteson[9], b. July 5, 1845 ; d. Jan. 13, 1849.

Sara E. Matteson–Kittelle[9], b. Dec. 14, 1846. She was married in 1872 to Albert Kittelle, her mother's cousin. Dinah Greene, sister of Deborah Greene–King,—see Chapter XX,—married Edward Kittelle. Albert Kittelle was one of the youngest sons of Asa, Dinah and Edward's son. There were no children born to Albert and Sara, to puzzle over their relationship.

Mrs. Sara Kittelle has furnished me with hundreds of names for this work. She has started right out, visited graveyards and copied inscriptions, and taken her kindred in rotation, visiting their homes, hunted up their records and family Bibles, and interviewed old people who knew of many unrecorded facts from their own recollection. She has literary ability herself, and writes verses that have something beside a jingle at the end to make them poetry. A booklet of her poems was brought out by the *Gleaner* press, (Phenix, R. I.) in 1903. Lack of space alone prevents me from giving some of her poems. The tribute to Mary A. Andrews, in this chapter, is from her pen.

Left a double orphan, she had her own way to make. She has done it, and helped others beside. Early in life she made up her mind that she would not be crushed ; she determined to be educated and awake to the happenings of the world about her ; to use her brains ; to do her own thinking ; to act for herself ; and she has done it. She is the type of a woman who may wear out, but will never rust out.

Aaron Weaver Matteson[9], [of John W.[8], Ruth[7], Hannah[6], etc.], b. Jan. 29, 1849. His first wife and mother of his children, was Anna Josephine Mitchell. His second wife was Matilda Rathbun, who died in 1903.

Eva Isabel Matteson–Woodmansee[10], b. Aug. 16, 1874. She m. Walter Woodmansee, and had Walter and Howard.

Rena Mabel Matteson–Johnson[10], b. Feb. 25, 1876. She is the wife of William H. Johnson. Their children are Jesse Francis, Frederick Eldred, Minnie Alice, and an infant.

Alma Matteson–Sweet,[10] b. Jan. 31, 1880. Wife of Marinus P. Sweet. They have Herbert Leroy and Hattie Josephine.

Lenora Matteson[10], d. in 1882, aged six weeks.

Leola Maud Matteson–Andrews[10], b. May 5, 1883 . m. Lucius E. Andrews in 1902.

Walter Howard Matteson[10], d. in 1885, aged six weeks.

Annie Laurie Matteson[10], b. Aug. 4, 1888.

Ruth Alma Matteson–Card[9], (of John W[8]., Ruth[7], Hannah[6], etc.), b. July 17, 1850 ; m. A. B. Card in 1891. He died early in 1904. They had no children.

CALEB HOWARD MATTESON[8], [Ruth Howard–Matteson[7], Hannah King–Howard[6], etc.], b. July 22, 1827, and d. Oct. 17, 1884. He married Dinah Hopkins, his second cousin. Dinah was the daughter of Gideon, son of Dinah King–Hopkins, a sister of Caleb's grandmother, Hannah King–Howard.

Susan Matteson–Johnson[9]. They have a son, Howard King, b. Feb. 17, 1903.

I   -   . . . .   Imperfectly reported.

David Matteson[9] Married his second cousin, Hortilla Belle Howard, daughter of Geo P , and grand-dau of Ephraim, and great-grand-dau of Hannah King--Howard They have no children Mrs. Matteson has a turn for genealogy, as have many of her family

Phebe Matteson-- ------[9] Married No children

John Charles Matteson[9] m Mary a daughter of Stephen Congdon s They have Walter Earl, b 1897, Frederick Lee, b 1899, Leon Francis, b 1900 , and Ida, b 1902

REV SAMUEL KING MATTESON[8], (of Ruth[7], of Hannah[6], etc), b May 4 1825 M (1) to Almira Spencer in 1849 His children are by her M (2) to his second cousin Julia Hopkins, a sister to his brother Caleb's wife Mrs Matteson has been an invalid for many years Elder Sammy , as he is familiarly called is well known Although he preaches he was for many years a millwright, one of the three great grandsons of Samuel King who inherited his peculiar talent in that direction He has put up all manner and all kinds of mills He is said to be the best posted individual now living on the intricate Matteson genealogy

Calvin Matteson[9] b June 28, 1847 m Laura Briggs in 1892 They lost two sons, Frank and Chester, 13 and 12 years old

Ava Matteson -Tarbox[10], b June 6, 1870 , m. Fones W Tarbox in 1893 They have Edith May, b Feb 9 1895 , Harold Boyd, b June 23 1896 and Earl Elmer b June 8, 1901 They lost an infant in 1898

Iva Matteson- Huling[10] b Aug 5 1871 , m to Ray Huling in 1892

Maria Matteson--Vaughan[9], [Elder S K[8] Ruth[7] Hannah[6] etc] b March 3 1849 She m Lorenzo Vaughan The Vaughans were originally Welsh, the name meaning little or of small statue In the old records it is spelled Vahan

Lillian V Vaughan--Bailey[10], b Sept 4 1869 Wife of John Bailey This is a common R I name I met it first in Mass records, where Gudo Bayley was living in 1657 These old New England families have a way of drifting together that is astonishing to the occidental mind Mrs Bailey became a widow in Feb 1903

Edward L Vaughan[10] b Dec 6 1874 , m Rosa Bates in 1894 They have Wesley Lorenzo, b July 18 1897 , Ernest Arthur b Dec 14 1899 , and Carl Edward, b Dec 7 1901

Frank L Vaughan[10] b Dec 3 1871 , m in 1891 to Zizalla Northup They have Cora A , Harry C and Ralph I

Arthur Garfield Vaughan[10], b Dec 27, 1881

Grace I. Vaughan[10] b Dec 20 1884

JOEL HOWARD[7], [of Hannah[6], etc] He was born about 1801 Married, when something of a bachelor, Calista Wheeler In 1842 he purchased the Roger Bromley farm of his cousin, Mercy King–Bromley's husband He built up a comfortable fortune on this place, where his grandchildren yet live In after years a post-office was established here, and was called Bromley after the former owner The post-mastership has always been held in the Howard family

There may be other men as good as Joel Howard, but there were never any better ones, nor any more respected, than he was in his community They had but one son

JOHN WHEELER HOWARD[8] He married Emma W He died in 1899

Warren Joel Howard[9] Present P M at Bromley

Julie Hazel Howard[9]

SAMUEL HOWARD[7], [of Hannah[6], etc] Born Aug. 2, 1802, or according to another account, in June, 1804, which is obviously wrong He

d. in West Greenwich, R. I., Jan. 13, 1880. He was married in 1825 to Susannah Harrington, dau. of Aaron and Amy Brown—Harrington. Susannah lived until May 8, 1903, reaching the great age of 96 years and 9 days. She was a fine looking woman even then.

ALBERT GREENE HOWARD[8], b. Aug. 14, 1826; d. May 25, 1883. His first wife was Juan Fernandez Smith, descended from the old Quidnessett Smith and Spink families. She was the daughter of Judge Harris and Hannah Spink—Smith, and grand-daughter of Judge Benjamin and Mary Austin—Smith, all of North Kingstown, formerly Quidnessett, R. I. This oddly named Mrs. Howard had marked artistic ability. She died in 1860, at 31, leaving three children. One month after her death, the babe for whom she gave her life, died also. Little Adeline died 3 years later, aged 7.

Mary C. Howard—Washington—Smith[9], the only surviving child of the first wife's was b. April 20, 1858; m. (1) to Pardon Arnold. They had no children. She was m. (2), in 1887, to Henry Washington—Smith, who was of Griffin, Georgia. They live in Mass. No children. Mrs. M. C. Washington—Smith is a well known artist.

Albert G. Howard[8] married for his second wife, Fannie B. Lamphear, of Daniel and Emeline Lamphear—Lamphear, of the old Huguenot family of that name who came to R. I. about 1687.

John J. Howard[9], b. Aug. 9, 1865; m. Fannie Young, who died in 1901. No children. Addie V. Howard—Berry[9], 1868—1893. She was the wife of Clark T. Berry, Jr., of New Hampshire. She died at 25, leaving no children.

LUCETTA HOWARD—TUCKER[8], [of Samuel[7], Hannah[6], etc.], b. Aug. 28, 1828; m. Alvin P. Tucker. She d. March 12, 1850, in her 22d year. No children.

AARON HARRINGTON HOWARD[8], [of Samuel[7], Hannah[6], etc.], b. Dec. 1, 1830; d. Nov. 17, 1894. He m. Almira Northup. No children.

DAVID HOWARD[7], (of Hannah[6], etc.), b. Aug. 12, 1804; d. Dec. 18, 1893, in his 90th year. He was a kindly and affectionate old gentleman. Because of an early love affair, he remained single all his days. He was so deeply attached to the old home that, after his mother's death, he kept house himself for over 40 years.

EPHRAIM HOWARD[7], [of Hannah King-Howard[6], Deborah Green-King[5], James Greene[4], John of Bristol[3], Lieut. James[2], John of Quidnessett[1].] He was born Sept. 21, 1807. He married Hannah Wicks Greene. This marriage brought a very mixed element indeed into the family blood.

Hannah was the daughter of Paris Greene and his wife, Hannah Wicks, and the grand-daughter of Nathaniel Greene, Jr., who was descended from John Greene of Quidnessett. [Nathaniel, Jr.[5], Squire Nathaniel[4], Maroon Swamp James[3], Lieut. John[2], John of Quidnessett[1].] Now Hannah's grandmother, Nathaniel's wife, was also of Greene descent. She was the daughter of Jonathan Matteson, and grand-daughter of Martha Greene-Matteson, own sister to James Greene, one of the ancestors of Ephraim Howard's mother. So that *that* line of Greene blood was nearly the same with both husband and wife. Hannah inherited Lascelle-Wardwell blood through her grandmother Patience, and an equal strain with her husband of Westcott, Straight, Holmes and Parsons blood.

Ephraim and Hannah W. Howard had three children that lived, two sons and a daughter.

JOHN WICKS HOWARD[9], b. Aug. 8, 1836. This son owns the old home. He is a typical Howard, quietly going his way through life. Rain, heat, or cold, 52 Sundays a year find him at Maple Root Church, 3 miles away, attending upon its services and superintending its Sabbath School. In everything else he is as punctual, as faithful, and as conscientious.

His first wife was Elizabeth M. Wood, daughter of Nicholas and Sylvia Sweet—Wood. She was the mother of his children. She died June 24, 1884, aged 40. He was marrid (2), July 12, 1887, to Hannah Eliza Sweet, by Bishop Hamilton of the M. E. Church. She was the daughter of William C. and Hannah Andrews--Sweet. See her pedigree in Chapter XIX. At the time of her marriage, Mrs. Howard was a graduate medical and surgical nurse in Boston, Mass.

A friend says of her, "Whatever Hannah Howard undertakes, she does well." Some years ago she became interested in Rhode Island Genealogies. She has collected a large amount of data. She helped Miss James to prepare her "Andrews Genealogy," and has unstintedly drawn on her memoranda to help me out in writing this book. Mrs. Howard is a correspondent for the leading newspapers of her state.

John W. and Elizabeth Wood--Howard's descendants are these :

Annie Elizabeth Howard--Franklin[9], b. Dec. 2., 1860. In 1878 she married her twice-over third cousin, John Clark Franklin the grandson of David and Thankful Hopkins--King, both cousins to Ephraim Howard, Annie E.'s grandfather. Both Mr. and Mrs. Howard are teachers. They have two children, Charles Sheldon and Sarah, who are enrolled in Chapter XXVI, among George King's descendants.

Frank Wheeler Howard[9], b. Dec. 3, 1862. In 1884, he went west. He settled at Reynolds, Idaho, and owns a large stock ranch. He was married in Boise City, Idaho, Oct. 12, 1897, to Mrs. Elizabeth Gardiner--Adams. They have no children.

Walter Eugene Howard[9], b. April 13, 1869. He is a telegrapher at Taunton, Mass. He was married Sept. 3, 1898, in Taunton, to Harriet Evelyn Read. They have one daughter, Ola Elizabeth, born Sept. 29, 1899.

Clarinda Howard--Bates[9], b. April 17, 1872. She was only 12 when her mother died, and she became her father's housekeeper. She married William H. Bates, a wheelwright of Phoenix, R. I. Mr. Bates, though never ordained, frequently preaches in Baptist churches. Her children are Leon Howard, b. Feb. 22, 1887, and Howard Frank, b. Nov. 17, 1900.

MARY E. HOWARD--ANDREWS[8], [Eph.[7], Hannah[6], etc.], b. Oct. 6, 1844. She married John Francis Andrews, distantly related to her three times over, twice on the Greene side, and once on the La Valley--King side. (See Chapter XVIII, descendants of John and Antha Sweet.) Mary's husband died when their children were small. She was a nob e woman. Her death, April 10, 1900, called forth this tribute :

> "We fond'y hoped that many years
>   Would yet be given thee below ;
> We needed thy dear presence here,—
>   How can we bear to let thee go ?
> . . . .
> . . . .
> No tears, no disappointments there,
>   Where we united soon shall dwell.
> No more sad partings over there,
>   O ! well beloved one, farewell !"
>
> —*S. E. K.*

John Francis and Mary E. Andrews have these descendants :

Mina Gertrude Andrews--Bailey[9], b. Sept. 15, 1868 ; m. William, **son of Daniel**

Bailey. She died March 22, 1901, partly, it is thought, from the effects of her long continued grief over her mother's death. She left Francis, born June, 1889, Hortense Isabel, b. Jan. 5, 1894.

Edward Blake Andrews[9], m. Nettie Shippee. They have Harold, b. April 2, 1892, and Eunice M., b. Sept. 28, 1897.

GEORGE PARIS HOWARD[8], [Eph.[7], Hannah King--Howard[6], Deborah Greene--King[5], James Greene[4], John of Bristol[3], Lieut. James[2], John Greene of Quidnessett[1],] b. Nov. 21, 1849. He lives near Hope, R. I. He was married on his 20th birthday. Like the rest of the family, he married a cousin, Tryphena Hoxie Johnson, dau. of Philip and Tryphena Greene--Johnson. Tryphena was thrice descended from John Greene of Quidnessett. A more complex-pedigree than hers would be hard to find. Those fond of Chinese-puzzle relationship are referred to her father Philip Johnson's line in Chapter XVIII ; her grandfather Hiram Greene's in Chapter XIV ; and her grandmother Abigail Johnson--Greene's in Chapter XVII. One can but pity the children of George P. and Tryphena Howard, as they try to make out their relationship to the rest of the tribe of Greene !

Mrs. Tryphena Howard died Aug. 21, 1899. She had been the mother of five chi'dren. Melinda died in infancy, and Edith at 18, in 1893. Those who lived to marry were these

Hertilla Belle Howard--Matteson[9], b. July 7, 1870. Married her twice-over cousin David Howard Matteson, son of Caleb and Dinah Hopkins--Matteson, this same chapter. They have no children.

George H. Howard[9], b. Dec. 3, 1873, m. Mary Grace, dau. of Alfred and Sylvania Colvin--Whitman. They live at Hope, R. I. No children.

Vivena W. Howard--Walker[9], b. Feb, 1, 1872 ; m. to Emery Walker of Robert and Susan Durfee--Walker. They live at Kent, R. I. They have Edith Belle, b. Sept. 5, 1894, and Charles Howard, b. Nov. 4, 1896.

BETSEY HOWARD[7], (of Hannah[6], etc.), b. in 1811 ; d. unmarried, Feb. 7, 1888.

MELINDA HOWARD[7], b. May 19, 1817 ; died unmarried, Oct. 30, 1850, in her 34th year.

CHAPTER XXVIII

FAMILY TREES. For descent from Alexander, Lord de Greene de Boketon, A. D. 1202, and Robert the Strong, Duke de France, A. D. 861, see Chapter XI.

For lineage from John Greene of Quidnessett, also from Captain Thomas Straight, Stukeley Westcott, Elder Obediah Holmes and Hugh Parsons, see Chapter XX.

For descent from John King, and Peter La Valley, see Chapter XXII.

Dinah King-Hopkins[6] was the seventh child and sixth daughter of Samuel King and Deborah Greene-King[5]. [Deborah[5], James[4], John of Bristol[3], Lieut. James[2], John of Quidnessett[1].] She was born about 1778. Her husband was Christopher Hopkins, of the old R. I. families of Hopkins and Whaley. He was the son of Ebenezer and Abigail Hopkins, and was born Dec. 6, 1776.

Hopkins is a very old name. It means literally Eoppa's kin or descendants. There were several Saxon Eoppas, princes and military leaders in England twelve and thirteen centuries ago. Their descendants centered in Wales, and the name became and is a Welsh name to this day. The R. I. Hopkins believe themselves descended from Stephen Hopkins, a Londoner of Welsh lineage, who sailed in the Mayflower in that memorial voyage of 1620. Unfortunately, the Hopkins family rarely recorded their dates with the town clerk, as the law required. This leaves a single link—or possibly, two—between Stephen Hopkins of the Mayflower and the first Joseph Hopkins of Rhode Island, where the name is presumptive only.

Stephen Hopkins' oldest son was Giles born about 1614. If he had any other sons who lived, they were born after 1622. Joseph Hopkins was born in the neighborhood of 1660. He is supposed to have been Giles' son or grandson, (Giles being 45 or so at that time) or else a son of an unrecorded younger brother of Giles.* The R. I. Hopkinses have always stood well. Hon.

---

*Stephen Hopkins, Signer of the Declaration, was the great-grandson of Thomas Hopkins, who came to Providence, R. I., in 1640, it is said. Though tradition makes Joseph to have been the grandson of the Mayflower Stephen Hopkins, he may have been a son of Thomas of Providence instead.

Stephen Hopkins, born 1707, was Chief Justice, Governor and Signer of the Declaration of Independence. Esek Hopkins, born 11 years later, was the first Commodore of the American navy. He was put in charge of our puny fleet of 17 vessels in the fall of 1775. We had no national flag then. Hopkins flung to the breeze a banner bearing 13 stripes; a rattlesnake stretched its length across them, and beneath it were these words,—"Don't tread on me!" He made that rattlesnake flag famous in its day.

To return to Joseph Hopkins, grandson, as supposed, of Stephen Hopkins of the Mayflower. Not far from 1695 he married Martha Whaley, daughter of Regicide Judge Whaley. Of this strain of Whaley blood thus brought into the family, Joseph's descendants are justly proud. It is claimed that the Judge was descended on the maternal side from William the Conqueror, and that he was also a first cousin of Oliver Cromwell's.

Miss Lois Hopkins says that Judge Whaley died in 1717, aged 106. According to this he was born in 1611. He was one of the Regicide Judges who condemned Charles I to death in Jan., 1649. In May, 1660, when Charles II was restored to the throne, these Judges were all in danger of their lives. Nine were hung, above twice that number imprisoned for life, and the others escaped. Four crossed the seas to America, Digsbee, Goff and Edward Whaley, who went to New Haven, Conn., and were hidden in the Regicides' Cave by sympathizers; and this Whaley who went to R. I. His christian name is variously given as Thomas, Theodore and Theophilus, the abbreviations for which are almost similar. Miss Hopkins says positively that his name was Theophilus.

With a price upon his head he lived as secluded as possible. There was a cave into which he retired, it is said, in times of danger. Long afterwards, it used to be told how he had mysterious visitors, and how at one time a ship from Boston sailed into the cove near him, and strange men disembarked and talked with him, sailing away again when he conference was over. The Colonists did not betray him, and he finally dared to openly occupy the home in which he died. One of the traditions handed down of him is that he used to say he never knew what it was until he was eighteen years of age not to have a servant bring him a silver ewer and a napkin whenever he wished to wash his hands. He was buried on his farm near Washington, R. I. This farm is yet in the possession of his descendants. He was 49 when he came to America. He married a Virginia lady and had children, one of whom was Martha, who married Joseph Hopkins.

Joseph and Martha Hopkins had one son Judge Samuel Hopkins. He had a son Samuel, whose son Daniel married Martha Matteson[2], daughter of she who had been Martha Greene[1], own aunt to Deborah Greene-King. Another son of the Judge was Ebenezer Hopkins, and his son Christopher is the one who married the Dinah King of this chapter. So the cousins, Daniel and Christopher Hopkins, married two cousins. Christopher and Dinah were married about 1797, and had these descendants: *

HONOR HOPKINS-CARR[7], b. Oct. 1, 1798. She m. Rev. Robert Carr. They moved to Ill. They left several children.

GIDEON HOPKINS[7], b. May 25, 1800; d. May 24, 1877. He married Susan[7], dau. of Ephraim[6], and Newie Briggs-Kittelle[6]. Ephraim's mother was a Greene, sister to Deborah, Gideon's grandmother, and Newie's mother was a King, sister to Samuel, Gideon's grandfather. So Susan was twice over his second cousin, and all of his line have a double strain of Greene, La Valley, and King blood. They had 12 children; 3 died in infancy and 2 in early manhood, and are not enumerated.

> PERRY A. HOPKINS[8], b. Aug. 24, 1824. He m. Mrs. Caroline Greene, widow of James Greene, and daughter of Burrill Hopkins. She died Dec. 27, 1890.
>> Susan A. Hopkins[9], b. July 10, 1877.
>> Lois C. Hopkins[9], b. Dec. 3, 1879.
>> John W. Hopkins[9], b. Jan. 6, 1882.
> DINAH HOPKINS--MATTESON[8], b. Feb. 15, 1827; Caleb H. Matteson, and line merged with his. See Chapter XXVII.
> SARAH A. HOPKINS--DAVIS[8], b. June 4, 1828; m. Wm. Davis, son of Comfort Greene--Davis. 6 children. See Chapter XX, descendants of James[7], of James[6], of Abel[5], of James[4].
> JULIA HOPKINS--MATTESON[8], b. June 27, 1830; m. Rev. S. K. Matteson, in 1859. No children.
> CHARLES HOPKINS[8].
> PHEBE HOPKINS--BRIGGS[8], b. Dec. 22, 1842; m. George Briggs. They have one son, Charles, born in 1871.
> HENRY C. HOPKINS[8], b. March 27, 1845. Unmarried.

THANKFUL HOPKINS-KING[7], b. April 17, 1802; m. her cousin, David King, son of George[6]. See Chapter XXX.

EBENEZER HOPKINS[7], b. May 5, 1805; d. Aug. 7, 1879; m. Julia Mawney, a descendant of the early Huguenots. The name was originally DeMorney.

> WILLIAM HOPKINS[8], 1844-1862. D. at 18.
> PETER HOPKINS[8], b. Oct. 15, 1845; d. Sept. 2, 1900. He m. Susan Wells. They had one child, Flora, born in 1885.
> JOHN HOPKINS[8], b. May 17, 1847; d. Oct. 23, 1900; m. Abbie Green. They had one child, Edwin Gardiner, b. 1876.
> MARY HOPKINS--POTTER[8], b. May 5, 1849; m. Willis Potter.
> CHARLES HOPKINS[8], b. May 12, 1851; m. in 1881.
> THEOPHILUS HOPKINS[8], b. Aug. 14, 1854; m. Abbie Wells.
> GEORGE HOPKINS[8], b. Feb. 18, 1858; m. Melissa Place, who died in 1900.

DEBORAH HOPKINS-WHITFORD[7], m. Elisha Whitford. Their sons Reuben and Joseph neither one left heirs. Elisha Jr. is married, but has no children.

---

* For the list of descendants of Christopher and Dinah Hopkins, I am indebted to Mrs. Sara E. Kittelle of Anthony, R. I., and to Miss Lois C. Hopkins of Washington, R. I.

ELIZABETH WHITFORD--EDWARDS[8], 1830--1895. She was the wife of George Edwards. They had Charles, who m. Mary Cottrell and has 2 children; Rhodes K., with 2 children; and Mary E., now Mrs. Fred. Straight, who has four children by her first husband, Whitford Reynolds.

HANNAH F. WHITFORD--POTTER[8]. M. Pardon T. Potter. They have Stukeley, who m. Abbie Clark; Rhodes F., who m. Evelyn Johnson and has 1 child; and Emeline C., wife of John Davis.

MARY WHITFORD--RATHBUN[8], wife of Nathan Rathbun. They have Hannah F., wife of Edwin Nichols, and mother of Mrs. Clara Northup, Mrs. John Nicholas and Mrs. Eva Capwell; Adeline, wife of Calvin Hopkins and mother of 4 children; and Jerome, who m. Hattie Brown, and has 6 children.

HOWLAND HOPKINS[7], 1808-1866. M. Phebe Lyon. One daughter, Phebe C.

ELIZA HOPKINS-KNIGHT[7], b. Mar. 18, 1810; m. Ezra Knight of Foster, R. I. I have no records of their son William's family.

MARY KNIGHT--SALISBURY[8], wife of Lemuel Salisbury. 1 son Elmer M.

EDWIN O. KNIGHT[8] and wife Mary have these children living; Susannah, Willard W., Hattie, and Estella.

EZRA A. KNIGHT[8], and wife Emma have Olney, Lucinda and Eliza.

LEWIS HOPKINS[7], b. Sept. 2, 1814. By first wife, Nancy A. Northup, had 6 children.

ELIZABETH HOPKINS--AUSTIN[8]. 1836--1867. She was the wife of James Austin.

MARIA HOPKINS--COLVIN[8], b. Nov. 16, 1837; m. Alfred Colvin.

PALMER L. HOPKINS[8], b. Sept. 14, 1839; m. Rebecca Young. He served in the Civil War. Their children are William and Claude. William[9] is married and has 2 sons, Raymond and Clarence.

MARY HOPKINS--BROWN[8]. 1842-1879. Wife of John Brown. 4 children.

DIANTHA HOPKINS--KENYON[8], b. Feb. 5, 1846; m. George Kenyon.

AMBROSE HOPKINS[8]. 1847--1865. Killed in front of Richmond, Va., during the Civil War.

EMMELINE HOPKINS--POTTER[8], wife of Peleg Potter.

CHAPTER XXIX

DAVID KING'S DESCENDANTS

FAMILY TREES   For descent from Alexander, first Lord de Greene de Boketon, A D 1202, and from Robert the Strong, Duke de France, A D 861, see Chapter XI

For descent from Lieutenant James[2], of John Greene[1] of Quidnessett; also from Capt. Thomas Straight of Watertown, Mass, and from Stukeley Westcott, Elder Obediah Holmes and Hugh Parsons, see Chapter XXII

For descent from John King, and Peter La Valley see Chapter XXII. The strain of Pierce–Lascelle–Wardwell blood is treated of in same Chapter, and more fully in Appendix

---

David King[6] was the eighth child and second son of Samuel and Deborah Greene–King[5]. He was born March 11, 1781, and died May 29, 1828, aged 41 years   He lived in West Greenwich, R I   He was married at about 22 to Mary Andrews, who was born Feb. 9, 1782.   She died Sept 21, 1837   She was a lineal descendant of the pioneer John Andrews of R I, the intimate friend of old John Greene of Quidnessett   There is a slight uncertainty as to one of the middle links   The line appears to be this   John Andrews[1], Charles Sen[2], Charles Jr[3], Sylvester[4], and Mary[5]. Her father's and grandfather's line removed to Vermont, not far from 1800, and I have not been able to trace them further

David and Mary had 9 children, 6 of them sons   Singularly enough there is but one descendant of their's alive to-day that bears the name of King, and of him practically nothing is known   A childless grandson, Edgar Cady[8], is yet living in 1904, together with his sister, Jane Cady–Nichols[8]   She, indeed, has five children, but as she married her second cousin, Fernando[8] of Nelson Nichols, her line is reckoned with his   So this record of David King is of a large family that in a century's time have become extinct as a family   Most of them lived in N Y

AVIS KING[7], b Nov. 27, 1804   Died Aug 30, 1877.   She was well versed in family lore, and ought to have been a historian.

GEORGE KING[7], b. Nov. 30, 1806. Died in 1851.

THOMAS A. KING[7]. Born March 18, 1808. Died in early part of 1865. He was a skillful carpenter, a good man and of sound judgment. He removed to Indiana some years before his death. His wife was Sallie Andrews, so noted for eccentricities that anecdotes about her will live for generations. An instance is where she stood by her husband's bed in his last illness, and calmly remarked,—" I'd like to have Thomas get well, for he is a good provider. But if he can't live, it would be better for his family if he would die right away !" The frank old soul outlived her husband many years, dying in R. I.

Their children were Sally Ann, b. 1837 and died in 1852 at 14 ; Caroline E. who d. at 8 months ; Caroline E. (2) who died unmarried in Rhode Island ; and Lucinda, a bright, beautiful girl of 14, who died early in 1865.

DEBORAH KING[7], b. Aug. 26, 1810; died in May, 1877, at her neice's, Jane Nichols, in N. D. She was deeply attached to her sister, Sally Cady, and at her death brought up her children as her own.

SALLY KING–CADY[7]. B. July 29, 1812. Died Dec. 21, 1851. She married Simeon Cady of N. Y. There was an epidemic of typhoid fever in this King family, and a half a dozen of them died in the latter part of 1851, among them Sally, her husband, and her 10 year old daughter Caroline.

> DAVID A. CADY,[8]. B. June 21. 1833. Died in the service of the Civil War, June, 1864.
>
> MARY JANE CADY–NICHOLS[8]. B. Aug. 17. 1836. Came with her aunt Deborah King to Indiana when a young lady. Married her second cousin, Fernando Nichols. Her line is traced with his in Chapter XL. In their old age she took care of three or four of her old uncles and aunts, until their death.
>
> EDGAR GEORGE CADY[8]. Born Feb. 25, 1838. He married his Uncle Paul's step-daughter, Sarah Bingham, May 18, 1866. She died within a year, and the child to which she gave birth died also. He never married again. He lives with his sister, Mrs. Fernando Nichols.
>
> CAROLINE E. CADY[8]. B. July 31, 1841. D. Nov. 29, 1851.

SYLVESTER A. KING[7], b. April 28, 1814 ; married Valeria Bewell in 1852, but separated from his wife. One son, George, of whom the last known was that he was living in N. Y., and was married but childless. Sylvester died at his neice's, Mrs. Nichols.

PAUL KING[7]. Born April 4, 1816 ; d. 1894. He married in middle-life a widow, Mrs. Louise Bingham. He left no heirs.

JOHN A. KING[7], b. Oct. 20, 1818. Never married. Died at his neice's, Mrs. Jane Nichols, in Feb., 1896.

DAVID KING[7], b. Aug. 3, 1820. He married Sarah T. Jewett in 1858. He had one daughter, Emily, who died in 1897. This entire family have passed away. He died in 1898.

CHAPTER XXX

FAMILY TREES. For the descent from Sir Alexander, first Lord de Greene de Boketon, A. D., 1202, and the descent from Robert the Strong, see Chapter XI.

For their lineage from John Greene of Quidnessett, through James Greene; also their lineage from Capt. Straight, Stukeley Westcott, Elder Obediah Holmes and Hugh Parsons, see Chapter XX. This family have a double strain of all this, as they are, through Joel King's wife, descended from Martha Greene, sister to James Greene.

For their descent from John King and Peter La Valley, see Chapter XXII.

Joel King[6] was the tenth child and fourth son of Samuel and Deborah Greene-King[5]. He was born Nov. 3, 1785, and died Dec. 12, 1867, aged 82. He outlived his wife by thirty years. He married at 24 to his second cousin, Esther Matteson, who was born June 18, 1783. Esther was a sister to Meribah, wife of Joel's brother George. The sisters' double Matteson descent, and also their lineage from John Greene of Quidnessett, is given in Chapter XXVI, pertaining to George King.

Joel King was a favorite in his family. He was frank and generous in his disposition, and of a genial, sunny temperament. His wife is yet remembered as one of the salt of the earth, patient, forbearing, and given to kind words and deeds.

He went to N. Y. in 1806, and lived for a few years with his sister, Mrs. Nancy Nichols. He went back to R. I. after his bride, but spent the rest of his life at Pompey, N. Y. Years after, when some of his own children were grown, he found that the then owner of his brother-in-law's old place was about to plow over the grave of this sister Nancy, with whom he had lived. He moved the remains to his own private burying ground. Then from Mill Creek he chose a smooth stone, dressed it into a slab, and chiseled her name and the date of her birth and death thereon. It was a long, hard task, but it was done so well that a regular stone cutter might have been proud of it. This incident illustrates his loyalty and devotion to his friends. His descendants are these:

HIRAM KING[7], b. Feb. 1, 1810; d. March 30, 1860. Married Julia Keeler.

ALEXANDER KING[8], b. Aug. 6, 1845. Went into the Civil War at 17, and died the next year, Feb. 19, 1863, at Fredericksburg.

FLORENCE F. KING-SEARLES[8], b. Feb. 13, 1857; m. to Charles Searles of New Bremen, N. Y. She has been a great sufferer for many years with a disease that settled in one limb, causing several amputations. No children.

THOMAS MATTESON KING[7], b. Aug. 27, 1811. D. Aug. 28, 1858. He married his double cousin, Celia King[7], May, 1836. She was the daughter of his uncle George and his aunt Meribah. They must have gone to Ohio at once, as a letter of 1837 speaks of them, then at Sharon Center, Ohio. They lived there until about 1852, when they removed to Wisconsin. They lost a daughter Florence when a child.

EDWIN KING[8]. Died in the Civil War.

JAMES HENRY KING[8], b. 1837. Died in 1866 from disease contracted in the Civil War.

ALBERT F. KING[8], b. 1840; d. Sept. 14, 1889, after an invalidism of 14 years, the result of disease contracted in the army. Earlier in life he was a teacher and farmer. About 1869 he married a young woman of Canadian birth, Philinda Moffit. They lived in Wisconsin until 1885, then in Nebraska, and a little later in Ohio, where he died in '89. After he was unable to work his two lads worked manfully to support the family. The oldest girl died the year after her father, in 1890. The mother died in 1893. Clifford, the second son, became ill in '92, and was sick for six years, dying in 1898. Edna King died in 1896, after a long illness.

Those were hard, bitter years for the old veteran's family. Herbert, the eldest son, kept the wolf from the door. When he was 21, the younger children now being in the Soldiers' Orphan's Home, and the widow in receipt of a pension, he was for the first time free to look after himself. With but $5.00 to his name, the poorly educated young man entered the common school, working for his board. At 25 he graduated from the High School. That same fall, with but $70.00 as capital, and a stout heart under his jacket, he started to take the full Ohio University course, including Civil Engineering. He boarded himself for $1.25 a week, and did odd jobs to earn his books and clothes. At 31 he received his well-earned degrees.

HERBERT SUMNER KING[9], b. May 24, 1870. He is a civil engineer, and holds an important and responsible position in West Virginia.

Clifford King[9], b. Dec. 12, 1872. D. in 1893.

Charles E. King[9], died at 1 year of age.

Erwin Norton King[9], died at 2 years.

Miona Atlanta King[9], b. Dec. 4, 1878, and d. Dec. 24, 1890.

Olive King[9], b. May 22, 1883. She graduated from both the Xenia and Urbana, O., High Schools by the time she was 17. She is a teacher, and is now living in Pittsburg, Pa.

Edwin King[9], b. April 1, 1888. He is living in Xenia, Ohio.

MARCUS NORTON KING[8], (of Thomas[7] and Celia, of Joel[6] and Esther). He is commonly called Mark. He is married, and lives at Oakfield, Wisconsin. He has a daughter Lutheria, born about 1886.

FRANK L. KING[8], youngest son of Thomas[7] and Celia. He lives at Grand Island, Nebraska. He has a daughter Mary, who married in 1901, and a daughter Gertrude, who is a trained nurse.

HENRY KING[7]. Third child of Joel and Esther King, b. April 6, 1814, and died Sept. 12, 1816.

DIANA KING–KNIGHT[7], b. March 7, 1816; d. June 26, 1871. She married Shubal Knight and spent her life at Pompey, N. Y. They had four children; Esther and Adelaide died young. Emma R. and Clifford live together on the old place, and have never married. The father died April 15, 1900.

Diana suffered greatly for 12 years with an aggravated rheumatic trouble. When Clifford, a promising young man, was about 30 he was attacked by the same dread disease. It has now run into hip disease, with no hope of cure. At the close of 1903 he had had 137 operations performed upon his hip, to remove the accumulation of pus upon the bone. Through it all he remains patient and cheerful. His sister Emma is giving her life to him, as she did first to her mother, and then to her father. All the heroes are not of the battle-field, nor are all the heroines those who have done world-famous deeds. Emma was born June 21, 1847, and Clifford in March, 1859.

DEBORAH KING[7], b. May 23, 1818; d. Dec. 18 1829.

CYRUS KING[7], b. Sept. 30, 1820; d. March 30, 1903. Wherever he lived, Cyrus King was held in the highest esteem. His life was absolutely clean. He had integrity, industry and ability. He died, as he would have chosen, in the bosom of his family, without a moment's pain or warning. He left behind him a record of a man active in all good works, and generous in his support of worthy causes.

March 21, 1848, he was married to Harriet, daughter of Timothy and Rachel Brown–Bennett. All of the Bennetts who were in N.Y. previous to 1800, were descended from Samuel Bennett, who came to the colonies during the great Anti-Laud Emigration, about 1635. His son Samuel went to R. I., and the next generation passed on to Pa. and N. Y. They were so intensely a patriotic family that 25 N. Y. Bennetts served in the Revolutionary War.* Several of this line moved to Ohio in an early day.

Cyrus and Harriet were married in Wadsworth, Medina Co., Ohio. He was a farmer and worked at the carpenter's trade. She lived but four years, dying in June, 1852. She left one son, Edmund Burritt King.

Cyrus married again, June 4, 1854. His second wife was Climena, daughter of Pliny and Betsey Rhodes–Porter. The Porters were of good family, and she had several heirlooms which she treasured highly. When a child, the author used to admire one of these. It was an antique bureau, its legs carved into fantastic knobs and flowers. Touch the knobs or flowers, and tiny concealed drawers would fly open. Mrs. King died Aug. 5th, 1897.

*See Bennett Book, page 9.

JUDGE EDMUND BURRITT KING[6], b. July 4, 1850. He was admitted to the Bar in 1873. Two years after this he removed to Sandusky, Ohio, where he has ever since made his home. He is one of the leading lawyers of the state. In 1894 he was elected Judge of the Circuit Court Bench, a Court of Appeals and Errors. After five years service he resigned, in order to devote himself to his law practice as one of the firm of King & Guerin. Excepting while he was Judge, he has always taken an active part in political campaigns. For the greater part of the last thirty years he has been a member of the County or State Republican Central Committee, and in 1888 was a Republican Elector, casting his vote for Benjamin Harrison as President. For 17 years he held successively the offices of Lieutenant, Captain and Major of the National Guard of the State, resigning in 1897, because his judicial position interfered with attending to its duties. He has also been prominent in the Masonic Order, belonging to all the Masonic bodies, including the 33d degree of the Scottish Rite, and has held most of the positions in the subordinate and local bodies. He is now Grand Standard Bearer of the Grand Commandary of Ohio.

Burritt King married Emma E. Hackett, Feb. 24, 1874. Of this marriage two children have been born, Cora King–Graves, wife of Thaddeus Graves, Jun., of Hatfield, Mass., born Nov. 16, 1875; and Clifford Marshall King, born Dec. 15, 1879, and now fitting himself at Cornell University for the profession of Civil Engineering. Judge King has one grand-child, Isabel Graves, b. Nov. 24, 1903.

IDA E. KING–WOLCOTT[6], born June 5, 1855; d. Oct. 9, 1879. She was married Dec. 4, 1878, to Samuel Melford Wolcott, son of Simon and Nancy Colding (or Coddington) Wolcott, and grandson of Joseph and Lucy Hills–Wolcott. This is the same Wolcott family to which the two celebrated Governors–Wolcott of Conn., and Oliver Wolcott, the Signer of the Declaration of Independence, belonged. His mother, Nancy Codding (ton) is descended from Sir William Coddington, one of the most noted of R. I.'s early colonial governors.

Ida King–Wolcott died leaving a 17-days old child, Winifred Ida. Her aunt, Mary King, took her, and has raised her in the Cyrus King home, giving her every advantage. She is a student of Hiram College.

DAVID PORTER KING[6], b. Oct. 23, 1857; d. Feb. 22, 1888. The mathematical genius that has again and again appeared in the family since the days of Robert Greene[11] of Gillingham, Eng., 350 years ago, was shown in this young man. He solved the most intricate problems on sight, and invented new methods of his own. He had graduated as a Civil Engineer, but his health failed him. He died at 30.

MARY ALMIRA KING[6], b. Oct. 24, 1859. A companion to her mother, a house-keeper for her father, a mother to her orphan niece, her life has been rich in deeds of love and duty. She lives in Medina, Ohio.

DELILAH KING–HAIGHT[7], b. May 29, 1823, and living in 1904. M. to James S. Haight, Dec. 22, 1847. Mrs. Haight is a gentle little old lady that all esteem. She was a teacher before her marriage. They came to Ohio in 1849, where Mr. Haight engaged in farming and the carpenter trade. They live with their son Clarence.

HERBERT D. HAIGHT[8], b. Nov. 29, 1856; d. June 12, 1880.

CLARA JANE HAIGHT–BRAINERD[8], b. Dec. 14, 1860; m. George M. Brainerd, April 3, 1884. He is a teacher, as was his wife before her marriage.

Edgar Preston Brainerd[9], b. May 8, 1885.

Edna Ruth Brainerd[9], b. Oct. 18, 1887.

Edwin Albert Brainerd[9], b. Jan. 28, 1893.

CLARENCE KING HAIGHT[8], b. Dec. 22, 1862; m. Gertrude May Phelps, Dec. 22, 1891. His birth and his wedding were each on an anniversary of his parents' marriage. His wife is a poet and magazine writer under the non-de-plume of Dame Durden. Since the advent of her children she does not write much. As she expresses it,

> " The hand well fit,.... ....
> · Finds truer work in wiping tears away.
> A woman, queen o'er destinies of men,
> May find her work is not with voice or pen ;
> To smooth the way that leads unto the grave,
> To train the child, and it for God to save ;
> Great things to do, and noble too, are these.
> The petty trials, the efforts vain to please,
> The upward strife, the failures too,
> That vex the heart e'en though 'tis true ;
> These all serve, and well He will repay·
> ......"

Clarence and Gertrude's children are these:
Howard Phelps Haight[9], b. May 30, 1896.
Derwin DeForest Haight[9], b. Feb. 11, 1898.
Helen Amanda Haight[9], b. Dec. 28, 1903.
Clarence Haight died early in 1904, aged 42.

ALMIRA KING–BUTTS[7], b. Nov. 25, 1825 ; d. May 14, 1875. She married Homer Butts, April 3, 1849. They had no children.

CHAPTER XXXI

FAMILY TREES. For descent from Lord Alexander de Greene de Boketon, A. D. 1202, and descent from Robert the Strong, Duke de France, A. D. 861, see Chapter XI.

For lineage from John Greene of Quidnessett; also from Stukeley Westcott, Elder Obediah Holmes, Hugh Parsons, and Capt. Thomas Straight, see Chapter XX.

For King and La Valley descent, see Chapter XXII. For the middle-ages history of the Mattesons, see Appendix.

Stephen King[6] was the eleventh and youngest child, and fifth son of Samuel and Deborah Greene-King[5]. He was born May 8, 1787, and died July 8, 1867, aged 80 years. He was married at 22 to Lydia Matteson. Her lineage on her father's side was this: Henry Matteson[1], the Emigrant, Capt. Henry[2], Ebenezer[3], Edmund[4], and Lydia[5]. On her mother's side she was of this descent: John Green[1] of Quidnessett, Lieut. Jas[2]., John of Bristol[3], James[4], Benjamin[5], and Virtue Greene[6], second wife of Edmund Matteson. As Stephen King was also a great-grandson of Jas. Greene[4], he and Lydia's mother were own cousins. He outlived his wife some 18 years.

Stephen King purchased the old Magdalen King place at West Greenwich. Here was where both he and his father were born. He had a world of trouble getting the title to it. The farm had "belonged" to Samuel, the youngest son of Magdalen, Stephen's father. But it seems to have been by a tacit agreement all around, and not by deeds. Stephen naturally wished a clear title. But the children of Magdalen were dead, and the grandchildren and great-grand-children were scattered over R. I., N. Y., Ohio and Ind. He commissioned his nephew, Joel Howard, to hunt up the distant heirs and get their signatures. I have before me a letter of Howard's reporting his progress. It is yellowed with time, and bears a seal, as that was before the days of envelopes and postage stamps. The letter bears date of Aug. 13, 1838.

His letter throws a light on their trust in each other, and the careful economy of those days. " I want to know if uncle Stephen will Accept the Deed without it. [Heirs' signatures.] It is not Convenient to take acknowledgements of Henry King and his wife, and Richmond Nichols and wife. It is agoing to be Considerable of trouble and 75 Cents Cost, but it Cannot be Done in York state by a Justice of the Peace. They firmly Declare to me that they will never trouble Him if he will Accept the Deed without it. I have the acknowledgement of 14, which Covers nearly all the blank paper there is on the Deed. If he will excuse us from taking any more, I will insure him as safe as though it was Done."

"Joel Howard."

In the above letter, the J in Joel had three mighty circles in the flourish of its tail. The H in Howard began with two large and two small convolutions, and the final d of Howard wound up with a string of 10-loop flourishes, which, with the many capitals, show that letter writing has its fashions, as well as other things.

Soon after this, Stephen sold the farm and moved to Pennsylvania, arriving there Jan. 2, 1840. The historic old house, while vacant, was in some way set fire to by a drunken man. Only the cellar and a few foundation stones are left to mark the home where Huguenot Magdalen King, and his wife Marie La Valley--King, breathed their last. The farm, once under good cultivation, is now overgrown by scrub oaks and pitch pine. It is in the hands of those who value it only for its quarry of rocks, and work that alone. It is a typical abandoned New England farm. The last Thursday in August each year, Magdalen's descendants meet at Indian Rocks and feast together ; and once a year these same people put in a day's work on the old family cemetery.

Stephen and his wife had eight children, two of whom died young. Two never married, and one left no issue. Nearly all his descendants live in Pa. Roger William King, a grandson, says, "None of this family have been famous or wealthy, but they have had the respect of their associates wherever they have been." They are a deeply religious family, nearly all Baptists, and have a general reputation for truth, honesty, and mathematical proficiency.

SAMUEL KING[7], [of Stephen[6] of Deborah Greene–King[5], James Greene[4], John of Bristol[3], Lieut. James[2], John Greene[1] of Quiduessett.] He was born March 6, 1810. He was married 7 years before they left R. I. to Mary F. Wood, May 12, 1833. He died April 1, 1862.

LUCETTA KING[8], b. April 22, 1834 ; d. Jan. 15, 1873, aged 39 years.

N. W. KING[8], b. April 28, 1843. He served in the Civil War, in the 46th Pa. Volunteers. Jan. 2, 1866, he married Nancy A. Baker. He is a contractor and builder on a large scale, taking contracts sometimes for 50 houses at a time.

Viola King-Avery[9], b. in 1868. Wife of Oliver Avery.

Carrie King-Harvey[9], b. March 22, 1870. Wife of John Harvey. She has a son.

Etta King--Egan[6], b. March 10, 1872 , m. John Egan. They have 3 children, and live in Brooklyn, N. Y.

Walter H. King[6], b. Aug. 27, 1875 ; m. and lives in Brooklyn. No children.

JAMES W. KING[6]. A twin, b. April 18, 1845. Died July 19, 1901. He m. Harriet E. McLaud, Dec. 24, 1870. Eight children, seven survive him.

JOHN S. KING[6]. Twin of the above. M. to Mattie A. McLaud, Nov. 9, 1872. They have 4 children, one of whom is dead.

ANNA KING-WHIPPLE[6], b. Dec. 26, 1850. Married James Whipple, March 26, 1889. They live at Silvara, Pa., and have one son, Earl J., b. Oct. 12, 1895.

WILLIAM KING[7], b. in June, 1811 ; married Harriet Dexter in 1859. He died Dec. 6, 1891. No children.

RAY KING[7], born Dec. 9, 1815. Died March 22, 1894. He was never married. He will be long remembered. For 60 years he was acknowledged as the best posted man on family lore in the King ranks. He was eccentric, peculiar in his dress, and plumped so abruptly into the subject in which he was interested that strangers would at first doubt his sanity. But he was shrewd enough, and never forget a date, or name, or incident. He would start on foot on one of his genealogy-tours, and would perhaps journey a 1,000 miles before he came walking back to his Pennsylvania home. He would be at Tully, N. Y., one day ; tarry three hours at another place ; stay with a cousin over night at Bromley ; another night at Pompey ; then shake the dust of N. Y. off his feet, and proceed in the same way to R. I. Wherever he went, he woke the kindred up on genealogical matters, and told them more in an hour than they had known in a life-time before. It is a thousand pities that a man so versed in family history, and with such a picturesque, succinct style of putting his knowledge, never put it down in black and white.

DEBORAH KING--BUNNELL[7], b. July 23, 1817. Married Edward Bunnell. No children. She d. in April 1882.

STUKELEY KING[7], [Stephen[6], Deborah Greene--King[5], James Green[4], John of Bristol[3], Lieut. James[2], John[1] of Quidnessett.] Born July 18, 1824. Died March 25, 1891. He married Fidelia Fish, Jan. 9, 1855. They were deeply religious people, Baptists, as were most of the Stephen King line.

CHARLES KING[8]. Died while young.

ROGER WILLIAM KING[8], b. Feb. 4, 1859. He is unmarried.

AMY L. KING--STURDEVANT[8], b. Aug. 3, 1861 ; m. Oct. 3, 1883, to Willis E. Sturdevant. Arva and Veva are dead. These children are living : Alma, b. 1887 ; Clark, in 1889 ; Carrie, in 1891 ; Webb, in 1893 ; and Sarah, in 1897. The Sturdevants live in Silvara, Pa.

CAROLINE E. KING-SCHMIDT[8], b. Dec. 26, 1865. She married C. Schmidt of Emporium, Pa., who died March 2, 1904. She has no children.

MARY DELPHENE KING--PLACE[8], b. Jan. 15, 1870 ; m. July 2, 1891, to Chas. A. Place, and died Dec. 25, 1901, leaving Claude, b. 1892, and Leah, b. 1900.

SUSIE JANE KING--LANIE[8]. Born Oct. 26, 1872. She was married March 9, 1904, to Clark Lanie of Rush, Pa.

CAROLINE KING[7]. Born 1834. Died single in 1862, aged 28.

CHAPTER XXXII

As the next eight chapters are really an elaboration of this one, it is thought best to give at the beginning a full pedigree of this family for convenience in consulting. Both husband and wife were descended from John Greene of Quidnessett, he through Lieut. John[2], and she through Lieut. James[2]. Both of them were descended from Marie La Valley and Magadalen King, he from their daughter Susan, she from their son Samuel. On his side comes the Lascelle, Wardwell, Waite, Hill, and Nichols descent. On hers comes the Straight, Westcott, Parson and Holmes descent, as well as a Lascelle, Wardwell, Waite and Hill descent also.

John Greene of Quidnessett had nearly eight centuries of certified noble and royal blood behind him. There are lords, dukes, counts and kings enough in his line to enthuse any title-hunter. It is a good line too. Nothing to be ashamed of. Chapters III and V give this in full. Chapter XI sums it up, and shows their relation to John of Quidnessett, the *stemmfader* Green of this book.

LINE OF LIEUT. JOHN GREENE[2]. The emigrant, John Greene of Quidnessett[1] (Wickford,) R. I., and Joan Beggarly; Lieut. John[2], whose wife was Abigail Wardwell; "Wealthy John[3]," and wife Ann Hill; Ann Greene[4], who married John Nichols[7]; Job Nichols[5], whose wife was Susan King, and David[6], their son.

LASCELLE–WARDWELL LINE. William Wardwell[2], believed to be the son of Richard and Mary Ithell–Wardwell, married Meribé, daughter of the French Huguenots, Gershom and Meribé Lascelle. Their son, Lascelle Wardwell[3], whose name was corrupted into Usal; William[4], his son, who came to America in 1634 and married Alice ———; Usal[5], born April 7, 1639, and married May 3, 1664, to the widow Mary Kinsman–Ringe; Abigail[6], their oldest child, born Oct. 27, 1665. She married Lieut. John Greene. Her line merged with his, running thus, John, Ann, Job, David, the 10th generation from Richard Wardwell and from Gershom Lascelle.

WAITE AND HILL LINE. Same as the above, to William Wardwell[2] and his wife Meribé. Their daughter Rosanna[3] married ———— Waite. Mehitable Waite[4] married Richard Hill of Great Torrington, England. They came with grown children to the colonies. John Hill[5], born 1613, and wife Frances had Jonathan[6], born about 1638. His oldest son was Henry Hill[7], born Jan. 27, 1661. His daughter was Ann[8], who married "Wealthy John" Greene[3]. David was the 11th generation from Gershom Lascelle and Richard Wardwell, by this line.

HILL–WESTCOTT LINE. (Wife's Side.) As above to Mehitable Waite Hill[4], then Rosanna Hill[5], (named after her mother's mother), who married Stukeley Westcott and followed Roger Williams to R. I. in 1636. (Stukeley Westcott's father, Richard Westcott of Great Torrington, England, m. Mary Parson in 1613.)

Stukeley and wife's oldest son was Amos[6], whose second wife was Deborah Stafford, whom he m. in 1670. Their daughter Rosanna, widow of Daniel Smith, married John Straight in 1705. The Straight[7] oldest daughter, Elizabeth[8], married James Greene[4], the son of John Greene of Bristol. Nancy King–Nichols was 10th in descent by this reckoning from the first Lascelle and Wardwell, and 7th from the first Westcott and Hill.

LINE OF LIEUT. JAMES GREENE[2]. (Wife's side.) John Greene[1] of Quidnessett and Joan; Lieut. James[2] and Elizabeth; John[3] of Bristol, and Elizabeth Holmes; James[4] and Elizabeth Straight. Deborah Greene–King[5] and Samuel King, Nancy King–Nichols[6] was their child.

PARSONS AND HOLMES LINE. (Wife's side.) John Greene of Bristol's wife Elizabeth was the grand-daughter of Elder Obediah Holmes who was so severely punished for his religious opinions. See Chapter VI. Her mother was Matilda (?) daughter of Hugh Parsons and his wife, formerly the widow of William English. Elizabeth Holmes–Greene was the mother of James Greene[4], the grandfather of Nancy King–Nichols. Elizabeth's relationship to Parsons and Holmes is not shown by official records, but rests upon family traditions and strong circumstantial evidence.

STRAIGHT LINE. (Wife's side.) Capt. Thomas Straight[1] of Watertown, Mass., by his first wife Mary, daughter of Joseph and Mary Long, had Henry[2], born 1652. He came to R. I. and married Hannah Tolman. Their son John[3] married Rosanna Westcott–Smith, and the latter couple's daughter, Elizabeth Straight Greene[4], was grandmother to Nancy King–Nichols, 6th in descent from Capt. Straight.

KING AND LA VALLEY LINE. Gershom[1] and Meribé, his wife; Anterés Lascelle–Pierce[2]; her daughter who married a King[3]; their son ————[4], who died of the Plague, 1665; John King[5] the Buccaneer, born 1654; Magdalen King who married Marie La Valley. Their son Samuel was Nancy's father, their daughter Susan, David's mother. Marié was the daughter of

Peter and Suzanné La Valley. See Chapter XXII, for the old La Valley history.

NICHOLS LINE. See Appendix and Ann Greene-Nichols section of Chapter XV. John Nichols[1], of Glamorganshire, Wales, died 1598 ; John the Mariner[2], and his wife Ruth ; Thomas[3] (probably); Hon. Thomas Nichols[4], the Emigrant, and his wife Hannah Griffin ; "Aristocratic John[5]," b. 1666, and wife Hannah Forman ; John[6], b. 1689; John[7] and wife Ann Greene[1] ; Job[8] and wife Suzanne King ; David[9] and wife Nancy King.

To most people this will be a dry list. But there is at least this compensation about it : The children of David and Nancy Nichols start out with 72 accredited and mentioned by name grand-parents of various degrees ; this exclusive of the eight centuries of ancestors back of John Greene of Quidnessett.

Nancy King was born Dec. 2, 1767. She was the oldest child of Samuel and Deborah Greene-King. Her chapter is given last because of the several chapters following it.

Nancy was not beautiful. She was naturally quiet and still-tongued, though a good talker on subjects in which she was interested. She was a placid, sweet-tempered woman of endless patience and forbearance. Her life was a sad one, because repressed and curtailed of what it should and would have been but for the absurd prejudice of her day.

Nancy King came nearer being a genius than any other one of the entire Quidnessett line. She had a strong brain. She was one of those mathematical prodigies whose mind grasps on the instant solutions of the most intricate problems, and she had a remarkable historical bent of mind. Nowadays she would have been a scientist or historian.

Our fore-parents had woman's sphere mapped out. She was to keep house and rear a large family of children. Never, never, was she to become a student, or above all, a writer. That would unsex her entirely. It may not be true that so strict were their ideas of propriety that a New England maiden fainted at the mention of undressed lumber, but it certainly was true that it was considered masculine, and therefore immodest, for a woman to write for publication. A friend of a poetess of that day, inserted without her knowledge one of her poems in a Boston paper. The lady expressed herself as so mortified that she could "hardly look anyone in the face." Mary Somerville was a model housewife. Yet because she engaged in scientific studies, a sister used this severe language so late as 1812 :" I hope you will give up your foolish manner of life and studies, and make a *respectable* and useful wife."

Samuel King and his wife emphatically sat down on their daughter's ambition. Her husband shared their views. She was not allowed to study mathematics, or to write anything beyond family letters. She was too sweet and tractable to resist. To the day of her death it was a common thing for puzzled neighbors to come to her to find out what a cistern would hold, how much stone it would take to build a house, or to know the number of acres in an irregular or odd-shaped tract of land. Baffled in her literary desires, she diligently searched out her family history anyway, interviewing old people who could remember back before 1700. She wove a verbal narration of this that is said to have been most interesting. The fragments that have come down to us show much care on her part. I have never found one of her statements that could not be verified.

This was the bright, cheerful girl with whom David Nichols fell in love when he visited her uncle's family after the Revolutionary War was over. David was quick-brained himself. He was good-looking, and had the stamp and breeding of a city man. He was a good conversationalist, and over-flowed with wit and mirth. He had the prestige of having been a Revolutionary soldier.* He was a fine singer, and an expert violinist. He was industrious, and a man of sound morals and principals. He was the son of Job and Susan King-Nichols, born in 1763, and had been brought up in Providence, R. I.

Nancy married him about 1787. She thought she was doing well. So did her parents. She had the French love of finery, and her wedding outfit was extravagant for a farmer's daughter. It was half a dozen years before the first cotton cloth was woven in R. I. A fine piece of cotton was then esteemed as much as silk. Her wedding dress was purchased in Providence. It was imported from England and cost $1.00 per yard, equal to about $3.00 at present money values. It was piece of fine chintz, thick and hand-woven. The creamy background was sprinkled with sprays of tiny pink flowers. Cotton goods like this can now be obtained for about 25 cents per yard.

But the auspicious marriage did not turn out so well. David could neither make money nor keep it. He was a fine workman, a deft hand at cabinet making, one of the half dozen men in the United States that alone at that time knew how to make a violin. But he could not turn his gifts to

---

*It is well known in the family that he enlisted twice during the 7 years' war. The first time he was only in his 16th year when he enlisted. He served this time as a bugler, in the same regiment in which were a dozen or more of his Greene cousins. The second time he served in the ranks, and the first lock musket that he carried he gave as a memento to his youngest son, Nelson Nichols, the author's father. Rhode Island's military records are too incomplete to throw any light on his second service. The former is a matter of record, as this will show :

"Record and Pension Office, War Department, Washington, D. C.
"Record No. 656329.					"July 1, 1901.

"It is shown by the records that one David Nichols served as a private in Captain Philip Traffarn's company of Col. John Tophan's regiment, R. I. State Troops, Revolutionary War. He enlisted June 14, 1778, and his name appears on rolls of that organization from July, 1778, to February, 1779, without remark.
"By authority of the Secretary of War."

advantage. He spoiled a first-class artisan to become a third-rate farmer. He could not plan. His family increased. He shifted from pillar to post, always in hard lines, never in easy circumstances.

David was buoyant and overflowing with life and hope, when he was wearing his rose-colored spectacles. But when the pendulum swung the other way he was morose, down-hearted and moody. He was never well, and subject to attacks of heart trouble and nervous prostration, at which times he was irritable and notional. It fretted and galled him that men without half his talent succeeded in life, while he was a failure. Poor, patient Nancy put up with all his humors, took the brunt of everything, worked like a slave for her dozen children, and never scolded or fretted. No wonder that her children thought her an angel. When she was young she had a physique that should have carried her to 90. She died Nov. 22, 1820, aged 53—worn literally out.

They seem for a short period to have lived in R. I. They lived mostly, however, among the Berkshire Hills of Massachussetts, until near the close of 1800. N. Y. was at that time offering great inducements to settlers in the northern part of her territory, in what were called the military districts. David caught the emigration fever. In the spring of 1801 they moved to Pompey Hill, N. Y., the highest point of land in the State, bitter cold in winter, and yet possessing many advantages. Here they lived, and here Nancy died. Her tombstone, cut and lettered by her brother Joel's hands, now lies prone and broken. But it can yet be deciphered where "Anna Nichols died, Nov. 22, 1820." Anna was really her name, but as she was always called Nancy, I have retained it always in speaking of her.

David Nichols married again. The last wife was Mrs. Abigail Brown. By her he had a daughter, Betsey. Becoming dissatisfied with N. Y., in 1831 he removed to Sharon Center, Ohio. Here he died and was buried. He died Nov. 5, 1839, aged 76 years.

David and Nancy had 12 children. There is a little uncertainty as to where the first George and Almira came in. I follow the judgment of those best qualified to place them. Nine children lived to grow up, and eight to marry. As the eight have their lives given in the next eight chapters, only their birth and death dates will be given here.

SUSAN NICHOLS[7], b. about 1788. Accidentally smothered in bed when six weeks old.

HENRY NICHOLS[7], b. Nov. 22, 1790. Died April 21, 1851.

JOHN NICHOLS[7], b. in 1792. He never married. He died **Dec.** 27, 1865. He was a fifer in the War of 1812. He was so frank and jovial as to be a great favorite with both officers and men. He was under Col. Scott, afterward General Winfield Scott. They were stationed for a time in

Canada. John used to delight in telling anecdotes of this period. All the
Nichols have a tooth for cream. The soldier boys were foraging one time,
when John could not resist slipping into a milk house, and helping himself
to cream. He was busy poking the cream into his mouth, when the mistress
of the house appeared, and the way she spluttered was a caution! On another occasion his mess helped themselves to a Tory farmer's honey. He
came the next morning, and raised so a great a kick that Col. Scott went
with him to find the secreted honey. When they came into the part of the
log barrack where Nichols' mess was, Col. Scott opened a sort of a cupboard,
and as luck would have it, awkwardly jabbed his hand right into the honey.
Fifer Nichols was a personal friend of his, and Scott was not minded to
make an example of him. Slamming the cupboard door to he whipped out
a handkerchief and began to wipe his hand.

"What do you mean, —— —— —— you!" thundered Scot, apparently
in a great rage. "Keeping your soft soap in with your victuals! ——
—— —— ——, I've a mind to send you to the guard-house for it! Don't
you let it occur again." The Tory did not find his honey, but Scott had
plenty of it for his dinner.

John Nichols was a noble man in every sense of the word. Upon her
death-bed his mother charged him to always look after his father, and gave
her 8-year old Nelson to him. He had thought of marrying a young woman
with whom he was in love. He resolutely turned his back on all this,
raised his little brother, and stayed with his father during the old gentleman's life time. Then he cared for his stepmother and half-sister, until the
latter married and left him. He spent the last 35 years of his life in Sharon
Center, Ohio. He was always called Squire Nichols. He was a fine
business man, and the soul of honor.

RICHMOND NICHOLS[7], b. Dec. 3, 1795; died Feb. 9, 1882.
CYNTHIA NICHOLS[7]–KING[7], b. March 4, 1796; died after 1870.
GEORGE NICHOLS[7] (1). Died in infancy.
MIRANDA NICHOLS–BARNES[7], b. Dec. 16, 1799; d. Jan. 7, 1852.
MARIAM NICHOLS–BRADLEY[7], b. Jan. 26, 1801; d. July 24, 1871.
SALLY NICHOLS–LAMSON[7], b. Feb. 13, 1804; d. May 20, 1879.
ALMYRA NICHOLS[7]. Died in early childhood.
GEORGE WASHINGTON NICHOLS[7] (2), b. about 1809; d. March
21, 1839.
NELSON NICHOLS[7], b. May 11, 1812; d. Feb. 4, 1865.

By his second wife David Nichols had a daughter Betsey. She married
a Mr. Breck. Both are dead long ago. She left at least two sons, Dr. Ira
Breck, and Dell Breck, of Cleveland, Ohio.

CHAPTER XXXIII

FAMILY TREES. For descent from the first Lord de Greene de Boke-ton, A D 1202, and descent from the royal Capet line of France, from A D 861, see Chapter XI For lineage from John King and Peter La Valley, see Chapter XXII For all other lines of descent, including two from John Greene[1] of Quidnessett, and lineage from Capt Straight, Stukeley West-cott, Hugh Parsons, etc , and from the Lascelles, Waites, Hills and Wardwells, see Chapter XXXII, and also the Appendix

Henry Nichols was the second child of David and Nancy Nichols, an infant sister dying before his birth He was born Nov. 22, 1790, in Berk-shire County, Massachusetts. When he was 11 years old his father moved to Pompey, N Y , then a new country He lived here until 1834, and then at 44, started out once more to live in a new country He came to what is now Wolcottville, Indiana, when no other white man was living in the town-ship, although his brother, Nelson Nicholas, and brother-in-law, Peter Lam-son, had entered land, and came there to live shortly afterwards He lived in Indiana from this time until his death, April 21, 1851, nearly 17 years after.

The oldest of a poor man's large family, and twice a pioneer in a new country, it goes without saying that he was used to hard work, hard times and hard lines in life He never let it worry him He had an odd habit, if much fatigued, of lying flat down on his back and sticking his legs straight up in the air. Then he would sing to the top of his voice, and by the time his song was over he was rested and ready to go to work again He cut short his honeymoon to enlist in the War of 1812–14, and as he used to say, never saw a battle or a scratch, as peace was declared three months after.

Henry was married July 10, 1814, to Eleanor Lord She was born in Deerfield, N Y , Dec 23, 1794 She was lineally descended from Thomas Lord, of Braintree, England, who was a noted man in his day, and helped to found the city of Hartford, Conn., in 1635 Hartford has erected a monument, a massive sandstone structure, to the honor of her founders, of whom Thomas Lord is named as one. Eleanor's father was killed by the Indians in 1801, when she was but 7 years old. The little orphan fell into cruel hands. To the day of her death she carried deep scars that marked the inhuman beatings and the knocking down with clubs that she had experienced. She was not sent to school, but picked up a knowledge of how to read.

Twenty years Henry and Eleanor lived in N. Y., and here 8 of their children were born; 2 more were born in Indiana. These children were Almyra, Ira, Nancy, Deborah, Halsey, Sally, Rachel, George, Margaret and John. There was not a break in this family until 1839, then in a year's time 4 died. Almyra died of consumption at 23, dying Jan. 26, 1839 or 1840 (both dates given). Nancy, the 19 year old daughter, died Feb. 5, 1839. The mother took a fatal cold standing by the grave in chill weather. She took pneumonia, and one week later, Feb. 12, 1839, she died also. John, the baby, died the next October.

The family had begun to thin out. In 1853, Sally died, aged 19. The father died in 1851, and Halsey, a young man of 27, died in 1852. Margaret died, March 27, 1864, Ira in 1865, Deborah died May 25, 1894, and George died Feb. 2, 1901. Rachel alone of all this family is yet living, in 1904. The old place passed into other hands after Henry's death in 1851. He had married again, nearly eight years after his first wife's death. He had no children by Polly—the last wife.

ALMYRA NICHOLS[8], b. Sept. 18, 1816; d. Jan. 30, 1839. She died unmarried, as did her aunt and great aunt, and her cousin, all of whom were Almyra Nichols, and all under 25 at time of death. It became almost a superstition in the family after that, that no Almyra Nichols would live to see a quarter of a century.

IRA VAN RENSEALLER NICHOLS[8], b. Jan 21, 1818. He was married Dec. 11, 1841, to Nancy Matteson, or Nancy Munger, as she was often called, having been brought up in the Munger household. She was a quiet, good woman. She died early in 1865. Her husband enlisted after her death, and was soon one of the many victims of the Civil War. They left 5 children, only one of whom was married.

LUCY NICHOLS-CHAFFEE[9], married and went out West.[?] Had a daughter, and a son Alvin, born about 1861. She died not far from the time her parents did.

ALBERT NICHOLS[9]. He married a Miss Dickinson, a daughter of Barrett Dickinson, of Wolcottville, Indiana. He is a farmer, and lives at South Milford, Indiana. His children are Elsie, Glen and Vernon.

FULTON NICHOLS[9]. He lives at Wolcottville, Indiana. He has buried three children, and has two living. Mabel is married, and lives in Kendallville, Indiana. She has a son. Fulton's youngest daughter is Pearlie.

ANNABELLE NICHOLS-NICHOLS[9]. Extremely modest and retiring, she was yet one of the sweetest girls the author ever knew. She was always as frail as a wildwood flower. She married William Nichols, no relation of hers, and had three children, Earl, b. about 1885, Alta, b. about 1887, and Irim (Ira ?) b. about 1896. She died of consumption in April, 1901.

Dr. Henry A. Nichols[9]. He was only 4 years old when his parents died. He was taken by Mr. and Mrs. Ira Meeker, of Wolcottville, Indiana. They were dear, good old people, who were real parents to the homeless boy. He owes much of his success to them. Henry became a physician, and has a large practice. He lives in Flint, Indiana. He was married in 1897 to Flora Benninghoof. They have no children.

NANCY NICHOLS[8], b. July 2, 1820; d. Feb. 5, 1839.

DEBORAH NICHOLS–ABBOTT[8], b. Jan. 1, 1823. Died after 1890. Deborah was one of those patient, gentle, domestic women that the world never half appreciates, because they blow no trumpet over their deeds. She married the Rev. Daniel Abbott, in 1856, and moved out West. She died at the home of her daughter, Ella Abbott Parker, May 25, 1894, a year after her husband's death.

Ella Abbott–Parker[9] was the oldest child of Rev. and Mrs. Abbott. Ambitious, resolute and independent, she was no more like her meek, never-speak-for-herself mother than as though a thousand generations rolled between them. Born in a new country, she breathed in her native air with a sense of freedom and a breadth of soul. Her father had an old-time distrust of learned women. But repression could not repress as dauntless a soul as Ella Abbott's. She studied, she taught, though she had to begin her first school in short dresses. At sixteen she ran away, so determined was she to go to school. She came 1000 miles alone to her aunt Rachel's. Here she was encouraged, and given the advantage of superior schools. Won over by her pluck, her father invited her back, and concluded it was a fine thing to have a scholarly daughter after all.

Aug. 16, 1883, Ella was married to W. H. Parker, of Long Island, Kansas. Together they have faced hard years, dry years, and no-crop years. Neither of them ever gave up. To-day they have a fine farm of over 400 acres, and all the comforts of life. They have had seven children. Carrie Pearl, their oldest child, died Oct. 9 1884, aged 7 weeks. Their living children are Ray K., b. Oct. 24, 1885, Hattie Mabel, b. Feb. 7, 1890, Henry Jay, b. Nov. 3, 1891, Lon Abbott, b. April 16, 1893, Ina Evelyn, b. Feb. 14, 1899, and Ira Theodore, b. Oct. 15, 1900. These children are chips of the old block. Mabel graduated from her home school at 3 months past 12, the youngest graduate ever in the country. Ray, the oldest son, who intends to be an engineer, was up with his studies to enter such a course when he lacked two full years of being old enough to enter any engineering school.

George Abbott[9], married Hattie Parker, a sister of Elia's husband. She was a most worthy woman. She died in March, 1900, leaving 4 children, Clyde, Clair, Una and Dee. George Abbott is a farmer on a large scale, owning 640 acres of land not far from his sister's home.

HASLEY NICHOLS[8], b. Aug. 23, 1825; d. June 17, 1852.

SALLY NICHOLS[8], b. Sept. 23, 1824; d. March 27, 1843.

RACHEL NICHOLS-BOOSINGER-HODGES[8], b. Aug. 28, 1830. After her father's death Rachel lived with her uncle Nelson until her marriage with Conrad Boosinger, Oct. 1, 1858. She has lived ever since in Rome City, Indiana. Mr. Boosinger died in 1870. Afterwards his widow married Nelson P. Hodges, and is again a widow. Rachel Hodges has given me almost all the dates and facts in this letter. She has never had any children of her own, but she has been almost a mother to her orphan nephews and nieces. She raised one of these, Ida Kesler, and this niece and husband live with her.

GEORGE NELSON NICHOLS[8], b. June 30, 1833, d Feb 2, 1901, went west when a young man. He was married in Iowa to Sarah Baxter, June, 1855 He died in Nebraska They had two children, Nellie, married and living in Hardin, Nebraska, and William in another part of Nebraska He has three sons, Charles, Paul and Fred. His sister Nellie is the mother of six children.

MARGARET NICHOLS–KESLER[8] She was the ninth child and the first one born in Indiana She married William Kesler at Rome City, Ind., in May, 1858 She died April 21, 1864

HENRY KESLER[9] Joined the regular army, 1862 Went to Fort Gibson, Arizona Never heard from again

IDA KESLER-TICE[9] She was brought up by her aunt Rachel, and has never been separated from her Her husband is William Tice of Rome City They have no children

JOHN NICHOLS[8], b Oct. 26, 1838, and d Oct 6, 1839.

CHAPTER XXXIV

Richmond Nichols[7], of Nancy King–Nichols[6], Deborah Greene–King[5], James Greene[4], John Greene[3], of Bristol, Lient. James Greene[2] and John Greene[1] of Quidnessett

FAMILY TREES For English pedigree, with descent from the first Lord de Greene de Boketon, A D 1202, and descent from the royal Capet line of France, A D 861, see Chapter III and XI. For lineage from Capt Thomas Straight, Stukeley Westcott, Hugh Parsons and Elder Obediah Holmes, together with the Quidnessett Greene descent on his father's side, and for both father's and mother's descent from John King and Peter La Valley, see Chapter XXXII This same chapter and the Appendix show Richmond's relation to the Lascelle–Wardwell, Waite and Hill families The generations in this chapter are numbered from John Greene of Quidnessett, counting from the mother, Nancy King–Nichols[1] side. The Nichols pedigree is also in Chapter XXXII

Richmond Nichols was the fifth child of David and Nancy King–Nichols He was born Dec 3, 1795 The family Bible was destroyed by fire Curiously enough in filling out the records in a new one, every date in it was placed exactly a year later than it really was I have therefore given his birth as the other Nichols records have it, in 1795 instead of 1796, and the births of the older children to correspond with these records also

In his sixth year his parents moved to Pompey; N Y, where he lived for 49 years longer He removed to Ohio, where he died, 32 year later, Feb 9, 1882, in his 87th year He was married in 1820 to Margaret Rice, remotely of Welsh, and more nearly of Rhode Island descent. Through a marriage of one of the early Rices, she was of Randall Holden lineage, the fiery, radical man, a refugee to R. I, because of the "damnable error," as the Massachusetts people put it, of his religious views, and who suffered arrest and imprisonment for the same. See Chapter VIII.

Margaret was born in Hastings, Oswego Co., N. Y. She came of a family of whom some reached the century mark. She herself died in 1889 aged 89. She was an active, independent, energetic woman, neat as a pin, and held in the family annals to be second only to Marie La Valley as a marvelous cook.

When the War of 1812-14 broke out, Richmond tried to enlist. He was but 16, and was rejected on account of his youth. He was rejected again in 1814, this time as physically unfit. The Nichols home at Pompey was in Western N. Y., near Lake Ontario, and the Canada line. The York State men realized that war was at their door, when General Prevost attacked Sackett's Harbor on Lake Ontario. Every civilian who could march or carry a musket, rushed to its defense. Samuel King, Richmond's own brother-in-law, says this 17-year old boy was one of those that helped defend this important fort. Patriotism was a marked trait in his family. The war record of his sons breaks any other recorded in this book. Six of his sons went into the Civil War. One died of wounds, one lost his eyes, two came back to die by inches, and two returned hale and well.

According to the old saying that every son is worth a thousand dollars to his parents, and every daughter half that sum, Richmond and Margaret Nichols accumulated quite a little capital in children, as they had 10 sons and 4 daughters. There was over 29 years difference in the ages of the oldest and the youngest sons, full brothers. Wealth in a tangible form never came to this couple, but no millionaire could have more hospitably welcomed friends to his home than did they.

Richmond kept a young heart to the last. Once a niece visited them. She was wretchedly homesick. He saw it. With a merry "now for some fun!" he took her in charge. Such a happy, lively day as they had! Such tricks as he played! Such droll stories as he told! She never forgot it. How many men of 70 would take that much trouble to give a 14-year old girl a day of pleasure?

Thirteen of Richmond's children lived to be grown. The fourth child died at 11. This family was called the best looking of the entire David Nichols branch. Two or three of the sons were particularly fine looking men.

GEORGE NICHOLS[8], b. March 19, 1822. The special turn of mechanical genius of his great-grandfather, Samuel King, was inherited by him. He is a mill-wright, and one who stands at the head of his profession. After he was 38 he gave up all other kinds of mill construction and confined himself to saw-mills alone. The finest and largest saw-mills on the North American continent he has constructed. From Canada to Louisiana he has built monster plants for Jay Gould and other capitalists. Twenty-three of these saw-mills have had a capacity of from 100,000 to 500,000 feet of lumber in

10 hours run. He has taken out various patents in his line of work, and has brought his sons up to be draftsmen and mill-wrights, also.

At the age of 30 Heorge married Hannah M. Coleman, of Pompey, N. Y. She was born in 1832 and died in 1894. Since then he lives with his sons in Canton, Ill. His oldest son, Frederick Adell, died in August, 1853, at 3 months. Eva Anna, died in 1864, aged 9 years, and Alfred J. died in 1881, at the age of 24. This left but two sons.

WINFIELD SCOTT NICHOLS[9], commonly called Scott, was born April 29, 1861. He has charge of the construction work of a large manufactory of Canton, Ill. Dec. 27, 1888, he m. Anna Beck. They have Bessie, b. Oct. 5, 1889, George Beck, b. Feb. 10, 1892, and Elmer Leroy, b. Aug. 31, 1897.

FREDERICK RICHMOND NICHOLS[9], b. June 14, 1863. He is the Superintendent of Machinery in a Canton, Ill., plow manufactory that employs 1200 workmen. Sept. 23, 1885, he m. Mary H. Manville. They have Eva Mary, b. July 17, 1886, Harry Manville, b. March 13, 1888, Margaret C., b. Oct 20, 1890, and Helen Jeanette, b. Oct. 26, 1892.

HENRY NICHOLS[8], [Rich.[7], Nancy[6], Deborah Green-King[5], etc.,] born Aug. 31, 1824. He came with his parents to Sharon Center, Ohio, when a young man, and has lived there ever since. Henry has the family records. As his older brother, George, has always been away from the rest of the family since he was grown, Henry is looked up to as the head of the Ohio Nicholses. He is a farmer. His wife was Huldah ————.

EDWIN O. NICHOLS[9], b. May 3, 1856. Married (1) to Catherine E. Long, in 1876. M. (2) to Eva A. Helmer in 1886. His son and daughter are by his first wife.

Myrtle L. Nichols-Wilkinson[10], b. Jan. 18, 1878 ; m. 1896 to Edwin E. Wilkinson. They have Lloyd C. b. June 8, 1897, and May Lavonn, b. July 5, 1901.

Bernard Nichols[10], b. Sept. 7, 1879.

EDITH NICHOLS-GRAY[9], wife of James Gray. Her children are Henry, who died at less than a year, George Deino, Lloyd William, and Richmond Henry.

GEORGE NICHOLS[9]. Married Nettie Buckley. She is the third or fourth generation from a Revolutionary War veteran, Benjamin Bentley, a pioneer settler who died at Sharon, O., in 1818. He was the great grandson of William Bentley, who was counted a leading citizen of Quidnessett in the early days. As such, along with old John Greene and 39 other prominent men of the Narragansett country, he signed in 1679 a petition to the King begging him to put a stop to Connecticut's claims, which invalidated the title to their land. Narragansett Wm. Bentley was the grandson of a William who came to the colonies about 1635.

PERRY NICHOLS[8], b. Aug. 8, 1825. Died not far from 1900. His wife was Melvina ————. He was a life-long hotel keeper. The more of hustle, coming and going about him, the happier he was. He knew how to be in sixteen places at once, how to manage a waiter's strike, or to care for a train-load of excursionists at two hours' notice. Nichols Junction, Mo., was named in his honor by the Frisco R. R. Co.

FRANK NICHOLS[9]. His wife is Emma ————. He is proprietor of the Nichols House, Norwalk, Ohio. They have a daughter, Geneva B.

KATE NICHOLS-CUNNINGHAM[9]. She lives in New London, O., and has several children.

AMY ROSETTE NICHOLS[8], d. in 1838, aged 11.

LEANDER NICHOLS[8], b. May 14, 1829. He married Eliza L. Martin, Feb. 9, 1854. She was the daughter of James and Ruamy Martin, Friends or Quakers who came from N. Y. to Ruggles, O. Leander Nichols is in comfortable circumstances. His wife was an expert amateur gardener and kept their home literally embowered in flowers. He has been a widower many years.

> ELMER NICHOLS[9], b. Nov. 14, 1854. He was married Nov. 16, 1875, to Evalyn Woolley. They have but one daughter, Lena D., born Nov. 15, 1878.

ANN NICHOLS–BATTERSON[8], b. Jan. 19, 1832. She was married to Simeon Batterson, Dec. 15, 1852. They live at Wanda, O. Mrs. Batterson has furnished me considerable data for this work.

> AMY BATTERSON-ROOD[9], b. March 25, 1854, and m. Feb. 25, 1892, to Warren Rood of Medina, O. They have a daughter Agnes, born May 10, 1898.
>
> HERMAN BATTERSON[9], b. Oct. 3, 1857, and m. Jan. 25, 1887. His children are Burdette, b. Jan. 8, 1888, and Carrie, b. Dec. 27, 1892.

ALBERT NICHOLS[8], b. Sept. 4, 1833. He was married Oct. 10, 1857, to Jane Gano, who was the mother of his children. He married his present wife, who was Mrs. Phebe Newton, July 18, 1901. Albert enlisted in the Civil War in Feb. 1864. He draws a total disability pension, as he sacrificed two good eyes for his country. He is almost entirely blind. He lives in Benton Harbor, Mich. The list of grandchildren was not furnished me.

> WILMER NICHOLS[9], lives at Bangor, Mich.
>
> GRACE NICHOLS-NEWTON[9], She was her father's housekeeper for some years. She married her step-mother's son, and lives in Chicago.
>
> MRS. LEAH NICHOLS-SHERMAN[9]. Wife of R. O. Sherman, Chicago.
>
> FLORENCE NICHOLS-JOHNS[9]. Lives in Genoa, Texas.
>
> LUTA NICHOLS[9], died Nov. 30, 1874.

DANIEL NICHOLS[8], b. Aug. 8, 1835. Daniel served three years in the 103d Ohio Volunteer Infantry, during the Civil War. He m. in 1880, when he was 45, Julia, daughter of Ephraim and Elizabeth Gaver-Cramer. She was born and raised in Frederick Co., Maryland. Their only child died at birth. Since 1895 they have had their orphan niece, Minnie, daughter of John Nichols, deceased. He lives at Chagrin Falls, Ohio.

LOUISE ROSINA NICHOLS–FOSTER[8], b. April 25, 1837. Louise was housekeeper for many years for her bachelor uncle, John Nichols. She m. William Foster, Nov. 30, 1870. Her husband's death and financial reverses came together, in 1890. Louise at 53, wasted no time in putting up a "poor mouth," but began to support herself as a housekeeper. As she expresses it, she "never borrows as long as she can buy, and always keeps enough money on hand to pay a doctor's bill, and buy the coffin she will need by and by."

CLARA A. NICHOLS–IRVIN[8], b. April 20, 1839; d. July 19, 1897. She was left a widow with two daughters, only one of whom is living.

> ELLA IRVIN[9], b. Nov. 11, 1862; d. Sept. 16, 1881.
>
> IDA M. IRVIN-STEFFEN[9], b. Feb. 29, 1860; m. Jan. 17, 1878. She lives in Hinckley, Ohio. Her children are Clara, b. July 1, 1879, Alta, b. Jan. 24, 1881, Harry J., b. Dec.

1882, Katie, b. Sept. 23, 1884, Ruby, b. Feb. 20, 1887, Ray, b. July 11, 1889, Daniel J., b. Dec. 1, 1891. and Georgie, who died in 1893, aged nearly 6.

WILLIAM H. H. NICHOLS[3], (Harrison,) b. Nov. 4, 1841. He was a soldier in the Civil War, one of six brothers in the service. He was struck with a shell at Antietam, and although he lived, he died a few years after from the effects of the wound.

JOHN NICHOLS[3], b. Aug. 6, 1844; d. in 1895. During the Civil War he was sent home to die. He rallied, but was never well again. He m. in 1874.

CHARLES NICHOLS[9]. He served three years in the Spanish-American War, 1898-1901. He is now living in Madina Co., O.

DEZ NICHOLS[9]. Lives in Medina Co., O.

MINNIE NICHOLS[9], b. June 22, 1885. She lives with her uncle, Samuel Nichols.

CHARLES NICHOLS[3], b. May 12, 1848. He was the youngest of the six brothers who went to the war. He died from a wound in the Civil War. He was under 18 years of age at his death.

FRANKLIN LEROY NICHOLS[3], b. May 28, 1851. When he was born, he had 8 brothers and sisters over 15 years of age, and one brother was in his 30th year. Frank himself is No. 14. He lives at Creston, Ohio. He has the largest family in the Richmond Nichols' third generation, having Leroy, Henry, Clarinda, Flina, Grace and DeForest.

CHAPTER XXXV

FAMILY TREES. For descent from Sir Alexander, first Lord de Greene de Boketon, A D 1202, and descent from the Capet Kings of France, from line beginning A D. 861, see Chapter XI. For the lineage of both husband and wife from the Kings and the La Valleys, see Chapter XXII For all other lines of the wife's descent, including two strains of John Greene of Quidnessett blood, also lineage from Capt Straight, Hugh Parsons, Stukeley Westcott and Obediah Holmes, together with lineage from Lascelles, Wardwells, Waites and Hills, see Chapter XXXII, and Appendix also

SPINK DESCENT, on husband's side (See Chapter XXII) Robert Spink[1], an early Quidnessett settler, Capt Ishmael Spink[2] and wife Deliverance Hall , Benjamin Spink[3] and wife Jane , Deliverance Spink[4], who married John King, grandfather to Henry King.

ALBRO DESCENT, on husband's side "Quaker John Alburro[1]," or Alborough, now pronounced Albro. He died at the Quaker settlement of Portsmouth, R I, Dec 17, 1712, aged 96 Hon John[2], Assistant President of Providence Plantations, the earliest name of R I. His wife was Mary Stokes, John[3], and Abigail Belloo, John[4] and Lydia Spencer, Job[5] and Deborah Andrews, who was probably of those Andrews (see chapter XVIII) who were of double Quidnessett Greene descent , Eunice[6], who married Job King, and Henry[7], their son

---

Cynthia Nichols[7] was born March 4, 1796, and died after 1870. She was married Jan 5, 1815, to her second cousin, Henry King, and thus their marriage gave *three* strains of both King and La Valley blood to their children. Henry was descended from John, son of Magdalen and Marie La Valley–King, Cynthia, on her mother's side, came from Samuel, John's brother, and on her father's side from Susan, their sister Cynthia's children inherited from her two strains of Quidnessett Greene blood, one line coming from Lieut James Greene[2], and the other from his brother, Lieut. John Greene[2] Their father, moreover, was almost certainly through his grandmother, Deborah Andrews–Albro, descended twice over from Lieut. John Greene[2].

Henry and Cynthia King's children therefore had the most crossed and most related blood of any of David and Nancy Nichols[7] grandchildren. In the family it was always understood that they partook largely of the Albro temperament, having their independence and their unyielding will. The oldern Kings had a thrifty side. The triple infusion of their blood has made this entire family money makers. Like their three-times-over first American ancestress, Marie La Valley, they have been tremendous workers. The La Valley reserve is also marked. Many of this line prefer the barest mention of their individual families, holding that their details are not for outside eyes. From the Nichols side not a few have taken a passionate love of music.

Forty years ago Job King, a brother of Henry, summed up his family's characteristics in these words: " They are long-lived, hardy, industrious, very fond of sports, hunting and fishing ; all very tenacious of what they believe to be their just and honest rights, and would willingly sacrifice time and money to defend the same, when attacked by an enemy. To friends, they are more than a common friend ; to an enemy, they are equally noted as un-yielding and unconquerable, not much given to compromise."

Of the heads of this line this may be said:

Henry King was born in the State of New York, May 11, 1794. He died March 25, 1865. His wife was born at Pompey, N. Y., March 4, 1796. In the War of 1812, Henry King served in the army along with Cynthia's brothers, John and Henry. His intimacy with the brothers ended in an attachment to the sister, whom he married Jan. 5th, 1815. Their large fam-ily were all born in N. Y. Most of their relatives having moved to Indiana or Ohio, their clannish feeling led them to follow them. In 1839 they moved to Huron County, Ohio, where the rest of their lives were spent. Here Cap-tain King, as he was called, purchased several hundred acres of land. A settlement grew up, called at first King's Corners. When it put on village and young city airs it changed its name to New London. Energetic from the crown of his head to the sole of his foot, Henry King set various en-ter-prises into motion and kept them there. Under his direction a large part of the first railroad was built that passed through northern Ohio. He built the first church in New London, according to the recollection of his children, paying for it out of his own pocket. At the time of his death his home paper said of him, " The poor man, provided he was industrious, was certain of finding in him a most excellent friend. The lazy always found themselves held in abhorence."

Mrs. Ascher, their youngest child, pays this feeling tribute to her parents: " My father was a man respected by all with whom he came into contact. He was foremost in every enterprise. My mother was methodical and self-controlled. She was fond of reading in a time when books were few and difficult to obtain. I remember her as a thoughtful woman who had an uncommon dislike of gossip and idleness. She seems to me to have been of the best type of the old fashioned New England woman. She was perhaps peculiar. She said and did things that I never knew any one else to say or do. One of her sayings was that all time belonged to God, and she must use it to the best advantage. She commenced the day with devotion. After breakfast she meditated, planning out the order of the day, and the way it should be done. After the regular forenoon's work was done she read her Bible and spent some time in reflection, for she said all reading and no reflection was not good.

"My brothers were industrious and intelligent. They were men of integrity, and their word was counted good anywhere."

Owing to their dislike of publicity, the rest of the family biography will be rapidly passed over. There were 10 children, 7 sons and 3 daughters, viz.: George, Vernon, Charles, Degoliar, Henry, John, Cynthia, Job, Huldah and Sabrina. Only one died young.

GEORGE KING[8], b. Jan. 12, 1816. He died in 1898, aged 82. He was married first to Susan Williams. By this wife he had 6 children, Eunice, who became Mrs. Morrill, and George, Henry, De Loss, De Golier, and De Witt. He married the second time.

VERNON KING[8], b. July 10, 1818. Married (1) to his cousin, Polly Ann Bradley. See Chapter XXXVII. 2 children, only one of whom lived to marry. He was married (2) to Regina Powers, who had no children. He and his family lived in Michigan. He died, March 29, 1895.

> HOMER W. KING[9], b. Nov. 13, 1844. Married on his 22d birthday to Ellen S. Gates. Two sons.
>
>> Wallace E. King[10], b. April 27, 1870. Married to Miss Emily S. Granville. They had Veva G., born Oct. 17, 1892, Sabra Verna, b. Jan. 11, 1895, and Rachel E., born Dec. 19, 1896.
>>
>> April 15, 1902, the father was away for the night. His second cousin Alma, the 18-year old daughter of Charles King (of De Goliar,) came to spend the night with them. The house took fire. Five year old Rachel alone escaped, the youngest occupant of the house. Her mother, her sisters Veva and Verna, and her cousin Alma, all perished in the flames. Two months later Alma's father died of grief, making this fearful tragedy to have blotted out five human lives.
>>
>> Jay S. King[10]. Married Miss Beckwith. They have twin sons born Jan. 15, 1903.
>> Elmer L. King[9]. Youngest son of Vernon, B. April 19, 1851; d. July 13, 1873, aged 22.

CHARLES KING[8], b. April 20, 1819. M. (1) Olivia Merrifield, Sept. 4, 1844. They had 6 children. M. (2) Myra ———, who d. in 1866. She had 4 children. M. (3) Julia ———, who had 3 children, and lastly m. Mrs. Harriet Kester ———. Of the first wife's 6 children, Celestine, Rosaιette, Charles W. and Charles D , (2) died young.

> MARYETTE KING–MILLIMAN[9], b March 6 1845   M Bryant Milliman, May 23, 1867
> They live in Kansas, and have no children
> URVINE KING–HOTCHKISS[9], b Nov 29 1851   M Dec 25, 1873, to Egbert C. Hotch-
> kiss   Their children are Lillie Elva b April 11 1875, Nellie Margaret, b June 18
> 1877, Daisy Edith, b April 9, 1880, and William Jay, b Dec 26, 1882

By his second wife, Charles King had these children

> CHARLES M KING[9], b July 6, 1857   He was the third son to be named Charles
> He married Alice A Wayman in 1885   He lives in Oakland, California   Their oldest
> child, Myrtle May, died in 1888, aged 15 months   Their other children are Mabel Lavinia
> b Jan 13, 1889, Chauncey Melrose, b Aug 21, 1891 and Lucile Elvira, b Nov 18
> 1897
> EDWARD AMHERST–KING[9]
> WALLACE LINCOLN KING[9], left home in 1873, and all trace of him lost
> CYNTHIA KING–POWERS[9], b March 26, 1863 , m at 20 to William H Powers of Ben-
> ton Harbor, Michigan   They lost a four-months old baby, Wallace Earle, b March 26
> 1886, and a bright little boy of 5, Karl Clyde, who died in 1896   Their only living child
> is Robin B , b Aug 22, 1896

By his third wife, Charles King was the father of these :

> HENRY OSCAR KING[9] b April 22, 1873   Usually called Oscar   He lives in Upper
> Sandusky Ohio
> GEORGE A KING[9], b Sept 9, 1874
> ANSON DeLOSS KING[9], b in Nov 1876   He lives in Lorain, Ohio

DEGOLIAR KING[8], b Jan 3, 1821 , d April, 1896   His daughter, Mrs Piper, gives these incidents of him   "At 18 his family moved from Jefferson Co , N. Y , to New London, Ohio. He was homesick for the old home. One night he slipped out of the house and started back on foot, all his belongings tied up in a red handkerchief, and an old-fashioned sixpence piece in his pocket   He reached his destination and the sixpence was yet in his pocket ! After some years he returned to Ohio   At 29, he married Mary Earl He used to joke about it, saying his children were surely well born, as they came from an Earl on one side, and a King on the other   After this wife's death, he married in 1855 his brother Henry's widow, who was also a sister to his first wife   By Almira Earl–King–King he had another family."

Soon after 1855 Degoliar moved to Michigan, where in Benton Harbor, he died, in April, 1896.   His wife died about 13 years before   He was postmaster at Sodus, Michigan, for some years   He was a just man, whose motto was "truth and honesty"   His daughter says he had one of the sweetest, strongest voices she ever heard , he could be heard singing a mile away

By his first wife Degoliar had four children, two of whom died in infancy   The other two were these .

> JOHN KING[9]
> EMELINE KING–PIPER[9]. Married to Dr Piper of Turtle Lake, Mich

By the second wife, there were several children, some of whom died young.

CHARLES KING[9], b. Jan. 7, 1857. He married Mary Carmony, March 12, 1881. His second child, Alma, a girl of 18, was burned to death, April 15, 1902. See under heading of Vernon King, this chapter. Charles grieved himself to death over the awful catastrophe, dying June 13, 1902, less than two months after.

    Claude King[10], b. Feb. 16, 1883.

    Alma King[10], b. Sept. 1884. Burned to death at 18.

    Emeline King[10], b. Nov. 17, 1886.

    Earl King[10], b. Jan. 9, 1895.

    Fern King[10], b. June 20, 1899.

ANABELLE KING-BURDICK[9]. Died about 1887, leaving three children, Myrtle, Roy and Hattie.

LIBBIE KING-CONKEY[9], of Benton Harbor, Michigan.

CHAUNCEY DEGOLIAR KING[9], b. May 12, 1872. Married Ida Megbon, in Jan. 1897. Their children are Lizzie, b. Aug. 2, 1898, and Mildred, born Jan. 27, 1902.

HENRY KING[8], b. August 29, 1822. He married Almira Earl. He died at about 30. His widow married his brother Degoliar. His children were Laura, who became Mrs. Cook, and Delila, who died young.

JOHN KING[8], b. Aug. 27, 1824. He spent his life at New London, Ohio. By his first wife, who was a Miss Case, he had a son John, who was brought up by his mother's people and took the name of Case. The second wife was Ann, by whom he had one son, Vernon, now living at New London.

CYNTHIA KING-AKEWRIGHT[8], b. April 19, 1826. Married to Mr. Akewright. They lived in Michigan.

    WINFIELD AKEWRIGHT[9], of Sodus, Mich.

    HENRY AKEWRIGHT[9].

    CELESTINE AKEWRIGHT[9]-OMWAG. Living at Sodus.

JOB KING[8], b. March 29, 1828. Died in Michigan.

    CHAUNCEY KING[9].

    BERT KING[9].

HULDAH KING[8], b. Dec. 1, 1830. Died young.

SABRINA KING-ASCHER[8], b. Aug. 17, 1835. She is the youngest of this family, a bright, alert and quick-brained woman. At about 17 she married Herman Ascher, who was born of Jewish parents in Konigsburg, Prussia. He was the son of a brave old Prussian soldier, who was decorated for conspicuous bravery. The Jew has an inborn love of music. Its strains, weird, sad, sweet and strong, voice to him his race's heaped up sorrow of the ages. Herman Ascher had this passionate love of melody, and passed it on to his children after him. Though he came to America, and married here, our land was never home to him. Finally he shook its dust from off his feet, and went to the far Orient. For many years he was in India, and is said to have accumulated a large estate there. He was on his way back to his family in America, and had reached France, when he sickened and died there. Some of his sons have travelled into strange and distant lands also, but all are now living in the Lake states.

    CECELIA ASCHER-CASSADA[9], b. March 4, 1853. Wife of Dr. Cassada, and mother of eight children.

SOPHIA ASCHER[9], b. 1855; d. 1878, aged 23.

EDWARD K. ASCHER[9], b. March 17, 1857. He married Martha McCook Rowley. They have Frances, Herman, Margaret and James.

OTTO K. ASCHER[9], b. July 3, 1863. He married Mary Stiles, and has Harry, Mary and Philip.

LOUIS K. ASCHER[9], b. March 1, 1865. He married Alice Bailey, and has one son, Norman.

CHAPTER XXXVI

FAMILY TREES. A general summing up of all lines is given in Chapter XXXII. For descent from the First Lord de Greene de Boketon, A D. 1202, and descent from Robert the Strong, Duke of France, A D 861, See Chapter XI For full particulars of lineage from John Greene of Quidnessett through his son, Lieut. John, see Chapter XV, through his son, Lieut. James, see Chapter XX ; all other lines, Nichols, King, La Valley, Straight, Westcott, Hill, Wardwell, etc., are in the first mentioned Chapter XXXII.

Miranda Barnes was born Dec. 16, 1799, among the Berkshire Mountains of Massachusetts. She was brought up in Pompey, N Y. She died in Wolcottville, Indiana, Jan 7, 1852 She was married on her 18th birthday to Samuel Barnes of Mass descent He was lineally descended from John Barnes, who came to Plymouth, Mass., in 1631 This John Barnes' immediate descendants intermarried with the Mayflower families of Gov. John Carver, Richard Warren and Gov. William Bradford Samuel's grandfather served in the French and Indian War. His father, Hartwell Barnes, served almost seven years in the Revolutionary War under Gen Putnam. His mother was Hannah Clark, who descended from Peter Wolcott, emigrant in 1630 She was the granddaughter of Governor Roger Wolcott of Connecticut, and neice of Oliver Wolcott, one of the signers of the Declaration of Independence

Samuel Barnes was a true son of the Puritans His character was as rugged, strong and enduring as the granite hills amid which he was born. He was unflinching in his convictions and called a spade a spade. Like a chestnut burr, beneath his brusque exterior was a heart of worth The Baptist Church at Wolcottville, Ind, of which he was a charter member, erected a beautiful memorial window in his honor. He was a soldier in the war of 1812 He outlived his wife 22 years, dying April 6, 1874

The Barnes remained in N Y nearly twenty years after their marriage.

Then with 10 children they moved to Indiana, at that time a new country. The rest of their life was spent in Wolcottville, Indiana. Mrs. Barnes died Jan. 7, 1852. She was a woman of fine mental powers and tireless energy. She not only cared for her 14 children, but found time, in this pioneer region where at first there were no doctors, to compound herbs and home remedies, in which she had great skill. She would never take a penny for her services. Their children were Nancy, Orville, Harriet, Samuel King, Mariam, Riley (1), Riley (2), Nelson, John, David Hartwell, Antionette, Richmond, and the twins, Theodore and Theodosia. Riley (1) died in 1828, aged 1 year. Theodore died in 1843, aged 3 weeks.

NANCY A. BARNES–EMERSON[8], b. Aug. 14, 1818; d. March 22, 1879. She lived up to the family tradition that a strenuous life awaited each Nancy. The oldest of a great family, when other children of her age were making mud pies, she was cooking the family meals, and standing on a chair to wash dishes. Twice she was a pioneer in a new country. At 16 she was a teacher. May 3, 1840, she married Alba Emerson, and became the mother of 12 children. Alba Emerson was a scion of the New England family to which the poet-philosopher, Ralph Waldo Emerson, belonged. He had the Emersonian ways of thought, and the Emersonian way of expressing them. This is reflected in his children who have much the same turn, and are also mostly Emersons in looks, being of slender build and of fairest blonde type.

Eight of their children live in Michigan, one in Minnesota, and one in Indiana. All are well-to-do, all are ambitious for their children. None of them use tobacco or intoxicating drinks.

JULIETTE EMERSON–SHUMAN[9], b. May 25, 1842, and m. Aug. 30, 1860, to William Shuman. Their home is in Benton Harbor, Mich. I am indebted to her for much of this data.

Eva E. Shuman–Shriver[10], b. Oct. 29, 1865; m. Oct. 27, 1887, to Charles Shriver. They have Gladys V., b. Nov. 18, 1889, and Uldene E., b. Aug. 18, 1891.

Leona M. Shuman–Koontz[10], b. Sept. 1, 1867; m. to George Koontz, Dec. 23, 1889. Their only child, Lester Emerson, died when a few months old, in 1895.

THEODORE A. EMERSON[9], b. Nov. 29, 1843; m. Mary Bower, Aug. 25, 1867. He was a soldier in the Civil War. For 36 years he lived on a large and well appointed farm at Brandon, Minn. Here all his children were born. He removed to Wolcottville, Indiana, in March, 1903.

Roxanna Emerson–Lauda[10], b. May 26, 1868. Married to James Lauda of Brandon, Minn. She died Oct. 21, 1895. Her children were Eunice, b. April 15, 1891, Myrtle, b. Dec. 21, 1892, Clarence, b. and d. in 1894, and Ralph, b. Oct. 21, 1895. Byron Todd Emerson[10], b. Sept. 30, 1875.

Lenora Emerson–Ewing[10], b. July 28, 1878. She is the wife of Rev. W. J. Ewing. Winfield, their oldest child, died in 1899 at 1 month old. They have a son Everett Emerson, b. March 8, 1903.

Eva L. Emerson–Wold[10], b. Feb. 12, 1880; m. Carl Wold July 4, 1900. They live in Brandon, Minn., and have a daughter, Blanche, b. Sept. 3, 1901. Her husband is a merchant.

Raymond Emerson[10], b. Sept. 26, 1881.

Mary Edith Emerson[10], b. Nov. 14, 1883.

Nancy A. Emerson[10], b. Sept. 16, 1887.

Elsie Viola Emerson[10], b. Jan. 17, 1889.

HON. JOHN O. EMERSON[9], b. March 6, 1845, has spent most of his life in Minnesota. He married Addie McKibben, a sister to John C. Nichols' wife. Something of her line is given in Chapter XXXIX. His wife frankly says of Hon. John, "I am proud of him, not because of his wealth, or his legislative record, but because his word is as good as a first mortgage on a gold bond."

MIRANDA M. EMERSON–SHIMER[9], b. Oct. 26, 1846; m. Isaac Shimer, Oct. 6, 1869. She d. April 16, 1891. Of her a sister says, "Few enjoyed a profitable argument better than she; few as enthusiastically studied the problems of human life or of our social system. She believed in making the world better." She left one son, Harry, b. Dec. 13, 1870.

CLARK S. EMERSON[9], b. Sept. 6, 1848. M. Margaret McCray, April 27, 1876. They live near Benton Harbor, Mich., on the old home place. He has two sons, Aden McCray, b. Aug. 25, 1878, and Ralph Waldo, b. April 8, 1880. Aden took the highest honors at his graduation.

HARRIET A. EMERSON–ROSA[9], b. April 23, 1850. M. to Abraham Rosa, Oct. 16, 1869. They have Alba, b. Sept. 4, 1870, and John, b. March 21, 1875. Their home in Benton Harbor, Mich.

LYDIA L. EMERSON–McCRAY[9], b. Feb. 14, 1852; m. to George McCray of Benton Harbor, July 3, 1879. No children.

POLLY A. EMERSON–MILLS[9], b. Jan. 28, 1854; m. Feb., 1872, to George A. Mills of Benton Harbor. They have no children.

MYRON EMERSON[9], b. Sept. 15, 1860; m. July 5, 1881, to May D. Finch. Their first children were twins, Ruth and Rae, b. March 1, 1885. Ruth died at 6 months. Their other children are Archie Lyle, b. July 29, 1888, Amy Elizabeth, b. Sept. 5, 1890, and Kathyrn, b. Jan. 24, 1898. This family live at Benton Harbor.

BERTIA A. EMERSON–NOE–MOLLHAGAN[9], b. Sept. 15, 1863. She was m. (1) to William Noe, April 2, 1882. M. (2) to John Mollhagan, Sept. 18, 1894. By this last marriage she has one son, Lloyd Emerson, b. April 4, 1896. She lost a daughter, Doris Mollhagan, at birth, Sept. 27, 1901. She lives in St. Joe, Mich.

ORVILLE S. BARNES[8], b. Aug. 21, 1819; d. Oct. 29, 1889. He was m. Oct. 1, 1845, to Amanda Culver, who d. in 1892. They had 12 children. Lewis Irvine, Henry Harrison, and the twins Susan and Sarah, all died in infancy. The others are these:

CHRISTOPHER COLUMBUS BARNES[9], b. Nov. 16, 1846; m. Sarah Stevenson, April 27, 1873. Their children are Grace, b. March 29, 1874, and Ida, b. Sept. 17, 1877.

WILLIAM IRA BARNES[9], b. March 11, 1849. He married his cousin, Emma J. Culver, Oct. 5, 1874. They have Alice A., b. April 6, 1875, Mabel M., b. Sept. 23, 1877, Francis Marion, b. Aug. 15, 1882, Elsie M., b. March 28, 1884, Beulah H., b. May 18, 1885, and Calcie C., b. May 19, 1889. Of this family one has said, "William and Emma have raised as fine a family as I ever knew."

SAMUEL C. BARNES[9], b. Sept. 11, 1850. M. Elizabeth Bull. She died 1891. They had William Irvine, b. April 14, 1875, James H., b. Oct. 21, 1876, Charles W., b. Sept 2, 1878, Albert C., b. July 8, 1880, and Francis M., b. Dec. 26, 1882.

LYDIA ANTIONETTE BARNES–NELSON[9], b. Oct. 24, 1855; m. John Nelson. 11 children, of whom 4 died in infancy. Those who lived are Archie A., Amanda E., b. Sept. 25, 1881, Sarah, b. June 3, 1883, Edith E., b. July 12, 1885, Merdie M., b. Dec. 24, 1887, Chester, b. Jan. 8, 1891, and Lester E., b. March 10, 1895.

JOHN RILEY BARNES[9], b. Aug. 18, 1859; d. Dec. 13, 1898; m. Amanda Butts. No children.

MRS. GERTIE BARNES-PALMER

MARGARET BARNES--PIERCE[9]. A twin. B. May 24, 1864. M. Monroe Pierce. 6 children.
LA FAYETTE BARNES[9]. Margaret's twin. He m. Flora Ripley.
FLORA BELLE BARNES–MERRITT[9], b. March 1, 1870. M. to Albert Merritt. No children.

HARRIET LA VALLEY BARNES–McNALL[8]. M. Hiram McNall,
of Mich. She left Celestia M., b. June 4, 1848, Harriet F., b. June 7, 1849, and Myron Irvine, b. Sept. 5, 1850. They live in Michigan.

SAMUEL KING BARNES[8], b. Oct. 6, 1823; d. Oct. 20, 1891. He
married Eliza Johnson, Oct. 1, 1848. She was born April 8, 1827, in Goshen, N. Y., and died March 13, 1897.

How plainly King Barnes' good-natured face comes to memory! His stubby grey hair that *would* stand straight up, and that genial voice that related his exhaustless fund of good stories! King was warm-hearted and large-souled, and successful in all he undertook. It is a peculiar coincidence that he was born, married and died in October, and that he and all of his children were married by the same minister, Rev. F. P. Hall. They lived for a time in Indiana, other years in Iowa, and their later life in Huron County, Ohio. Both of them, by their own request, are buried in Iowa, by the side of their daughter Lottie, in beautiful Oakland Cemetery. They had but one son, who died Aug. 2, 1851, aged a little over 2 years.

LAURA JOSEPHINE BARNES–EVANS[9], b. Sept. 21, 1852; d. April 10, 1884, aged nearly 32. She was always called Lottie. She married John C. Evans, Sept. 20, 1877. They removed to Iowa, where he became a leading man. He is the founder of Evanston, and is a grain buyer and capitalist. They lost their first child at birth, July 23, 1878. Lottie left two others, Edith Mae, b. Sept. 16, 1880, and Edna E., b. Sept. 12, 1882, whom she requested should be raised by her sister Mary. This sister has been indeed a mother to these children.

MARY ELIZABETH BARNES–EVANS[9], b. Oct. 5, 1854. She married J. C. Evans, whose first wife was her sister Lottie, March 8, 1885. They have one daughter, Lottie Josephine, b. Sept. 22, 1888. The Evans have an elegant home in Fort Dodge, Iowa.

GERTIE A. BARNES–PALMER[9], b. July 1, 1860. She was m. Oct. 1, 1879, to Abner Eugene Palmer. The Palmers go back to crusading days. Their name itself means palm-bearer, i. e., one who having made the journey to the Holy Land and back, was entitled to bear palms in procession upon Palm Sunday. The first American Palmer was Walter, who came to Massachusetts in 1629 in charge, with John (Governor) Endicott, of six ship-loads of colonists. He settled eventually in Connecticut. At Stonington, Conn., is a monument to the three founders of the town, one of whom was this Walter Palmer. From Walter[1], came Abijah[2], William[3], William[4], Abijah[5], Hiram[6], and then Abner Eugene. Mr. Palmer has been very successful in all his undertakings. They live in Fort Dodge, Iowa, where the two sisters, all that is left of their family, can be near each other. Their oldest child, King Barnes, d. Sept. 14, 1881, aged 15 months.

Mabel Fern Palmer[10], b. May 22, 1881.
Jesse Wetmore Palmer[10], b. Sept. 30, 1883.
Chester Ray Palmer[10], b. April 29, 1885.

MARIAM M. BARNES–TERRY[8]. B. March 30, 1826. She was
m. Nov. 15, 1856, to Rev. George Terry of Mich., who left her a widow in 1861. She returned to Wolcottville, Indiana, and was her father's housekeeper. June 2, 1874, a little over a month after his death, this dutiful

daughter who had so tenderly cared for her father's declining years, followed him to her grave. Her son returned to Michigan. He is a railroad man and lives in Kalamazoo.

GEORGE NELSON TERRY[9], b. Aug. 14, 1860. His mother's death threw him out to do for himself at 14. He m. Cora B. Golden, Aug. 31, 1882. He is the Foreman Car Inspector for a Michigan Railway Co. George lost his first son, Leon at 5 months old, in Oct. 1884. He has one son living, Roy William, born August 30, 1898.

RILEY RINALDO BARNES[4], b. June 1, 1829. Died unmarried Feb. 1, 1892, aged 63. He had something of a roving disposition in his younger days and spent the years from 1858 to 1862 in California, Oregon, and the Rocky Mountains, when these regions were considered quite outside of civilization. He was a mill-wright, and a good one. He put up many mills in the states that border on Canada. For 14 years he made his home with his nephew, T. A. Emerson, of Brandon, Minn. The last ten years of his life were spent with his brother and brother's family, the widow and children of Hartwell Barnes in Iowa. He was totally blind for nine years. Riley was turned like his father, abrupt of speech, but kind of heart. He was well read and observant. He served 3 years in an Oregon company during the Civil War.

NELSON IRVINE NICHOLS BARNES[4], b. Nov. 15, 1830, and d. Nov. 29, 1850, aged 20. Unmarried.

JOHN O. M. BARNES[4], b. Feb. 25, 1833; d. Jan. 13, 1862, aged 29. He was married April 12, 1856. He left two children, Theodore Irvine and Harriet. The widow married again and moved away, and all trace has been lost of these heirs.

DAVID HARTWELL BARNES[4], b. Aug. 9, 1835; d. March 7, 1891, aged 56. Hart Barnes, as he was commonly known, adopted teaching as his life profession. He bore a striking resemblance to Daniel Webster, having the same massive brow, square jaw, thin-lipped mouth and dark complexion. He was a man of intense energy and resolution. He was married June 22, 1856, to Mary Jane Strayer, the oldest daughter of Michael and Melinda Nichols–Strayer. She was, and is, a comely woman, fair and blue-eyed, with rippling, curly hair that frames in a face always illumined with smiles.

Hartwell suffered long from asthmatic, heart and nervous troubles. He taught for years, when only sheer will power kept him up. No man ever had a more devoted family. Jane Barnes did man's and woman's work, indoor and out, to spare him. When even his iron will had to yield to physical weakness, Emma, the oldest daughter, began to teach at a month past 14. Frances, the second daughter, commenced teaching at 15. The children all worked hard, but their struggle but bound them the closer together. The entire family moved to Iowa in 1880. Here Hartwell's health improved,

ABNER EUGENE PALMER

and he prospered also.

There was a romance connected with the older daughter's marriage. Her husband used to say that he fell in love with her before he ever saw her, because she was so good to her parents. He proposed the second day after he met her, and wooed with such earnestness that they were married two months and a day from the time they first met.

EMMA J. BARNES--SOCKRIDER[9], b. March 11, 1858 ; m. John W. Sockrider, Feb. 26, 1879. Mrs. Sockrider is now a widow, and lives at Jennings, Louisiana, near the Gulf, on a rice farm.

Guy W. Sockrider[10], born in the summer of 1880. M. Myrtle Belle Clark, of Louisiana, Jan. 16, 1901. They have a son, Clyde, born in 1902.

Norah Gay Sockrider–Norton[10], b. June 30, 1882. She is the wife of Carl G. Norton, of Jennings, Louisiana. They have one son, Ernest, b. in 1902.

FRANCES J. BARNES–SELLS[9], b. June 16, 1860, and m. to B. W. Sells of Webster, Iowa, Sept. 21, 1881. He belongs to a prominent family. They live on an extensive farm four miles from Webster City. Their only child is Mary Elma, b. Nov. 18, 1886.

CHARLES BARNES[9], died Oct. 22, 1862, aged 7 weeks.

WILLIAM HENRY BARNES[9], b. Jan. 19, 1864, m. Alice Whistler, Oct. 30, 1888. Their children are David Hartwell, b. March 31, 1890, Katie Belle, b. Nov. 2, 1893, and Mary Jane, b. Feb. 18, 1897.

GEORGE MELVIN BARNES[9], b. Feb. 18, 1866. He m. Arvena Traver, Feb. 24, 1891. They have Lula Jane, b. Jan. 20, 1892, Bennie W., who d. in 1894 aged 9 months. Helen J., b. July 22, 1895, Leslie Traver, who died young. Ada Leona, b. March 7, 1900, and Kittie Melvena, b. Dec. 16, 1901.

JOHN MICHAEL BARNES[9], b. April 13, 1875

SAMUEL KING BARNES[9], b. Aug. 3, 1880.

MIRANDA ANTIONETTE BARNES–ELLIS[8], b. Dec. 27, 1836. Married William Ellis, Aug. 26, 1866. They went to Nebraska where she yet lives. She is a woman who despises shams, affectation or toadying to wealth and title. She speaks of herself as a "white haired old woman," but she still has the energy and enthusiasm of a girl. She is the last survivor of 14 children. Mrs. Ellis gives this boiled down paragraph as to her children :

"William R. is the County Attorney of Knox Co., Neb. He has a good wife and two bright boys. He is a copy of his uncle King, and succeeds in whatever he undertakes. Hattie Dennis lives in Iowa on a farm. She has a kind husband and four of the brightest kind of children. John has the Barnes *penchant* for the frontier, and has been in Montana for several years. Carrie lives with me, in Madison, Neb. Her husband is a shoemaker, and does a good business. Her husband is Peter S. Olin, a Swede."

ANNA M. ELLIS[9], d. at birth, Sept. 6, 1867.

WILLIAM RILEY ELLIS[9], b. Sept. 10, 1869. M. Edna Cooper, March 28, 1894. They have Leslie, b. Jan. 1, 1896, and Paul Cooper, b. June 9, 1897.

HARRIET ELLIS–DENNIS[9], b. May 11, 1871. M. to Edgar Dennis, Dec. 8, 1889. They have Millie, b. July 6, 1891, Stella, b. July 18, 1892, Gladys, b. Nov. 22, 1893, and Lily, b. March 31, 1898.

JOHN SAMUEL ELLIS[9], b. Oct. 28, 1872

CURTIS W. ELLIS[9], a twin. He d. Aug. 23, 1878, aged 2 years.

CARRIE W. ELLIS[9], twin to Curtis. Born June 11, 1876. M. to Peter S. Olin, April 5, 1899.

GERTIE A. ELLIS[9], b. Jan. 21, 1877, and d. July 24, 1879.

JAMES RICHMOND G. BARNES[8], b. Oct. 26, 1840. Killed before Petersburg, Va., June 9, 1864. Unmarried. Had Richmond lived, he would have made his mark in the world. He was running over with mirth and wit, had a fine mind, and poetical talent. His first verses were mostly clever squibs and parodies. After his effervescence of fun had worn off, he would doubtless have settled down to serious literary work, had he lived.

He was a soldier in the Civil War. A favorite army amusement of his was to improvise rhyming letters, written as fast as the pen could travel. From a newspaper account of a raid, written by him, I give a single extract :

> " The way we scratched the gravel
> Was anything but slow !
>   *   *   *   *
> The rain commenced to pour,
> And till ten o'clock that night
> We trod Pamunkey's shore,
> And were on the march next morning,
> At the dawning of the day."

Poor boy ! His war experiences were soon over.

At the attack on Petersburg, June 9, 1864, by a blunder, an impossible assault was ordered. Captain Ringland says, "it was a slaughter pen." The officer refused to send men, but asked for volunteers. Only three men followed their lieutenant to what was certain death. "As they came up to the rifle pits," says the Captain, "Barnes' was the first foot planted upon the barricade. He was instantly killed." Later the Federals captured this outpost, and an officer and men were at once detailed to inter the brave soldier. His captain thus describes it. "They dug his grave with bayonets, and laid his body in a shallow grave. They left it to sleep upon the battlefield. *   *   *   *   We all mourn the loss of Barnes, with his cool determination and intrepid heart. If I am to fall in defense of the Old Flag, I do not ask for a more honorable death than his."

THEODOSIA ALMYRA BARNES[8], a twin to Theodore Almyron who d. at 3 weeks. She was b. Aug. 10, 1843, and d. Oct. 25, 1858, in her 16th year.

CHAPTER XXXVII

FAMILY TREES For descent from Alexander, first Lord de Greene de Boketon, A D 1202, and descent from the royal Capet line, A. D. 861, see Chapter XI For the old time history of King and La Valley families, see Chapter XXII For all other lines, including two of descent from John Greene of Quidnessett, Straight, Westcott, Nichols, Parsons, Hill, Waite, Wardwell, Lascelle, etc , see Chapter XXXII

Mariam Nichols[7], fourth daughter and eighth child of David and Nancy (Anna) Nichols, was born Jan 26, 1801, in Rhode Island Her parents moved to Pompey, N Y, when she was but a few months old Here she lived until middle life, when she came to New London, Ohio, where both she and her husband finally died She died July 24, 1871

One of the playmates of her childhood, and her early lover, was a boy a few months older than herself. He was a native of Massachusetts, and his father had been a Revolutionary soldier This Josiah Bradley was not born with a silver spoon in his mouth. He had his own way to make. Love, however, makes light hearts and willing hands, and January 3d, 1820, the boy and girl lovers were married She was just under nineteen, he a few months under twenty Nearly a year after, by a singular coincidence, one of the greatest joys and one of the deepest sorrows of her life, came to her upon the same day On the 22nd of November, 1820, Darius, her first born, was laid in her glad arms, and on that same day, her good, patient, loving mother died.

Five children were born to them, all of whom grew up Josiah and Mariam Bradley were an industrious, thrifty couple. She was a perfect type of a quiet, mind-her-own-business woman, as neat as wax, and orderly in everything In those days people did not expect a boy to sow his wild oats as a step toward getting on in life, nor did they expect a girl to promenade the streets while her mother was at home bending over the washtub So the Bradley sons were early trained to work, and the Bradley daughters became as skilled housewives as their mother.

We never have heard the slightest whisper against Mariam Bradley. Her strong Christian faith and pains-taking disposition were exemplified by her last hours. She calmly specified all that she wished to have done after her decease, and arranged the details of her funeral, even to selecting the minister, the text for her memorial sermon, and the hymns that were to be sung. Her husband survived her many years, dying at a ripe old age.

DARIUS BRADLEY⁷. Darius Bradley is an optimist. He has always looked on the bright side, and always will. He is a hale old gentleman, now several years past eighty, doing the daily work of a usual man of fifty, and writes and talks as though but in his prime. Such a life points a moral. The man who keeps a young heart, who lives healthfully and contentedly, and goes without fuss or worry through the world, when he reaches the autumn of life, will find it a mellow Indian summer that retains the flowers of summer and adds them to the fruits of fall.

At twenty-one, Darius married Hannah Merrifield. There is a touch of pathos in this record that he gives.—"I lived with Hannah sixty years and fifty-eight days," as though even the days were so precious that he would record them. Hannah Bradley was indeed a good woman. The one sorrow of their wedded life was their childless home. There was a bevy of pretty children at David Bradley's home, and the older brother and sister finally persuaded David and his wife to allow them to have Estella, one of that family, as their own. They gave her every advantage. She grew up an attractive young woman, and a fine musician. Estella is the wife of George Morton, of Wellington, Ohio, and her foster father makes his home with her. She is an enthusiastic lover of art, and until her health failed gave much time to it.

DAVID BRADLEY⁸. David Bradley was born in Pompey, N. Y., May 21, 1823. He married his brother Darius' sister-in-law, Polly Merrifield. Their entire married life was spent in New London, Ohio. David was a hard-working man, a good provider, and affectionate in his family. His good wife did all in her power to make a happy home. There was a large family, of which the girls were particularly fine looking. After being long unbroken, the family's ranks were thinned fast. In seventeen months, four of the family died. Ettie, a lovely girl, was first. Then the mother died. Louisa, the oldest married daughter, a young woman dearly loved by her associates, was the next to go, and after her, Luella, the youngest child. Isadore (Mrs. Barnes), whose pretty ways and winsome girlhood we remember well, died in 1894, leaving six motherless little ones. Last of all the father died March 26, 1899. Over half the family have now passed away.

Gertie Bradley, after her mother's death, took her place as housekeeper and home-maker for her father. A trimmer, neater, livelier little body than she no one need ever expect to see. She is a good sister as well as a good daughter. After Isadore's death, Gertie brought home Georgie, the baby boy, and tenderly cared for him until his death in 1901. She is now living in Wellington, Ohio, with her sister, Mrs. Morton.

The sons of this family are personally unknown to us. But they are said to be upright and respected citizens, with the Bradley trait of not being afraid to work. Alfred Bradley was a soldier in the Civil War. He is now a Master car and locomotive painter of the Baltimore and Ohio Railroad, and lives at Washington, Indiana.

ALBERT NEWLAND BRADLEY[9], b. Nov. 23, 1845, at New London, Ohio. He married Ella A Gregory, June 11, 1867. His two older children were by her. He married again, Nov. 26, 1870, to Ida Chapman, and by her has five children.

David Albert Bradley[10], b. March 30, 1868; d. Sept. 10, 1890.
Fred. Bradley[10], b. Sept. 18, 1869.
Maud May Bradley–Porter[10], b. Aug. 7, 1872. Married June 18, 1899, to W. L. Porter.
Sadie Ellis Bradley[10], b. July 27, 1874, at Pana, Ill.
William Edward Bradley[10], b. Nov. ———.
Nina Adaline Bradley[10], b. Jan. 16, 1886, at Cochran, Ind.
Benjamin Harrison Bradley[10], b. Oct. 10, 1888, at Cochran, Ind.

JAMES ERSKINE BRADLEY[9]. He is married, and has a family. He lives in Newark, N. J.

MARY LOUISA BRADLEY–MATHERS[9]. She was married to D. T. P. Mathers. She died June 3, 1878, leaving one son, John A.

GERTRUDE H. BRADLEY[9].

FLORA ESTELLE BRADLEY–MORTON[9]. Married in La Grange, Indiana, to George Morton. No children.

ISADORE MARION BRADLEY–BARNES[9]. She was married June 14, 1873, to G. W. Barnes. She died in 1894, leaving Hugh, Vera, Glenn, May, Cecil and George W. The latter died Jan. 16, 1901, in his eighth year.

CHARLES LEWIS BRADLEY[9]. He married Electra Bruce. They have Viola, b. in Oct. 1886, Freemont and Willard.

ETTA BRADLEY[9], died April 6, 1877.

LUELLA BRADLEY[9], died Sept. 23, 1878.

WARREN BRADLEY[8]. He was a man well spoken of in all relations of life. He was a soldier in the Civil War. He was born in Sept., 1826, and died May 27, 1882, in Ohio. He married Ann Day.

ADA BRADLEY–CALL[9]. She lives in New London, O., and has a son Charles,
ALICE BRADLEY–BARRETT[9]. She m. Ranson Barrett. Lives in New London.
JOSIAH BRADLEY[9], m. ——— Noble. Lives in Grand Rapids, Mich.

POLLY ANN (PAULINE) BRADLEY–SEGUR[8], b. Oct. 15, 1828. Polly Ann, or as her husband calls her, Pauline, was married when but sixteen, to her cousin, Vernon King. Two children were born to them, one of whom died when a young man. Her marriage proved unhappy, and it was dissolved. Her second husband is Joseph Segur. They live in a pretty, well-kept home in New London, Ohio. Polly Ann is a capital housewife and has enough French about her to arrange everything in the most inviting way. She and her husband both have the knack of making a visitor feel at home. It was with this daughter that Josiah Bradley lived until his death. Her children's line is given in the Cynthia King chapter. It was her grandson's wife and two children that were burned to death in 1902, as described in that chapter. But one of her sons lived to marry.

SARAH ANN BRADLEY-HEMENWAY. B. May 28, 1834. Died Jan. 26, 1904. Sarah Ann Bradley was one of those fortunate mortals in whose cup of life the wine was ever rich and sweet. She was married at twenty to Charles Hemenway, son of Daniel and Marinda Hemenway. He was born Nov. 24th, 1829, in Massachusetts. Charles Hemenway was a fine man, a home-loving man, and what some would regard even more, a financially successful man. He used to be thrice busy with sawmills, brick-yards and much real estate to look after. He died in the summer of 1903 at Wellington, Ohio. His wife was first of all a faultless housekeeper. But she had leisure to indulge her love of the beautiful, and her husband encouraged her to do so. Nearly all who share the Greene blood retain the characteristic Greene love of nature, of trees and flowers. Now and then the old passion breaks out in full force. Sarah Hemenway was one of the Greene descendants whose flowers were her meat and her drink. Rare plants were in her windows, beautiful flowers upon her lawn. Indoors was beautiful fancy work of every kind, a collection of curios and blown glass, wax-work, and dainty bric-a-brac.

WILLIAM T.,[9] their only son, was born Sept. 30, 1855, and married Feb. 1, 1882 to Addie Tripp. They live in Wellington, Ohio. They have two sons, George Courtland, b. Nov. 4, 1884, and Sidney Tripp, b. Nov 3, 1888.

CHAPTER XXXVIII

FAMILY TREES   Her full pedigree, from Alexander, first Lord de Greene de Boketon, A D 1202, Robert the Strong, Duke de France, A. D 861, on the grandmother's side from John Greene of Quidnessett, including descent from Capt Thomas Straight, Stukeley Westcott, Elder Obediah Holmes and Hugh Parsons, on the grandfather's side from John Greene of Quidnessett again, including Lascelle–Wardwell, Hill and Nichols descent, —also their King and La Valley pedigree from both father and mother of said Sallie Lamson, is given in Chapter XXXII.

Sallie Nichols was born in Pompey, N. Y., Feb. 13, 1804.   She died May 20, 1879   She was a quiet, even-dispositioned, home loving woman, and a sincere Christian.   She was married in her 21st year to Peter Lamson, in Lorain, N. Y.   He was the son of Jonathan and Ann Cobb Lamson, both of whom were Massachusetts people   His mother's family, the Cobbs, went back to nearly the first years of New England settlement, and were noted for the number of clergymen in their ranks

The Lamsons were of English descent   Peter's ancestors are said to have lived in London at the time that city was visited by three great calamities in two successive years,—the Black Plague in 1665, that killed 70,000 people, and the same dread disease again next year, killing 30,000 more, but brought to a sudden end by the Great Fire of London in September, 1666   Three days and nights the fire burned, destroying a third of the city.   After this, the government, or as some say, the Colonial Emigration Society, chartered a ship and offered free passage to America to all able-bodied men and boys of the burnt district   The Lamsons have it handed down that one of their ancestors came over in this ship, and settled in Mass, late in 1666.   We know that Sallie Lamson's great-great-grandfather, John King[1], came to Rhode Island in 1665, the sole survivor of a plague-destroyed family of London.   It is a singular coincidence that the fore-parents of this couple should have landed in New England within a year of each other, and that each should have owed his coming to the horrors that overlook London in 1665–1666.

Sallie's husband was well thought of.   There was plenty of Down–Eastern grit and moral backbone about him.   He was honest and upright and so strong in his convictions that during the anti-slavery agitation, he cast one of the four sole abolition votes in Lagrange Co., Ind., his brother-in-law, Nelson Nichols, and his son-in-law, Ozias Wright, being two of the other three.   Aside from his rock-ribbed principles, however, there was little of the New England granite in his make-up.   He was brimful and boiling over with mirth.   He was never blue or discouraged, though he commenced life with with no possessions beyond a pair of willing hands and a stout heart.

Seven years after their marriage they moved to Sharon, Ohio.   Believing there was a better opening farther on, in the spring of 1834 Lamson and his brother-in-law, Nelson Nichols, explored the whole of northern Indiana.   "They took their foot in their hand," to use an Irish expression, passing through trackless forests, and around great swamps and quagmires, seeing many Indians, but meeting not a white man in all that time.   In what is now Lagrange County they found land to their liking.   The government had appointed a Land Office at Ft. Wayne, 40 miles away.   A second trip on foot had to be made before they found the office open.   Theirs were the second entries in their county, and Nichols' the first in their township.   The men then returned to Ohio.

In the fall they returned, with Lamson's family.   Two ox wagons held the household goods.   Cows and other stock were driven through a roadless region, and through the dreaded Black Swamp, which was but 31 miles across, but took five days to cross.   In the boggiest part but three miles were covered in two days' time.

When they reached their destination they found that Henry Nichols, Mrs. Lamson's brother, was already there.   Nichols' family of eight were living in a log cabin 16x16.   There were eight of the newcomers, making a total of sixteen, one to each square foot of space; but they found a home for a time, somewhere and somehow, under that humble roof.   Such were the struggles and hospitalities of our forefathers.

An incident will show something of the conditions of the early settlements, and suggest a little of the romance of pioneer days.   There was a Pottowatomie Indian village a few miles away.   It was surrounded by large old apple orchards.   The seed of these trees had been planted by Jonathan Chapman, the famous "Apple-seed Johnny" of tradition.   Before the Revolutionary War and for many years after, this half demented wanderer regularly appeared each fall at the Pennsylvania cider presses, and filled sacks full of apple seeds which he carried off to the wilderness. Over the present territory of Ohio and Indiana, wherever he could find an open glade, there he planted his apple seeds. The Indians never molested him, as they believed insane people under the special protection of the Great Spirit. The Indians were not slow to appreciate "Apple-seed Johnny's" gift when the apples began to fruit.

This particular village was called Mongoquenong, which means the White Squaw. Peter Lamson had a faculty of getting on with the red man, and often let Indian hunters "sneap" (sleep) before his own fire. So with his wife he visited Mongoquenoug, he to visit the orchards, she to see the famed "White Squaw" that had given name to the settlement. The Indians loaded their good friend with apple grafts and with fruit, and Sallie Lamson was taken to see the white Indian. Seated on the ground in her wigwam, her grey hair hanging down in two long braids, and a blanket wrapped around her in Indian fashion, was an old woman, blue eyed and fair skinned. In a foray upon the whites she had been captured, and adopted into the tribe when an infant. All through the border states a report had gone forth of a white Indian. Once a brother presented himself, and through an interpreter asked her to return with him to her kindred. But she refused to leave her Indian husband and sons and lived and died with her adopted people. Soon after their visit the White Squaw was taken ill. The Indian doctors stripped her to her waist and stretched her before a fire with her naked back to the blaze to roast the disease out. She died under this heroic treatment.

Peter Lamson died in July, 1846. There had been a land transaction between he and a neighbor, and a trifling irregularity gave the grasping neighbor a chance to harass the widow. Lawsuit after lawsuit he brought against her. Having secured in some way a hold, he served 10-days' execution on her land at the beginning of wheat harvest. In pioneer days ready money in a lump sum was hard to get hold of, and by rushing it through in this way he hoped to get her land for himself at a third of its value. The widow was a favorite with her kindred. They rallied to her assistance and told her persecutor that they would pay the amount, however unjust, as soon as their harvest was over and the grain marketed. He refused to give them a day's time.

Her younger brother, Nelson Nichols, at once left his harvest with hired hands, and set out on foot for Sharon, Ohio, 200 miles away, as there was no public conveyance. He reached there after night fall on the fourth day. John Nichols, Sallie's wealthy brother at Sharon, advanced the money, and at daybreak the next day the younger brother started back, getting home at the close of the eighth day, but in time to save the sister's land. Incidents like these show that the pioneer's path was not all roses, and that there were rascals in those days as well as now.

Some years after the widow married Rev. William Hall and removed to Iowa, where she died, May 20, 1879. Her children were all by her first husband. Her only surviving sons were in the Civil War, and her only two grandsons old enough to see service, also were in the war, and both died for their country. Although she had a large family, her descendants have been few.

THERESA LAMSON–WRIGHT[3], 1825–1853. Died at 28. She was the wife of Ozias Wright. Her brother says that none of her kindred ever saw her ruffled or angry, so serene was her nature.

JANE LAMSON–PERCELL[3], b. May 12, 1826; died July 13, 1882. She was married Dec. 8, 1844, to William Percell, who was born Dec. 19, 1822, in N. Y. They spent the whole of their wedded life in Michigan. Jane as a child, a girl and a woman, faced pioneer hardships and privations. She was ambitious and hard-working, and lived to see a good home in what had been a wilderness. Her latter life was saddened by the untimely death of her two older sons, scarcely half grown-lads, both of whom died in the terrible Civil War that made wreck of so many homes.

FRANCIS WILLIAM PERCELL[9], b. April 17, 1846. Went into the army at 15. Died at Campbell Hospital, Washington, D. C., on March 3, 1863, in his 17th year.

JOHN CALVIN PERCELL[9], b. Nov. 25, 1848. Enlisted at 15. Died from homesickness, at Huntsville, Alabama, Feb. 28, 1864, aged 15 years, 3 months and 3 days.

HENRY PERCELL[9], b. Jan. 8, 1852. He married Belle Burt, Sept. 14, 1871. They live on the old Percell homestead.

Carrie Percell–Garner[10], b. Jan. 3, 1873. Wife of Went Garner. One daughter, Bessie, b. Nov. 28, 1903.

John Percell[10], b. July 31, 1874. Married Maud Davis, Jan. 13, 1898. One dau., Irene, b. Sept. 19, 1898.

Charles Percell[10], b. Oct. 2, 1876. M Lottie Elligot in 1900.

Mary Percell–Brown[10], b. Nov. 4, 1878. M to Harley Brown. They have Charles, b. Sept. 14, 1898, Nellie, b. Aug. 4, 1900, Cassie, b. June 2, 1902, and Louise, b. Nov. 16, 1903.

William Percell[10], b. March 22, 1883.

JULIA THERESA PERCELL[9], 1853–54. D. at 10 months.

GEORGE CURTIS PERCELL[9], 1857. D. in infancy.

BELLE PERCELL–SLANKER[9], b. June 18, 1859. M. to Samuel Slanker. They live in Stanton, Mich. Her husband was a teacher for many years.

Bertha Slanker–Grill[10], b. Jan. 3, 1876, and m. to Allen Grill in 1893. Their children are Hazel Lucile, b. Dec. 3, 1898, and Mabel, b. Mar. 7, 1901.

Theresa Slanker–Stroudt[10], b. July 31, 1877; m. to Eli Stroudt in 1895. Their children are Letha Belle, b. Aug. 7, 1896, Lyle Edmond, who died at 15 months, and Eunice Ethel, b. June 26, 1901.

Gertrude Slanker–Kinsman[10], b. Nov. 17, 1882; m. to Jay Kinsman in 1903.

J. Lee Slanker[10], b. and d. in 1889.

Raymond H. Slanker[10], b. Nov. 13, 1892.

JUDGE JOHN COBB LAMSON[8], b. Nov. 29, 1827. Left an orphan in his teens, the oldest son in a large family, and in a new country, he had to literally make his way. He studied, starved and economized, worked and taught, and pushed himself through Oberlin College and the Law Department of Albany (N. Y.) University. Under Lincoln's first call he joined the 17th Indiana Infantry and served four years and four months in the Civil War, coming out with the rank of Captain. In 1866 he located at Pineville, Mo., and engagd in the practice of law. Here he was successively elected County School Commissioner, Representative, Prosecuting Attorney and Judge of the Twenty-fourth District. He is the largest taxpayer in his county, and can truthfully say that not a penny of his fortune has been built upon speculation, or get rich schemes.

At 45 he married Lois A. Santley, of Ohio. She is of English and Virginia parentage, and is a woman of more than ordinary ability. On the English side, she can boast of what few people on the globe can claim—kindred blood to Shakespeare. Remembering his own early struggles, in the last quarter of a century the Judge and his wife have taken into their home not less than a dozen deserving young men and women, and helped them to get an education and to make something of themselves.

BELLE (ARABELLE) LAMSON-GUERNSEY[8], was b. June 5, 1831. April 17, 1852, she married Curtis Guernsey. Her husband was for some years a merchant in Freeport, O., and then for 19 years lived in Kansas. They are now living in Fostoria, O. The Guernseys are intelligent, whole souled people that it is a pleasure to know.

JOHN PETER GUERNSEY[9], d. at 8 years of age.

CHARLES L. GUERNSEY[9], b. Jan. 31, 1858. Married Malina C. Brown on his 22d birthday. He lives in Fostoria, O., and is a successful lawyer with a large practice.

Ethel Guernsey[10], b. Jan. 3, 1882.

Charles A. Guernsey[10], b. July 17, 1884.

Marion Bernice Guernsey[10], b. Feb. 28, 1886.

Curtis Guernsey[10], b. May 17, 1888.

John Philip Guernsey[10], b. April 29, 1891; d. in 1892.

CARRIE CLEORA GUERNSEY-WARNER[9], b. Aug. 19, 1864, and d. June 16, 1900. She was the wife of N. Warner, and spent all of her wedded life in Kansas. Her death was a grief from which her parents have never recovered. Her energy and vim was wonderful. She was housekeeper, book-keeper for the firm with which her husband was connected, and was a musician and a church-worker. She left no children.

FRANCIS LAMSON[8], b. in 1833, and d. at 6 weeks.

FRANKLIN LAMSON[8], 1834-1850. Died at 16.

MARILDA FOSTER LAMSON-WIREBAUGH[8], b. Nov. 22, 1837. She was the second daughter of this name, as a sister born 6 years before her had borne the name of Marilda F. during her short life. Rilla inherited her father's wit and liveliness. She was a teacher for more than 20 years. Aug. 20, 1877, she married Nicholas Wirebaugh. They live at

17

Prairie Depot, O. I learn from others that Mr. Wirebaugh is liberal toward religious and educational objects, and has several times made gifts to them which requires four figures to express the amount.

BETSEY MIRANDA LAMSON⁶. A most estimable young lady. Died at Pearce City, Iowa, in 1866.

HUBERT THRACEA LAMSON⁶, b. June 3, 1841. Married Emily Fanning, July 1, 1868. Hubert T. is a man fond of reading, of travel, and of the companionship of his friends. His wife is a cherry, active little body, who will never let things stagnate about her. Their home is in Girard, Kansas.

> JOHN LAMSON⁹, b. Nov. 2, 1870. M. Winne Reese, Sept. 3, 1901. They have one son. They live in Kansas.
>
> MARY LAMSON–GROVE⁹, b. Dec. 2, 1873. M. to Frank Grove, Aug, 16, 1894. They are living at Jamestown, N. Y. She has had two children, one of whom died.

CHAPTER XXXIII

FAMILY TREES. For descent from the first Lord de Greene de Boketon, A. D 1202, and descent from Robert the Strong, Duke de France, A.
D 861, see Chapter XI

For full particulars of descent from John Greene of Quidnessett, through
Lieutenant James[2], including lineage from Hugh Parsons, Elder Obediah
Holmes, Capt Thomas Straight and Stukeley Westcott see Chapter XX
For particulars of descent from John Greene though Lieut. John[2], including
lineage from the Wardwells, Hills and Nicholses, see Chapter XV. King
and La Valley descent will be found in Chapter XXII A summing up of
all is found in Chapter XXXII.

ALBRO DESCENT (of wife) is this. "Quaker John" Alburro or Alborough, of Portsmouth, R I, was the first The name soon became Albro.
He d in 1712 at 96 Hon John Albro[2], Assistant President of Providence
Plantations His wife was Mary Stokes Samuel[3], who m Ruth Lawton,
Rev. Samuel[4], who m. Jane Cole, Samuel[5], who m. Sarah Conves; James[6],
whose daughter was Eunice, the wife of George Nichols Eunice died in
1902, aged 86.

George Washington Nichols[7], was born about 1809, and married Eunice
Albro about 1833 He died March 21, 1839. They had but three children,
Sarah, born March 2, 1834, John Convass, born Aug 9, 1835, and Juliette,
next younger, who died in the spring of 1839 in her third year George's
wife was but 17 at the time of her marriage She was a cousin and namesake of the elder Job King's wife, whose son Henry married Cynthia,
George Nichols' sister This brought about a double relationship between
the familes of George Nichols and Cynthia Nichols–King In the fall of
1835, the young couple with their two small children, moved to northern
Indiana, where several others of George's family soon afterwards followed
them At that time, however, the only white inhabitants were the families
of Henry Nichols and Sally Nichols–Lamson, and a single brother, Nelson
Nichols. All the hardships of pioneer life fell to their lot.

In the fall and winter of 1838-9, a strange epidemic swept the country. Eight of the Nichols relatives died. George Nichols wore himself out taking care of the rest, then sickened and died. The youngest child soon followed her father. The disheartened widow sold out and returned to the East with her remaining children, Sarah and John.

Eleven years later Mrs. Nichols married David Lake. Sometime after her mother's marriage, Sarah married Jackson Leighty. Mr. Leighty died in 1865. Sarah married Samuel Miller for her second husband, and is again a widow. She had two sons by her first husband. Emmett Leighty was an engineer, and was killed in a railroad wreck. Frank Leighty married and has children.

JOHN CONVASS NICHOLS³. The marriages of his mother and sister broke up the home ties of the son, John Convass Nichols. He drifted back to Indiana, and became an inmate of his uncle Nelson Nichols' family. October 8th, 1863, he enlisted in Company C. of the 129th Indiana Infantry, and served during the rest of the Civil War. It showed his patriotism. For from an injury received when a child, his left arm was shortened, and he could never have been forced into service.

In 1866 he removed to Douglass Co., Minnesota, then just opened to settlement. The rude fort or stockade and soldiers' barracks were still standing, and cellars and heaps of rubbish marked where the adventuresome settlers before them had been massacred by Sioux Indians, and their homes burned. However, the new-comers were not molested, and the country was soon thickly settled. Oct. 11th, 1868, John C. Nichols was married to Jane McKibben. He was thirty-three, she fifteen and a half. As this was the first of three marriages between our family and the McKibbens, a paragraph about them may be of interest.

About one hundred years ago a family by the name of Jennings came into that part of Illinois commonly nick-named Egypt from the abundance of its corn. This family has of late years acquired prominence because one of its scions, William Jennings Bryan, has twice been candidate for the presidency. A daughter of this house married Francis Stanley, a brother of the man who brought up the celebrated African Explorer, Henry M. Stanley, and whose name the explorer adopted.

Among these Jennings–Stanley children were two daughters, Mary and Lucinda. They married two brothers, Zebulon and Henry McKibben. Zebulon McKibben died in the army. His widow with her double brother-in-law and his family, came to Brandon, Minnesota, and took up a homestead. John C. Nichols married one of the Widow McKibben's twin daughters. John Emerson of the Barnes–Emerson line, married Addie, the youngest daughter, and Amasa Pierce of the Stephen Pierce line, married

Martha, the double cousin of the other two, making a triple tie between our families.

Jane McKibben-Nichols measures up to the standard of our family tradition as to what is required of our Janes. Her doors are open to all of the kin, and she delights in doing all in her power for her own. John C. himself is a man deeply attached to his own fireside. One special incident is a pleasure for us to record. When the widow of the uncle with whom he had so long had a home, came to Minnesota to stay for a time with her children, he insisted on being considered as a son, and his aunt and little cousin—the author—spent the entire winter of 1869-70 at his hospitable home. He has by industry and economy secured a competency. They now reside upon a prairie farm near Holmquist, South Dakota. They have a large family of daughters, but only one son, the youngest of all.

Mary Eunice Nichols, the first-born, was a favorite child. Love, that comes to all, came to Mary in the first flush of womanhood. David Parks, her sweetheart, was not liked by her parents. When all remonstrances were of no avail, her father gave a reluctant and bitter consent to their marriage. Poor Mary, that had scarcely known what a care was, became the mother of more children in a given length of time than any other woman mentioned in this book. Her health failed. She died at twenty-eight, leaving nine children of whom the youngest was six weeks old, and the oldest but eleven years of age. Her last wishes were that her people might have an oversight over her little ones, and that her sister Julia would raise the youngest two children.

Her husband, however, could not forget old grievances. He kept Withue, Lucy and Ray, the three older children. Ada was given to his wife's uncle, J. McKibben. The other five were given away to strangers. James was given to a family that moved to the state of Washington. Minnie and Reuben were given to a family that moved to Montana. The two smallest ones had both their Christian and surnames changed. One of these was adopted by a Methodist minister, the other by a Bristol, South Dakota, man. All this has been a great grief to this family, as it has wiped out half Mary's descendants from all connection with their line.

Four more of their daughters are married. Alice is Mrs. Swanson, Sarah is Mrs. Burg, Elsie, Mrs. Faulkner, and Myrta is Mrs. Lake. All of them live reasonably near their parents, the farthest but ten miles away. Julia, Grace, Josie, Frankie and John S. are yet at home.

MARY EUNICE NICHOLS-PARKS[9], b. Aug. 2, 1869. Wife of David Parks. Died Dec. 23, 1897.

> Withue Parks[10], b. Aug. 26, 1886.
> Lucy Parks[10], b. Oct. 8, 1887.
> Ray Parks[10], b. Feb. 28, 1889.

Ada Parks[10], b Oct. 7, 1890.

James Parks[10], b. March 5, 1892.

Minnie Parks[10], b. July 7, 1893.

Reuben Parks[10], b. Nov. 20, 1894. } Given away. Lost to the family.

Sarah Parks[10], b. June 23, 1896.

John Parks[10], b. Nov. 10, 1897.

ALICE NICHOLS SWANSON[9], b. July 16, 1871. M. to Ole Swanson of South Dakota, March 26, 1890.

John Swanson[10], b. Jan. 9, 1890.

Hannah Swanson[10], b. Feb. 17, 1892.

Maggie Swanson[10], b. Aug. 4, 1893.

Albro Swanson[10], b. Jan. 4, 1895.

Hendricks Swanson[10], b. Feb. 9. 1897.

Evarts Swanson[10], b. July 24, 1899.

JULIETTE NICHOLS[9], b. July 16, 1873.

SARAH NICHOLS–BURG[9], b. May 20, 1876; m. to Henry Burg, Feb. 18, 1896.

John Nicholas Burg[10], b Jan. 8, 1897.

Arthur Burg[10] b. Aug. 8, 1898.

Florence Burg[10], b. March 8, 1900

Perry Edward Burg[10], b. May 4, 1902.

MYRTA NICHOLS–LAKE[9], b. in Feb. , 1878; m. to her cousin, George Lake, April 27, 1901.

Hazel Irene Lake[10], b. July 10, 1902.

ELSIE NICHOLS–FAULKNER[9], b. July 31, 1880. M. to Lur Faulkner, June 23, 1899.

Edith Faulkner[10], b. Feb. 9, 1900.

GRACE NICHOLS[9].

PERRY NICHOLS[9]. d March 2, 1885; aged 12 days. The first son.

JOSIE NICHOLS[9]. b. Aug 9 1886.

FRANKIE NICHOLS[9], b. March 24 1888.

JOHN EMMETT NICHOLS[9], 11th and youngest child, and only living son, b. July 19, 1897.

CHAPTER XL

DESCENDANTS OF NELSON NICHOLS[7].

FAMILY TREES. For descent from royal Capet line from A. D. 861, and descent from Sir Alexander, first Lord de Greene de Boketon, see Chapter XI. For lineage from John King and Peter La Valley, see Chapter XXII. For all other descent, including two lines of Greene, Waite, Hall, Lascelle, Wardwell, Straight, Westcott, Holmes, Parsons and Nichols, see Chapter XXXII; also Chapters XV and XX and Appendix.

[All who read this chapter are warned to make full allowance for my partiality. There is not an intentional over-statement in it. I always believed my father and mother to be remarkable people, and my brothers and sisters to be the salt of the earth. I have probably been too enthusiastic. I freely acknowledge this. I am thankful that those nearest and dearest to me are good enough and wise enough that I dare enthuse over them.—L. S. L.]

Nelson Irvine Nichols[7] was the youngest of a family of twelve, half of whom were grown at his birth. Years after his death, a cousin of his said this of him: "We were always proud of Nelson. He was good looking, bright and keen, and had a moral record as clean as any woman's. On Sundays he used to look as though he stepped out of a band-box, so spruce was he in his broadcloth and beaver. But he was not afraid of work, and always had an eye out to the main chance." To this we may add that he had his mother's even disposition. With strangers he was still-tongued, but among his friends he was boiling over with life and merriment.

In February, 1831, this young man of nineteen came with his father's family to Sharon, Ohio. Three years later he went to Indiana, then newly opened to settlement, and opened up a farm near the present town of Wolcottville. In due time he returned to Ohio after his bride, and on January 23d, 1837, was married to Kezia Waltman.

She was of this ancestry: Her great-great grandfather was Valentine

Waltman of Germany, who married Barbara, the heiress and last of the line of a family of barons. The second son, Valentine, eloped with his wife, Miss Bierly, crossed the ocean and settled in Pennsylvania. Their son John served in the Revolutionary War. To this John and his proud little wife, Anna Marie Marguerite, (Surface,) was born, in 1790, a son named Valentine, and this son married Achsa, daughter of Andrew and Rebecca Wilson.

Achsa Wilson-Waltman's maternal uncles won in the Revolutionary War the title of " The three fighting Colonel McLanes." One of the uncles, Major Allen McLane, rose to high distinction under General Wayne and General Henry Lee. These Scotch-Irish McLanes suffered great loss during the war, the British laying waste their estates near Philadelphia in reprisal. The mother of the "fighting McLanes" withstood them to the last, throwing it in their teeth as her houses burned, that her sons were making greater havoc for them than all the injury the British could do to her. Hearing of her distress, one of the sons returned to aid her. She quickly sent him back to his command, tersely telling him she could look after herself, and expected him to attend to the fighting.

Kezia, oldest daughter of Valentine and Achsa Waltman, was born Oct. 8th, 1814, at Huntington, Luzerne Co., Pa. She was said to resemble her resolute Revolutionary grandmother in both looks and disposition. She was beautiful, fair as a lily, with eyes and hair as dark as midnight. She never lost her birth-right of good looks. At eighty, her eyes were as bright as ever, her cheeks pink, and her fair skin almost transparent in its whiteness. Her brain was quick, her memory astonishing. At twelve years of age she could repeat Milton's Paradise Lost and Young's Night Thoughts, word for word. She often said that if the Bible were blotted out of existence, that with the exceptions of the genealogical tables, she could write it again from memory.

All of her life, Kezia was eccentric in many of her way. She never did anything because others did it. She was absolutely independent in her thinking. She believed in progress, and as thoroughly disbelieved in the old hide-bound "woman's sphere " beliefs. She had the honor of being one of the pioneers among western women teachers. About this time also, she completed a volume of verse of merit, which she would never allow to be printed.

It was this radical but winning teacher that Nelson Nichols fell in love with, won from many competitors, and married. He never lost his faith in her goodness, or admiration for her talents. After 28 years of wedded life, when death faced him, he could not bear to have her out of his sight. By his side she went with him to the very brink of the grave, and for 31 years after remained in widow-hood, true to his memory. All of their married life was spent on their farm at Wolcottville, Indiana. Nelson had all the Greene love for well-kept premises, and his husbandry showed in orderly fields and meadows, orchards and woodland. Kezia's yard contained more flowers and more rare plants than any other home in the township, if not in the county. Here their nine children were born, six of whom, Fernando, Attie, Valentine, John, Nancy and Lora, lived to grow up and become heads of other families. Besides these, two orphan nephews, John Lamson and John C. Nichols, and an orphan neice, Rachel Nichols, had their home with their uncle and aunt, and were considered full members of the family.

It was pleasant in after years for their children to recall the high moral ground their parents took. The Nichols' home was one of the regular stations of the famous Underground Railway of anti-slavery days, harboring escaped slaves and anti-slavery agitators. Nelson had the courage to vote the Abolition ticket when but four such votes were cast in the county. His influence is seen, in that all three of his sons and his two adopted nephews, fought in the Civil War for the Union. The last time he ever left his room he was carried to the polls to cast a vote for Abraham Lincoln's second term.

Kezia Nichols was never so busy that she could not do Christian work, encourage the weak or fallen, or care for the sick and the poor. To the last, it was never too muddy or cold for her to meet her Sunday school class, and at eighty she was still an angel of mercy at the bedside of the sick. When her last day dawned upon earth, the watchers at her bedside caught the faint words—"Thy will be done!" and Kezia Nichols had crossed to the Great Beyond. She died Dec. 3d, 1895, and was buried in Pineville, Mo.

> Her eighty years of life
>   Were spent in doing good;
> By deeds she proved her faith
>   In human brotherhood.
>
> Death came and breathed his icy chill
>   Just where our Mother's footsteps trod;
> Her throbbing heart grew cold and still—
>   Her work is done. She rests with God.
>   —*Mrs. Stowe.*

Their children were these:
Fernando, b. Jan. 20, 1838.
Maranda, b. Sept. 1, 1839, d. Oct. 7, 1839.
Almira, b. Nov. 27, 1841; d. Sept. 30, 1858.
Attie A., b. Oct. 30, 1843.
Valentine David, b. Oct. 26, 1845.
John Joel, b. Sept. 13, 1848.

Nancy Theresa, b. Dec. 14, 1850.

Myron, b. Nov. 14, 1853 ; d. Oct. 10, 1861.

Lora Sarah, b. April 2, 1857.

As might have been expected with parents of such marked personality, their children presented diverse temperaments. A waggish relative once gave "character" names to them, which were so pat that they have come down in a sub-rosa way to this hour. Attie, dignified, and faultlessly correct in her manners, was The Duchess ; Nannie, whose keen eye took in every detail, and who wanted everything done precisely right, was Inspector General ; Valentine was Tine the Good ; his younger brother was Happy-go-lucky John ; Fernando was The Singed Cat. The reference was to a cat which had been scorched and bore a rough and touzled coat in consequence, but could out-mouse and out-rat any of his slick brethren. The allusion was plain to anyone who ever saw Fernando Nichols arise in church—necktie knotted under his ear, and his hastily-pulled-on coat sagging six different ways at once—and deliver a red-hot talk that set everyone aquiver to get into church or Sunday school work instanter.

FERNANDO NICHOLS. His children are all of them successful and respected, and all are fortunate in their home ties. "Our children are every one a comfort to us," says their mother, and their father, as though something was left unsaid, adds this unusual testimony,—"All of my children-in-law are pure gold, also."

So Fernando Nichols has a right to be called a successful man, although with all his industry he has never accumulated material riches. His fortune has been in his family. January 22, 1859, he married his second cousin, Mary Jane Cady, whose genealogy is given in Chapter XXIX.

The curious family superstition that every Jane among them would be a care-taker of the friendless or infirm among her connection, reached high-water mark confirmation in her case. Her father and mother died within six weeks of each other. For a time the orphans lived at the old King home in New York, a perfect nest of old bachelor uncles and old maid aunts. Then their Aunt Debbie (Deborah) took the children with her to Indiana, and here Jane married. The only other one of her family, her brother Edgar, came to live with her, and her house is yet his home. The aunts and uncles became too old to live by themselves. Good Jane, that never lost her gratitude, that never tired of them, took care of them all, of feeble Uncle John, infirm Uncle Sylvester and childish Aunt Debbie, who at the last had to be waited on as a babe. Jane never paraded as a martyr ; she never thought herself a saint ; she was too busy patching, cooking and sweeping to take a leading part in church or mission work. But the Master who counts the cups of cold water given in His name will surely give her the reward of her deeds.

Fernando Nichols has lived in Indiana, New York, North Dakota and Tennessee, and is now at Warren, Arkansas. He has always worked for the betterment of the community in which he has lived. He is a Deacon in the church. Not one christian in a thousand is as efficient and tireless a worker in the church as he. He is an ideal, up-to-date Sunday school superintendent. His speeches are short, crisp, sawed-off right in the middle, but they hit the mark every time. His prayers are earnest, brief, face-to-face petitions that touch the most indifferent. He spends no time seeking a mission, but does the work nearest his hand, and does it with all his might. He has five living children.

Minnie (Mrs. Rose,) is a fine woman, in her traits happily combining the best characteristics of both her father and mother.

Charles has one of the kindest hearts that ever beat in mortal frame. Quiet and still-tongued, he is like his mother's people. His wife was a reporter before her marriage.

Allen G. Nichols is the printer son. He has done much reportorial work, and has made a specialty of fraternal writing, particularly of that pertaining to the Odd Fellows and Knights of Pythias orders, in which he has risen to high rank for so young a man. He wields a vigorous political pen also, and was rewarded for his political services by the position of Collector of Customs, at Sabine Pass, Texas. He was here when the dreadful Galveston Flood swept hundreds of homes and human beings into the ocean's waters. A perverseness of fate dogged this young man, to which he alluded, upon his recent removal to Los Angeles, California, after this manner:

"I am a builder of houses for fires to burn and floods to wash away. What with fires, floods and hurricanes, I am in the position of the man who had that taken from him that he seemed to have. The only things I have left are the sweetest wife and the two finest children on earth, a wrecked nervous system, and a determination to build me up another home."

Harry E. is *sui generis*. A letter from him is a treasure. Something like his father's prayers, it begins without a beginning, and ends without an ending. He jumps right into the middle of what he is interested in, and goes after it, up and down, tooth and toe-nail, hip and thigh, but the interest never lags. We gratefully acknowledge that this indefatigable digger, who plunged into old books, dry official records and out-of-the-way references, has helped the making of this history materially. He is a postal clerk on the Iron Mountain R. R., and lives in St. Louis, Mo.

Eddie F., born in 1880, proved himself in his teens an exceptional student, and has already given good earnest of being as exceptional a business man. He is honest, quick, steady and tireless. Already he holds the important position as manager of a certain territory for a large lumber company.

Fernando's table of descendants is this :

NELSON NICHOLS[9], born dead, Dec. 16, 1859.

MARY LINCOLN NICHOLS[9]. b. May 18, 1861 ; d. Jan. 14, 1863.

MINNIE O. NICHOLS-ROSE[9], b. May 15, 1866; m. to Wilber Rose at Jamestown, N. D., March 9, 1886. Their first child, Charles Wilbur, was born April 12, 1887. Their second son, Clifford Allen, died May 25, 1890, aged 14 months. They live at Warren, Ark.

CHARLES DICKINSON NICHOLS[9], b. Jan. 24, 1868 ; m to Bernice Bennett, Nov. 3, 1890, at Jamestown, N. D. They have Henry F., b. Dec. 17, 1895, and Ruth, b. Oct. 6, 1900.

ALLEN GEORGE NICHOLS[9], b. Dec. 5, 1869. Married Emma S. Reichmann, Nov. 3, 1892. They have two children, Harry George, b. Oct. 17, 1894, and Gladys, b. April 21, 1899.

MARY E. NICHOLS[9], b. June 10, 1871 ; d. Aug. 17, 1871, aged 10 weeks.

CORA NICHOLS[9], b. July 25, 1873. Died the next day.

HARRY ELTON NICHOLS[9], b. Aug. 12, 1874 ; m. Clara Deihl. They have one daughter, Marjory D., b. Jan. 2, 1900.

EDGAR FERNANDO NICHOLS[9], b. Sept. 22, 1880. M. June 11, 1903, to Ida Godwin, o Oakdale, La. They live in Louisiana.

ATTIE A. NICHOLS-STOWE[8] will not allow us to say as much about her as we would like. She puts a special bar upon us as to her poetical efforts. We submit the more cheerfully that her stanzas interspersed through this book are her own best interpreters. If anyone can read them and not believe her a woman of intellectual power and high ideals, our words would be idle.

Mrs. Stowe is dignified, self-controlled and well-poised. Her affections are true as steel to her own. She holds life as a sacred trust, and believes it a duty to make the world happier and wiser by all possible efforts. She must allow us to use this poem of hers, written when her heart was sad, and when the world seemed to her to have passed by and forgotten her. It shows how free from envy or sordid littleness are the impulses of her heart.

> Because another's muse
>   Gives her a sweeter lay,
> Shall I, then, dare refuse
>   The words mine bids me say ?
>
> Because another paints
>   With touch and skill more free,
> Shall I hold in restraints
>   The talent God gave me ?
>
> Because another's path
>   Seems brighter far to me,
> Dare I assume God's wrath ?—
>   Refuse His love to see ?
>
> Because another's work
>   Lies in the focus light
> Of fame, dare I to shirk
>   My duty to the right ?

> Because some other mind
>> Received the talents ten,
> Shall I, with envy blind,
>> Hide me in darkest den?
>
> No ; let me rather ask
>> God's blessing on my one ;
> If I do well my task,
>> I'll hear Him say, " Well done."
>>> —*A. A. Stowe.*

Mrs. Stowe has done good descriptive work for *Collier's Weekly* and *Leslie's Monthly*, and various other magazines. Her best work is in verse, however, and of this her patriotic poems are probably the best. Her work rings true, because she puts her heart in it, and writes only what she feels.

Attie A. Nichols was married in 1863 to Fletcher H. Noble, her second cousin on her mother's side. He lived but a few years. Naturally restless, and always seeking a region where his health would improve, they moved from point to point in Ohio, Indiana, Michigan and Minnesota. Three children were born to them, Myra and Clara in Indiana, and Ralph in Minnesota. Little Clara died early. Ralph, restless as his father, wandered from state to state. In Colfax, Washington, he married Effie Benton, March, 1891, and in November of the same year he died, leaving a widow of seventeen. Five months after his death a posthumous child was born, who was named Ralph for the father he had never seen.

Myra, the remaining child of the first marriage, has unfortunately been handicapped all her life by inherited disease, but is growing stronger as the years pass by. She married Ernest E. Everett, October, 1886, and has been the mother of five children, all of whom are dead. She is living now in flower-environed Pasadena, California.

Attie A. married for her second husband, Captain Martin Stowe. He was born at Princeton, Mass., 1830. He had a brave war record and was a man of distinction in every way. He was magnetic, polished, large-brained, and had traveled extensively in South America and the U. S. He had made two large fortunes and lost them, only to make a third. After his marriage he became a merchant. He represented his district in the Minnesota legislature several terms. All their children were born in Brandon, Minnesota. He moved to Hailey, Idaho, in 1882, and in mining operations again became embarrassed. Before his usual good fortune returned to him, his health failed. His plucky wife stepped into the breach, and put her scholarship to use. She soon rose to be assistant principal of the Hailey schools, refusing the principalship as taking too much time from her home duties.

June 6th, 1891, Captain Stowe died from injuries received in a fall from his horse. The accident was superinduced by an attack of heart trouble, the direct result of his arduous army experiences. Mrs. Stowe could never bear to live in Hailey afterwards. Her home is in Los Angeles, California, where she is active in church and club work.

Mrs. Stowe's descendants by her first husband are these:

MYRA ESTELLE NOBLE-EVERETT[9], b. Feb. 23, 1864; m. at Jamestown, N. D., to Ernest E. Everett, Oct. 25, 1886. Their children are all dead. They were Irene, an unnamed infant, Edith, Myra, Grace and Ernest Earle.

CLARA NOBLE[9], b. Aug. 22, 1865. Died, March 13, 1868.

RALPH NOBLE[9], b. July 17, 1868. Died in State of Washington, Nov. 22, 1891, leaving a young wife and posthumous child, Ralph.

By her second marriage, Mrs. Stowe has these descendants:

CORA ALLEN STOWE-DAVEY[9], b. June 11, 1871; married to Edward Davey.

EUGENE M. STOWE[9], b. Dec. 4, 1872; m. Oct. 28, 1903, to Stella Gimble.

ARTHUR WILDER STOWE[9], b. Aug. 29, 1874. His home is in Alaska.

GEORGE WALTMAN STOWE[9], b. Aug. 28, 1876. He lives in Alaska.

VALENTINE NICHOLS[8]. It is a singular paradox that the most thoroughly good child out of this Nelson Nichols family should have been the one who delighted most in war and bloodshed. Even as a small boy, Valentine (or Tine) was everlastingly poring over the history of some war, or the biography of some fighting general. The only time he disobeyed his father in his life, he ran away to be a soldier. He was rejected four or five times on account of his size, but persevered until he found a more compliant recruiting officer. When asked his age, he frankly told, and when he was warningly re-asked, unflinchingly answered:—"Not quite seventeen." Not all the gold of Australia could have made Tine Nichols tell a lie. The officer smiled as he looked at the eager, conscientious lad, slight, boyish, and weighing not a hundred pounds. "We'll take him," said he. "That boy's got the making of a soldier in him."

He served three years, and saw hard campaigning. He could have been lieutenant or captain, but with characteristic self-effacement refused to accept either office because of his youth. Twice he was called out of the ranks and publicly thanked for exceptional bravery.

One of these occasions was late in November, 1863. In a forced march across the Huston River, in East Tennessee, a gun was caught in a crevice of a rock in a deep and dangerous ford, and behind it were four more cannon, a wagon train of supplies, and the ambulances of the sick and wounded. If abandoned, these would fall into the enemy's hands, who were near. Volunteers were called for to dislodge the cassion. Not even its own gunners responded. The night was dark, the water swift and deep and full of needle ice.

Nichols stepped out. "Come boys!" he cried, and nine followed him. They worked for six hours, but saved the gun and waiting trains. Then it was that General Garrard called Nichols out, still in his frozen garments, and publicly eulogized him. "If we had a thousand men like you," he said, "we could take Richmond." They took up the march again, when he suddenly sank to the ground from exhaustion. To this day he suffers severely from rheumatism and heart trouble contracted in that fearful night's exposure.

In 1868, Tine Nichols removed to Braudon, Minnesota, where he lived for 35 years. He is now living in East San Josè, California. He has prospered financially, and his valuable Minnesota farm of about four hundred acres is so well kept that not even a thistle or burdock is tolerated. As a man, he lives his Christianity, and his charity reaches from his neighbor to the distressed of the nations beyond the seas; for in his creed, all mankind are brothers.

His first wife, Antionette Stevenson, of New York, was unfortunately an invalid. When her youngest child was twelve days old, she died from a sudden return of her old malady. She left five children, Harold, Hubert, Clyde, Rosa and Lucien. Clyde was drowned while a child. Harold is an engineer on the Nothern Pacific Ry. Hubert and Lucien are also railroad men. None of the first wife's children are married, except Harold.

V. D. Nichols' second marriage was to Mrs. Katherine Landa-Bartoss. She was born Nov. 11th, 1853, in Vesely, Bohemia, and came to America when seven years old. The Landa family were of gentle blood, of the upper middle class. This daughter was always a person of distinctive character. She was energetic and forceful in other matters. Quick, resourceful and self-reliant, she is always ready for an emergency. If a machine breaks in the fields, she is ready to repair it; and if a castastrophe occurs, she keeps her presence of mind, and is the first to suggest a practical alleviation. With it all, she is a keen business woman, hospitable in her home, and kind to the poor. Her husband is very proud of her.

By his second marriage, V. D. Nichols became the father of four children. Besides these, his wife was the mother of a daughter by her first husband. This daughter took the name of Nichols, and was considered as entirely belonging to the family.

Valentine's children by the first wife:

HAROLD NELSON NICHOLS[9], b. Sept. 20, 1869. Married, March 6, 1898, to Mrs. Anna Rosedal.

HUBERT V. D. NICHOLS[9], b. Oct. 21, 1871.

CLYDE BOWMAN NICHOLS[9], b. Oct. 9, 1873. Drowned April, 1878, aged 4 years.

ROSEMOND E. NICHOLS[9], b. Aug. 16, 1875.

LUCIAN MARTIN NICHOLS[9], b. Sept. 4, 1877.

His children by the second wife are these:

ETHEL NICHOLS-THORSON[9], b. Aug. 28, 1879; m. Jan. 24, 1899, to Theodore Thorson.

BENJAMIN FRANKLIN NICHOLS[9], b. Dec. 14, 1880.
LORA KEZIA NICHOLS[9], b. April 12, 1885.
MARCUS M. NICHOLS[9], b. Nov. 25, 1887.

MARY BARTOS-UKESTAD. Adopted daughter, and second wife's child by first marriage. Born April 17, 1874. M. Dec. 24, 1897 to Julius Ukestad. Died Jan. 31, 1903, leaving two children, Marcus, born Sept. 2, 1898, and Valentine David, b. June 9, 1901.

JOHN J. NICHOLS[8] was the jolliest boy alive, laughing, joking, and singing from morning until night. He entered the Civil War at the age of seventeen, and served until its close. In 1866, when but eighteen, he went to north central Minnesota, then newly opened to settlement. His romantic disposition led him to Fort Abercrombie, in the heart of the Sioux Indian reservation, where he lived with the Indians for some time, learning their language and much of their wood and prairie craft.

At twenty he returned to Brandon, Minn., and was then married to a French frontierman's daughter, Josephine, the sixteen-year-old daughter of Antoine and Samantha Pelissier. She could shoot, hunt or swim, and in backwoods' parlance, was "as smart as a steel trap." Six children were born to them.

After a time John Nichols joined a surveying corps working in the then unexplored territory of North Dakota. Believing home-seekers by the tens of thousands would flock in as soon as the region would be opened to settlement, he engaged in a unique business. He moved his family into this unsettled country, near the present city of Jamestown. Then for years he traveled over the wide territory, preparatory to guiding parties to it later. His Indian training had developed almost a sixth sense, a sensitized memory of locality. He could not be lost and he never forgot lake or wood stream, or soil. No other man, Indian or white, ever knew North Dakota as he did.

He had a hundred adventures. He had a score of narrow escapes from drownings, stampedes of buffaloes, and terrific blizzards. Several times he was reported killed and scalped. He drove with his faithful greys 12,500 miles a year, or as he expressed it, " Put a belt around the earth every two years." He was not in the least of a cow-boy type. He was a gentleman always, and an expert in his line. He became a member of an opulent real estate firm, and when the rush of emigration began, fortune in her most gracious mood smiled upon him.

There are those to whom all the misfortunes of a lifetime come in one terrible storm. It was so with easy, trusting John. Business reverses swept away all. Trouble and death came into his home. North Dakota proved the charnel house of his hopes. When he married again, he sought his fortune anew on the Pacific coast. He now lives at Palo Alta, California.

His second wife was Miss Jeannette Emond, daughter of Robert and Elizabeth Emond. She was born August 7th, 1855, at Fergus, Canada.

She came to the States in 1890 and two years later married. She is of good English and Scotch blood, and takes a pride in her family ancestry. She has a literary talent, but writes only for her friends. We have room for but two stanzas from a memorial poem of hers.

> "The Master walked in His garden,
>   In search of the flower most rare.
> Amid all the flowers in His garden,
>   He found one exceedingly fair.
>   Gladly he gathered the blossom,
>   'Twas a lily of spotless white,
>   Pure as the riven snow it shone
>   In the darkness of the night.

> "Grieved was the gard'ner's heart and sad.
>   But the Master in tenderest tone
> Said, 'I've need of this one sweet lily,
>   To adorn a place by my throne'.
>   A voice like a dream of the morning,
>   Said 'Beloved one, come, come away;
>   The Master hath need of thy presence,
>   Then why dost thy coming delay?'"

Mr. Nichols' children by his first wife all lived to be grown. At twenty, George was killed by the kick of a horse, and Fannie died at nineteen from an attack of heart trouble. Clara married early, and was left a young widow with two or three little daughters. She is noted as being one of the best cooks in this family of cooks. This results from her double French blood, as they, of all people, elevate cookery to a fine art. Emma, a successful teacher, married her distant cousin, Merritt Pierce, and lives at Wolcott-ville, Indiana. Nelson is a promising young man, and prominent in fraternal orders. Before he was nineteen he married a girl of fifteen. He was but twenty when his only child was born. He lives at Jamestown.

Antoine, the remaining son of the first marriage, inherited a love of travel. In 1896, at the age of seventeen, he enlisted in the naval service, cruising to Central and South America and the Hawaiian Islands. When the Maine was blown up in Havana harbor, the Baltimore, on which he belonged, was ordered to Hong Kong, China. Here she sailed away with Commodore Dewey for Manila. What follows is in Tone's own words, a graphic picture of the famous Manila Battle of May 1st, 1898.

"April 30th we lay just outside of the Bay. We waited until the moon went down near midnight. Then we put out all the lights only on the stern

13

of the ships, and steamed in, waiting about seven miles out from Manila for daylight. Then we saw the fleet and started for it. The Spanish ships commenced firing, but Dewey's orders were to reserve our fire until within 3000 yards. This we did. We turned broadside, steamed slowly and poured shot into them lively, for nearly three hours. Nearly all the Spanish ships were on fire, and two of them sunk. Then Dewey signalled to get out of range and get breakfast.

"At 11:30 a. m. we steamed back. We soon had the Flagship Reine Christina and the other ships destroyed. Then the Baltimore opened fire on the fort at Cavite. The second shot knocked one of their ten-inch guns more than two hundred feet high in the air. At 2:00 p. m. we landed. One of the first things I saw was a big bunch of keys, very ancient and curious, hanging in the door of the arsenal. I have them now."

Antoine was one of the men chosen to return to America with Admiral Dewey. He was one of his Orderlies, and was one of the five who went with Dewey wherever he went,—Asia, Europe and America, they were lionized, and attended parades, receptions, and court presentations. Congress voted them special medals, and they were personally presented to them at Washington, D. C., by President McKinley himself. Having had enough of globe trotting, Tone accepted a discharge, and is now a machinist at San José, California.

John Emons is the only surviving child of the second marriage. This "last little one" is younger than some of his own nieces. This last John is not only the son of a John, but from one line to another, the descendant of a dozen Johns who have lived upon American soil. He is a baker's son and completes a baker's dozen that have borne this good, old-fashioned name.

CLARA EVELYN NICHOLS-WILLIAMS[9], b. May 2, 1870. M. at Jamestown, N. D., to Harrison M. Williams. She is a widow with three children. The two oldest are Harriet M., b. Aug. 27, 1887, and Dolores, b. June 25, 1889.

GEORGE ALBERT NICHOLS[9], b. Oct. 21, 1871. Died, Nov. 9, 1891, killed by a kick from a horse.

EMMA N. NICHOLS-PIERCE[9], b. March 8, 1873. M. Aug. 1896, to her third cousin, Merritt Pierce, of Wolcottville, Indiana. They have a daughter, Marjorie, b. Aug. 16, 1897.

FANNIE LORA NICHOLS[9], b. Jan. 5, 1875; d. Oct. 23, 1893, aged 19.

NELSON PETER NICHOLS[9], b. Dec. 31, 1876; m. Nov. 4, 1895, to Bertha Lebo. They have Elizabeth Irene, b. Dec. 7, 1896.

ANTOINE NICHOLS[9], b. Sept. 15, 1879.

By the second marriage John Nichols has:

JOHN EMONS[9], b. Aug. 26, 1893.

LINTON AND LOMORE[9], twins, b. Jan. 4, 1895. Died, Jan. 6, 1896.

MRS. NANNIE T. NICHOLS-TUCK[8]. Mrs. Tuck had the forethought to make out a list of her faults, and send them on in time to be used in this work!

Mrs. Tuck has always protested that the name Nancy fitted no one but a fat, black, bandanna-turbaned cook. Therefore her friends have softened her name to Nannie. She might well afford to put up with the homely old family name, for she took the lion's share of all that was good, that the family blood could give her.

She is fine-looking, with the coveted Marie-LaValley expressiveness of features. There's a world of meaning in a single flash of her eye, and her face reflects every shade of animation or emotion, even though not a word be spoken. Her tongue and brain are ready, and her wit as quick as an Irishman's, though never bitter, for she has the kindliest of hearts.

Her husband is James Tuck, born December 20th, 1842, at Clyde, Ohio. He is the son of Shubal and Mary Tuck, and is an original character. He is a Free Mason, an Eastern Star man, a G. A. R., and an old soldier from head to foot. He is a seven-times-dyed-in-the-wool Republican, a Baptist to the bone and marrow. But he is so hail-fellow-well-met with all, that no one takes offence at his ultraness.

Mr. Tuck was a successful druggist. He was badly injured during the Civil War, and has for years been an invalid. He put his business in charge of one he trusted. His confidence was misplaced. There was a sudden crash, and the sick and disheartened man faced what seemed absolute ruin, every dollar gone, and heavy debts against him.

Mr. Tuck was too sick a man to do anything. His wife promptly put her household in charge of her daughter, conferred with the creditors, and soon convinced them that she had the vim and the brains to build up a new business from the wreck of the old. She was given a chance. She still conducts the drug store and its allied departments. Long ago Nannie Tuck paid off every cent of debt with full interest. She has been full of original ideas. All this time, church, temperance and Sunday school work has been actively engaged in. Nor have business cares made her dull, narrow, or ill-tempered. She is particularly charitable toward her sister-woman, and at forty-nine was able to say, "I have almost completed a half-century, and no woman can ever say I have spread an unjust report against her good name, or ever pushed a weak sister down."

This woman who has stood so loyally by her infirm husband, and been a pillar of strength to every good cause, she it is who sent a list of her faults to be recorded in these pages!

Mrs. Tuck's first two children, both sons, died at birth. Besides them she had these decendents:

MARY LORA TUCK–BAIRD[9], b. Sept. 13, 1875 ; m. to Riley Baird, June 25, 1893. They have Donald Keith, b. April 8, 1897. Their home is in Oklahoma.

GRACE TUCK–ILEFF[9], b. in June, 1880. She is the wife of Charles Ileff. They have one son, Gerald Tuck, b. Sept. 21, 1899.

LORA SARAH NICHOLS–LA MANCE[3], born April 2nd, 1857. Married April 14th, 1880, to M. N. La Mance. She is the author of this book. As to what manner of woman she is, when she dies this might be inscribed on her headstone :—

LORA S. LA MANCE.

HERE LIES a woman with more hobbies
than she had fingers and toes.

*   *   *

She always went at things as though killing
snakes.

*   *   *

She found the cup of life full and rich, and
enjoyed it to the last drop.

*   *   *

She departed this life, firmly believing it but
the prelude to an infinitely fuller and
deeper life beyond the grave, with
God and Christ our Saviour.

In the words of the Psalmist, "The lines have fallen unto her in pleasant places." As daughter, sister, wife and mother she has all of her life met with more than ordinary affection. She has had time for study; opportunity to gather about her flowers, books and curios, and a chance to work for the reforms and beliefs she cherishes. In middle life she began to write for the press, her first efforts being along floral lines. Of her series of floral booklets, "Beautiful Home Surroundings," "House Plants," and "Pansies," 75,000 copies have been sold. She has written historical sketches, etc., and one novel, "When Roses Have Fallen," a romance of early Ohio. She is now at work on "Our First Inheritance," a book on surnames, and a religious biography, "Jesus, the Christ." This last she esteems as the best thing she has written.

Lora S. Nichols was married April 14th, 1880, to Marcus N. La Mance, of Pineville, Mo. One daughter, Lora Lee, was born to them, January 27th, 1881. Oak Lawn, the home of the family, lies at the foot of Battle Mountain, from the summit of which Pineville was shelled during the Civil War. It owes its name to the lawns upon the one hand, with their background of shrubs, roses and flowers, and a long slope upon the other, this declivity clothed with noble forest trees.

M. N. La Mance* was born October 16th, 1844, of Huguenot—French descent. His father was Lieut. James P., son of Jacob and grandson of John La Mance, who crossed the ocean. His mother was Cynthia H., daughter of Adam and Jane Given Caldwell. His parents were married in Georgia. Marcus, however, was born in the same county where he now resides. He shows the Scotch characteristics of his mother's side of the house, being conservative, prudent, farseeing, firm as a rock, and honest to the core.

Marcus enlisted in the Confederate Army in 1863, and remained with it until the war ended. After the war was over, father and son returned to find the town nearly all burned, and the streets white with the bloom of the dog fennel. So destitute was the land that during a considerable part of that summer of 1865 the family's sole diet was branshorts mush and wild blackberries.

In the spring of 1866 M. N. La Mance opened up a dry goods store in Pineville, following the same occupation as his father and grandfather before him. For many years he was Post Master, and he served four terms as County Treasurer. A man of more integrity cannot be found anywhere, or one more deeply respected.

Lora Lee, the only child, has all her life been one of the dearest and most affectionate of daughters. She holds one silver and two gold medals, won in her school days. She has always been a popular young woman, because of so generous a disposition, so warm a heart, and her entire freedom from affectation of any kind.

Lora Lee La Mance was married April 14th, 1902, to Joseph C. Watkins, of Galena, Mo. He was born September 1st, 1877. He is the son of Joseph C. and Betty G. Watkins. The father was a well known educator, and for twenty-one years before his death was superintendent of schools at Ennis, Texas. It is in his honor that the Joseph C. Watkins Library of Ennis, Texas, is named. The mother has made a life specialty of music, and is the author of an elementary work upon piano forte playing.

Joseph C. Watkins, Jr., is an exceptional young man, a Christian, a scholar, and a gentleman. He holds several diplomas and is professionally

---

*Several have asked the meaning of the family name, and also how La Mance is pronounced. It is an old and rather uncommon French name. Originally it was La Normance or Le Normance, i. e., The Norman, or of Normandy. In time, the Catholic branch, who remained in France, mostly shortened the name to Mance. The Protestant wing, in eastern France, after the Massacre of St. Bartholomew, Aug. 24, 1572, fled in terror over the border into Switzerland. Here their name became shortened into La Mance. 200 years after this, John La Mance, native of a French-speaking canton of Switzerland, came to the United States. He pronounced his name as though spelled La Mönz, with the last consonant prolonged until almost La—Mon—ze. Whereupon his Southern neighbors made a mess of the name, twisting it into Lamonts and Lemons. Lemons was so sour a surname that the next generation Anglicized the pronunciation as La Mance to rhyme with la chance. So don't try to Frenchify the author's name. It has Americanized itself, and that is better.

a Civil Engineer and Mineralogist. He is the General Manager of the McDonald Land and Mining Co.'s interests in Stone and McDonald Counties, in Missouri.

LORALEE WATKINS[10], born August 2, 1904.

APPENDIX

Appendix

AN ACCOUNT OF THE MATTESON, LASCELLE–WARDWELL,
WAITE AND OTHER FAMILIES.

A CORRECTION   On page 17 Robert the Strong, the head of the royal
Capet line, is spoken of as a Saxon leader in England.   It should have been
"a Saxon leader in *Germany*."

Fully one-third of the Quidnessett Greenes are of Matteson descent also
Nearly as many are of Lascelle-Wardwell extraction   Toward a half are of
Waite blood.   All that I can learn of these lines is therefore given here
This is the first time the Lascelle-Wardwell or Matteson lines have had their
British history traced   The task has been most difficult, therefore.

THE MATTESONS

Matteson, Madison, Mathewson and Mathis are all surnames derived
from Matheson.   The Mathesons were a sub-clan of the royal *siol clann*
(great seed or royal clan) of McAlpine   This clan united in its blood two
rival royal lines, that for hundreds of years had divided Scotland's territory
between them.

Scotland lies to the north of England.   From 55 B C to A D 448 the
Romans held England as a conquered province.   But this land of North
Britain stubbornly resisted and perpetually harassed them.   It was held by
a Celtic people originally from the Orkney Islands   They were sun-wor-
shippers, living in tents.   They were fierce and savage, daubing their bodies
with paint, or hideously staining their skins with the juice of the woad or
dyer's weed.

The historian, Dion Cassius, speaks of the annoyance the Emperor Severus received A D 208, from Mæatæ in the vicinity of Hadrian's Wall, a
fortified rampart, one hundred and eighty miles long, built to keep the barbarians off the Roman territory   Severus lost forty thousand men trying to
overcome the Caledonians and this tribe.   This is the first mention in history

of the Mæatæ, presumably the nucleus of the Matheson clan. The Romans later gave the name of Picts to all the North Britain tribes, including the Mæatæ.

After the Romans left Britain, in 448, the Picts plundered the Britons. This unwarlike people appealed to the Saxons in Germany to help them. The Saxons came, sent the Picts about their business, and gobbled up Britain for themselves. With them began England and English history.

The Picts were no longer savages. They had already picked up—no pun intended—a few glosses of civilization, when in A. D. 400, Saint Ninian preached the gospel to them and converted the South Picts. From that time their advance was rapid. But they had scarcely settled down to peaceful pursuits when a rival nation appeared contending for Pictavia or Caledonia, as North Britain was variously called.

A few centuries before Ireland had been conquered by the Gael, said to have been Milesians from Spain. They were a Celtic people, for they could, though with some difficulty, converse with the Picts of North Britain.

The city of Tara was their capital, and at Tara's court were gathered an imposing number of bards, sages, sooth-sayers and law-makers, showing that, though heathen, their civilization was of a high type for those days. Macfirbis, who died in 1400, quotes one of the old Irish bards as saying of this ruling class :—"Every one who is white of skin, brown of hair, bold, honorable, daring, prosperous, bountiful in the bestowal of property, wealth and rings, and who is not afraid of battle or combat—is the descendant of Milesius in Erinn." This is flattering, but graphic.

A. D. 426, Saint Patrick the Missionary began his labors in Ireland. He was so earnest and faithful that King Laogaire McNeill became a convert, and the whole nation followed the King's example. The good bishop spent the rest of his century or so of life in Ireland. It is said that he himself baptized more than twelve thousand persons. One of these was a boy of royal blood, Fergus McEarc, son of Earc (or Ferchard), King of Meath, the principal kingdom. Patrick was attracted to the lad and gave him his patriarchal blessing, a circumstance of which the prince was not a little proud and to which it is said he attributed much of his good fortune in after days.

Fergus raised an army of men to conquer himself a kingdom in the land of the Picts. The Irish king seems to have helped him, perhaps glad to be rid of so ambitious a spirit so near his throne. It was A. D. 503 when the Irish army crossed the North Channel in their skin boats, and landed in what is now Argyleshire, Scotland. Fergus went forth prepared both to conquer and to colonize. He had his priests and his *Seanachaidhe*, men skilled in herbs and remedies. He had his bards, one set of which chanted the laws, and one the chronicles of the nation. These were his harper-heralds, that led his army into battle. He had, as his rank required, his *Oclamh Fila*, the Master Poet, whose office requires him to know three hundred and fifty songs of wars, destructions, adventures and battles, and to have at his tongue's end poems of *Tir Tairngair*, the Land of Promise, and Magh Mell, the Plain of Honey, the half-heathen, half-christian Paradise, and the Isle of the Blessed, with a wonderful palace of glass that floats in the air. Only a ruler could wear the peaked hat of thin, beaten gold; but the *Oclamh Fila* might wear the fringed and 6-color robe, lawful beside but for the king to

"STONE OF SCONE" IN CORONATION CHAIR

wear. These high honors show the control exercised over Erin's rude warriors by the learned class of that day.

According to most authorities, Fergus McEarc carried with him also a sacred stone from Tara. According to others it was brought to Iona fifty-eight years later by Saint Columba. To the modern eye it is but a slab of dull red sand-stone, twenty-six inches long, sixteen inches broad, and ten inches thick. But this inanimate stone has played no small part in history. In after years fabulous stories gathered about it. It was said to have been the stone upon which Jacob pillowed his head when he saw the vision of angels ascending and descending a ladder from Heaven. It was claimed the stone was carried from Palestine to Egypt by the Prophet Jeremiah,* who

* See "To-day in Syria and Palestine," by William Ellery Curtis.

acted as a guardian of the Princess Circa or Scola, who fled to that land
shortly after her father, King Zedekiah, was taken captive to Babylon,
B. C. 580.

The story goes that Princess Circa went from Egypt to Ireland, where
refugees from the lost ten tribes had already established themselves. She
took the precious stone with her because all her ancestors, the kings of
Israel, had been crowned upon it. She married a royal prince, and from her
time all the Irish kings were crowned upon it to the time of Fergus McEarc,
who carried it to Scotland.

Still another account of this "Holy Pillar of Jacob," is that Hiber or
Iber, the Phoenician, came from Palestine and Egypt to Spain, bringing the
relic. From there he came with Miletus, and helped to conquer Ireland,
which is sometimes called Hibernia in his name. Whatever its real history
it was venerated as sacred. It was called the Stone of Scone, because the
Scotch Kings were crowned on it at Scone, and *Lia Fail*, i. e., the Stone of
Destiny, because it was held to insure the supremacy of the kingdom that
possessed it. In 1296, Edward I., King of England, captured the stone from
its shrine at Scone, and carried it to England, where he had a magnificent
cornation chair built to receive it. Every English monarch since then has
been crowned at Westminster Cathedral, sitting upon the sacred stone that
Fergus McEarc brought across the channel fourteen hundred years ago.

King Fergus wrested West Scotland from the Picts, and founded the
kingdom of Dalriada, or New Scotia. Tradition says both he and his son
Eugenius were slain in battle.

Half a century later a son of the royal Irish house became a missionary
priest. This Columba, or Colum Ceille, sailed away to the new kingdom
across the sea in 563. The king then upon the throne was Conal, a great-
grandson of Fergus. Columba asked of King Conal, and of King Brude of
the rival Pict nation, a grant of the quiet little island of Iona, that he might
build a monastery and a priests' college there. His favor was granted, and
he immediately erected his ecclesiastical buildings. What Iona did for Scotland is beyond computation. For centuries it was, as Dr. Johnson has said,
"The luminary whence savage clans and roving barbarians derived the bene-
fits of knowledge and the blessings of religion."

King Brude himself, and all of the North Picts, were yet heathen. He
granted Columba permission to preach before him, but connived at his pagan
priests and sages raising an infernal din as soon as the sermon began. Columba had a voice of extraordinary compass. He immediately chanted the
forty-fifth Psalm in a voice so clear and loud that all the shrieks and yells of
the Picts could not drown it. King Brude thought it a miracle and at once,
with all his people, embraced Christianity. This good priest of the royal

house we are tracing did a wonderful, noble and lasting work. And he died, as became his life, on his knees at prayer.

The two lines of Dalriada and Pict Kings were both now Christians. None the less they remained rivals at perennial war between themselves. Neither was able to expel the other, but for two centuries or more the Pict kings were the stronger.

The history of these Pict kings is most obscure. Sir Walter Scott in the sixth chapter of The Antiquary touches off in ludicrous fashion the unpronounceable names of some of their kings,—Trynel McLachlin, Drust McTallargam, Golarge McChanannail and Eachan McFungus, that made Sir Arthur sneeze but to speak them. Whereupon sarcastic Jonathan Oldbuck put in a fling about "numbering in genealogy all the brawling, bulletheaded . . . . . . since the days of Crenttreminachcryme,—not one of whom could write his own name!"

Occasionally a name stands out with more distinctness. There was another King Brude, who in 685 killed the English King Egfred in battle, and gained great victories. There was pious King Nectan, who held great religious councils, and built churches. After him, in 730, came King Angus McFergus, the most active of all. He conquered his rival, King Selvach, of Dalriada. The fortunes of the Scottish or Delriada kings were at low ebb, indeed.

Not far from A. D. 800, Alpine came to the weak Scotch throne. He was both a warrior and statesman. He had the sagacity to see there could never be peace with two royal houses to claim the same territory. Having obtained an advantage over the Picts, he compelled their king to give him the Pictish crown princess in marriage. The Pictish crown descended each time through a daughter. The oldest son of the oldest daughter inherited the crown from his grandfather, instead of it going to the kings' sons. Alpine's heir was Kenneth, and Kenneth was, of course, the heir through his mother to the Pict Kingdom. King Kenneth succeeded his father in 836. Seven years later he succeeded the old Pict King, and the two kingdoms were united. It was Kenneth's policy to incorporate the Picts with the Dalraida, henceforth known solely as the Scotch, and their land as Scotland. It is said the Highland dress owes all its distinctive features to the Picts, and that the red hair and grey eyes, so often seen in Scotchmen, are from the Picts, also. On the other hand their language and customs gave way to the Irish.

Kenneth was a lineal descendant from Fergus McEarc of more than 300 years before. So far as we know, the oldest tribe among the Picts was the Mæatæ. It was a particularly warlike tribe also. It is reasonable that from this old and heroic clan the royal line should spring. When the two peoples were merged together, the king's own lines would be naturally placed together in one royal clan. That there was such a royal line we know, which was called the Clan of McAlpine, in honor of King Kenneth's father. The Mathesons were a division or sub-clan of this. Their tradition has ever been that they were of markedly royal blood; their name means "sons of heroes," and is apparently derived from the obsolete term of Mæatæ itself. It is supposed, therefore, that they are descendants of the royal Pict clan, intermarried with the McAlpine line until equally of their own blood also· All of the Scotch kings are descended from Kenneth, as are also all of the English kings from James I. The King of England counts among his progenitors the Pict and early Scotch Kings. These far-away kings, however, are as truly the fore-fathers of those who bear the Matheson or Mattison name as they are of England's royal family.

A Scotch clan consists of tribesmen who intermarry until the humblest of the clan has of the blood of the head of the clan who gave it its name. Clan pride was great. The old Scotch traced their kinship to fourteenth cousins, or five hundred years to a common ancestor. The head of each clan was called *The* McIntosh, *The* McDonald, *The* Matheson, etc. His word was law, above the king's own. When the chief would summon his men to war, he took a cross of wood, marked it with fire and blood, then gave it to the first man he met, naming a day and the field of rendezvous. He who received the "fiery cross" fled as though for his life, until he reached another one of the tribe, to whom he gave the cross and message. The largest clan in this way was assembled in two days' time. In time a large clan divided into sub-clans, who never, however, forgot their common tie.

The royal clan of McAlpine divided into the sub-clans of McGregor, Grant, McKinnon, McNab, McPhie, McQuarie, McAuley and Matheson. They had many customs in common, and all wore in battle or parade the clan badge, a sprig of pine or Scotch fir. Scott in his Lady of the Lake, that has for its motif the pride and power of the McAlpine chief, put this song of the pine in the mouth of a hundred clansmen, as they sing of their chief, Rhoderic Dhu.

> " Hail to the chief who in triumph advances !
> Honored and blest be the ever-green Pine !
> Long may the tree, in his banner that glances,
> Flourish, the shelter and grace of our line !
> Heaven send it happy dew,
> Earth lend it sap anew,
> Gayly to bourgeon and broadly to grow,
> While every Highland glen
> Sends our shout back again,
> ' Roderigh Vich Alpine dhu, ho ! ieroe ! '

"Ours is no sapling, chance-sown by the fountain,
  Blooming at Beltane, in winter to fade :
When the whirlwind has stripped every leaf on the mountain.
  The more shall Clan Alpine exult in her shade.
    Moored in the rifted rock,
    Proof to the tempest's shock.
Firmer he roots him the ruder it blows ;
    Mentieth and Breadalbane, then,
    Echo his praise again,
' Roderigh Vich Alpine dhu, ho ! ieroe !'" *

The seat of the Matheson clan is supposed to have been in the Highlands of Rosshire, in Northern Scotland. They had their own clan music that their bag-pipers played, and they rushed into battle with a wild *cath-ghairm* or battle cry, "*Dail acha'n da thear nai!*"—"The field between two hills!" This was their clan rendezvous, a valley plain where they always assembled to muster for warfare, for every Matheson believed that ill-luck would attend them did they muster elsewhere. They had their own tartan plaid, that only a Matheson might wear, and the men wore buskins, or short boots of deer-skin after a pattern of their own.

For hundreds of years they had their great clan gatherings, a feature of which was the dancing of the clansmen. Expert dancers not only could " do the spring," as the Scotch say, in reel, fling and strathspery, but could wind through the intricate step of " Kemshoal, Kemkossy, Lamatrast, Kenbradenoch and forgladln."

After the Reformation the clan embraced the most straight-laced Presbyterianism. Under James I., about 1608, there was a great emigration of the Scotch to Ulster, in the northern part of Ireland. Some of that branch of the family in which those who read this sketch are interested, were among the number. It was two grandsons of these emigrants that came to New England in the early days, and whose descendants are now so numerous. One of these came to R. I., probably about 1668. This was Henry Matteson, born in Ireland. Oct., 1646. He married Hannah Parsons, and became the head of a large line that has largely intermarried with the house of Greene. A large part of the Josiah Matteson line adopted the spelling and pronunciation of Mathewson. President James Madison was of Scotch-Irish ancestry also. At the time of his election, a part of the family, because he was the most eminent of the blood, adopted his form of the name in compliment to him. But Matteson, Mathewson or Madison, all are of the same general descent.

There was a James Matteson who came to R. I. before 1650. His de-

* Black Roderick, descendant of Alpine, Lerwick !

scendants are yet about Newport, and southern R. I.   His line was easily enough traced, but as it has not intermarried either with the Henry Matteson branch, or the Greene's, it is not given.   He is supposed to have been the uncle of Henry Matteson.

Many have asked for a genealogical table of the Mattesons.   I will give the men of the family for the first three generations, and sometimes beyond that.   Almost any one of the Mattesons can trace their ancestry back to Revolutionary times, so that this will be ample for them to complete their pedigree.   Henry, the father, born in 1646 in Ireland.   Married Hannah, daughter of Hugh Parsons and his wife Elizabeth, widow of Wm. English. Henry died in 1690.   They had a daughter, Hannah, and six sons, Henry, Thomas, Francis, Joseph, Josiah and Hezekiah.

CAPT. HENRY MATTESON[2], b. 1670; m. Judith Weaver in 1693. He had 10 children, 6 of them sons.   Two of his children m. Waites, 3 sons and 3 grandsons m. Sweets.   Line much crossed with the Greenes.

HENRY[3], m. Ruth Sweet, 1720.   His line was continued by Henry, Ruth, who m. John Greene[4], (see Chapter XV.), Caleb, Dinah, who m. her cousin Jonathan ; Nathan, who m. "Wealthy John" Greene's step-daughter Freelove Bowen; Thankful, who m. William Waite, and Jonathan, whose 1st wife was Alice Sweet, and 2d Meriba Waite.   By his last wife this Jonathan had Jonathan, Jr., whose line is traced with the Howards, in Chapter XXVIII.

JOHN[3], b. 1706 ; m. Elizabeth Hunt.   They had Thomas, who m. Hester Arnold ; John, Henry, who m. Dinah Spink in 1760 ; and probably Joseph, who m. Catherine Hatheway.

JAMES[3], b. 1712.   He m. Enfield Greene.   See Chapter XV.   Their son, Uriah, m. Mrs. Waite Sweet.

EBENEZER[3], b. 1718; m. Susannah Comstock.   Their son, Edmund[4], m. (1) Susannah Matteson, of the Thomas Matteson[2] line ; and (2) Virtue Greene.   See Chapter XX.   This Edmund[4] had John, Rowland and Ezra, and by the last wife, Stukeley.   Another son of Ebenezer[3] was Ebenezer[4], who m. Sarah or Susan Fish, or both.

HEZEKIAH[3], m. Mary Sweet, 1639.   He had 7 d., 4 sons.   George[4], was the father of Reuben, b. 1780.   Reuben m. Barbara Bowen.   Thomas was b. 1762, no other record.   Jeremiah, b. Dec. 31, 1743, m. Ruth Sweet at 19.   He had Caleb, Jesse and Jeremiah ; Solomon, who m. Rosanna, of Josiah Matteson line ; and Reuben, b. May 9, 1767, who m. Sarah Matteson.

It will be seen there were two Reuben[5]s, cousins to each other ; Reuben[5] of George[4], Hezekiah[3], Capt. Henry[2], b. 1780, m. Esther Burleson.   They had Archibald, John, Reuben, James, and 3 dau.   The oldest of the sons, Henry[7], m. May Angelyn Rouse, and had Walter H.[8], who m. Eliza J. Hope. and has Minnie Angelyn and Susie Elizabeth.

THOMAS MATTESON[2].   Probably the second son, as he was m. Nov. 14, 1695, to Martha Shippee.   They had 7 or 8 children, 3 of them sons.

THOMAS MATTESON[3], b. 1703.   He and his sister Mercy, married brother and sister. His wife was Susannah, the daughter of Frances, and granddaughter of John Briggs.   Her mother was Susannah, daughter of John and Susannah Griffin–Spencer, and granddaughter of William Spencer, the emigrant.   The first 3 sons are by her.   The second wife's name is not known.   His 5 daughters I do not give.

David Matteson[4], b. March 26, 1726.

Richard Matteson[4], b. Sept. 22, 1728.   Father of Susannah, who m. her second cousin, Edmund[4] of Eben[3], Freelove and Richard, Jr., who m. Mary Spencer in 1775. Jonathan Matteson[4], b. June 16, 1730.   He had Josiah and two dau,

Solomon Matteson[4], b. Oct. 5, 1730.   Married 3 times.

Francis[5], (Prob.) born, 1763.

Oliver[5]. Prob. by the second wife. Born, 1787. Removed in 1808 to Otsego Co., N. Y., and became the head of a well known family there. By his first wife, Hannah Brownell, he was the father of Celinda (Mrs. N. Tolls), Anson and Henry. By the second wife, Lydia Draper, he had Catherine (Mrs. W. Toll), Electa (Mrs. Bresee), Andrew P., Clynthia (Mrs. J. Angel), Edward and Martha (Mrs. D. Radley), all heads of families.

The last wife of Soloman[4] appears to have been Sarah, the dau. of Jeremiah and Hannah (Matteson) Waite. By her he had Joseph, born 1792 ; Thomas, born 1794, (who was the father of Oliver, born 1820), and Sheffield, born 1796.

JOSEPH[3], b. 1705. A Revolutionary soldier. His sons were Benjamin, who m. Mary Pierce, and Elias, b. 1746.

HENRY[3], b. 1707.

JOSEPH MATTESON[2]. His first wife was Rachel ———. By her he had Joseph, b. 1707. His second wife was Martha Greene. He had a large family of children by her, whose line is given in Chapter XX.

FRANCIS MATTESON[2], b. March 15, 1680 ; m. Sarah, daughter of Richard and Phebe Nichols, May 1, 1700. 10 children, 5 of them sons. Their daughter, Hannah[3], m. Pasco Whitford, and had George[4], who m. Dinah Whitford, his cousin. George and Dinah's only child, Esther[5], m. Joseph Tarbox. Roby Tarbox[6] became Mrs. Spencer, and Amanda Spencer[7] became Mrs. Job Briggs. See Chapter XX.

JOHN[3], b. 1704, had John[4], who m. Comfort Weaver, and had son Eleazer. By a second wife, Martha Phillips, of Greene descent, he had Joshua, John, and 4 dau. See Chapter XX.

FRANCIS[3], m. Dinah Tibbetts, 1740.

HENRY[3], b. 1712 ; m. Rachel Greene of Nathaniel and Anna Gould, Warwick Greenes. She d. 1740, leaving prob. Rachel, who m. Wm. Richmond.

JOB[3], b. about 1714 ; m. twice. He had 4 dau. and 2 sons.

Allen[4], by his first wife, was b. Jan. 20, 1755. Removed to Berlin, N. Y. He was a Revolutionary soldier. His wife was Jermima Johnson. He had David, Job, who m. Rebecca Wilcox ; Ebenezer, who m. Roxanna Greene, and Allen, who m. Lucy Thomas. All of N. Y.

Capt. David Matteson[5], of above, m. Anna Fuller, descended from Dr. Samuel Fuller, the only physician who came over in the Mayflower. The line came thus : Dr. Samuel[1], Robert[2], Samuel[3], Abial[4], Jeduthan[5], Amos[6], Daniel[7], and Anna[8]. They had 8 children, but only 2 continued the line. David O.[6], by second wife, Helen M. Rose, has Martha and Amanda. Job O.[6] m. Hannah Nichols in 1848. She was descended from Hon. Thomas Nichols (see Chapter XV) thus : Hon. Thomas[1], Deputy Governor Benjamin[2], John[3], Jonathan[4], Capt. John[5], George[6], and Hannah[7]. Job O.[6] and Hannah had Edwin[7], who m. Alma Shaw, and Albert O.[7], a farmer and surveyor, who lives on the homestead taken up by his great-grandfather in 1788. He has many relics, and is keenly interested in genealogy. He married his cousin, Amanda E. Matteson, dau. of David O. They have Allen, Harold, Phyllis and Stephen. Job O.[6] had also a daughter, Eunice[7], who m. Owen D. Fuller, like herself, descended from Daniel Fuller, the 7th in descent from Dr. Fuller of the Mayflower. They live in West Shelby, N. Y., and have Albert, Floyd and Eunice.

Joab[4], (by last wife), m. Deliverance Spink. He had daughters, and sons Ishmael and Titus.

THOMAS[3], had Joseph[4], who m. Ruth Jones, 1762.

JOSIAH MATTESON[2]. Next to the youngest son of Henry Matteson, the Emigrant. Named after his mother's people. Born about 1685. He lived for many years in Foster, R. I., but his line are nearly all of West Greenwich. He married Rosanna, daughter of Zerubabel Westcott. [Richard Westcott[1], Stukeley Westcott[2], (see Chapter VI), Robert[3], Zerubabel[4], Rosanna[5].] He had Nathan, who m. in 1738, David, who m. in 1739, and Josiah, who m. in 1746. He probably had John who m. in 1740, James, who m. in 1749, and possibly William, who m. in 1752.

DAVID[3], Lived in West Greenwich, R. I.

Silas[4], m. Patience ———— 1766. Had Rosanna[5] who m. Solomon[5] of Capt. Henry[2] line, and Christopher[5], whose son was James McKinsey[6]. Also James Oliver, Gardiner, Royal, John and Josiah Gifford.

David[4], b. Oct. 25, 1763. A Revol. Soldier. He m. Dorcas, dau. of Silas Waite. They had Andrew and Waite, who moved to Pa.

Amos[5], moved to Mich. Had David, Joseph, a Chicago capitalist, and daughters.

Peleg[5], m. Polly James. 13 children. Rebecca[6] m. Calvin Wilcox. Philip[6] by two wives had 9 children (See chapter XVIII for line of David of these.) Simon[6] had 1 child ; Hannah[6] m. Daniel Lillibredge and had Thurston, Rhoda, Amy and Hannah; Peleg Jr.[6] m. Hannah, dau. of Col. Edward Barber; his children are Mary M., widow of Charles S. Nichols, and mother of Nettie May Nichols, and David Edwin, who m. Alice A. Greene, (see Chapter XXI., line of White Hat John), and Phebe C., wife of J. J. Greene. 4 children. Of the other children of Peleg[5], Dr. James' line are all dead ; Fanny[6] and Polly[6] m. Bradford and Welcome Barber, and had 6 and 7 children respectively, of which Fanny's are all dead ; Albert m. twice, children all dead. Andrew[6] has 2 children, and Charles[6] is a bachelor.

Jeremiah[5], m. Sallie Bennett. John, William, Benjamin, George and Jeremiah married.

Benoni[5], m. Alice, dau. of Col. Edward Barber. Had Phebe and Dorcas, and Eunice, who m. Reynolds Waite, and had a dau., Mabel E. A. See Chapter XVIII.

JOSIAH[3], m. Mercy Nichols, March 5, 1746. She descended from Hon. Thomas Nichols thus : Thomas[1], Thomas[2], b. 1660, and m. to Mercy Reynolds ; Stephen[3], m. to Sarah, and Mercy, their daughter, born, 1722.

Stukeley[4], m. Mapleb Hopkins. Their dau. Sally m. Caleb Shippee.

Rosanna[4], m. Ezekiel Matteson, of Joseph[2] Line. See Chapter XX.

Rachel[4], m. Burton Sweet. See Chapter XXII.

Russell[4], b. April 18, 1774 ; m. Mary Straight. Had beside these given below, Luther, Abel and George.

David A.[5] He had Bradford, David S. and Sarah.

Wilbur[5], m. Hannah Potter. Took the name of Mathewson, followed by all his descendants.

Ezekiel[6]. Had George, Daniel, John, Charles, Byron, and 4 dau.

Syria Wilbur[6], m. Anna Eliza Hill, descended from Roger Williams, the Warwicks, Greenes, Hills, Allens, Lascelle–Wardwells, and other first families of R. I. He is the proprietor of The Mathewson, Narragansett Pier, R. I. See illustration. Their children are Mrs. Ida B. Benson, Thomas Greene, m. to Celia Madison, (see Chapter XX, line of Martha Greene Matteson), Syria Wilbur Jr., Walter H., and Everett Irving.

THE MATHEWSON HOUSE, NARRAGANSETT PIER, R. I.

Peleg Clarke[6], who has Lucius, Albert, Lorenzo and Carrie.

Wanton[5], who had Horace, father of Jas. and Wanton.

John[3], prob. of Josiah[2], m. 1740, had Job, Joshua, Abel and Thomas.

James[3], prob. of Josiah[2], m. Hannah Sweet 1749. They had Rufus who m. Lucy Spink and had Thos. who m. Maria James.

HEZEKIAH MATTESON[2], m. Margaret, daughter of Zerubabel and Jane Westcott. See under heading of Josiah.

Abraham[3]. M. his second cousin, Freelove Phillips. See Chapter XX. Sons John, Abraham, Daniel and Thomas.

The other sons of Hezekiah Matteson were Amos, Zerubabel, and Samuel. It is supposed they mostly moved to N. Y.

THE LASCELLE–WARDWELL LINE

There are no kings or princes to fall back upon in this line, or even lords. Nevertheless it has given to the world President Pierce, Susan B. Anthony and Gen. Nathaniel Greene, which is glory enough for one line. It has furnished progenitors for the Pierce, Wardwell, Anthony, Waite, Slocum and Hill families. The entire line of Lieut. John Greene[2] is descended from them, through Abigail Wardwell, his wife. I confess the old records are tantalizingly obscure and chopped off. It has taken long and patient study to weld the links together. There may be minor errors, but practically this account is correct.

Both lines have been hard to trace because pronounced and written so many different ways. Wardwell is the correct form of the name of the Welsh-English line. It is an old compound word meaning the guard's spring, pointing to the feudal landmark near which the first name-bearer lived. We find the name recorded in English, Welsh, Mass. and R. I. records under 24 different spelling, viz.: Wardwell, Woodall, Udall, Warrell, Woddle, Wardell, Wordell, Wardall, Werdell, Woddall, Waddall, Wadle, Wadell, Wardel, Wardayle, Werdall, Woddell, Worrall, Udell, Wriddell, Warrall, Wodell, Wadel and Wadall.

Lascelle, the other original line, was French. When the name-bearer came to England, pronouncing the name as he did, with his Frenchy slurred consonants, and burry accent on the terminal syllable " celle," his English neighbors in despair gave him various names ending in sounds of zell, sell, or sall, [Mitchell's History of Bridgewater.] It became Hazell, Hazeal, La Zelle, La Zalle, Yazell, Youzell, Yousiel, Uzzell, Uzel, Uzzall, Uzal, Usal, Usual, Lasell, and Uzzele ; or as Savage in his " Genealogical Dictionary of New England " says, after enumerating five U-capitaled variations, " or any other outlandish name !" The Wardwell line, and Lieut. John Greene[2] branch of the Wardwell line, adopted Lascelle as a given name, and for seven generations used it and spelled it every possible wild way that could commence with a capital U or Y.

About A. D. 1480, one ———— Ithell, of North Wales, married a Miss Pierce. They had a son, Pierce Ithell, whose daughter Mary was m. about 1540, to Richard Woodall, Udall, Woddall, Worrell, or Wardwell, of War- wick, England. One of their sons, Dr. John Wardell, and a grandson, who crossed the ocean in 1594, had much to do with early Virginia settlements. An older son, William, was married by 1565 to Meribé Lascelle, the daught- er of a French couple, Gershom and Meribé Lascelle.

Reading between the lines of the records, it is evident that the French- man came to England with his wife and family of grown children about 1560 at the first muttering of the storm that finally broke into bloody wrath against the Huguenots, or French Protestants. Gershom had many namesakes for more than a century, and Meribé, her name anglicized into Meriba or Merib- ah and Meribeth, still has her namesakes scattered over New England. The next two generations of the family intermarried with the Slocums, Kings, Waites and Hills. Their names were so peculiarly odd and Frenchy, that they can almost be traced by that alone. Anteres, another daughter of these Huguenot refugees, married a Pierce. There is more about her line in Chapter XXIV.

There was a good deal of restlessness in the blood of these allied families. Before the New England settlement some of the Pierces and Wardwells went to Virginia, where the older generation of the Wardwell's had invest- ments. Some of these then drifted to the Barbadoes, where later we read of one of the Pierces owning many acres of land and 80 slaves. All of the Lascelle–Wardwell line seem to have been Independents in religious mat- ters, and under religious oppression quite ready to cross the sea for con- science's sake. Some of the Pierces were in Plymouth in 1623. And re- belling against Laud's tyranny about a score of the allied families of this line came to Mass. in 1633-5.

There were three great-grandsons of Gershom Lascelle and Richard Wardwell among these. Two of them, William[1] and Thomas[1], were brothers, sons of Lascelle Wardwell[3]. The other was their cousin, William[4], son of Gershom Wardwell[3]. The fathers of these men, Lascelle and Gershom, were sons of William[2] and Meribé Lascelle the younger, mentioned in a preceding paragraph. William, son of Gershom, went to Portsmouth, R. I., and be- came a Friend. Two of his daughters married Anthonys, one of them, Frances, who married John Anthony, became the fore-mother of Susan B. Anthony.

Thomas of Boston was the father of Samuel[5]. This Samuel's wife, Sarah Hawkes, in a fit of religious enthusiasm, in order to "mortify the flesh," appeared at church one day in the costume that Eve wore in the gar- den of Eden. The town authorities had her soundly whipped for it. When the witchcraft excitement broke out in 1692, Sarah Hawkes-Wardwell and her daughter were both arrested as witches. Badly frightened, they said it was Samuel, the husband and father, who had been bewitching people. He denied it, but was hung Sept. 20, 1697, as "an impenitent witch and possessor of a familiar spirit."

William, of Boston, brother to Thomas, was born in 1610. Came to the colonies in 1633, as "Our brother, Edmund Quincey's servant," (Church records.) He married Alice ——— and had 5 children, of whom the second was Uzel (Lascelle), b. April 7, 1639. When the church banished Rev. Mr. Wheelwright for heresy, William, for being too friendly with him had his arms and freeman's privileges taken from him for a time. William died either at Wells or Boston in 1670. One of the entries in the Wells records gravely assigns a pew in the church to him, "To sitt in ye sixth of ye men's long seats in consideration that his son Elihu sitt in ye same seat."

William of Boston's two sons, Uzel and Elihu Wardwell, both served in King Philip's War, 1675-6, as the Mass. archives show. Uzel, the ancestor of all of Lieut. John Greene's line (of Chapter XV) served under Capt. Nicholas Paige, and the state of Mass. still owes him for his services, 5£, 10s ($25.00). [Mass. Archives, vol. 68.]

Uzel was m. May 3, 1664, when 25, to the young widow of Daniel Ringe, Mary Kinsman-Ringe. They lived at both Bristol and Ipswich, Mass. At the latter place, Abigail, their oldest child, b. Oct. 27, 1665, was married at 19 to Lieut. John Greene of R. I. I shall not attempt to give of the other Wardwells, except to say that William of R. I. also had a Uzel, born the same year as the Mass. Uzel. He married Grace ——— and their lines are entirely different.

I will not attempt to trace in this the Kings, Pierces, Motts or Slocums. One other line needs to be spoken of.

Another child of William and Meribé Wardell was Rosanna, who married ——— Waite. They had several children who came to the Colonies, Mehitable, the oldest, who married Richard Hill, of William, and was left a widow soon after coming to the new country; Richard Waite, born in 1596, Gambiel, b. in 1598, and Thomas, b. 1601. All of these came about the height of the Anti-Land emigration. One of the sons, Thomas, went to Portsmouth, R. I., in 1639, and from him all the R. I. Waites are descended. D. Byron Waite's "Waite Genealogy" takes up their history, so it need not be given here.

There were a number of the Hills came at the same time that Richard Hill and his wife Mehitable did. A nephew of Richard's, Valentine Hill, (of John of William), a wealthy and prominent man of Boston and Dover, Mass., was the head of a line from whom Frances E. Willard, that peerless soul and apostle of temperance, was seventh in descent. All of the lines of "Wealthy John" and Usal Greene (Chapter XV, XVI, XVII) can claim blood kin to her—an honor greater than kinship to a queen.

Richard, who died in 1639, left two children that concern us, John and Rose (Rosanna), both born in 1613, and who came together to the colonies. John married Frances, and lived at the "Great Lotts" i. e. Dorchester, Mass. Their oldest son was born about 1638. He married while yet in his teens Mary ———, and removed to Portsmouth, R. I. Here Jonathan, Jr. was born in 1657, to a nineteen year old father. Jonathan, Jr. was the father of Patience Hill who married Daniel Pierce. See Chapter XXVI. He was also the father of Caleb, Ebenezer and Thomas, all heads of R. I. Hills, and probably of Capt. John Hill, also.

Jonathan Hill's second son, Henry, brother to Jonathan Jr. of above paragraph, was born Jan. 24, 1661. He was the father of Ann Hill, and Susanna Hill, who married the brothers "Wealthy John" and Usal Greene, Esther Hill who married John Nichols, and Mary Hill who married William Nichols.

Rosanna Hill, the emigrant, undoubtedly married Stukeley Westcott. They were both old friends at Great Torrington, England, and nearly the same age. Stukeley's descendants carried the name of Rosanna down for a half-dozen generations. For more than 100 years the name was never found in R. I. records except in families that sprang from the Westcotts. Stukeley and his wife followed Roger Williams to Providence, 1636. (See Chapter VI.) They had Amos, who m. two Stafford sisters, Jeremiah, who m. Ellen England, the step-daughter of his father's cousin, Hugh Parsons—see Chapter XX—Robert, who m. Catherine ———, Mercy, who m. Sam. Stafford, and Damaris, who m. Benedict Arnold. All these became heads of prominent families.

THE WAITE FAMILY

WAITE COAT-OF-ARMS

Rognvald, Jarl (earl) of More, was a friend of Jarl Harald Haarfagar (Harold the beautiful haired). But when Harald in 872 made himself king of Norway, he put down Rognvald and all the other jarls, with a high hand. One of Jarl Rognvald's sons was Ganger Rolf (Ralph), also called Rollo, and Rolf the Dane. Deprived of his dominion, Rollo entered upon a gigantic scale of roving, plundering piracy. Harald expelled him. Rollo with his followers, A. D. 876, sailed to France and compelled the king to cede a large territory to him. Here he settled with his followers, becoming the first duke of Normandy.

After him in succession came William, Richard and then another Richard. This last Richard, fourth Duke of Normandy, died in 1026. Among the grandchildren of the fourth duke were three that concern us. One of these was William the Conqueror; the other two were brother and sister, cousins to the Conqueror. In 1075, nine years after he had conquered England, William the Conqueror made this cousin Roger Earl of Hereford. The Earl's sister was Emma, named after her great-aunt, Queen Emma, the wife of two kings and the mother of two others, all four of whom in turn ruled over England.

This Emma, so closely related to earls, dukes and kings, gave her hand to one Ralf (Ralph) de Waiet. We only know of this man that his father was Ralf also, and was the son of an English father and Welsh mother. For the fourth of a thousand years' Ralf's and Emma's descendants are traced under various spellings, Waiet, Wate, Waight, or Wayght, Wayt, or Wayte. Richardus (Richard) who, in 1315, was by Edward II. made Escheator over five counties, wrote his name le Wayte. During the reign of Henry VI., 1421-71, the le was dropped from the name, and never resumed.

The home of the Waites was mostly in south central England and in Wales. A scion of one of the North Wales families was Thomas Wayte, a cousin to Mehitable Waite–Hill, and Thomas Gamaliél and Richard Waite mentioned under Lascelle–Wardwell heading. This Welsh Thomas was a member of Parliament, and was one of the regicide judges who signed the warrant in Jan., 1649, for the execution of Charles I. The family hold that upon the restoration of Charles II. to the throne in 1660, Judge Wayte was hung. His descendant, the late Chief Justice Waite, owned the death warrant on which the regicide was apprehended. In it the execution was ordered " Tomorrow, being the 30th day of the instant month of January, [1661 ?] between the hours of ten in the morning and five in the afternoon of the same day."

Nevertheless, history says he was not hung. There were 59 judges signed the instrument. In the eleven years that intervened between the execution of King Charles I. and the restoration of his son, quite a number of these died, four fled to America, several escaped to the continent, twenty-seven were apprehended in England, and a death warrant issued against them. But Hume says explicitly that but nine were executed, Scott, Carew, Harrison, Clement, Jones, Scope, Berkstead, Cobbet and O'Key. The other eighteen, which would, of course, include Wayte, were imprisoned for life. D. Byron Waite furnished me with this cut of the Waite coat-of-arms.

From the five sons of Thomas Waite of R. I., Samuel, Joseph, Jeremiah, Thomas and Reuben, the R. I. Waites are descended. I am indebted to D. Byron Waite's interesting work for many of the facts here related.

OTHER FAMILIES

THE NICHOLS FAMILY

The derivation of name, description of coat-of-arms and reference to the founders of this line is given in the Ann Greene-Nichols section of Chapter XV.

Late researches indicate that all of the original lines of Mass. and Rhode Island Nichols sprang from the same stem father, John Nichols of Glamorganshire, in the south part of Wales. He died late in 1598, leaving much property. His sons lived in Wales and the near counties of south England. Very likely this man was the same John Nichols, a friend of Sir Walter Raleigh's, to whom that nobleman made a grant of land in 1587. This is the more probable as several of his sons were concerned in various colonial enterprises. William, a merchant, 1610, was a charter member of the Virginia Co.; Christopher and Thomas, merchants, were also charter members. John, a fourth brother, is supposed to have been he who made a West Indies voyage in 1606, which he described the next year in his book of travels, which bore the odd title of "An Houre Glasse of Indian Newes." A dozen years later we find John[2] living at Tavenstock, Devonshire, near Wales. Most of his children and grandchildren came to the Colonies. The indications are that Francis Stafford Nichols (b. 1595), William, Richard and Kendall (or Randall), all emigrants, were all sons of John. His daughter, Prudence, m. Thomas Fones in 1620. Their son, Capt. John Fones, was one of the pioneers of Quidnessett, R. I., and head of the company of whom John Greene was also one, that secured first from the Indians and then the General Assembly, the celebrated "Fones Purchase" region, 1772-7.

Yet another son of John Nichols[2] was Thomas (?), who lived in Wales. His son was Lieut Thomas Nichols, the same recorded in Chapter XV. This Thomas came first to the Barbadoes in the West Indies. Then he came to R. I. about 1658 or 1659. His cousin Kendall (or Randall) Nichols was at Newport, and another cousin, Capt. Fones, at North Kingstown. Thomas himself settled at Newport by 1660. He was married the year before this to Hannah Griffin, born 1642, a girl of Quaker parentage. Susannah, a sister of Hannah's, married John Spencer, the first of the name in R. I., making a bond of relationship between these two pioneer families. Chapters XXXIII to XL inclusive are all of descendants of Greene and this house of Nichols. A very large branch of the Mattesons are of this line, Josiah Matteson Jr.[3] marrying Mercy, daughter of Stephen, who was the son of Thomas, oldest child of this Hon. Thomas Nichols. The houses of John, Perry and Joseph Greene[5] (see Chapter XXI), each an important line, are also of this blood, these three brothers having married Catherine, Sarah and

Hannah Nichols, daughters of Jonathan, grand-daughters of Deputy Governor Benjamin, and great-grand-daughters of Hon Thomas Nichols

None of the rest of the original Nichols colonists concern us save Richard[3], already spoken of as the probable son of John[2] of John[1] of Wales   He was in Ipswich by 1630. His son, Capt Richard of the Indian Wars (Pequot ?), married Rebecca, daughter of John and Eliza Eaton   Their son, Richard[3], m. Phebe ———, and their daughter, Sarah, in the year 1700, m. Francis Matteson[2], head of one of the branches of that family

An uncle of Hon Thomas Nichols[3], Robert Nichols of Mass , together with his wife, were killed by the Indians, Sept 2, 1775, in King Philip's War

THE COGGESHALL FAMILY

As Humility Coggeshall was the foremother of the " Tribe of Benjamin," the largest family of the Greenes, many will wish to know of her line.

The family dates back nearly to the Conquest, to a certain Lord de Coggeshall, a noted Crusader   The town of Coggeshall, in the County of Essex, England, perhaps marks the ancestral home. In the oldest records the name is also spelled as Coxsall or Coxall

Hon John Coggeshall, the first president of Providence Plantation— equivalent to governor of R. I —was born in the County of Essex, England, in either 1581 or 1599. He sailed in the ship Lion, and landed in Mass Sept 16, 1632, with his wife Mary and three children   In 1638, when Mrs. Anne Hutchinson and her followers were banished from Massachusetts for heresy, he went with the rest to the Island of Aquidneck, which they purchased from the Indians, and where they settled Pocasset (Portsmouth) that same year.   Portsmouth became the storm center of Quakerism

One of Hon John's daughters, Wait, married Daniel Gould   This Daniel Gould, Mary Dyer, the wife of a Portsmouth neighbor, and President Coggeshall's own son Joshua, introduced the Friends' doctrine into R I. Mary Dyer was hung as a " pestilent heretic," while in Mass preaching   Daniel Gould also passed into that forbidden territory, and " ye 22 of ye 9th month, 1654," was whipped in Boston, receiving 30 lashes from a cat-of-nine-tails

Joshua Coggelshall[2] did not fare as ill   He married Joan West   Their next to the youngest child, Humility, married Benjamin[2], the youngest son of John Greene of Quidnessett.

SPENCER

There is a tangle of Spencer-Briggs-Matteson and Greene marriages in some lines   The head of the New England Spencers appears to have been William[1], who probably came to the colonies during the Anti-Land emigration   He was a married man with a family   After living for a time in

Massachusetts he removed to Connecticut, where most of his children re-married. It is supposed that one of his older sons was John[2], first of the name in R. I., who became the head of the old and well known family of Spencers in that state. He married Susannah Griffin, a sister-in-law of Hon. Thomas Nichols. His son John married Audrey, daughter of Deputy Governor John, and grand-daughter of Surgeon John Greene of the Warwick line. His daughter Susannah (Mrs. Richard Briggs[2]) was grandmother of Capt. Thomas Briggs who married Mary Greene of Quidnessett blood. See Chapter XXI. Two other sons, Michael[2] and Robert[2], by the intermarriage of their grandchildren, Daniel Briggs[4] of Susannah[3], and Welthian Sweet[4] of Susannah[3], of Robert[2], headed a line that two generations later intermarried with the N. Y. branch of Quidnessett Greenes. There were many intermarriages in later generations.

THE BRIGGS FAMILY

John Briggs, pioneer and intimate friend of old John Greene of Quidnessett, was Secretary of the Colony, 1671 ———, and shareholder in the various land companies of that day. His great-grandson, Capt. Thomas Briggs[4] (Francis[3], Richard[2], John[1]), m. Mary Greene[4]. See Chapter XXI. Another great-grandson, Daniel[4] (Benj.[3], Daniel[2], John[1]), m. the Welthian Sweet mentioned in Spencer paragraph. Very many cross marriages occurred between the Quidnessett Greenes and the Briggs family.

It is handed down in the family that there were three of the Briggs brothers who came to the colonies. Also, that as they sailed away their friends were kneeling upon the shore, praying for their safety. Their small craft was disabled, and from June to September they were afloat upon the then scarcely traveled ocean, the captain (who was one of the brothers) and his eighteen men having to depend upon their oars most of the journey. As usual, tradition has assigned this to a later generation, Capt. Thomas Briggs[4] being made the hero of the incident that really happened to his great-grandfather.

VAUGHAN FAMILY

Intermarried largely with the Quidnessett Green and branch families. The name is Welsh, and means "little." In the oldest records it is written Vahan. The first family of the name in R. I. was that of John Vahan. To him and his wife Gillian were born John[2], 1644, and Davy, 1646. Gillian and Davy are Welsh names, and would indicate that the family emigrated from there. While there is no positive proof, it is supposed Mrs. Gillian Vaughan was nearly related to Hon. Thomas Nichols, also of Wales. Both lines head the same family names, and there were five intermarriages within the first 100 years after the Vaughans came to R. I. John Vaughan[1] and his wife were Quakers.

HILL FAMILY

See Lascelle-Wardwell article. Of the American line, Henry, son of Jonathan and Mary, and grandson of John and Frances, was the ancestor of all the R. I. Hills.

Rosanna Hill, named for her grandmother, Rosanna Wardwell-Waite, m. Stukeley Westcott and had any amount of namesakes in the next 150 years. See Westcott Family.

INDEX

Index

The first three generations of R I. John, Benjamin and Joan Greens are marked to distinguish them, a Q standing for Quidnessett line, and a W for the Warwick members.

The Greene Tree
and Its Branches

A New Book on a New Plan
Nothing Else Like It

This book gives the only full account of the rise and early history of the House of Greene. It brings the narration down the centuries to the coming of the Greenes to the American colonies, and to the part that the Warwick and Quidnessett Greenes took in the stirring pioneer days of Rhode Island. It is the fullest history that has every appeared of the large, but hard to trace line of the Quidnessett Greenes. So peculiarly is the story of this House the story of Rhode Island and the other New England colonies as well, that COPIES OF THIS BOOK HAVE BEEN

Ordered for Reference by the Astor Library, R. I. Historical Society, N. Y. Historical Society, and Other Public Libraries and Historical Societies.

When this edition of 1200 volumes is exhausted, no more can be obtained. An historical and chronological work of this kind is an expensive undertaking. The author has small hopes of getting back in dollars and cents what this book has cost her. She will never repeat the experiment.

Price, $5.00 Each, Prepaid

ADDRESS

MRS. LORA S. LA MANCE,   PINEVILLE, MO.

Milton Keynes UK
Ingram Content Group UK Ltd.
UKHW020115030823
426179UK00005B/127